THE SELECTED LETTERS OF ROBINSON JEFFERS

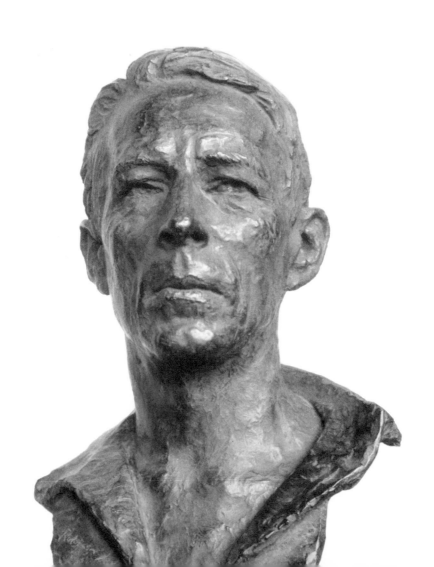

THE SELECTED LETTERS OF
ROBINSON JEFFERS

1897-1962 EDITED BY ANN N. RIDGEWAY

FOREWORD BY MARK VAN DOREN

PHOTOGRAPHS BY LEIGH WIENER

THE JOHNS HOPKINS PRESS, BALTIMORE

95346

For Fred

". . . the calm to look for is the calm at the whirlwind's heart."

—Robinson Jeffers, "Be Angry at the Sun"

FOREWORD

As the editor of this volume remarks in a Preface that leaves little to be said—everything is there, in the fewest possible words—Robinson Jeffers thought he was a poor letter-writer and yet was not. He seems to have been unaware of the extent to which he was like other people when he faced a pile of correspondence to be answered. He shuddered and put off the evil hour. There was something unique, however, in the way his eloquence on the subject mounted from occasion to occasion. It mounted through levels of humor which suggest, now that his voice is silenced, a mixture of amusement and despair. "It is ridiculous, and I can't understand it." "I am one of those fish-like objects that can't write a letter." The difficulty, or perhaps the obsession, was something he developed as a poet develops a theme. It was a "chronic disease," a "born imbecility," a "narcotic addiction," "a kind of insanity." In a word, it was "constitutional." "I am a worm," he confessed once to Arthur Davison Ficke, whom clearly he liked and considered a close friend. That was in 1929; but in 1958, almost thirty years later, he was writing to Dr. Hans Barkan: "I wish I knew why I can't write letters. I love my friends, who are very few, but I can't write to them." This in the course of a letter which itself was very fine, and full to its edges of the author's character.

The author's character. Those are easy words to set down, but it is not so easy to define the rich thing they refer to: the deeply moving, the lonely, the loving and lovable thing that a few persons can be envied for having known. The chief of those persons was of course Una Jeffers, who is the heroine of this book as her husband is its hero. What was it that she said to him, or did to him, on November 17, 1912? He asks her a month later and we do not know what she replied, if she replied. Neither one of them may have known, and yet it must have been in effect everything for them both. His love letters to Una are among the most touching in the world; and so are his letters about her after she died. Without her he would not have been the person he was: the powerful poet, the complex man whose every sentence in these letters comes up out of a depth where playfulness is by no means inconsistent with a seriousness that no doubt could be terrifying even to him. The seriousness nobody has ever questioned, but the playfulness will now be evident to some readers for the first time: the playfulness, the courtesy, the affection, the exquisite consideration for others. All of which might seem to be illicitly there if we heeded only his pronouncements concerning the human race, whose days in the universe were numbered, he thought, and a good riddance too. "I don't enjoy meeting people," he once remarked. Not that he hated people—he denied that he did—but neither did he "respect them excessively." Human nature for him was already an "anachronism" in a civilization that had no further use for it. Therefore he had no business embodying it, as certainly he did.

It was hidden in him even from himself: an antique of great price, an heirloom, a fossil. This misanthrope was in fact an old-fashioned gentleman who never in his own life willingly hurt a soul, though to people he thought silly or wrong he could "speak plainly." And even then he hedged. "As to 'pessimist'; that should mean believing in the worst—that things are as bad as possible. I can imagine them a great deal worse. Things are as they are; and the world is full of wretchedness yet very beautiful. And not all wretched."

His theory of the world was not borne out, that is to say, by his behavior in it. He was two men in one—at least two—as Thomas Hardy was. Hardy had the bleakest possible view of nature and man, yet many of his poems seem to be written by a warm-hearted man who has forgotten what he was supposed to think. Few things are more attractive than this: than feeling in someone who has put feeling aside, than tenderness in a person of tough mind. The mind of Jeffers had been hardened in hot fires—just when, it may be possible some day to determine. In his Foreword to *The Selected Poetry of Robinson Jeffers* he spoke of two "accidents that changed and directed my life." One of these was his meeting with Una, and the other was their coming to live near the Monterey coast mountains. There must have been other "accidents," too, including a collision with ideas that transformed him from the more or less commonplace poet of his first two volumes into the stunning one of "Tamar," "Roan Stallion," "The Tower Beyond Tragedy," and the other long poems that followed. In 1938 he reminded Una of "the accidental new birth of my own mind" which she had witnessed years before and which he now hoped, in a dark moment of self-doubt, might with good luck be repeated. Una, writing to Lawrence Clark Powell four years earlier than this, had tried to say what happened to her husband in the great days when he was finding himself, and it was not easy for her to be certain on the subject. It might have been World War I that "made the world and his own mind much more real and intense to him." But also it might have been the building of Tor House, which brought him to be "aware of strengths in himself unknown before." Anyhow, she concluded, "at the age of thirty-one there came to him a kind of awakening such as adolescents and religious converts are said to experience." Whatever it was, we can be reminded of Walt Whitman, who went to sleep as one kind of poet and after five or six years woke up as the other kind we know. The experience in either case was something like an earthquake or a lightning stroke. And the Jeffers who survived was the man who was two men: he who loved hawks and he who could smile about "my damned serious nature."

The second of these men had friendships which he valued: with Dr. Lyman Stookey and his brother Byron, with Frederick Mortimer Clapp, with George Sterling, with James Rorty, with Arthur Davison Ficke, with Benjamin de Casseres, with Frederic Ives Carpenter, and later on with Judith Anderson and with Eva Hesse, his German translator. "What a fellow James Rorty is!" he exclaimed to George Sterling in 1925. And with good reason, for it was Rorty who took "Tamar" to New York with him and did not let the reviewers rest till they had read it and responded as they should. The reputation of Jeffers began then and there, and Jeffers never forgot it; though his liking for Rorty grew to have other grounds, so that in 1934 he could say to him in a letter from Taos: "You are the only person to whom I can write."

With reputation—Jeffers called it "notoriety"—came letters from strangers, and these were the hardest of all to answer. Yet he tried, and some of his best letters are attempts either to say what his "philosophy" was or to deny that he had one—only one; or to define poetry as he understood it, with glosses on his own. He was never wiser than when he insisted that the proper function of poetry was not to express but to present; or when he said: "Poetry does not necessarily have a 'message' except 'How beautiful things are'—or 'How sad, or terrible'—or even 'How exciting.' These are the only messages that Homer and Shakespeare have for us."

Homer and Shakespeare. In what more fitting company could we leave him?

Mark Van Doren

PREFACE

When I first proposed to assemble Robinson Jeffers' correspondence, I was warned that it was Una who wrote most letters in order to assure her husband time to write poems. I soon discovered that, no matter how much Jeffers disliked answering mail, no matter how ruefully he admitted his vice of procrastination, no matter how scant he thought it, his correspondence was nonetheless considerable. There are nearly 500 letters in university and public libraries and in private collections. They provide some interesting details about Jeffers' life and work, as they might be expected to, but what is more important, they declare a personality not commonly known.

Nothing surprising in these letters, then, except the man who wrote them. Little here of the stereotype which has been drawn from his poetry. No hawk's wings shudder these pages, and whatever granite they contain proves remarkably sentient. The man who wrote these letters was a loving suitor, a devoted husband and parent, a courteous friend, a grieving widower. He was a man dedicated to a life of personal and artistic excellence, a man who spent his life to poetry. These are the letters of a gentle, detached, devout, and humorous man.

Humor is bound to be surprising from so stern a demeanor as Jeffers'. Though there are occasional puns and rather bizarre elements of humor in a few of his poems, such a neo-Jeremias does not naturally strike a comic pose. In his letters, however, Jeffers often deliberately attempted to amuse his correspondents with verbal playfulness and with anecdotes that, in their brevity, demonstrate a narrative skill very different from that which formed his long poems.

Jeffers' social and political convictions were firm. He enjoyed exchanging them with several correspondents. But he was no philosopher, and he preferred writing about animals and trees to explaining his work and his "philosophy." His "inhumanism" was a rejection of the exclusiveness he saw in prevailing "humanistic" attitudes: Robinson Jeffers valued human nature only so far as it participated in the natural world which contained it. The God who lived in that nature was more dear and more real to Jeffers than his readers have appreciated. Piety does not readily subject itself to intellectual or critical examination, nor even to self-analysis, but some of Jeffers' comments reveal him as at once more orthodox and more original in his religious responses than he himself might have recognized. Although intellectually he accepted mankind's religions only in their historical and social settings, his ability to maintain this detached view did not minimize the devout love he felt for the "beautiful God of the world."

It was his detachment that misled many to judge Jeffers as overproud and aloof. Yet his letters show that he was never really careless about what he said to friends and critics or about what they said of him. Only through experience did he come to accept and even to defend their right to interpret his work and to speculate on his intentions. Through experience he came to trust his work to stand its own tests. His apparent indifference to political and economic movements, which were to him no more than inevitable expressions of human history, was actually thoughtful appraisal and reappraisal, commitment through continual exercise of free choice. He made certain to be an informed observer, attentive to the moral significance of independent thought and action. He considered the judgments and advice of others with an equanimity born out of a singular merging of assurance and deference. His letters give evidence of the rare degree of self-possession Jeffers achieved.

But self-possession did not reduce his capacity for tenderness. Tenderness marked all his concern for Una and his children. And compassion moved him to rebuke what seemed to him a misdirected humanity. He was sensitive to beauty and to pain, could find them in each other. He admired bold energy and he knew violence, but because he knew also their danger, he exacted from himself graciousness and gentleness beyond his nature. That gentleness, hard-bought as were most of the goods he found in life, he took much care to preserve. Not the words but the spirit of his letters tell us this.

It is probably true that Robinson Jeffers' vision ranged among and focused upon more evils than goods. The goods that came to him, however, he embraced with dignity and full appreciation: Una, his twin sons, his grandchildren, a few firm friendships, "the beauty of things." And the goods that he chose were of such importance that he sometimes battled even Una for them. These letters record his choices and acceptances, record an ordinary life met by an extraordinary man. Before I looked into these letters, I admired Robinson Jeffers' poetry, and I imagined some affinity with his thought. Now I am pleased to have had this opportunity to know him, for I like him very much.

Ann N. Ridgeway

Bowling Green, Ohio
June, 1967

ACKNOWLEDGMENTS

Acknowledgment is gratefully made for permission to publish from the following collections and libraries in which manuscripts are located: Academy of American Poets; American Academy of Arts and Letters; Brooklyn Public Library; Poetry Collection, Lockwood Memorial Library, State University of New York at Buffalo; Bancroft Library, University of California at Berkeley; Special Collections, Library of the University of California at Los Angeles; Harriet Monroe Modern Poetry Library, University of Chicago; Special Collections, Columbia University Library; Special Collections, Emory University Library; Houghton Library, Harvard University; Henry E. Huntington Library; Lilly Library, Indiana University; Special Collections, University of Kansas Library; Manuscript Division, Library of Congress; Los Angeles Public Library; Rare Books and Special Collections, University of Michigan Library; Albert M. Bender Collection, Mills College Library; National Institute of Arts and Letters; Henry W. and Albert A. Berg Collection of the New York Public Library, Astor, Lenox and Tilden Foundations; Lewis M. Isaacs Collection, Manuscripts Division, New York Public Library, Astor, Lenox and Tilden Foundations; Edwin Björkman and Burton Emmett Papers, Southern Historical Collection, University of North Carolina Library; Mary Norton Clapp Library, Occidental College; Charles Patterson Van Pelt Library, University of Pennsylvania; James D. Phelan Foundation; Ridgely Torrence Papers, Rare Books and Special Collections, Princeton University Library; Gleeson Library, University of San Francisco; Charlotte Ashley Felton Memorial Library, Stanford University; Academic Center Library, University of Texas; Clifton Waller Barrett Library, University of Virginia; Beinecke Rare Book and Manuscripts Library, Yale University.

Individual librarians I should like to thank for special assistance include Helen H. Bretnor (Bancroft), Alexander P. Clark (Princeton), Donald L. Gallup (Beinecke), Ralph W. Hansen (Stanford), Tyrus G. Harmsen (Occidental), Ruth V. Hewlett (Tufts), Mary M. Hirth (Texas), Mrs. Matthew Josephson and Felicia Geffen (American Academy of Arts and Letters), Kenneth A. Lohf (Columbia), Janet Lowrey (Chicago).

To the following I am indebted for assistance in locating manuscripts and establishing identifications, and for permission to publish private and business correspondence: Brother Antoninus, Dame Judith Anderson, Kamil Bednář, Mrs. Van Wyck Brooks, Rev. Robert Brophy, S.J., Mrs. Hugh Bullock, Frederic Ives Carpenter, Dorothy Chauvenet (for Witter Bynner), Francis Gardner Clough, Mrs. Louis Henry Cohn (New York House of Books), Mrs. John W. Collins, Mrs. Saxe Commins, Mrs. Douglas Cummings, Babette Deutsch, Jean Kellogg Dickie, Fraser Drew, Gladys Ficke, Sara Bard Field, William M. Gibson, Allen Griffin, Herbert Heron, Eva Hesse, Philip C. Horton, Jeremy

Ingalls, Dan Burne Jones, H. Arthur Klein, Benjamin H. Lehman, William Turner Levy, Theodore M. Lilienthal, Joyce Mayhew, Ernest Moll, Dr. John W. Nevius, Mrs. William H. Norton, Glenn W. Rainey, Selden Rodman, Arthur Leonard Ross, James Rorty, Richard J. Schoeck, Karl Shapiro, Radcliffe Squires, Dr. Byron Stookey, Walter G. Tolleson, Mark Van Doren, Hyatt Howe Waggoner, Isabelle Percy West, Stanley D. Willis (for Rudolph Gilbert), and Ella Winter.

I should like also to acknowledge the permissions granted by the following publishers and copyright holders:

S. S. Alberts for Letters 103, 122, and 160, and for several excerpts from *A Bibliography of the Works of Robinson Jeffers* (New York, 1933, 1961, 1966).

The American Humanist Association for Letter 359, from *The Humanist*, XI (October, 1951), 200–1.

P. W. Chase for the Audubon Society of Sewickley, Pennsylvania, for Letter 42, from *The Cardinal*, I (January, 1926), 23n.

Melba Berry Bennett for Letters 1, 11, 122, 173, 180, 275, 280, 381, 396, and for many excerpts from *The Stone Mason of Tor House* (Los Angeles, 1966).

Allman J. Cook, publisher of the *Carmel Pine Cone,* for Letter 339.

E. P. Dutton for the Van Wyck Brooks letters in the University of Pennsylvania Library.

Geoffrey Grigson for Letter 237, from *New Verse*, II (December, 1934).

Bruce Humphries, Publishers, for Letter 169, facsimiled in Rudolph Gilbert, *Shine, Perishing Republic* (Boston, 1936).

Franklin B. Folsom, for the League of American Writers, for Letter 276, from *Writers Take Sides* (New York, 1938).

The Louisiana State University Press for the quotations and paraphrases in Letter 303, from R. W. Short, "The Tower Beyond Tragedy," *Southern Review*, VII (Summer, 1941), 132–34.

Odyssey Press for Letter 180, from Andrew Smithberger and Camille McCole, *On Poetry* (New York, 1931).

Henry A. Christian for Letter 291, from the *Princeton University Library Chronicle*, XXVIII, No. 2 (Winter, 1967), 90.

Bennett Cerf, for Random House, for the above listed letters from S. S. Alberts' *A Bibliography of the Works of Robinson Jeffers* (New York, 1933), for the Random House correspondence in the University of California, Bancroft Library, and for quotations from Jeffers' works.

Sheed and Ward, Inc., for Letter 235, from Sister Mary James Power, *Poets at Prayer* (New York, 1938).

Remsen Bird, David Hagemeyer, Tyrus Harmsen, J. B. Tompkins, and Brett Weston have been helpful in locating and making available Johan Hagemeyer's photograph of the Jo Davidson bust of Jeffers, reproduced on the dust jacket and title page of the book; and Sadie Adriani has been generous in permitting the use of her photograph of Jeffers which he once recommended to Random House for publicity purposes. Mark Van Doren and Leigh Wiener have so enlivened this book, each by his special contribution, that it will say something new to me as well as to its other readers: a singular gift, surely, to anyone who makes a book.

Donnan Jeffers has been especially conscientious in searching out material and supplying me with copies of letters, as have Una's sisters, Mrs. Violet Hinkley and Mrs. Daisy Bartley (who has also provided several of the family photographs for this volume). I am deeply grateful to them as well as to Donnan's wife, Lee, to Garth and Lotte Jeffers, and to Hamilton and Barbara Jeffers. For Mrs. Hans Barkan, Melba Bennett, Frederick M. Clapp, Blanche Matthias, and Lawrence Clark Powell, who have given unstintingly of manuscripts, time, encouragement, and practical assistance, an appreciative word must say in little what is more largely felt. Finally, quiet thanks to my editor, Miss Barbara Parmelee; to the book's designer, Gerard A. Valerio; to Stanley K. Coffman, Jr., who nudged me into this book; to Stafford Whiteaker, who nudged me into the Johns Hopkins fold; and to Frederick Eckman, to whom this book is dedicated, in trifling barter for generous gifts of instruction, friendship, and poetry.

CONTENTS

A NOTE ON THE EDITING

Robinson Jeffers always found it easier to compose with pencil than with pen and easier with pen than at a typewriter. Many of his letters and notes for others are in pencil; other letters are in ink, some copied from penciled notes; a few are typed, again from notes. I have worked from Xeroxed copies, from handwritten and typed copies made for me by the owners of the originals, from published copies, and from originals themselves. The term *letter* here extends to postcards, telegrams, answers to questionnaires, and inscriptions on manuscripts and books which seem worthy of inclusion. A few of Una Jeffers' letters and a few letters which supply the context for Jeffers' responses are also entered here. Jeffers' correspondence dwindled as Una took over more and more business mail and as, after her death, their friend Melba Bennett came to the poet's aid. Correspondence of the later years, therefore, has somewhat scant representation, and apparently a number of the notes and drafts made during this period were never finally composed for mailing. Most of these notes and drafts I have utilized in footnotes and in explanations of ideas found in completed letters.

In all cases I have deleted and editorialized very little in order to preserve the integrity of the individual letter; whenever possible, I have allowed the content of the letter itself, or the text of other letters, to clarify references to individuals and events. I have not annotated misquoted lines and misapplied quotations, nor have I identified sources of quotations or references unless they seem especially obscure. I have agreed to select sparingly from letters to Una, especially from those written during the period of courtship, only because these may make a separate volume one day. Personal details and references to friends and relatives in these and other family letters I have edited not so much for discretion's sake but more often because some names and events, had they been retained, would be of little interest except to the addressee. I have deleted very few passages merely to avoid monotony. A double slash (//) indicates a deletion of a sentence or more. Though I have used footnotes or headnotes to furnish bibliographical material and identifications of some length, remarks which could be limited to a few words I have simply bracketed within the text. Unless otherwise indicated, then, such brackets are mine.

With the exception of the kinds of deletions mentioned above, I have tried to reproduce the manuscripts precisely as they are in the original or in the copy given me. The only other types of changes are as follows:
(1) Robinson Jeffers consistently placed periods and commas outside quotation marks and haphazardly punctuated titles, exaggerated or multiplied dashes, and indented so irregularly that it is often impossible to be sure where a new paragraph is intended. I have left titles as he wrote them, restored gen-

erally accepted American usage in other punctuation, and indicated probable paragraph divisions by standard indentions. Una's more energetic style eliminates apostrophes in contractions and possessives and omits occasional commas and periods, but if no misreading is likely, I have retained her mechanics. (2) I have corrected the rare misspellings, except for proper names, by bracketing inserted letters or the accurately spelled word. A bracketed question mark stands in place of each illegible word. (Occasionally a guess can be made: then brackets and a question mark accompany my conjecture.)
(3) Jeffers frequently neglected to date his correspondence. If I have been able to discover the date from examination of postmarks or consideration of internal evidence, I have inserted and bracketed it. I have also made consistent the form in which the date is given. All letters lacking any other heading originated from Carmel. A few correspondents are unidentifiable, the letter giving only the last name. When possible I have identified first names from other sources and inserted them in brackets. Salutations and complimentary closes are here separated from the body of the letter by a space.

I have been unable to locate letters to Edna St. Vincent Millay, Edgar Lee Masters, Genevieve Taggard, Horace Liveright, and Peter Boyle, though Jeffers certainly wrote to most and probably to all of them. The papers of S. S. Alberts and James Rorty have not yet been sorted. Henry A. Christian has graciously permitted my use of a letter from the Louis Adamic collection, which he is cataloging for the Princeton University Library. Margaret Carpenter has also consented to my use of a letter to Sara Teasdale from her collection of Miss Teasdale's correspondence, not yet published. The Robinson Jeffers Collection in the University of Alabama Library is restricted from general use, but I have copies of some of these letters from the files at Tor House.

Bibliographical listings of Jeffers' works and of reviews and criticism of that work, begun in S. S. Alberts' *A Bibliography of the Works of Robinson Jeffers*, recently reprinted by Cultural History Research, have been selected, annotated, and made current in Frederic Ives Carpenter's Twayne Series *Robinson Jeffers* and have been further expanded in Melba Berry Bennett's *The Stone Mason of Tor House*. These have been invaluable aids in the preparation of this volume of letters.

THE SELECTED LETTERS OF ROBINSON JEFFERS

1897 *The ten-year-old John Robinson Jeffers, who wrote the first letter in this collection, was born in Allegheny, a section of Pittsburgh, Pennsylvania, where his father taught at Western (Presbyterian) Theological Seminary. The family lived there, in Sewickley, and abroad until 1902. This earliest extant letter was written during one of Dr. J's trips on parish business. The letter makes reference to J's younger brother Hamilton, born in 1894, to William Hicks, the Js' driver and gardener, and to Philena Robinson, not really J's "grandma" but the wife of his mother's cousin. The letter is also included in Melba Berry Bennett's* The Stone Mason of Tor House *(Los Angeles, 1966), p. 7.*

1: TO WILLIAM HAMILTON J

Sewickley, Pa.
August 23, 1897

Dear Papa,   The baby and I were out in the garden when I saw a snake
which afterwards measured 22 inches. I called William and ran to get a club.
But William called me back to help him hunt for it. I ran back and found it
and he got it under his hoe and I ran away to get a stick. When
I came back he was about two rods away and I thought he had killed it but
when I asked him he said no it was in the row of beans just above the
garden. I saw it in the beans and William poked it out with the hoe and
then I killed it with my stick. I think, it was a garter snake. It was
white under neath, black with green speckles on top, a greenish yellow band
ran along its back, and large brown stripes ran lengthwise along its sides.
Mr. Shannons road is being filled up fast. We go out for a ride every
morning; before Grandma went away we took her; since then we have been
taking Mrs. Knox. Yesterday we went to the U. P. Church. Goodbye.
Your loving son, John Robinson

John Robinson

1912-20 *After a brief attendance at the University of Western Pennsylvania, J moved with his family to Long Beach, California, in 1903. In 1905 he was graduated from Occidental College and began graduate work at the University of Southern California, where he met Una Call Kuster. He studied at the University of Zurich in 1906 but returned to the United States to enroll as a medical student at USC in 1907. J's contributions to the Occidental student magazine, the* Aurora *(from 1904 the* Occidental*), and to the* Youth's Companion *were published during these years, 1903–7.* ❧ *Continuing their studies at USC, J and Una Kuster grew more and more troubled over their deepening relationship; J also became increasingly uncertain that a medical career would allow him time to write. In 1910, therefore, he decided to begin the study of forestry at the University of Washington, and he and his parents moved to Seattle in August. Correspondence with Una gradually dwindled until both began to think that the separation had accomplished one of its purposes. Less than an hour after his return to California in 1911, however, J saw Una on the street, and their lives were soon more complicated than before. Una's husband, Edward Kuster, questioned her about gossip he had heard and, when she corroborated the rumors, persuaded her to spend a year in Europe in an attempt to rescue their marriage. The separation once again served only to delay rather than to alter the progress of the affair, which eventually brought the Kusters to a divorce in 1913.* ❧ *Meanwhile, J published his first book of poems,* Flagons and Apples, *in 1912 and returned to Seattle. He and Una were married in Tacoma on August 2, 1913. After a September visit with J's parents, who had moved to Pasadena, they rented a small house in La Jolla, where they remained until their first child was expected, at which time they moved to Los Angeles.* ❧ *The next few years were marked by personal loss as well as by achievement. Una and J's daughter Maeve, born May 5, 1914, lived only one day. In December of that same year, J's father died. After a long illness, J's mother died in 1921. (Regrettably, the letters J wrote her before her death have been destroyed.) A few months after Maeve's death, in September, 1914, Una and J rented a small log house in Carmel, where, in 1919, J began building Tor House and, later, Hawk Tower. Twin sons, Donnan and Garth, were born in 1916, the same year in which Macmillan published* Californians.

2: TO UNA CALL KUSTER

*When she returned from her trip abroad, Una took lodging
in the St. Francis Hotel, San Francisco, informed J of her
return, and asked him to meet her there. A brief residence
in Berkeley was also expedient during their courtship.*

Hermosa Beach
November 5, 1912

This is the line you asked, to say that I am well; and that I am ready to
go north next week, and impatient to go.

Pardon this stub pen, which deforms my already enough deformed
handwriting.

I am having a book of verse brought out, under John S. McGroarty's
supervision, by the Grafton Pub. Co., who publish the West Coast
Magazine. McGroarty (of the Mission Play, etc) is become a good friend
of mine, and praises my productions in an exaggerated and satisfactory
manner,—as he might, being friend, and publisher's reader, and
Irishman. The book should be out by Christmas.

Also, I have an Ayrdale terrier pup, who looks as much like Bernard
Shaw as is possible for a dog.

—This is all the news till I see you. The photo from Tivoli is beautiful.
Good-bye—till soon—   Yours, R. J.

3: TO UNA CALL KUSTER

Seattle, Washington
Monday Evening
November 25, 1912

Dearest, two letters from you,—of Nov. 21 from S.F. and of Nov. 22
from Berkeley,—are lying in front of me; and I haven't opened either
one of them yet!

And you may believe that I want to open them—I'm thirsty for letters from
you, always—but first I want to write the things I have in mind.

Sweetheart—I love you—that's the first thing. The second is that I just
this morning engaged my berth on the Unatilla for tomorrow, and shall
be in S.F. to see you—they tell me Friday afternoon—but I fear not
until Saturday morning. However, if we have a good north wind, the ship
may possibly get in on Friday.—You'd better not try to meet me; I'll
find you as soon as possible after arrival.

Third is, that I love you, and more than ever—dearest—dearest—

Fourth—I've just had a letter from my mother, to whom I wrote from S.F.
telling her all. She is happy—very *very* happy, she says,—to know that I
have an aim in life at present—something to work for. She promises
to love you as she loves me; and she wants to know when I'll bring you
home—how soon she can see you. She wants to see you—she loves you. But
not as much as I love you dearest.

Finally, before I open your letters, I'll tell you about what I did yesterday.
I went for dinner to the Phi Delt house, as I told you I was going to.
Then, in the evening, I went with a couple of brothers, to a high-brow party
where a woman with the skin stretched tight over her large forehead
read and talked about the economic status of women. The great
Hannibal once went to a lecture of this kind, and said; "I've heard many
an old fool talk: —but such as this—never."

While we listened—as reverentially as possible—to the talk and the
conversation which ensued, came an earthquake. We were up in the
sixth story of a building down town, and there was a very considerable
vibration! In fact, I thought for a moment that we were all going
down with the building.

Then Glenn Hoover—the socialist ∈χ of whom I told you (Good
God!—if there *is* a God!) —spoke up quietly, and said in his drawling
manner: "Well, I guess we're just about as ready to meet our Savior as we
ever will be."—So the threatening stampede was quieted.

After the lecture, etc., was over, another of my brothers, Chester Warner,
went with me to the Rathskeller, where we had some crab à la Newburg,
with beer. The beer was served in a peculiar manner. According to
police restrictions in Seattle it's against the law to serve anything alcoholically
drinkable on Sundays. So the beer came in a tea-pot, and was poured
into tea-cups. It was really laughable, as you can imagine, sweetheart, —and
I saw two men at another table drinking wine out of egg-cups!

Now, dearest, I've told you almost everything that has happened, except
that I've written some verse, in between times, which I'll either send you
or bring to you.//

I never ask you a question? —NO: because I know everything necessary
without any asking at all. —I love you—you love me—what more do
we want?// Robin

4: TO UNA CALL KUSTER

Pasadena, California
December 4, 1912
Tuesday night

Dearest-in-the-universe, it's one-forty-five AM, and I've just returned to Pasadena from town [*Los Angeles*], and found your letter of Monday morning, and clipping, and catalogue fragment, awaiting me.

To-day I had lunch and a good talk with McGroarty—then saw Dr. Stookey[1] and gave him a copy of the Great Book—then found Anderson—and then Willard Huntington[2]—saw Miss Buckmann—saw Wright again, and was instructed to write a review of my own book for the book-number of the Times, which is due next Sunday. So I wrote the review, and Wright is going to revise it to-morrow and make it sound like himself. —Afterwards, Wright and I went down to the Bristol Cafe for an hour, and drank Würzburger.—Then I started home, and am just arrived.

When the Times book number comes out, I'll send you it, and also my review of myself as written originally—for sake of comparison. —For I don't know what Wright will do to my very eulogistic article.//

Now I'm going to bed, because I promised to meet Wright to-morrow morning and help him with what's left of the book-number, which goes finally to press to-morrow. Andy and he have been losing sleep working on it, and are fearfully irritable, snarling at each other like two strange dogs. They tried to find me, a week ago, to assist them. But I wasn't in town; I was occupied with something better—dearest—dearest//

5: TO UNA CALL KUSTER

Pasadena, California
December 6, 1912

This morning, dearest one, when *our* mother woke me up, I saw the post-man approaching from down the street, and sent our mother to get the letter that I knew would come for me.//

As you remarked, most beautiful, Emerson's a great and good man. We've only had two great men yet in American literature. —Poe is the other.

[1] *Dr. Lyman Stookey was J's physiology teacher at USC, 1907–9. Several letters to Dr. Stookey follow, beginning with Letter 12.*
[2] *Antony Anderson served as art critic for the* Los Angeles Times *until 1926; Willard Huntington Wright also wrote detective stories under the pseudonym S. S. Van Dine.*

But I think that Emerson treats experience in a too "pessimistic" manner. He ought not to grieve that griefs don't affect him; he ought to rejoice— with us, sweetheart.

The souls of a few of us fortunate ones—you and I—Alcibiades and Emerson—are a little too high—too *divine* to be more than ordinarily troubled by the ordinary human accidents.//

I think I'll go see Parker[3] this afternoon, and get him to take charge of some of my books. Andy wants to introduce me to him—Wright wants to introduce me—so does McGroarty. But I think I'll cut the Gordian Knot, and introduce myself. That will be easier, and, I imagine, just as effectual.//

Andy says that Flagons and Apples sounds like a cider-press. That the title is a great deal too cheerful for the book.

When I'm next in San Francisco, dearest, I'm going to introduce to you my friend Bill Yager. You don't like him, sweetheart, but you will. For, seriously, he's *one of us*. Not educated the same way, of course; —but of our family—our *type*. He's blue-eyed and reckless; has Scotch-Irish sanity; and our own proper aloofness—irresponsibility, perhaps. I think Archibald will resemble him; —but—of course—we'll bring Archibald up better. Bill Yager and Alexander the Great—Marlowe and Mary Queen of Scots—Sulla and Alcibiades—you and I and Archibald—we're a fine company, sweetheart, aren't we? A blue-eyed and reckless and irresponsible company.

Dearest, I am weak to the verge of imbecility. I'm uxorious—I need you so much. There's no living—no delight or adventure—nothing but a bad blank—until we're together—for good.   Robin

6: TO UNA CALL KUSTER

Pasadena
December 8, 1912

I'm mailing you today, sweetheart, the Times book-number; which contains, on page 17, the maiden review of my verses—written by myself. Wright has made in it only a very few changes—purely verbal changes, of no importance—so there's no need after all, of sending you my original draught (or should it be draft?) The thing seems to me very fair

---

[3] *J's book was at first to be placed with the Los Angeles bookseller, C. C. Parker, but was finally distributed from Holmes' Book Store. See Letter 59.*

and impartial and truthful—except for the suggestion, at the end of chapter first, that Wright's verse equals mine—"except, of course, my own." That's very poor criticism, you know; but not to be complained of—since I wrote it myself. However, I'm *not* responsible for "—not lascivious, be it noted, but psychologic." *Those* words are of Wright's insertion.

It'll be interesting to compare McGroarty's Irishness, when he reviews us in the West Coast, with the Wright-Jeffers collaboration.

Sunday's a dreary day, most beautiful one; but I've escaped half of it by staying in bed until noon.

This P.M.—it's 2 o'clock now, and we've just come back from lunch—I think perhaps I'll write some verse; or else start the novel I spoke about in San F. I'm not sure what the story of the latter will be; but I've already chosen a most thrilling theme, and a catchy title, and an adorable heroine; who, as I told you, is to be a libel on yourself. —Her name is Mona McLeod. —If I weren't sure of your sense of humor I wouldn't dare contemplate this slander; which shapes itself as a kind of high-burlesque-melodrama, a little on the order of Mlle. de Maupin. The title is "Man-Maker." The heroine falls in love several times; and makes each of her victims amount to something worth while—even, now and then, in spite of themselves. But she isn't the least *Ann*-ish—just the *Ewig Weibliche*, which *zieht uns hinan*—in this case, *hinauf*. It's a good theme; but, since it's a little *popular*, I'll have to drop in a suspicion of burlesque, so that people won't be quite sure whether I'm in earnest or not. "Irony," somebody says, "is the final achievement of art." —But not too much irony, nor too evident.

You shall see this libel, when I next meet you. —That is, if it isn't still-born.

To-morrow evening, dearest one, I think I'll go down to the [*Hermosa*] Beach for a few days. But you'd better still address me at Pasadena; for I'm not sure of going, nor for how long.

Meanwhile I send you all my truest love, solitary star,—and forever. You are the one shining thing in the world for me; and you have brightened all the rest.

It seems strange to be hopeful again, and full of happy laughter. I've always considered recklessness as the one great virtue; but I see now that it must be a positive and forward-looking recklessness,—not a desperate negative disregard of consequence. —The gay and laughing courage of D'Artagnan on his daffodil-colored hack; not the sombre death-and-devil-defiance of Athos.   Dearest, from your own—with his seal: Ⓧ

7: TO UNA CALL KUSTER

December 15, 1912
Saturday night

This morning, dearest, we got up pretty early—that is, for me,—and
drove down to Hermosa—our mother, Hamilton, Paddy, and I. We visited
Mrs. Nash[4] for awhile, and I got some manuscripts I wanted, and
my typewriter, which was to be returned to the shop, because it's broken,
and I don't want it any more at any rate. (I'll rent one here in Pasadena,
perhaps, for a month.) Mrs. Nash seemed very happy to see us, and Paddy
overjoyed to see her—he almost ate her up.

Coming back, we arrived in Pasadena about four P.M., and your letter—
beautiful was awaiting me. Its first words were: "I'm going, sweetheart,
to Seattle." —Do you wonder, heart o'me, that I think it one of the
nicest letters yet?//

Who is Galey-on-Euripides, sweet? —I never heard of him; so you can
exult over me. —But then I don't care much for Euripides, Una; nor
for any Greek drama—save in a spirit of pure dilettantism—except the
Prometheus. —Even *that* has its *longueurs*.[5]

But the Greek lyrists are the *thing*. Archilochus—Sappho—Alcaeus—so
the good pedants have handed us down just a few miserable patches of
their old magnificence. A pedant or grammarian, I think, is the worst possible
judge of literature—except the general public.

The MSs—that's dangerously close to *Messes*!—which I brought from the
beach were the ones I need to compile "Songs and Heroes"—*your* book.
I'll while away to-morrow therewith. Clun is going to have a book by
himself—later—so I don't need anything about him at present.
And anyway, I think I have practically all of that polygynist
now, in rough draft.

Mona McLeod—or whatever her name is—has been somewhat neglected
during these latter excitements; but she's started best foot foremost, and
hopes to complete her journey in time.

Anderson, whom I saw for a fleeting two minutes this afternoon while
we passed thru' town, is going to run a couple of pieces of verse in
the Sunday Times Magazine over the signature: "From Flagons and Apples
by J—— R—— J." McGroarty is going to do the same in the West Coast.
Parker, I understand, has sold a few volumes. Wright, who wishes it

---

[4] *Melissa Nash was J's landlady when he stayed at Hermosa Beach. See Letter 11.*
[5] *An undated (1941?) note to Agnes Meyer in the Tor House files specifies, "As for
Oedipus, poor man, I seem to like him less the more I think of him. But he
has some secrets still, which Sophocles perhaps overlooked. Sophocles is too careful, too
planned; I prefer Aeschylus drunkenly (as was said) heaping mass on mass."*

understood that he knows everybody of literary importance in the country, offers to do some logrolling for me with the eastern reviews. So we'll see.

—Wright is preparing an article on L.A. for the Smart Set, which is running a series of portraits of cities: —this month it's Chicago, by Constance Skinner. —If Wright's article is published before he leaves town for good, I'm sure there'll be a lynching bee among those hot-headed Southerners. L.A. likes advertising;—but—honestly, I never heard a city so bedevilled as in the pages Wright read me of his description. And this just as our Ishmael is getting back into the good graces of society and Mrs. Edison!

—Next letter we're going to begin our Seattle planning; but of course won't arrive at any decision until we get there—or later.

—I love you with all that's in me, dearest one. —Each little brain-cell is crying to all the others: "Praise thou Una!"

8: TO UNA CALL KUSTER

Los Angeles, Cal.
December 16, 1912

Dearest, this is just another "Irregular, out-of-town note to talk about loving"—like your sweet one of Sat. morn. I've just come from lunch with Andy, and want to talk to my dearest—about nothing—just loving— which is *not* nothing, but everything. So I came in here to the— "College o'sin," the boys used to call their cafe of the same name in Seattle. —But this is no cafe—just a bar, with seats back of it, and a Jap to serve.

I was just thinking, sweetheart, how fortunate was my anti-matrimonial prejudice of the past. If I hadn't had it I would probably have married some nice young girl with a milkmaid complexion several years ago. Before I knew you, sweet. —And afterwards things were so long so hopeless. —But now—there is no happiness like my happiness, joy of me, —and no hope like mine.

Do you remember—even less than a year ago—on Mt. Lowe—*when you proposed to me (N.B.)*—how hopeless I was? And when you were in Europe I was hopeless.

I think you're a witch, dearest. —What was it you did, Nov. 17, to make hope and joy rise all at once, like a sun in the tropics? —And permanently! —What incantation—what charm—did you use overnight, dearest, so that the world grew golden instead of gray? I am sure, if you set your mind to it, you could.

After he was graduated from Occidental College in 1905, Robinson Jeffers began medical studies at the University of Southern California.

—Tame the morn with peeled gray hazel-wands. Witch! you've done a bigger thing than that.

—Loveliest, we're very much like each other, and yet unlike. This morning I'm studying your photo, and comparing it with my own face in the mirror. Our faces *do* resemble each other—greatly. Except that my brows are heavier, and hang lower over the eyes. And my nose is more prominent. Our souls are very much alike, too. But yours has qualities which mine hasn't. Confidence and hope *was* one of them; but that is mine now also—you've given it me. *Social* courage is another—*social* courage—to be distinguished from moral and physical. (We both have the latter). —*Readiness* is a third. I have to think before I can act; but you have the great gift of being able to do the right thing at the first impulse. This comes from your purity—your *wholeness*—of soul, dearest. Mine, in the past, was split into a thousand pieces, and is just now reuniting. I used to have to take each of those pieces up, and balance each, one by one, against the others. But my soul is growing whole, now,—thanks to you, sweet.

*Jeffers met Una Call Kuster in
a German class at the University of
Southern California in 1906.*

And there are many, Una—many other gifts that you bring me.
—Wonderful gifts, that I never could have gained without you.—//

I want to talk a little about disintegration of soul. I saw an article the
other day—somewhere—which just expressed what I had often thought. It
was about writers. Said that men of action—captains—politicians—
Caesar—Alcibiades—had an *immediate* motive, and hence acted immediately
and with the whole mind. —But writers, etc., having no *direct* motive—
no immediate stimulus—which could appeal to the whole mind—
need something else to integrate their personalities. —Toxins of some kind.
(The author of this article didn't explain that the value of toxins—
alcohol-tuberculosis-opium-syphilis—lies in the fact that they are always
depressants, and exert their influence first on the weaker fragments of
personality, so that the stronger is free to act by itself, without friction. And
that's the whole point of the theory.)

Then the writer went on to cite Keats, Stevenson, etc., who were subject
to tuberculosis. —And London, who was a victim of the gout, and
Johnson (Samuel) who suffered from scrofula, —etc., (Most of these

examples I'm inventing at present.) After these, he said, came the fairly healthy ones, who *being* healthy, needed an artificial toxin. Such as Poe and Burns with their alcohol—DeQuincey and Coleridge with their opium, Tennyson with his tobacco, et al. Said also that Wordsworth, for instance wouldn't have missed inspiration so often if he had only resorted to some artificial toxin.

And all of this is very true. It's strange that a man could cite so many facts leading to one hypothesis, and never cite the explanation— which I've given at the head of this page, between ( ).

But the personal point of the affair lies in this, dearest,—that you—as I've told you—are integrating my own personality. You furnish an immediate motive, sweet, and are a great deal more worth while than *toxins.* Dearest, you don't merely paralyze the weaker fragments of soul: —you unite them with the stronger, so that the whole soul's become one. You have given the *big motive.* So at last, sweet, I have the single soul and the single eye (of Holy Writ). —(The clergyman's son in me *will* show itself now and then.)

I'm going back to Pasadena now, to continue making Heroes into a book.

Dearest, I'm sending this without revision. The voices of revelers here have distracted me—so you'll forgive the inconsequence of this epistle— which started out to be a mere couple of lines of "hello" and greeting.

Body and heart and soul, Una-sweet, I'm yours.   Robin

9: TO UNA CALL KUSTER

Pasadena, California
December 21, 1912
Friday afternoon

Most sweet, I just had an interview with *our* father—it's *our* father now, as well as our mother, dearest—because everything went well, and he appears quite reasonably content. I was terribly frightened, Una, at the prospect; because I thought he might say something to make me angry, and had visions of myself going up like a sky-rocket and making an awful row. But he said nothing wrath-provoking, dear-beautiful,—was on the contrary most kind; and even a little enthusiastic. He's been afraid

*"Think of me as one of those friendly natural objects
like a tree outside the window, that hasn't much means
of communication but all it has is well intended."*

(Letter 196)

15

that my anarchic ideas were going to ruin me, and is comforted now
by the prospect of firm anchorage ahead. Also he likes you—for four things
especially—and with fine diplomatic foresight, sweet,—I was careful to
emphasize these things right at the first. 1. Your Scotch-Irish descent—father
thinks the Scotch-Irish are the best people God has made yet—[6]
2. That you were born and partly brought up on a Michigan farm—he's
delighted that you're not city-bred. 3. I showed him your pictures, and
could see that he was impressed, tho' he didn't say much. 4. I told
him that you had your M.A. in philosophy. He likes brains; and
was delighted.

   —So it's all well settled, dearest-under-heaven. —Before our interview
ended he was telling me that I must persuade you to leave Berkeley,
and study in the University of Washington while I'm there. —Don't things
come out nicely for us, my beautiful one?

   And he said not a word against you for being divorced. —However, he
asked me if I didn't think I'd better give up smoking and occasional
drinking in order to please you and be worthy of you! —Sweetheart!
—I would—if you want.//

   —I've only looked—yet—at the outside of the two books you sent me.
But I read [John Collings] Squire's verse—without much appreciation,
I fear. The metaphysical doesn't appeal to me—usually—especially
not in verse. My theory (however much I may depart from it in practice)
is that poetry should be a blending of fire and earth—should be made
of solid and immediate things, of the earth earthy, which are set on fire by
human passion. Archilochus—Villon—Marlowe—these understood
the art of poetry as I understand it. (They'll forgive me the profane
comparison.) And I'm not very keen on beautiful but ineffectual
angels. —Squire seems to me (from this solitary example) a compound of
Browning and Emerson—only he understood versification
a great deal better than either.

   —I love you—more than I do myself—and that's saying a great deal!
O my dearest and most beautiful, let me see you soon. Love love love.

---

[6] *In a letter to the editor dated December 15, 1966, Una's sister, Daisy Bartley, has
corrected this continuing misimpression: "Because Una was so devoted to Irish poetry
and music I think she wished she were Irish—but I heard mother telling her
several times that 'You are not Irish—just because my parents lived in Ireland' and
this, of course, we found very true when we were researching the family blood lines."*

10: TO UNA CALL KUSTER

Pasadena, California
December 21, 1912
Saturday morning

Sweetheart, last night I read the Secret Woman and the four plays of Tchekoff. And I'm moved to criticism—of the former—as compared with the latter. I have the same objection to the S. W. that I had to The Tragedy of Nan, and those other two English plays we read on Mt. Lowe. (We had *such* a good time there, you know, dearest,—in spite of— sword of Damocles—) —I couldn't formulate my objection then; and I'm not sure that I can now. But—these English plays seem to me to be *machine-made*. Does that express it? —It's all very well for Russians— Gorky—Tchekoff—etc. to strew dust and ashes, and stick their heads into a tragic *mud*. Because that's native to them—indigenous—it grows out of Slavic nature. Also, there's bound to be suffering, and hopelessness, and *dirt*,—when a struggling intellectualism tries to grow up in a huge, mediaeval, disintegrated nation. "Dirt is just matter out of place"—and surely the intellectuals are out of place—in Russia. So this sordid and unrelieved *Welt-ekelon* (I'm making a new word out of Weltschmerz) has its own justification. It's the thing they can do *well*. It's not exotic; but *belongs*.

But when you come to the "Tragedy of Nan," e. g.—you—I mean, I,— feel as if it's another (forgive me! his name is forgotten)—as if its author had said: "If these benighted Slavs can take a sordid horror of the peasants and make a wonderful thing—even a beautiful thing—out of it—a piece of living literature—go to!—Why can't a free-born Englishm*u*n do as well, or better?" so he goes and tries to do likewise. And the result is that it's second-hand literature—very dramatic, certainly, (more dramatic than the Russians) and very well-written—but still second-hand. You feel that it doesn't grow out of the country, nor out of personal emotion; but out of modern literature, and a good mechanical craftsmanship. And the Secret W. gives the same impression; altho' it partakes more of Ibsen than of Andreyeff. Also Phillpotts's last act is dangerously close to anti-climax—tho' I'll admit that it contains some fine dramatic irony.

—But after all I don't think I've really hit the bull's-eye of my criticism. Perhaps this is more to the point: —when Ibsen or Strindberg or Tolstoi or Tchekoff or Synge sticks a nasty tragedy under our noses (I don't mean nasty as literature, but nasty as life) we feel that there are principles at stake—that a philosophy or a racial character is being dissected and explained. But with the S. W. or the Tr. of Nan, you feel as if the author said: "Here's a peculiar mix-up that ends in a specially disastrous climax. Isn't it horribly interesting? But of course it doesn't mean anything much: There's no harm intended." —The two types of author compare like two physicians demonstrating two different post-mortems. Says the first physician: "This man died of syphilis. —You see the gummata in brain and liver: you see the opacity of the cornea. And here, under the microscope, is a fresh culture from his blood. Here you can see the spirochetes themselves. I'm not showing you this case because it's exceptional, but because it's typical. It's fearfully typical: one man and often, is affected in just this manner. —What are you going to do about it?"

But the second physician, a police-surgeon, says: "Look at this poor man who fell from the 15th story of the Flat-iron Bldg. Isn't it terrible? And isn't it interesting? —You'll observe that the right femur has been driven completely thro' the pelvis, and has ruptured the sigmoid flexure of the colon. —A very strange accident: —couldn't happen again in a thousand years."

—Dearest,—have I bored you horribly? —My brain has no fingers this morning—just thumbs.// Your Robin

11: TO MRS. MELISSA NASH

See also Melba Berry Bennett, The Stone Mason of Tor House *(Los Angeles, 1966), pp. 64–65.*

Hotel Tacoma
Tacoma, Washington
August 1, 1913

My dear Mrs. Nash: Tomorrow we'll be mailing you the announcement of our wedding, and I suppose you'll receive it at the same time as this letter. It hardly seems possible that we are really going to be married tomorrow; so great a happiness is almost incredible. But it is true. This morning we left Seattle and came to Tacoma, and this afternoon we went to the court house here and got the marriage license. My mother, as Una has told you, has been with us in Seattle for the last three weeks; she is staying with us now, and will start for California early tomorrow afternoon, soon after the ceremony is performed. We are very glad that she is going to be here to see us married, and I think that she has very much enjoyed her stay in the north. I wish you too could be here, my foster-mother.

You'll be surprised, I'm sure to hear that Una and I intend going to Europe this winter. Una enjoys England and her English friends so much

*Robin and Una Jeffers lived for several
months in Seattle after their marriage in
Tacoma, Washington, in 1913.*

that I think it will give her great happiness to go there again and to
live there for a year or two. And I shall be able to work as well there as
in America—perhaps better. At any rate the experience will be helpful
to me, and I look forward to it with great pleasure. We'll come back
to visit California after a year, I think; but probably a good deal of our future
life will be spent in England and on the Continent.

Our plan is to remain in Seattle until the middle of September; then to go
to Los Angeles—and Hermosa—for almost three weeks. After that we'll
go straight to Europe, stopping only for a few days in Michigan, where Una's
parents live. And perhaps for a few days in New York.

So we'll see you, Mrs. Nash, in September; and I'm looking forward with
more pleasure than I can tell you to staying a fortnight in Hermosa.
You have always been so good to me, and I have a son's affection for you—
how anxious I am to see you and talk to you!

It is almost midnight, and I shall have to close this letter—the last I
shall write before my marriage. I'll write again very soon, and more fully,
about our plans and our experiences.

Thank you ever so much for your sweet letter which I received yesterday
morning.   Goodnight, my dear Mrs. Nash, Robin

12: TO DR. LYMAN STOOKEY

December 15, 1915

Dear Dr. Stookey—   Last week we drove by mail stage some forty miles
south of Carmel—"down the Coast," they say here—into the valley
of the Big Sur River. A mile or so this side of our destination the stage-driver
pointed out what is called the "white redwood"—a quantity of bushy
redwood growth, pure albino, around the stump of a big tree. I am
enclosing a sprig of the albino (with one of the normal for control), thinking
you may be interested. Albinism seems very unnatural in plants, since
their life depends on chlorophyll. All the saplings of this stump have white
needles; there are no other albinoes, so far as anyone knows, in the
forest. It is not caused by lack of sunlight; for the other redwood saplings,
growing in much denser shadow, are quite normal. The stage-driver's
theory is that the parent-tree was struck by lightning, and that turned white
the foliage of the root-sprouts: —I suppose on the principle of a man's
hair turning white with terror!
　　—We had a delightful drive, and returned the next day. The scenery
was marvelous—a hardly inhabited country—mountains 4000 feet
high standing on the ocean-cliff—streams in every canyon—and the
immense sombre redwood trees, towering straight up, with trunks thirty
feet or more in circumference. Here in Carmel we have gigantic
pine-trees; but they are pygmies compared with those redwoods.
　　Carmel has been our home now for over a year, and we are as little tired of
it as we were at first. I am steadfastly writing poetry—good poetry, I
think—and shall publish it in due time. I'll be most happy to hear that
you and Mrs. Stookey are well and prosperous.   Your friend, Robinson Jeffers
　　The albino is turning a little brown, I see. It was pure white when
fresh, like new ivory.

13: TO DR. LYMAN STOOKEY

822 Garfield Avenue
Pasadena
January 18, 1917

Dear Dr. Stookey—   It is my turn to ask pardon for not having sooner
answered such a friendly and delightful letter as yours. I have been
expecting to visit you at your office, and have been quite occupied, too,
spending the mornings and midnights at work, and the rest of the day
admiring and attending my young sons. Had you not heard, when you wrote

to me, of that particular and reduplicated happiness? The boys are ten weeks old to-day, very vigorous and pleased with the world, and have doubled their birth-weights. They are as fat as any Mellin's food baby, but get only what nature provides, plus a little boiled water.

I'm very pleased that you think well of my book; and the fault will not be of intention or of effort if your flattering hopes of my future ones are disappointed. "To this end," as Dante says, "I labor all I may."

You spoke of *vers libre*, etc. I have a theory as to its origin. You know that French translators, realizing the next to impossibility of rendering verse worthily into another language, have these many years been translating foreign verse into domestic prose, but line for line, separating the lines so as to indicate the original form. Thus divided, a prose paragraph acquires a pleasant deceptive sort of jingle, and I think this must be the fountain-head of the free-versists. But I object rather less to such a senseless way of printing prose than to the effeminacy and hysteria, as of a tea-party gone mad, that seems to have infected all of them.

I was very pleased, and very surprised to meet Byron [*Dr. Stookey's younger brother*] at the Good Samaritan Hospital. He has had some wonderful and enviable experiences; I'm devoutly glad, though, that he has safely returned to this state. You must have spent some nervous months for his sake.

Una and I have had two idyllic years in the Monterey pine forest and are not tired of it, but often homesick for the north. We shall return, and I think build a home up there, as soon as the spring is firmly enough established to make motoring safe for babies. We bought a Ford last June for the trip south, and have used it a good deal since, without ever changing a tire, or any repair except one spark-plug and two fan-belts. They are vulgar and snub-nosed, but they are hardy and economical as goats or jackasses.

I shall visit you as soon as I can, and remain very faithfully your friend.
Robinson Jeffers

14: TO ERNEST G. BISHOP

See "The Belled Doe" and "The Mill Creek Farm" in Californians; *"Fawn's Foster-Mother" in* Cawdor.

July 31, 1917

Dear Mr. Bishop: As a matter of fact, the belled doe was brought up (on condensed milk!) by a solitary who lives in Palo Colorado Canyon, some twenty miles south of here. She is still living, and visits her benefactor.

She bore twin fawns this season, and they appear to be growing up as tame as their mother. I transplanted the incident to the south, I hardly know why—perhaps in order to speak of places that I love but had no story about them, having been always alone when I wandered there, and talking to no one.

As to the rearing of stray fawns: —there is an old woman here in Carmel—eighty years old and swollen with dropsy—who has lived most of her life in wild places hereabout. Once her husband captured a fawn while she was nursing a baby. She had an uncomfortable excess of milk; the fawn shared with the child and both grew up happily, nuzzling the same breasts.

The waterfall and the little farm below it,—I suppose must be called imaginary, though they seem real enough to me. I probably had Hoyt's in mind when I wrote of the ranch on Tujunga Creek, but I didn't mean to designate Hoyt's or another. Likewise I thought of Fox Creek in inventing the name Foxbrook Flats. It's ten years, unfortunately, since my last campfire in your mountains, and my memories of them are not definite so far as names are concerned.

The Mill Creek farm is not in the south, but in Monterey County, between Palo Colorado (mentioned above) and the Little Sur River. There's a tremendous number of Mill Creeks in our state, both north and south; and all that I know of are lovely streams.

I am glad my verses have pleased you.   Sincerely yours, Robinson Jeffers

15: TO DR. LYMAN STOOKEY

[*August 21, 1920*]

Dear Dr. Stookey—   I would have written you earlier—at least an acknowledgement of the Christmas card we received from Mrs. Stookey—but I know your aversion to correspondence and feared you might think a letter called for a reply. This one does not.

We have builded us a little house on the sea-cliff here; it is just a year since we came to live in it. A delightful place we think, cormorants on the sea-rocks in front of us, and pelicans drifting overhead; a most graceful hill-range to the south across a neck of water;—it is a promontory, with water on three sides of us. The house and garage and walls are gray granite—sea-boulders, like the natural outcrop of the hill. In foolish frankness, it is the most beautiful place I have ever seen. I mean, to my taste.

We have two and a half acres; I hope we shall be able to afford more in course of time.

The infants are flourishing; they will be four years old next November, and are growing mightily in this free space and free air.

My work progresses (I believe) in spite of appearances. I'm tolerably satisfied with it, the first time in my life, and shall perhaps be ready to publish a book pretty soon; magazine publication I don't care for; not indeed to publish anything until I become quite sure that I shall care for it twenty years from now.

I spend a couple of hours nearly every afternoon at stone-masonry, having still much to build about the place; or bringing up stone from the beach, violent exercise; and physically I'm harder than at any time since that delightful unforgotten summer when you and Byron and I wrestled at Hermosa.

Pray give my cordialest greeting to Mrs. Stookey; and to Byron when you see him or write—I don't even know whether he's in Los Angeles.

If you are ever in the north, and have time, or pass our village—the coast road goes through Salinas, only twenty-three miles from here—I wish heartily that you would come to see us. And stay more than one day if possible.   Yours, Robin Jeffers

OVERLEAF:

"No man can make an invention or a poem by willing it. . . . We can only prepare the way a little—sweep out distractions."

(Letter 284)

1924-28 *By 1924 the Js were well-established members of their small community. J's work began to attract attention, and his career was encouraged by his developing friendships with James Rorty, George Sterling, Benjamin de Casseres, Mark Van Doren, Albert Bender (a generous patron to several San Francisco area artists), and others. Peter Boyle published J's first major work,* Tamar and Other Poems, *in 1924, and Boni and Liveright republished it with "Roan Stallion" in 1925. In 1927, Liveright published* The Women at Point Sur *and, in 1928,* Cawdor and Other Poems. *J's work was anthologized in 1925 in the Book Club of California's* Continent's End *and in Robert H. Schauffler's* The Poetry Cure, *in William S. Braithwaite's* Anthology of Magazine Verse *for 1926, in Harcourt, Brace's* A Miscellany of American Poetry: 1927 *and, in 1928, in Braithwaite's* Anthology . . . , *in Louis Untermeyer's* Modern American and British Poetry, *and in Mark Van Doren's* An Anthology of World Poetry. *Individual and small groups of poems appeared during these years in* Nation, Measure, Overland Monthly, New Republic, American Mercury, San Francisco Review, New Masses, Literary Digest, *and* Poetry. *J also reviewed James Rorty's* Children of the Sun *for* Advance, *XII (April, 1927), 12, and Mark Van Doren's* Now the Sky *for the* New York Herald Tribune Books, *December 2, 1928, p. 4, and he contributed a prose eulogy of George Sterling, "A Few Memories," to the* Overland Monthly, *LXXXV (November, 1927), 329, 351.* ❧ *J's sadness over the death of George Sterling in 1926 suggests the reach of their brief and curiously detached friendship in which each respected the other's work, personality, and opinions but was very little influenced by any of them. The friendship with Sterling did lead J further and further into self-evaluation, however, and prepared him for the many explanations his work began to demand. During this period J's intentions and motives took shape and began to justify themselves for him: his confidence in the propriety of the incest symbol, his sense of the rhythm and verse line best suited to him and to his material, his willingness to attempt poems for dramatic reading, if not for dramatic performance, and to experiment with dramatic forms all increased. He became, also, more and more aware of his growing audience as a body of individual readers with individual and varying responses to his work, and he occasionally consented to help educate them to its appreciation.*

16: TO GEORGE STERLING

July 5, 1924

Dear George Sterling— Your letter quite toppled me over, like that poor
city in Ohio the storm visited lately; and now after two or three days I am
still trying to creep out of—not a desolation—a terrible splendor. One *can't*
accept such praise—and I'm not inhuman enough to put it aside—or
mean enough to be critical where you have been so generous. What can I
say—except that if power comes I shall try to deserve
some part of what you have written.

You have long been a fixed star in my sky—since for my delight I came
on Wine of Wizardry in some magazine [Cosmopolitan] many years
ago—and living about Carmel the past ten years I have felt myself again
and again an intruder in your domain, but now the lord of the region
has made me welcome. But how can I thank you for a letter that has the
eagle-sweep and the clear sweetness of your odes, and such generosity
as I think isn't recorded before in the dealings of poets with each other?

Our friend James Hopper[1] used to tell me now and then that you had been
here; perhaps I may see you if you visit this place again. Rorty is staying
with us over the week-end; if the privations he will describe don't
appear too formidable, maybe you will honor us sometime. I wish you would.
If you come I shall get a young cypress tree and ask you to plant it for a
memorial—to be distinguished forever among the two or three hundred
others we have planted here—so there is warning.   In all
sincerity yours, Robinson Jeffers

17: TO GEORGE STERLING

Sunday, [1924]

Dear Sterling: My young brother, who is an astronomer but disagreeable,
and pervades the house with damned radio experiments, is stopping here
on his way to Lick Observatory and I've been fighting several days
for an hour to write to you. Before he came there was a man
laying linoleum—

Forgive me for questioning whether you don't take fashions too seriously.
You have Shakespeare for precedent—you remember the sonnet that

[1] *Hopper was on the staffs of* McClure's Magazine *and* Collier's. *With his journalist
friend, Frederick Bechdolt (see Letter 18), he wrote the novel* 9009, *which
prompted early California prison reforms.*

says he would have been equal to the others if he had "grown with this growing age" but then one wonders whether the age very much outgrew him.

What is good in the "modern movement in poetry," as in most earlier "modern movements," is a return to reality I think; and precisely reality is one of the qualities that makes your "Old Anchors" such a splendid poem; they are not heraldic anchors but real ones in a junk-yard and you see them lying there with the rust on them. This is one of your poems I wish your grandfather the whale-killer might have read; yet he could never have loved as I do the superb last stanza and last line of it; nor indeed any one of the lines, for it is perfect.

To return to theory: I think two essential qualities of poetry are that it be rhythmic (and not in the sense in which we talk about rhythmical prose, but with fairly regular recurrences, metrical or other, making at least a tidal regularity; the tides don't follow the clock nor yardstick but they are regular if you see enough of them)—and that it deal with things and emotions that are permanent or capable of perpetual renewal.[2] Perhaps you have noticed how much of the modern movement fails to be rhythmical and deals with God may know what. It's not the movement but the man—perhaps I've spilled enough pedantry.

Laffler[3] was here once to see my stone-work and told a buried treasure story that had a beautiful picture in it, of a ship wrecking on Point Lobos, bales of rich-colored Chinese silks spilling on the waves, and vaqueros on the rocks fishing for them by tossing out their spurs tied to the ends of their lariats. —I'm glad he is seeing "Tamar."

Long ago I read Neihardt's "Man-Song"; I have never read "Hugh Glass" nor "The Song of the Three Friends" though of course I know about them. To my shame, I have never read "Lilith" nor the volume of your "Selected Poems"; I certainly shall read them soon in any case; I'd be extraordinarily happy if you'd send them but how have I deserved it?

Rorty had two things among others to say about you; that you have a fault of humility, and I see it is true; and that your work grows steadily better still. Perhaps that fault is one of the sources of the excellence: —but it will take much to outshine the splendor of the great suns of your "Testimony."

Astronomers are curious folk: my brother is a mathematical one, and I

---

[2] *For related discussions of this subject, see J's Foreword to* The Selected Poetry of Robinson Jeffers *(New York, 1938), pp. xiv–xv, and his "Poetry, Góngorism, and a Thousand Years," New York Times, January 18, 1948, Sec. 6, pp. 16 and 26, which was reprinted as* Poetry, Gongorism and a Thousand Years *(Los Angeles, 1949); in Bennett, Stone Mason, pp. 202–7; and in "The Creative Artist and His Audience: A Symposium," Perspectives USA (Autumn, 1954), under the title "Poetry and Survival," pp. 102–7. See also Letters 182 and 183.*
[3] *Harry Laffler, one of Sterling's Bohemian Club friends, edited Argonaut Magazine.*

doubt whether he could point out Orion on a clear winter evening. There is a great deal more I want to say, but I hope there will be another opportunity. Don't forget us if you come to Carmel.

"Pro Christi et ecclesia" reminds me of the Latin we have just had cut in marble to set in the parapet of the granite tower I'm building here—R. J. suis manibus me turrem falconis fecit—we call it the Hawk's Tower for the sake of a sparrow-hawk that used to perch daily on my scaffolding, so we have hawk gargoyles and a key-stone with a hawk carved on it.   Well—pro versa ecclesia—tuus remanebo, Robinson Jeffers

18: TO GEORGE STERLING

August 10, 1924

Dear Sterling: I'm unhappy to think of your having taken so much trouble about the books for me; pray don't buy the "Selected Poems," but when your next book is published maybe you'll send me a copy and I shall be very proud, and call in all our friends to see it, [Frederick] Bechdolt among them.

I didn't know that his opinion of you was not what it should be; when he has spoken of you I thought his manner rather distant, but it was certainly not hostile; but in ten years we've never yet learned to understand the ramifications of Carmel opinion.

Yesterday Heron[4] lent us "Lilith"; he did her up in white paper and lent her reluctantly, begging us to be careful of her. A terrible and beautiful poem; I have only had time yet to read carefully the first two acts, and dreamed of the vaults and the lake; you make horror shine. And there is no gulf in which you forget beauty.

Thank you indeed for "The Wiser Prophet"; you use astronomy to some purpose; there is peace I think deeper than any terror in this thought of the end: *it is as it ought to be.* It's hard to express comprehensibly— existence would be rather a shallow affair without non-existence to back it—

Those true words of Bierce's are matter of history and you ought to keep the page; but if you won't take it back when you are here, we will keep it, and safely.[5]

You'll stay with us a couple of nights, won't you, when you come to

[4] *Herbert Heron, proprietor of the Seven Arts Bookstore and founder of the Forest Theater.*
[5] *Ambrose Bierce, "A Poet and His Poem,"* Cosmopolitan *(September, 1907). The article was republished in Volume X of* The Collected Works of Ambrose Bierce *(New York, 1911), pp. 177–86.*

Carmel? I wish I could ask Harry Laffler, or whoever brings you, also; but our house is such a little one, though it will be bigger some day if I keep on building.

Totheroh's innocent Salome is to be staged next week-end in the new theater our friend Kuster has built here;[6] maybe you'd like to see it; the theater at least will be pleasant to look at; and the lighting; and Ruth Kuster will be charmingly ingenue as Salome. —The play I won't speak of: Kuster read it to us. But I'm not a judge of plays.   Yours always, Robinson Jeffers

Monday morning.   I have read through the poem, though not finished it, and am grateful to you for it. It is most nobly conceived, and has in it some of the most beautiful passages I have ever read. That is a haunting vision of the twin drops, of blood and dew, whence phenomena evolve—the whole world subjective—it might be the Book of Genesis for a new religion.   R. J.

If you care about seeing the Salome will you let me know soon? It is Saturday evening, and it appears the house will be even more sold out than usual.

19: TO GEORGE STERLING

September 21, 1924

Dear George Sterling: You've heard of course about Hopper's house being burned; possibly you've seen him lately, as he was on his way home and I think intended stopping in San Francisco. The house was not entirely ruined, enough left to start rebuilding with. It was a solemn and splendid blaze, lighting all Carmel Bay at 9 PM; we enjoyed the spectacle from our tower-top, not knowing until next morning whose house it was. We weren't happy when we knew.

I'm glad you didn't come this way when we hoped you were coming as the "Salome" is said to have been not very good; I didn't see it. But pray come sometime—any time—not too far hence.
Yours always, Robinson Jeffers

Thank you much for that admirable Bedouin sonnet on the "city of illusion." "Talk of where we go and whence we come"—activates the mind at least. How constantly the beauty of your manner flows through every avatar.   R. J.

---

[6] *Una's ex-husband, Edward Kuster, liked to promote young talent. Dan Totheroh was a drama student at the University of California at Berkeley.*

20: TO DR. LYMAN STOOKEY

September 23, 1924

Dear Dr. Stookey— The post-office wrote a last line to my chapter of absurdities by sending your letter to Catalina! whence it has just reached me, post-marked Avalon. I'm most awfully sorry you've been bothered with this foolishness.

George Sterling, who is extraordinarily kind to this book of mine, wanted me to send a copy to Masters; and my natural reluctance to write to someone I don't know would no doubt explain the mistake to a Freudian, but not quite to me. I'll send Masters his letter, and ask him to destroy yours, unless it's already on its way back to me.

Very likely the title poem of the book ["*Tamar*"] won't please you, but perhaps one or two of the shorter ones will. At any rate, don't trouble to acknowledge them further; you've already written me a letter, a delightful one, and I remember how you detest writing them. But if you're ever up this direction do visit us, and if possible plan to spend a day or two. It's really a very beautiful place, four or five acres of the best of a little promontory just in the middle of Carmel Bay, Point Lobos on one side and Pebble Beach, etc., on the other, the sea three quarters of a circle around us, the little hill the house is on running down to beautiful granite cliffs and skerries. The house and garage, almost-finished tower and courtyard walls are granite sea-boulders, built mostly by me. Also brought up the cliff by me and my wheelbarrow. (170 pounds a cubic foot). But the carpenter work I leave to others.

Please give my kindest remembrances to Mrs. Stookey, and I hope she may be with you if you come up our hill sometime. I'm almost sure you will; for we'll always be here; except a half year in England, two or three years from now, after all my building is completed. Una joins me in hoping for a visit from you both; I've just asked her.

Here are pictures of my worthless sons and me and the place we live in. Yours always, Robinson Jeffers

21: TO GEORGE STERLING

November 22, 1924

Dear George Sterling: Perhaps you are tired having letters from me, but I can't forbear telling you how glad we were of your visit. At your pleasure I hope you'll come and stay a couple of nights instead of an hour; our Ford is even older than the Hoppers', and much rustier, and you can ride up and down in it.

We have had carpenters in the tower all this week panelling Una's little
room with Japanese oak, and it is such a wonder of a little place now
with its deep window-embrasures and carved hawks and unicorns
and motto from Virgil, that I'd like to show it to you, and am
sure that she would.[7]

Monday they'll begin on the boys' room down-stairs, and that will soon
be habitable; though the parapets are not finished and most of
the winter will go by before my turret is.

I've made, though not completed, a poem about Clytemnestra and her
family that I'd like to inscribe to you, if you'll let me, when—and if—it comes
to publication. I'll show it to you when you come—not read, I can't
read but I can typewrite—also we'll provide the young tree that you've
promised to plant for us.   Yours always, Robinson Jeffers

I'm enclosing the Ambrose Bierce page, which I failed to speak of when
you were here. Sorry to part with it; but I feel you ought to keep
it—if only because your biographer will want it.   Yours, R. J.

22: TO GEORGE STERLING

January 21, 1925

Dear George Sterling: Here is the poem I thought of inscribing to you, and
here are stamps to send it back with when you're done looking. I think I
shan't offer it to be published, I don't see why anyone should want
to read about Mycenae. And the best part of publication is showing it to
G. S., which I do herewith. Sometimes I'll write something more
amusing, and dedicate it to you, if you'll let me.

This is my first letter of 1925, or indeed for awhile before, we've been
so occupied with the little rooms in the tower, and celebrating
the children's holidays.

Una loved the poem you sent her; so do I; we have many treasures from
you. Wonderful to have made so many beautiful things, all stamped
with the maker's signet, so that one would know them in Arabia.

I could hardly believe it when that other page of Ambrose Bierce tumbled
out of your letter. He was a good friend; and a wise critic.

When are you coming to see us? Or do you really intend to wait for
spring-time and the twinkling blue lupine? I hope not.
Yours always, Robin Jeffers

[7] *See Una's note to Letter 23.*

23: TO MAURICE BROWNE

February 11, 1925

Dear Maurice Browne—   It is a wonderful thing to receive a letter like
yours, and tell myself that such a man may be mistaken but in judging a poem
he can't be *utterly* astray—and grow intolerably haughty. No, humble
rather, at any rate agitated and grateful. *I* enjoyed very deeply *your* poem,
that was played here, and didn't tell you so. I knew there were enough
voices praising it. Una must have spoken for me, however, she came
home glowing and shaken from the reading when she first heard it.

That you should read "Tamar" through such a divine hazard, in the oasis
by Santa Maria, is more luck than I think any writer deserves.

I'd have given you a copy of the book when you were here, but I knew
well you were too busy to read it. The one I send with this has
nothing written in it, so that you may feel free to give
or mislay it, having read it already.

You will be in Carmel again sometime, and then you'll come and see us. You
and Una will talk and I shall listen, it's not in my nature to have much to
say but indeed I should enjoy your presence, and may Miss Van
Volkenburg be of the party.[8]   Yours, Robinson Jeffers
[*Addition in Una's hand*]

Yes, *do* come to the Hawk's Tower and talk! My little oaken room is all
carved round with hawks and unicorns and its an enchanted place—
and it says over the fireplace "Ipsi sibi somnia fingunt." Come
and fashion a dream there!   Cordially Una J.

24: TO GEORGE STERLING

February 12 (is it?), 1925

Dear George Sterling—   It's a lovely gift, and I'm not a little ashamed of
not having said "yes" when you first spoke of it. I thought you meant to
lend, not give, and I thought it would be a bother for you to wrap
and address, and—well, I'm grateful, at any rate, for the gift *and* the
inscription.

This is the first book of Frost's that I've seen, and as yet I've only read
rapidly the first pages. It sounds a bit like "Bishop Blougram's Apology," but
also the man has a humor of his own, and I think the Notes and so forth

---

[8] *With Browne, Ellen Van Volkenburg founded and directed the Chicago Little Theatre
in 1912; in 1918 they took their repertory company to the West Coast.*

are going to be even better than the pleasant beginning. —I was
right, opening again I've just read the picture of the little colt
afraid of a snow-storm, it is *delightful*.

You overwhelm us with gifts, I'm still admiring in memory the ghostly
beauty of your "Pavement," and not only Una but I too delighted in
the sonnets about Helen. And "Archer and Arrow"—why did
people ever imagine that truth and beauty were enemies?

I was thinking that your name sings too. Una's idol George Moore
remarked long ago the ugly names of novelists and the beautiful ones of
poets—I forget the passage—Thackeray sounds "like a clatter of
plates falling"—and Dickens, Scott,—but Algernon Swinburne "a reed over
which every wind blows music." One can't carry the comparison
very far, but how about George Sterling?

I'm pleased that you were going to show that Oresteia to the Lafflers and
[*painter Xavier*] Martinez.   Yours always, Robin Jeffers

25: TO MARK VAN DOREN
                                                    March 15, 1925

Dear Mr. Van Doren—   Let me thank you for your very kind notice in
the Nation of my book called "Tamar."

Our friend Rorty was confident several months ago that you'd like it if
you saw it, and I think you must agree with me in admiring
his persistent energy!

I've met much generosity lately, especially from poets—yourself, Rorty,
George Sterling, Robert Nichols, and several others, —which is very
upsetting to the notions that one learned from Horace.
Sincerely yours, Robinson Jeffers

26: TO GEORGE STERLING
                                                    March 18, 1925

Dear George Sterling: It's two weeks to-morrow since young Garth Jeffers
got up from a tumble (happily not off the tower) and showed me without
a whimper his left forearm all bent over backward. We got the bones
set in an hour but the household remains upset a little, and that's why I've
been thinking letters to you instead of writing one. Your praise of the
verses pleased me more than I can say, but you know how happy it would
make me. Since they were absent I've thought of all sorts of things to change

in them—I mean, that ought to be changed—whether I'll be able to
is another question. The title, to begin with. My idea was to present
as a part of the action, the culminating part, that liberation which the witness
is supposed to feel—to let one of the agonists be freed, as the audience is
expected to be, from passion and the other birth-marks of humanity.
Therefore *beyond* tragedy—tragedy and what results. It occurred to me
with a sort of horror that others—not you, I know,—might imagine
"beyond" was meant in a foolisher sense, like Man and Superman—my God!
So that will have to be changed, at any rate. The incest theme—you are
right of course. I never had a sister, and here is what inexperience
does to one! I think of two reasons why it occurs to me; first because it
breaks taboo more violently than the other irregularities and so *may* be of a
more tragic nature; and more important, it seems to symbolize human
turned-inwardness, the perpetual struggle to get ahead of each
other, help or hinder each other, love each other, scare each other, subdue
or exalt each other, that absorbs 99 per cent of human energy. For
instance the man who discovers a mountain isn't happy until he collects other
men to admire it, or until he fights other men for possession of it. This
excess of introversion is a sort of racial incest, or so I imagine, but
we'd better find another symbol.[9]

I'm ashamed to say I haven't read "Rosamund," but I intend to, it will be
in the library here, or Heron will have it. I know well how beautifully you
would do it. And I pray you, don't spoil nice things you say about my work
by dispraise of your own. It isn't true. The sun of blank verse hasn't set,
certainly not, has the sun of the hexameter?—if Greek were still a
living language? It was many a century between Homer and Theocritus,
and the hexameter still rolling on, because it belonged,
as much as young Marlowe's invention in English.

About Theocritus, I had a nice letter the other day from Robert Nichols,
in Hollywood, who talked about "Theocritus of the Pacific Slope"! I
didn't know him but no doubt you will—Georgian poet, friend of
J. C. Squire of the London Mercury, to whom he sent a copy of "Tamar."

Thank you very much for talking about me to [*William Rose*] Benét; and
to C. Erskine Scott Wood, from whom I had a note yesterday, which I
must answer, with a copy of "The Poet in the Desert." And what a
fellow James Rorty is!

And thank you for "The Cynic."[10] It is beautiful and desolating—a last
word indeed! Touches bottom, to the very stretch of the intelligence:

[9] *See also J's discussion of the incest symbol in Louis Adamic,* Robinson Jeffers: A Portrait
(Seattle, 1929), p. 28, and Letters 53, 122, and 169.
[10] *Library of Congress retains the manuscript of the poem, which was sent to J
with Sterling's notation, "Illustrating how I waste my time!"*

—only a lost mystic may imagine that the bottom drops out somehow, and
the mystic and the plumb-line and the whales and the scattered ocean
all flow down deeper. They are hauntingly beautiful lines—
"Sorrow once with slumber there"—
    We still hope a visit from you sometime. But a hundred some miles is no
trifle, I should be overwhelmed at the thought—   Yours always,
Robin Jeffers

27: TO GEORGE STERLING

March 26, 1925

Dear George Sterling: I was quite overwhelmed by your gift, coming with
such royal suddenness, and I read it through the night of its arrival.
In my awful ignorance I'd thought it was the Rosamund whom "those dragon
eyes of injured Eleanor" pursued, the King of England his mistress,
do you remember her epitaph?

> Hic jacet in tumba   ⌈ the rose of the world, ⌉[11]
>   rosa mundi, non rosa munda.   ⌊ not the clean rose.   ⌋
> Non redolet sed olet,
>   quae redolere solet.   (mediaeval morality!)

    Glad was I to meet this earlier, more primitive at once and modern, more
satisfying story. And now I remember that I read it somewhere in a
paragraph, years ago, and thought that was just the subject for me, but I
didn't know enough about the times and people. It was in some
writing about Italian cities: I've never even seen the outside of the
Decline and Fall: I wonder how that happens!
    What a feeling there is to those times. Besides the blood and splendor and
distance, a feeling of great bursts of air into a stuffy room; it anticipates
the Renaissance, and beats it for grandeur. And your poem carries the
feeling, besides being admirable for beauty, as I knew it would be. And for
direct telling of the story it is straight as an arrow. The other thing
that I most admire among many is the quietness—innocence—of Rosamund's
mind. The beautiful half-savage girl being moulded by circumstances;
hardly conscious of any possibility of choice; she does what is right, and

---

[11] *These brackets are J's.*

"Great men have done their work before they were
thirty, but I wasn't born yet."

                                        (Letter 111)

then what is necessary, and makes no pretences. One always instinctively thanks God for a poem—even more for a play—without sentimentality.

My mind, as I read the wonderful last page, thought that she would have taken death more loudly—more like a harlot, less like a queen—but your way is certainly the more heroic, and I can see in your rendering a psychology deeper than would ever have occurred to me. It is a glorious poem, and I am very grateful, and more proud than I can say of the inscription you wrote in it.

What a fragrance and contrast the sweet small quintessential Iris-Hills song brings into it.

Thank you again, most devotedly.   Yours always, Robin Jeffers

28: TO GEORGE STERLING

April 8, 1925

Dear George Sterling: The manuscript came home, and I'm grateful to you for reading it, and quite respect it now for the kind things you said. Thank you very much for offering to speak to the Grabhorns.[12] The thing needs attention before I think of publishing it, and I'm horribly involved with another long thing, and haven't had time even to look at this one. Except leafing it through to look for your marginalia, for which thanks, but there aren't enough of them. As to the Grabhorns, after the third edition of Lilith is printed—(stipulation not out of regard for you, be sure, but for them and the rest of humanity)—after that, if they think they might want anything of me, they might choose between this manuscript and a story called "Peacock Ranch,"[13] rhymed, Locksley Hall meter, which is hardly half so long and might suit them better. It's the Big Sur instead of Mycenae; Jimmy Hopper liked it and lamented it was left out of the Tamar volume.

I still want to inscribe my next one to you, if you can stand it, whether it's either of these or the one I'm in a mess with at present.

You're perfectly right of course about the priggish verses "on a book of poems." I mean about suppressing them; I don't want to endorse the volcanic island hypothesis, which is a beautiful metaphor just the same.

There is nobody in the world but you could write a sonnet like "The Meteor"; it gave solemn delight to Una and me, and we're very grateful for it.

[12] *Edwin and Robert Grabhorn of the Grabhorn Press published the Book Club of California's* Poems, *by Robinson Jeffers in 1928 and several other of the Book Club's selections.*
[13] *See Letter 57, J's reference to the "story written just before the Coast Range Christ. . . ."*

The Hoppers are drawing plans for a new house, maybe you've heard,—
the only new house in Carmel that I wish good luck to. —Bechdolt
stopped me on the street the other day to quote some wonderful words of
yours about me. He expressed deep and due respect for your critical
judgment. Really, I've never known him to speak ill of you,
several times quite the opposite.

I wish the Lafflers would stop in as they go back and forth to their domain.
And you—I'm sure you'll come sometime. I'm sorry that I've such a
wretched handwriting.   Yours always, Robin Jeffers

29: TO BENJAMIN DE CASSERES

April 11, 1925

Dear Mr. De Casseres: Your letter came like a jet of fire, and I was too
overwhelmed for a couple of days even to say thank you. Though the
generosity of poets is not so new and strange to me as it was this time last
year, when I'd had no proofs of it, and fancied that Horace—or was it
Pope?—knew what he was talking about.

That you date from Hollywood is astonishing too; we live rather solitary
here and never know until we get letters from them what splendors are
south of us. If ever you happen up this way you could quite crown
your kindness by stopping in; the coast is rather beautiful here, you might
like to see it.   Sincerely yours, Robinson Jeffers

30: TO MARK VAN DOREN

April 30, 1925

Dear Mr. Van Doren: Rorty *is* a good salesman; but indeed I had no idea
that he would add this to other kind offices when I sent him the verses
to look at. Yet I'm delighted that you liked the four well enough to
gather them into your drawer.[14]

When I was seventeen I sold some verses about a vulture;[15] for a year
afterwards I tried in vain to sell some more, and swore off; the oath has been
kept a long time and now you and Rorty have broken it for me,
thank you.   Sincerely yours, Robinson Jeffers

14 *"Birds," "Haunted Country," "Fog," and "Boats in a Fog" appeared in*
Nation, *CXXI (September 23, 1925), 333.*
15 *"The Condor,"* Youth's Companion, *LXXVIII (June 9, 1904), 284.*

31: TO BENJAMIN DE CASSERES

June 5, 1925

Dear De Casseres: You knew we'd be delighted to hear from you, and so we are, and thank you for the invitation to an affair that it took the continent's breadth to keep us away from. It's pleasant to think you've promised to come back here sometime and stay awhile—and will send the books for hostages—that also is something to look forward to.

George Sterling was here the other day, and sorry to have missed you when you went through San Francisco, but remembered with pleasure the other time, parading arm in arm with you, singing old songs, himself (he said) entirely sober, and merry.

A friend has just sent me the New Republic, May 27, with some nice talk about "Tamar" in it.[16] I came on a pleasant fantasy of Huneker's the other day, about you and Flaubert at a desk together reading proof, you rapping the Norman's knuckles, teaching him a thing or two about literature.   Sincerely yours, Robinson Jeffers

We want to be remembered very cordially to Mrs. De Casseres.

32: TO BENJAMIN DE CASSERES

June 15, 1925

Dear De Casseres: A library of lightnings: it has been a great experience to look through them, and we're very grateful. I said *look* and not *read*, for the books are packed full, and the reading will not be done in a few days. I think I can say that I've read the book about Huneker, which is very fine. I knew him pretty well of old, but there was much in the volume that I didn't know, and a splendid enthusiasm that you've renewed for me. And the Shadow-Eater—every word—but that is Promethean— and one is not to say that it has been read, until after a whole cycle of returnings. I have never seen anything like it. Chameleon is tremendous too, made of the like splendors, and I was going to say that it is poetry but then what beyond-word could I find for The Shadow-Eater?

The Mirrors is a great book, in its other way, I liked it and I laughed; but I'm not to say that it was appreciated as it ought to be; our sense of

---

[16] *Babette Deutsch's "Brains and Lyrics," New Republic, XLIII (May 27, 1925), 23–24, reviewed new books by John Drinkwater, John Crowe Ransom, and George Moore, as well as J.*

humor is not strong, and our rural intelligences find so much to be bewildered
at. But one carries away an impression of grotesque energies and
multitudinous atomic swirls—vortices—and currents; which is part of
what you intended. You'll not be pleased—but Teufelsdroeck's (is
that how to spell it?) lonely brain in his garret, containing and combatting
the great city, is the similitude that occurs to me.

A wire three days ago from Boni and Liveright offers to republish the
Tamar book, of which there are no copies left, in one volume with some later
poems of mine, this autumn. They wanted a name for the book, and I
wished you were here to help me find one, and finally thought of calling
it "The Stone Coasts of Desire." You could have done better.

So perhaps in a few months I can begin—reprisals—by giving you a copy.

We look forward joyfully to seeing you and your wife in this country
again, sometime. And Una joins me in thanking you earnestly for
great gifts.   Yours, Robinson Jeffers

33: TO GEORGE STERLING

June 17, 1925

Dear George Sterling: I've wished you were along on two or three
"pilgrimages" lately; one to the abandoned coal-mine away up Mal Paso
Canyon, where there were more wild flowers, familiar and not, than
we ever saw before,—and a few range-bulls, to Una's horror;—one yesterday
up Robinson's Canyon, that opens southward seven miles up the valley; fine
stands of redwood; hard sandstone boulders, full of shells and bones, in
creek-beds; we brought some home. The ornithologist one of our twins
counted hawks and vultures. You might have seen a hawk's nest for us.

Let me thank you for that noble poem; of a kind that I wish the one or two
a century capable of it would give more of. The *talk* of genius. Shelley's
"Julian and Maddalo" is of the same kind. The great hawk's-cry line
or passage every so often is the more unforgettable because it comes
naturally, in conversation, like a star's image in the lift of a wave.

Una and I took turns with the poem; then I read it aloud to the children
and they enjoyed it as we did, and want to thank you.

Boni and Liveright are to republish the Tamar book this fall in one volume
with some later work. The wires are obscure as to how much, or whether
all, of the later material is to be included. Life the past week has been
a nightmare of telegrams, night letters, air-mail, getting photographed, trying
to write an amusing "biography." I'm not fitted for any of these horrors.
Yours always, Robin Jeffers

34: TO BABETTE DEUTSCH

June 17, 1925

My dear Miss Deutsch: I don't suppose it's customary for writers to say thank-you to reviewers they're not acquainted with; but if this reaches you perhaps you'll forgive the intrusion. I'm grateful not only for kindness to me, but for the intelligence of all your article—though I've quite loved for a dozen years, and do still, that "aging sybarite in Elroy Street."

I'd have written this sooner; but Boni and Liveright have decided to republish the "Tamar" book in one volume with some new work this fall, and have made the past ten days hideous with telegrams and air-mail, getting photographed, trying to write an amusing "biography." Perhaps it was your comment that determined them; they sent it to me.
Sincerely yours, Robinson Jeffers

35: TO ALBERT BENDER

June 21, 1925

My dear Mr. Bender— I shall be very happy to see the book; George Sterling showed us the noble-looking announcement of it when he was here three or four weeks ago; spoke, too, of your hard work on the preparation of it.[17]

My address remains Carmel, as I expect it always will. Perhaps it may interest you to know that my book "Tamar," in which what I contributed to the Anthology appeared also, has run through its edition and is to be republished this fall by Boni and Liveright, with some later poems.

I'm well pleased to be among the contributors to the Anthology.
Sincerely yours, Robinson Jeffers

36: TO ALBERT BENDER

June 28, 1925

Dear Mr. Bender: It is a most beautiful book, and I want to say thank you very cordially to the Book Club for sending me a copy. And the high level of the poetry in it surprises (I'm rather ashamed to confess) and delights me.

[17] *The Book Club of California's anthology of western poets,* Continent's End, *edited by George Sterling, Genevieve Taggard, and James Rorty in 1925. Bender was at that time secretary of the Book Club.*

Your postscript is a little puzzling on account of a slip of the pen: — "a manuscript of yours for my Mills College College"—is what you wrote, and I don't know whether the second "College" should have been magazine, anthology, or some sort of collection. Perhaps I can make it right either way by copying in my most legible handwriting an unpublished sonnet that I still have a fondness for, though it was written several years ago.

Boni and Liveright's wires and contract have not set any nearer date than "this fall"; I'll be happy to let you know the date more definitely as soon as it's revealed to me. And thank you for your interest in it.
Cordially yours, Robinson Jeffers

37: TO SARA TEASDALE

August 8, 1925

My dear Miss Teasdale: It was rather wonderful of you, whose name carries such a fragrance of manifold beauty and clear singing, to write me about the book "Tamar," and I am very sincerely grateful. That you found it in the same room with Samson Agonistes is almost too much for me; people speak of the Samson as gray and black, but to my private feeling it is the poem that wears best—I was going to say of any in English, but of course one oughtn't.

We shall have many questions to put to Mr. [*Ralph Radcliffe*] Whitehead about you, when he returns nightingalelike to this "Abyssinian vale" for the winter.

I think no one else ever had a more active friend than James Rorty has been to me the thirteen months I have known him; whether in San Francisco or New York, or at the MacDowell Colony in New Hampshire where he is now, he apparently meets everyone that interests him, and talks of that work of mine. It is marvelous, to me, who stick to this beautiful sea-cliff like a barnacle, and can't talk at all.

Mr. [*John Hall*] Wheelock I've never met; and know of his writing only through reviews, but sometime I shall come to it.

You probably wouldn't care for the only other book of mine, poems called "Californians," Macmillan, nine years ago. I don't like it; it is out of print, permanently I hope. Boni and Liveright are republishing "Tamar" this fall, in one volume with some later work, to be called "Roan Stallion, Tamar, and Other Poems." Late this fall I think, for no proofs have been sent me yet.

Let me end as I began, by thanking you most earnestly for the great kindness of a letter that coming from you is the more valued.
Sincerely yours, Robinson Jeffers

38: TO GEORGE STERLING

Dear George Sterling—   I planted 99 cypresses a few weeks ago, yesterday four blue-gums; whenever there are trees to plant I propose to put one in a pot to save for your coming, and Una says no, we'll get something more important, a cedar of Lebanon or the like;—your tree is still at the nursery but the sheltered spot is chosen; all our saplings live, yours should grow tall.

I've been reading your poems in the anthology over again, that was what reminded me to write to you, and am as always overcome with the simultaneousness of lyric rush and clear descriptive vision, wings and eye too, it is given only to you and the eagles perhaps to have both at once.

Haven't I written to you since the anthology [Continent's End] was sent me? There are many fine poems in it; you knew of course already, but I had my moments of delightful surprise.

A letter from Robert Schauffler the other week said that we have a friend in common he thinks, G. S. I suppose you hear sometimes from Rorty, who has been spending the summer with Mrs. MacDowell's colonists. And who but Sara Teasdale wrote the other day to say that she liked "Tamar"; I shouldn't have thought she would. She met it in the Catskills.

Liveright sent me some prospectuses a couple of weeks ago; I enclose one. Their publicity man (one Isidor Schneider) asked me for letters from readers, I sent copies of parts of a few but said I thought it would hardly be ethical to use them without asking permission. Yet I wonder whether permission was asked. If not, forgive me. It's rather horrid at best if books have to be advertised like baking-powder.

I feel disappointed too that the Greek thing I was going to inscribe to you has got absorbed into this book prededicate to Una. I don't want to inscribe a fragment to you. Probably there'll be another book sometime, and there I'll put your name. Meanwhile the loss is mine, and yours the exemption.

There was a fine landing of liquor here night before last, lights and signals from ten o'clock to dawn; and—someone told us—the traffic blocked on Ocean Avenue for fear of its interfering with the smugglers.

August 19?

So far I wrote awhile ago, and your kindness in sending the "Poetry" reminds me to finish and mail. Things move slowly here.

James Daly has exchanged a couple of letters with me, and told me three months ago that he had written this review, the first in his life![18]

---

[18] "*Roots under the Rocks*," Poetry, XXVI (August, 1925), 278–85.

I supposed he'd send a copy, but none has come except from you. Thank you. Daly meditates coming to Carmel. I think he will be the only person except you that hasn't come here this summer!

The galley proofs of the stallion book came the same day as "Poetry," and I've sent them back now.

That was a great and terrible sonnet about Thirst—I'm not sure of the title—it's down-stairs and I can't go look at it because there are people down-stairs—but I remember the lines—like the language that the vultures speak in their dreams.   Yours, Robin Jeffers

39: TO BENJAMIN DE CASSERES

September 4, 1925

Dear De Casseres—   I'm ashamed to have enjoyed two post-cards, I think, and a letter of yours without acknowledgment. It is the fault of the sun. Summertime increases labors and diminishes energy. I've four hundred little trees to water in the afternoons, besides stone-work, and have even been watering them by moonlight lately. Also we have had an abominable number of guests and visitors this summer.

The tower is finished, except two little jobs of paving. I laid the last stone in the parapet of the turret yesterday. Wish you'd walk around here and see it. Now we're planning a dining-room. Also the boys speak wistfully of a stable that I promised them, to keep their saddle-horses in when they get them.

It is not the love of a horse for a woman, that poem, but of a woman for a stallion which is more reasonable if not more moral. Also the affection is platonic—which makes it perhaps less absurd.[19] No doubt the book will be out in a couple of months, and then I'll send you a copy.

You complain of "psychic dumps"—my trouble is mere dummheit, psychic or other. I have begun a story four times, and each time but the last it has

[19] *On page 112 of* The Stone Mason of Tor House, *Melba Bennett quotes the following notes for a letter dated November 5, 1944, to an unidentified addressee:*
"Personally I think the woman fell in love with the stallion because there was no one else she could fall in love with: and then because the love was physically impractical and the stallion seemed infinitely superior to any man she had known she identified him half-consciously with God. First with the God she had heard religious stories about, the Conception and so forth; and then with a more real God— not a human invention but the energy that is the universe. She was glad to sacrifice her husband to him—for whatever the man was worth. But at the end she slipped back into ordinary life, 'obscure human fidelity'—an animal had killed a man— she must kill the animal. Though the animal was also God. As to Christine's fetching the rifle—it was obviously because she saw her father in trouble and knew that was the only way to save him. . . ."

turned into a novel on the way, and been scrapped. It's perhaps because
I'm trying to write about more or less educated people this time, and
it's hard to set fire to too much thought. Ideas and passion don't live together
willingly. However, I hope it's coming out of the nebula at last.

You are "flirting with Europe"—you don't speak of coming west again.
We shall be sorry if you don't[.]

Boni and Liveright sent me three or four prospectuses of "Roan Stallion"
and Una sent one of them to you, via a relative of mine in the east
who was to forward it.

Do you know a young woman bookseller in Hollywood named Unity
Piqués or some such spelling? She was a rather more agreeable one
of our thousand visitors this summer.

Thank you for telling us about Keyserling and his Reisetagebuch
[Das Reisetagebuch eines Philosophen] —I was interested already, having
seen it reviewed—but have not got to it yet. No doubt this winter.
Good books don't deteriorate.

Remember Una and me to Bio [de Casseres' wife], and let us hope that
both of you will come and see us again sometime.   Yours always,
Robinson Jeffers

40: TO ALBERT BENDER

September 25, 1925

Dear Mr. Bender: I promised some time ago to let you know when the new
printing of "Tamar" and the other poems was to be published. Lately I
was informed that it was to be October 15th. Here's a prospectus that the
publishers and not I must be held responsible for; the last of several
that were sent me a month ago.[20]

I've wondered whether the page of manuscript that I offered for your Mills
College collection was quite the sort of thing you wanted. You were kind
enough to say it was; but if anything else would be preferred you
have but to let me know.

We'd be delighted to have you come and see us, if ever you're in this
neighborhood. It's a beautiful bit of coast, and my stone tower beside the
house is notorious, people have watched me building it the afternoons
of four years, and now it is finished!   Sincerely yours, Robinson Jeffers

[20] See S. S. Alberts, A Bibliography of the Works of Robinson Jeffers (New York,
1966), pp. 29–31.

"It's surprising to be nearly seventy-two years old all
of a sudden; I'm not sure that I like it."

(Letter 394)

46

41: TO BENJAMIN DE CASSERES

September 26, [1925]

Dear De Casseres—   I dare say [Brett] Page sent one of these clippings, and
I don't know that any of them will interest you much, but—les voici.
And thanks for the page about Peter Boyle and me.

I planted 100 eucalyptuses this week, and 100 more cypresses.

There is a Carmelite convent—a nunnery—building on this Point within
sight of us, a ten-foot wall around it. A house of virgins engaged in
perpetual prayer and adoration—was all that was lacking here.
Yours, Robinson Jeffers

42: TO BAYARD H. CHRISTY

November, 1925

Dear Mr. Christy: I was delighted to hear from you, and from Sewickley,
where I wish I had lived longer and more consciously. Childhood seems half
dream and half stupor when you look back—though it doesn't appear
so when I consider the sparkling energies of our nine-year-old twin sons.
—However, I'm sure I remember seeing you; and the family of course
I remember, your father was very important to mine.

I'd be very glad to have the verses reprinted;[21] I was waiting for *The
Cardinal* to come before answering but it hasn't arrived yet; probably it will
be there when this goes to be mailed. The birds make a fine part of our
lives here, all the little land-birds thronging a sandstone basin full of
water on the courtyard wall, song-sparrows and phoebes, red and gold finches,
bluebirds and buntings; the swallows are the only ones that go off in
winter; and seaward of the house are always gulls and a solemn convocation
of cormorants on the rock, pelicans at least half the year, and lately
miles and miles of thousands of shearwaters, which hadn't been about here
for ten years but returned in multitudes. The great blue herons are grand
creatures too, and the night-herons, the various hawks,—I was
forgetting the meadow-larks!

There are some vivid pictures of Sewickley and Edgeworth in my mind; if
ever we go east I'd like to stop there and compare them with reality. And
if you should be in the west, I wish you'd come and visit us, the coast
hereabouts is very beautiful.   Cordially yours, Robinson Jeffers

21 *"Birds" was reprinted in the January, 1926, issue of* The Cardinal, *the journal
of the Audubon Society of Sewickley, Pa., with an accompanying footnote quoting
a portion of J's letter.*

Carmel, California
November , 1925

Dear Mr. Christy:

I was delighted to hear from you, and from Sewickley, where I wish I had lived longer and more consciously. Childhood seems half dream and half stupor when you look back — though it doesn't appear so when I consider the sparkling energies of our nine-year-old twin sons. — However, I'm sure I remember seeing you; and the family of course I remember, your father was very important to mine.

I'd be very glad to have the verses reprinted; I was waiting for the Cardinal to come before answering, but it hasn't arrived yet; probably it will be there when this goes to be mailed. The birds make a fine part of our lives here, all the little land-birds thronging a sandstone basin full of water on the courtyard wall, song-sparrows and phoebes, red and gold finches, bluebirds and buntings; the swallows are the only ones that go off in winter; and seaward of the house are always gulls and a solemn convocation of cormorants on the rock, pelicans at least half the year, and lately miles and miles of thousands of shearwaters, which hadn't been about here for ten years but returned in multitude. The great blue herons are grand creatures too, and the night-herons; the various hawks, — I was forgetting the meadow-larks!

There are some vivid pictures of Sewickley and Edgeworth in my mind; if ever we go east I'll like to stop there and compare them with reality. And if you should be in the west, I wish you'd come and visit us, the coast hereabout is very beautiful.

Cordially yours, Robinson Jeffers.

43: TO ALBERT BENDER

November, 1925

Dear Mr. Bender: Day after day I have intended to thank you for the kindness of your letter; there's a destiny conspires against me, and even the most essential letters fail to get written. But I've been hoping very earnestly that you are well recovered from that attack of illness.

It was not clear to me until rather lately how singly the California Anthology was due to your initiative; and perhaps you'll let me thank you for it in more personal terms than I did before. I was reading last night an all-American one and was impressed with its inferiority to this one. Besides a certain patchiness the general level I thought was lower; we were fortunate in your editors.

I had a note lately from James Rorty; he is getting well established in New York and expects to be able to give all his time to literary work within a year or so. Is interested in a new magazine, which will begin its issues in two or three months, and he will probably be one of the editors. Yours always most cordially, Robinson Jeffers

44: TO GEORGE STERLING

November 3, 1925

Dear George Sterling: To-day I received some copies of the "Roan Stallion, etc.," and one would go to you with this if it hadn't occurred to Liveright to print a special little edition of twelve copies on more luxurious paper, not for sale, the title pages of which were sent me to write my name on. Eight of these for members of the firm, four for me to give, and as my four should arrive any day now I'm going to ask you to wait (not that you're impatient!) for one of these. One for you, one for Una, I don't know for whom the other two, but I think Una is laboring with a suppressed desire to send one to George Moore. —These are promised to arrive within a day or two, but now I shall be on edge until yours is sent to you.

We were all delighted with the ballad of the whaling-ship, and thank you. I read it to the boys as soon as it arrived. They have a somewhat tolerant sympathy for verse, but a tremendous admiration for the scion of your grandfather, and not they alone hope that you'll come and see us some day not too far hence.

R. L. Burgess came in one day when I was planting trees. He was lately from your presence, and I was glad to see him not for that reason alone, but for a fine enthusiasm about poetry that reminded me of Rorty's, and a vital solidity that is pleasant to meet. —Two or three days ago a note, not answered yet, from Rolfe Humphries on behalf of The Measure; he also mentioned the magic three syllables that make your name. —Harry Laffler was here a month or so ago, Mary with him, they seemed cheerful together and we don't know to this day whether they have agreed again or are only good friends.

A Carmelite nunnery has established itself on our horizon, a bit too near, considering the look of the building, but it's quite exciting to have this austere colony of prayerful virgins for neighbor, prayer going on in hour shifts, we're told, night and day, without a moment's intermission, one expects it to wear out the roof.

I think there's no more news from here, except that we've bought a brand new shiny Ford, to be delivered to-day. The tower's finished, come and climb it again. Now I'm getting stones to build a dining-room, which we hope will look like an old inn-kitchen.   Yours always, Robin Jeffers

45: TO GEORGE STERLING

November 12, 1925

Dear George Sterling: Una sent off your book yesterday as soon as it arrived, and I want to thank you for—many things, but most recent—your wonderful talk in the Overland-Out West, which I wish Tamar and I were worthy of.[22] It came the day after I last wrote to you.

I answered Rolfe Humphries this morning, sending a few things for the Measure.[23] Yesterday I started laying foundations for our inn-kitchen of a dining-room, between the garage and the house. Now I have to go to the dentist, which is worst of all, but since the rain I'll probably not have to water trees any more this year, and that may console me.   Yours—in haste this time—but yours always, Robin Jeffers

[22] "Rhymes and Reactions," Overland Monthly, LXXXIV (November, 1925), 411.
[23] "Two Garden Marbles: Alcibiades, Alexander," "Adjustment," "Clouds at Evening," and "Summer Holiday" were published on pp. 3–5 of the December, 1925, issue of the Measure, then edited by Humphries.

46: TO DONALD FRIEDE (Horace Liveright, Inc.)

November 25, 1925

Dear Mr. Friede: I'm awfully sorry that I burned the typewritten manuscript of Tamar soon after it was printed. There was only one set of proofs, which I returned to Peter Boyle and he is very unlikely to have kept it. The pencil-scribble must have been burnt too, though I don't remember doing so, for not a sheet of it can be found.

In looking wildly through drifts of paper on my table this morning I found the enclosed great sheet,[24] which contains:

   1) The first germ of the Tamar story, dramatis personae (several of whom were lost or changed in the telling), incidents, metrical indications . . .

   2) The first, and final, draft of "Continent's End"—the last poem of both the Tamar and the Roan Stallion volumes.

   3) Fragments of two other short poems that were never finished.

   4) Plans for the stairway of a granite tower that I have built with my hands beside the house here. —Etc.

You are very welcome to drop this illegible medley in the waste-basket. But if you can put up with such things I'd be happy to send you the almost equally illegible pencil-scribble of "Roan Stallion," or of the "Tower beyond Tragedy," both of which came to light during my search this morning. It's probably Tamar you want, though, and I'm very sorry not to be able to produce it.

I still have two copies of the Peter Boyle edition, and could send you one, but that isn't what you want.

Let me thank you most cordially for the kindness of your letter and the invitation to visit you. If you should ever be in the west we'd be delighted to receive you here; it is a rather beautiful coast; at any rate I may hope to see you sometime.

And I'm glad of this opportunity to thank you as a member of the firm for having produced my book so beautifully, both the regular and the little editions, and for your generosity in sending me copies of them.

If you wish, I'll write to Boyle about the proof-sheets; but I have little doubt that he destroyed them.   Sincerely yours, Robinson Jeffers

[24] *The manuscripts referred to in this letter and the galleys for* Roan Stallion *are now deposited in the Beinecke Rare Book and Manuscript Library at Yale University. See also Letters 58, 127, 154, and 363. Alberts includes detailed descriptions of these manuscripts with his descriptions of their respective published volumes in his* A Bibliography.

Following is section 1 of the note-sheet which J describes in his letter.
Its purpose as an author's outline accounts for the illegible words, the
abbreviations and fragmentary phrasing, the uncertainty about characters'
names, and the final notation suggesting that J intended to list
for himself specific settings for the story's action.

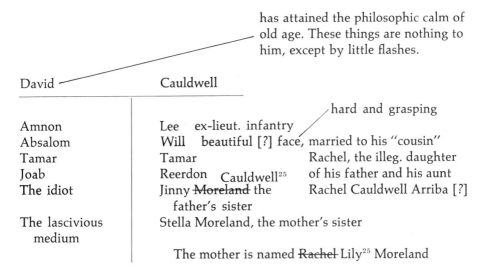

has attained the philosophic calm of
old age. These things are nothing to
him, except by little flashes.

David   Cauldwell

hard and grasping

Amnon	Lee ex-lieut. infantry	
Absalom	Will beautiful [?] face, married to his "cousin"	
Tamar	Tamar	Rachel, the illeg. daughter
Joab	Reerdon Cauldwell[25]	of his father and his aunt
The idiot	Jinny ~~Moreland~~ the	Rachel Cauldwell Arriba [?]
	father's sister	
The lascivious	Stella Moreland, the mother's sister	
medium		

The mother is named ~~Rachel~~ Lily[25] Moreland

The conflict is in Will's mind chiefly. He is protagonist. He is going
to punish her, his aunt and his father's [?] family's are [*gradually?*]
unfolded to him.

Tamar's rape by Lee had happened before Lee went to the war, now on the
eve of his return—she is shyly [*slightly?*] excited. Stella admires her.
She confesses to Stella.
Stella is medium, Lily is ghost, Jinny is suppressed idiot, hark back a
generation.
David is dotard, harks back another and identifies himself with David his
father who came on a [?] ship from Scotland, in 1820.
5 beats to the line
   doubled in a few passages to [?] 10s
   quickened to anapests, [?] anapestic
  ᴗᴗᴗ——— lyrical passages, [?]
       to 8s

places?

[25] *These corrections are J's.*

47: TO GEORGE STERLING

December 1, 1925

Dear George Sterling: You disclaim "genius," but I was reading Le Gallienne's new anthology last night, which Liveright just sent, partly for an advertisement on the jacket, partly perhaps thinking I needed education, —and your Black Vulture stood out in it like a mountain-peak. Tell me who else? The Pathfinders has the same—I'll affront you with another word— sublimity. Other poets have sublimity, but yours is of a different nature, more literal to the word, more abstract perhaps, I've no analysis but I recognize yours. The Pathfinders is a magnificent poem, the same lift of enormous wings, and yet I feel that your more metrical manner is too beautiful to be abandoned. Have you experimented much in regular lyrical meter without rhyme, like Collins' Ode to Evening, more modulated perhaps? I think my thoughts would tend that way again, if I could ever work free of the tiresome story that won't be finished for months yet.

We look forward to your coming soon to see us, I was hoping you'd have come before this.

Thank you for the Nation and Saturday Review and to-day the [San Francisco Call-] Bulletins—though it did give me a ghastly feeling to see that face—and afterwards when I began to read the absurdities.

A note lately from Rorty says that he expects in a year or so to be able to leave commercial work. He is interested in the New Masses—no propaganda —expects to start next January. He will probably be an editor. They have $17500 from the Garland fund, and are looking for 8500 more.

My sons have a bantam hen and three chicks, a terrible burden on us all. The family lived in the tower the first few days, and had a fine morning and evening; now they sleep in the garage. Our old stone-cutter's wife inflicted them on us.//   Yours always, Robin Jeffers

48: TO GEORGE STERLING

December [19], 1925

Dear George Sterling: No, I've never been on the Soberanes reef, only followed the road there. This is your country, it will be a great privilege if you'll show us that bit of it. What's more, I've never gathered an abalone, except to remove it from a stone I wanted; and only one sackful of

mussels, nine or ten years ago. But even better than new
adventures is your hoped-for coming.

It's splendid news about your Lilith. We had to borrow Heron's copy in
order to read it, and Oh but he was reluctant. And the book of lyrics to
follow that great poem—I'm glad the house of Macmillan were
careful bargainers.

Finally the new dramatic poem—tell us about the subject when you
come—or are you as sensitive as I am and shrink like an old-fashioned little
girl from talk of prospective maternities? You've tougher fiber, I hope.

Your letter was a delightful one to receive, swarming with good news,
I even think it's nice that the mop-manufacturers appreciate
literature.

Thank you for the extra clipping from the Nation; Una often has
mysterious uses for those things. And thank you for The Voices, illumined
by your beautiful sonnet, by two or three other things that I thought
surprisingly good, and by that ingenious young woman who has such a
delightful way of making amends in her final paragraph.[26] I think a
conversation between her and Rorty must be good to listen to.

Night before last we had to take the children to see the animals in Conan
Doyle's Lost World; so yesterday I enjoyed my regular post-cinema
head ache; to-day the remnants of it perhaps are the cause why this letter
is rather scattering—

There was something more I meant to say, but it won't come to me,
perhaps it will wait until you're here.   Yours always, Robin Jeffers

49: TO ALBERT BENDER

December 21, 1925

Dear Mr. Bender: I meant to have thanked you before this for the booklet
you sent me, containing Markham's beautiful poem and his inscription.
George Sterling was with us most of last week, showing us places on this
coast that I had never seen before—but long familiar to him—and there was
no time for me to write a letter. Now your lovely Japanese memento
has come, and I have that also to thank you for, very sincerely, and am
sending you my best thoughts and wishes for this midwinter
season.   Most cordially yours, Robinson Jeffers

[26] *Virginia Moore reviewed* Tamar *and* Continent's End *in* Voices, V
(November, 1925), 70–72.

50: TO GEORGE STERLING

December 31, 1925

Dear George: I have hoped with a sort of craziness for some clear time to write you a decent letter, and it hasn't come yet. Three days ago we went down the coast and visited the Point Sur light; phantasmagoric situation on the round rock three or four hundred feet high, over half a mile of almost tide-flats from the shore. Buildings on top of heavy squared sand-stone, great blocks, retaining wall of the same to make their terrace; the sort of masonry that is never done any more, since concrete. The journey brought me awake and I went back to that long story and have been rather productive.

How can I thank you with any fit words for the beautiful books of poems, your gifts? There are honey and wine for many a winter evening—the richness of poems like the Carmel ones—the lonely height that is one of your peculiar powers—the melody and color: You made us very happy.

Tell me whether you have a copy of that "Californians" book of mine. We still have two or three and I'd like to send you one if you haven't——with a very different feeling from the pride of authorship!

And perhaps your copy of the first Tamar has escaped. It is rather a secret that I saved a couple of those; I'd love to write in one and mail it, if you haven't one. I didn't inscribe the one I sent you.

The boys burst with pride in their great knives; they took them along down the coast and felt ready for anything. One of them indeed was used on the Ford—the screw-driver blade.   Yours always, Robin Jeffers

51: TO DR. LYMAN STOOKEY

January 2, 1926

Dear Dr. Stookey: I was happy—of course you know—to hear from you; and want to say thank you too for the card that Mrs. Stookey sent in your name and hers. I ought to have written long ago to thank you for the portrait sent last year, which we treasure quite religiously; I would have written, but you might have thought the letter required acknowledgment, I didn't want to bother you.

We often think it would be very pleasant if you, and Mrs. Stookey if possible, would stop here sometime and spend a day or two with us. It's a wonderful coast, we've lived here eleven years and are more than ever bewitched with it. And you'd be amused to see the stone-work

I've accomplished—and perhaps to see the very noble-looking young persons, our nine-year-old sons.

Your plea for the sonnet is just E. A. Robinson's, who concluded a very kind letter awhile ago by wishing I would write a short book of sonnets. Well: there have been very good ones.[27]

Last week we drove down the coast twenty-five miles of wild road to the Point Sur lighthouse, a wonderful place that no one visits, great sandstone buildings and retaining walls topping a round volcanic rock three or four hundred feet high, half a mile across almost tide-flats from the shore. The week before Christmas George Sterling was with us three days, his first visit except one or two flitting ones. He was consumed with an incredible passion for sea-food, led us to the remotest reefs of the shellfish, cooked abalone for breakfast since no one else would. Another excitement we have is to watch the whiskey-smugglers, this broken coast is a favorite working ground of theirs. Signal-lights continually, sometimes a landing near us; two or three months last year we were kept in kindling by the empty whiskey and grain-alcohol cases washing ashore, all properly labelled; there must have been a good deal of breakage for the woodshed would smell like happy Scotland. Our share was merely the aroma; but this is a pleasant savor to close a letter with.

Please speak of us to Mrs. Stookey. I'd like to tell her what pleasant memories remain of the house on the sands at Hermosa.   Yours always, Robin Jeffers

52: TO GEORGE STERLING

Saturday
[January 16, 1926]

Dear George: I am a poor and useless creature, bound up in chains of habit, and if the bottom should drop out of the sea I couldn't touch a mussel, unless inspired by starvation or by your immediate presence as we were last month.

No primitive instincts; no enterprise; try to forgive me. Jimmy Hopper

---

[27] *I did experiment with and modify the sonnet form: undated (1938?) notes to R. H. Elias in the Tor House files explain "Shiva": "A 'Shakespearean' Sonnet has four quatrains and a couplet, and so I suppose 'Shiva' is an irregular (or degenerate) sonnet in form. And it is a sonnet in the unity and shape of its content. It is the latest, I think, of a series of such fourteen-line poems that began in 1918 or earlier— (see 'The Truce and the Peace' in my* Roan Stallion *volume)—and were then quite regular, but have been increasingly careless of metrical and rhyming regularity.*

"It seems to me that we have come to distrust regularity. In the poetry of classical times we value it; I don't know why. It appears either dull or meretricious in our own time." See Bennett, Stone Mason, *pp. 168–69.*

walked by here yesterday, and we lamented our laziness together, and
the tide ebbed toward evening. Another thing is that I don't like to leave the
place during low tides on account of the ragamuffins that gather along
our shore and incline to steal fire-wood. The stakes that shelter the trees
attract them irresistibly unless someone's here to shoo them off. Someone
stole a big log of a fence-post, for instance, while we were at Soberanes
with you last month. It wouldn't do to burn, I can't imagine what
they did with it.

Grace Wallace brought a poetess named Helen Hoyt to visit us a couple of
weeks ago. Una was away, so it was rather hard on me; but
I liked her husband.

Rolfe Humphries wanted me to greet you for him, in a note recently. And
Rorty writes that "California is a flop" so far as supporting the New
Masses is concerned, but that you had contributed an amazingly fine poem.
They are almost out of the woods now financially, he says, in spite
of California.

George West's kind and exciting article[28] hasn't brought any of the
sorrows you foreboded, neither letter nor visitor thank God, only the barber
began to talk about it when he cut my hair; but was willing to talk about
Bergson and Schopenhauer instead, a philosophical barber, a Carmel barber.

That is a wonderfully beautiful poem about running on the sands, Greek
and shining, clear simple marble against the blue elements. So beautiful
that I rather resent Miss T.'s connection with it; not that I've anything against
her: she may even be worthy of the honor: only, a literary young
woman— Thank you for it.

I expect you received the couple of books a week ago or so. I wish "Tamar"
were better and "Californians" sunk in the sea, but I'm glad to give
them to you.   Yours always, Robin Jeffers

53: TO GEORGE WEST

January 22, 1926

Dear West: I expect any reasons one can give for choosing a theme are
superficial ones;[29] it isn't chosen, of course, but intrudes itself, and perhaps
it would take more than a "life and times" to explain why. Which would
be taking the question too seriously.

[28] *"Great New Poet, Jeffers, Arises at Carmel, Voices Real Californian Lure,"*
San Francisco Call-Bulletin, *January 2, 1926, pp. 9, 13.*
[29] *See also Letter 26 and accompanying note 9.*

But for a rationalizing attempt: In the first place, Tamar is only one in
a string of stories; it isn't as though one were choosing a theme for a
life-time. It's perhaps the best story in the book, probably because when
it was written I had more sense than I had before, and more time than
I've had since. —I mean for anything published yet. But if it isn't the best
in the book, I hope it isn't the best in *me*.

Now to defend the theme. Of primitive motives—hunger, fear of death,
etc.—sexual desire is surely the most poetized and dramatized in the
normal consciousness, therefore the readiest for use in a poem, as every young
person knows. Of environments the family is the most familiar, and original
and universal—the good old family. So the theme that combines these
elements (supposing it's decent in execution) ought to reach rather deeply
into people's consciousness. That's what one wants of a theme.

Then from the point of view of responsibility: There are such strong
resistances against incest in every normal person that one can feel rather
safe as to seduction or perversion. Various inhibitions may be resolved
or more likely excited; but this is not a crime that people are easily
tempted to.

From a personal point of view: The theme isn't worn out with use like so
many others, and what use it has had has been at the hands of rather decent
people,—Sophocles, Ford, Shelley, and Byron, and Wagner. The theme
has got to be handled seriously or it's a little too abhorrent; and I haven't
any talent for the light or humorous. Also I never had a sister; and
perhaps, for that reason felt the more free to use it.

Last, a somewhat esoteric reason: Incest seems to me a fairly appropriate
symbol of the immoderate racial introversion which needs pointing out
and protesting against. These words are elephants! But I mean the
ninety-odd percent of people's activities turned in on other people instead
of outward on the world. All the waste time of picking quarrels and looking
for praise, trying to get the better of each other, being sociable, making
war, politics, bargaining, commerce, making laws and making love, hatred,
philanthropy,—writing books!—Of course all these things are necessary, but
don't you think too much human energy goes back into humanity; and
the farmers who subdue the earth, the scientists who widen horizons, even
the merely contemplative person admiring mountains have chosen a better
way? They live outward.

So having sufficiently clouded wisdom with words, I'll draw a line. My
ideas are still in process and therefore muddled. My next theme I think
is parricide. There's something to be said for this, too, as a theme.—   Yours,
Robinson Jeffers

59

54: TO GEORGE STERLING

January 26, 1926

Dear George: We were much excited about your fire yesterday, when
Saturday night's paper reached us; but in the afternoon I saw Jimmy Hopper
walking on the shore and he had it from another paper that your room
and belongings were not damaged, at least not at all seriously. I hope it is so.
But the trouble and the mess must have been a rude experience.

He doesn't feel that the [Austen?][30] was ever hostile to you, though he
says there was some controversy about the theater—what a root of disorder
in this village! How unconsciously clever we have been not to care about
the theaters—three of them now! He was interested in the review, and
thinks it pitiful that Mary abandoned her first and proper field. I never met
her, though Una has, but I have heard tales.

Thank you much for sending the [San Francisco] Review, and for All's
Well with your grand and lovely conception, the figure seen across
crowded millennial vulture-wings. I read the story of Marco Polo's rival—
remembering Wells's nice early phrase about the "convincing air of unreality"
that journalism hangs over the most actual happenings. There was a
reference to unicorns in the story, Una pounced on it like a hawk. Thank
you too for your beautiful North Wind in the Quarterly. Miss Deutsch's is
good too; two bad words in the last line might so easily have been
changed.   Yours always, Robin

55: TO GEORGE STERLING

February 5, 1926

Dear George: Like yours this is "but a note," I'll write to-morrow, I hope.
It's late and I've just finished reading your article for the S.F. Review.[31]
It's altogether beyond belief generous and resounding and Olympian—good
Lord, if one were worthy of the tenth of it. The comparisons with Frost,
Robinson, Masters, —all three are friends of yours more or less, aren't
they?—and I should be very sorry to think that your unmeasured kindness

[30] *Herbert Heron suggests that this may be an ironic reference to Mary
Austin's rather imperious air.*
[31] *"A Tower by the Sea,"* San Francisco Review, I (February–March, 1926), 248–49.

*"I announced then that I wanted the luxury of dying
in that bed. But of course I'm willing to postpone it awhile."*

(Letter 168)

to me was doing you harm with them. The paragraph could be taken
out and the article would still be a flaming lyric. You understand it's of you
I'm thinking. For myself, that first letter of yours to me so tipped me
over that not even your praise, and there's no one's I could possibly value
more, will turn my head after that. You can appreciate what Swinburne said
about not knowing any reason for writing criticism except for "the noble
pleasure of praising."

Well, consider the paragraph. Whitman doesn't matter, nobody will send
the article to Whitman.

We're very glad the fire did you no harm. I haven't read the correspondence
yet, except Humphries' racy letter, of which more soon, and I'll remember
to return it all.   Yours gratefully and always, Robin

Una says to thank you for the Nations, which she is reading at this
moment. I do. And we both thank you for the beautiful sonnet "Intimation,"
the spirit of autumn caught in a crystal glass. What a joy this crystal
clearness is compared to—so—many—to Masters on a Death-Mask, which
Una is scolding at this time and I was half-heartedly defending. You told
me you would write a sonnet on the train, and I couldn't quite believe.

56: TO GEORGE SYLVESTER VIERECK

February 13, 1926

Dear Mr. Viereck: It was good of you to send me the page from The
American Monthly, with your generous mention of "Roan Stallion, Tamar
and other poems."

I read with interest the other reviews on the page, and sympathize with
your appreciation of Leonard's "Two Lives," only dissenting from your
suggestion that part of the story should have been told in prose. The idea is
attractive but I think not practical; Dante in the Vita Nuova may say
"this event so interested me that I made a canzone about it," but Dante was
describing visions, and an unearthly passion; Leonard is presenting actual
life and could hardly say "my wife's menstruation at the time of her
suicide seems so pathetic as to require expression in a sonnet." —In other
words, the convention of verse may be accepted once for all in a depiction of
actual life, but to reserve it for the pinnacles would almost inevitably
suggest self-consciousness and over-emphasis. Of course in Elizabethan
drama the prose and verse blend into each other—their special quality—the
verse is unrhymed and often irregular, the prose is lyrical and
approaches the condition of verse.

Long ago I met an early volume of your poems, with a preface; ever since

then your works and your fortunes have interested me, and it is pleasant
to have this chance of writing to you.   Sincerely yours, Robinson Jeffers

57: TO BENJAMIN DE CASSERES

February 19, 1926

Dear Ben De Casseres: It would be splendid if you could write the pamphlet.
A letter came from Donald Friede the day after yours, and I'm answering
it to say I'd be delighted, and that you write brilliant things, which
of course he knows.[32]
   I burned the manuscript of Tamar as soon as the book was printed; there
were so many papers lying around. Friede asked me for it awhile ago,
and in telling him the same sad story I offered him the pencil-scribbles of
"Roan Stallion" and "The Tower beyond Tragedy." He has just claimed them,
with kind words about "unbelievable generosity." I suspect you both
are amusing yourselves.
   However, here's the first draught of the poem to Night, third in the
Liveright volume I think, and the only thing I can lay hands on. Mark Van
Doren quoted a bit of it in the Nation. You may light your pipe with the
scribble, I wish I had something better if you're in earnest.
   George Sterling is here overnight; you know he's an active person and I
can't write more at present.   Yours, with our best greetings to
Bio, Robin Jeffers
   The typing on the back of these scraps is a bit from a story written just
before the Coast Range Christ; I don't know that it will ever be published.[33]

58: TO DONALD FRIEDE

February 19, 1926

Dear Mr. Friede: Here are the scribblings, smudged paper that I'm quite
ashamed to give but you are welcome to keep. Many of the sheets have
typewriting on the back which I hope you won't notice, it's mostly a scrapped
old puerile manuscript I used the back sides of.[34] Evidently one should use
clean paper!

[32] *George Sterling's* Robinson Jeffers, the Man and the Artist *finally served Boni and
Liveright as publicity pamphlet; see Letter 66.*
[33] *"Peacock Ranch"; see Letter 28.*
[34] *Alberts prints the "Introduction to Brides of the South Wind" (verso manuscript
sheets of* The Tower beyond Tragedy*) on pp. 109–14 of his* A Bibliography. *Typed on
versos of "Roan Stallion" is a portion of "The [An?] Alpine Christ" with the note: "Here
ends the poem called* The Alpine Christ, *which is the first part of a poem to be
called* Witnesses"; *see* A Bibliography, *p. 229, and Letter 111.*

I'd be delighted to have De Casseres write the pamphlet you speak of, if you really think it's worth while. He sent me a note from Hollywood about "Tamar," and when he was in Carmel a month or two later I drove him around a bit of the coast in our Ford and was well repaid by his conversation and enthusiasm. He has written brilliant things.

Your letter makes me quite hope that you'll come visiting us sometime. It's a pleasant wild coast. The roads are washed out a bit at present but they'll be in shape again, and we'll see splendid things down the coast and up the valley. The stonework I've done here with my hands might amuse you too. Here's a picture of the place, perhaps you can see a bit of Point Lobos beyond.

I haven't offered verse to a magazine since I was nineteen, though during the past year I tried to oblige when asked to. However, I'll go over my papers and see whether there are things I can send you. There may be a few. Lately I haven't written anything short, so taken up with the story that I hope to have ready this summer. Certainly it's surprisingly good of you to offer attempting to place anything for me.

Besides "Californians" in 1916 and "Tamar" and "Roan Stallion" I had a little book of verse called "Flagons and Apples" (!) printed in Los Angeles in 1912. Little young verses somewhat after the manner of Heine. I gave away a few copies but did not place it on sale. Eleven years later the printer wrote to ask what he should do with the 450 copies and I said to throw them away. He sold them to a second-hand book shop for twenty cents apiece and sent me the money![35]

Forgive the hurry of this letter, we've a guest in the house. George Sterling brought Sinclair Lewis to see us yesterday, and Lewis went back to the hotel but Sterling is stopping here. Life is short and crowded, but he's a pleasant companion.

I'm very glad to hear that the family of Friede is returning to health again.

Oh, Point Lobos. Lobos means wolves, in this case sea-wolves, i.e., sea-lions or seals; there are lots of them still.   Cordially yours,
Robinson Jeffers

59: TO DONALD FRIEDE

March 9, 1926

Dear Mr. Friede: I looked all about here and found two copies of the queer little "Flagons and Apples" (besides one inscribed to my wife) and have presumed to write yours and Mr. Liveright's names in them. They are mailed

[35] *Compare J's account in "First Book,"* The Colophon: A Book Collector's Quarterly, X (1932), 1–8, reprinted in Alberts, A Bibliography, pp. 153–56.

with this. The 450 copies were sold to Jones' Book Store; I don't know
the street in Los Angeles but it's an old shop and a letter would probably
reach them. Perhaps you have the address. I think the printing firm is
extinct. Queer things are wanted for collections!

The little books are addressed to you: will you be kind enough to give
Mr. Liveright his—if he wants it? —I've just remembered that a copy of
this, brought me to autograph a month ago, was stamped as from
Holmes' Book Store, another old one in Los Angeles.

If you still consider a pamphlet on the subject of me—I can only think of
George Sterling to suggest as author of it. He's done some fine things in
prose for the American Mercury, is almost hyperbolically indulgent toward
my productions, comes here avisiting sometimes, is very friendly though
our friendship's not quite a year old yet. I don't know whether he'd consent,
I'll ask him if you want. —My wife could do it very competently, but I
don't think she'd be willing.

Certainly I haven't done anything about the English rights of "Roan
Stallion" etc.; and I'd be very much interested if you could dispose of them:
though indeed I can't imagine what England would think of the book.
They buy many worse ones.[36]

Will you forgive—and can you read—this writing? I can't think through
the noise of a typewriter.

It was good to hear from you of the delights of New York. I read with
pleasure—without envy.   Cordially yours, Robinson Jeffers

60: TO GEORGE STERLING

[*March 14, 1926*]

Dear George: Your Braithwaite article[37] is a triumph, thank you for sending
it—the manuscript—but I'm not sure we should keep it, you must tell me
if you'd like it back in spite of that kind "needn't return." I was thinking
what a hideous thing it would be to have to write, and you write it as
if it were the easiest, and so exhaustive, and Olympianly
good-humored, it is wonderful.

Una brought home Powys' "Verdict"[38] and I glanced through it a little, I
like him better for the nice way in which he speaks of you and of Col.
Wood: who was in Carmel a couple of weeks ago, with Sara Bard Field and
her daughter and the young professor her fiancé: they were delightful to

[36] *The Hogarth Press distributed J's works in England.*
[37] *"The Poetry of the Pacific Coast—California,"* Anthology of Magazine Verse for 1926
and Yearbook of American Poetry, ed. *William Stanley Braithwaite*
(Boston, 1926), Part I, pp. 84–103.
[38] *Llewelyn Powys,* The Verdict of Bridlegoose *(New York, 1926).*

meet, and the old lion as great and leonine as I knew well he'd be.

We didn't know about the burning of the books until your letter came. You speak so philosophically it lessened the shock—just the same it was dreadful to think of, compensation and all.

What do you think of our [?] healthy children? It's not only sad and uncomfortable—scandalous too. First Garth has measles, he is just recovering and this tonsil infection brings higher and longer fever, with knobs like oranges on each side of his throat; he is just recovering from that and Donnan, who escaped measles, gets a violent intestinal infection that lasts a week; Donnan recovers, we still have to be careful not to let Garth exercise violently; three days ago he got the intestinal infection and is now in the midst of it—not quite so bad a case as Donnan's, but so bad that he hasn't eaten successfully for three days. I think he's begun to get better, and please God when this is over we'll have healthy boys again. Except that in six or eight weeks from now he must have his tonsils— "pulled"—the boys call it.

Three afternoons ago the tide looked so low I went down to try for mussels, but I couldn't jump from Scylla to Charybdis. This coming full moon surely it will be possible.

George, I wanted to finish this; but Una is going to the post-office and I'll send it off, on the principle that half a letter is better than none. Thank you for the weeklies, and for sending [Percy] Hutchinson's letter, and for much else.   Yours always, Robin

61: TO WITTER BYNNER

March 15, 1926

Dear Witter Bynner: It was good of you to write, and I'm grateful to Clara Evans for speaking of me to you.

Lucky perhaps that we didn't meet in 1911, I remember humbly a rather queer young person called by my name then. But I'd be very happy if you could stop in Carmel this summer; we're always at home; meanwhile I look forward to sending you a book (for better or worse) as soon as you're in Santa Fe to receive it.

I don't know whether you've ever visited this village. It's a beautiful coast, and this sea-fog should be a fine foil for your desert suns. We've been enjoying and admiring some of your lovely Chapala poems lately—El Musica for one—I think in Saturday Reviews that George Sterling sent us. He was here and noticed a lack of periodicals in the house.

I who know very few people have heard praise of you from many; and yet have been unlucky and foolish enough not to have seen a book of yours for a long time.   Sincerely yours, Robinson Jeffers

62: TO BABETTE DEUTSCH

March 18, 1926

My dear Miss Deutsch: This doesn't need answering—I have five
unanswered letters in front of me and know how it depresses one—it is
only to thank you for the review of "Roan Stallion" in the [*February 10*] New
Republic, and to congratulate you on the great poem in the Nation. How
can I say anything about the review, except that you know what Swinburne
meant by "the noble pleasure of praising"? But the iron passion and
beauty of your poem hardly allow praise, not in a letter to you, it would be
too much like patting an eagle. But I may thank you for it, very
earnestly.   Sincerely yours, Robinson Jeffers

63: TO RIDGELY TORRENCE

March 29, 1926

Dear Mr. Torrence: There's nothing better to offer you than these three
enclosures;[39] two of them seven years old; at least they've never been out of
my drawer before. I've been busy with a long thing and have written
nothing for a good while that the New Republic could use. Whenever
anything emerges I'll send it.

   I was proud to be addressed over your signature; and I'm glad of the
opportunity to thank the New Republic for publishing Miss Deutsch's very
kind reviews of my recent books.   Sincerely yours, Robinson Jeffers

64: TO GEORGE STERLING

April 13, 1926

Dear George: We were sorry not to see you; too bad it rained when you
were up the valley—though the rain was a great blessing. The boys
enjoy their history and can't quite believe until it shall happen about the
water-ouzel nests.

   I appeared to be elected to take H. Monroe to Pt. Lobos. We stopped at the
Mission by (her) request, and passing San Jose Creek I told her G. S. says
there are water-ouzel nests up there. She was much interested, not
having heard of them west of the Sierras. I didn't know she'd written verses
about them. I was quite pleased with her, she was so much more decent
than I expected. But those who went to her lecture were not. Una went, not

39 *"Promise of Peace" appeared in* New Republic *on June 9, 1926, and "Noon"*
on July 21, 1926.

I. It appears in a tired hour and a half she said only one thing of interest—that G. S. knows all about water-ouzels! She talked vaguely of poets of the east, and of the mid-west. At the end of the lecture up and spoke Grace Wallace, "What do you think of Mr. Jeffers?"—"I think a great deal of Mr. J., I've been talking to him all morning." For which reticence one may forgive her anything except (I speak from hearsay) her own verses, which occupied half the lecture. No one else's were quoted.

I must thank you again for that wonderful and I wish it were deserved article in the S.F. Review. Also for the other magazine you send us so faithfully.

I wish we had news of some kind—not that I'd like anything to happen more than is—but to write amusingly. I'm not progressing very well with my verses, and Tom Cator is going to marry the Hilliard girl—but this is more in Una's line to tell than mine, and I think besides it was in the Examiner. We look forward to having you here whenever you're able. Yours always, Robin

65: TO DONALD FRIEDE

April 24, 1926

Dear Mr. Friede: The poem is called Point Alma Venus.[40]

I began it quite cheerfully, soon after Tamar was written I put it aside because it was too exciting, and ever since has been a struggle to keep it out of my mind by writing something else.

The story, like Tamburlaine or Zarathustra, is the story of human attempts to get beyond humanity. But the superman ideal rather stands on top of humanity—intensifies it—ends in "all too human"—here the attempt is to get clear of it. More like the ceremonial dances of primitive people; the dancer becomes a rain-cloud, or a leopard, or a God. The protagonists are a paralytic old farmer, a preacher who has renounced his faith, a weak imaginative boy who kills his father. The episodes of the poem are a sort of essential ritual, from which the real action develops on another plane.

The story grows rather intimately from the rock of this coast. Someone said to me lately that it is not possible to be quite sane here, many others feel a hostility of the region to common human life. Immigration overpowers a place, at least for a while, but where the coast is thinly peopled it seems really to have a mood that both excites and perverts its people.

There will be a few short poems, somewhat related in theme to the long one; and perhaps, like their chief, conceived a little too barbarously in earnest.

[40] See Letter 67.

68

The name of the book. There's a headland with a lighthouse on it, of some importance in the story called Point Aumentos; and one of the people, (he reads Lucretius), dreams of it and thinks of it to himself as Point Alma Venus. I haven't been able to find any better title. This is for your private information. The origin of the name appears in the poem, and I don't suppose needs to be explained beforehand.

I'm afraid it's rather a poor description; but you wouldn't want me to tell the story of the poem; and perhaps this can be edited for the catalogue. I'll give you more information, if you want, later. I must stop in order to get this in the mail, and shall answer your recent very kind letter to-morrow.   Cordially yours, Robinson Jeffers

66: TO GEORGE STERLING

[April 30, 1926]

Dear George: We haven't given up your coming.

Yesterday I received a copy of a letter written you by Donald Friede. He asked me a month or two ago whether I'd be willing to have De Casseres (who'd been talking it over with him) write such a pamphlet as suggested. I said "of course," both to him and De Casseres, who wrote at the same time. Then Friede wrote that they'd decided against De Casseres: could I suggest someone? There was no one but you to suggest (unless Una would do it!) and he asked me to speak to you about it.

I was waiting for your arrival to speak about it, but his letter has reached you first.

If your hands are full of more serious work I hope you'll refuse. Otherwise there's certainly no one I'd rather owe this kindness to; and no one could do it half so beautifully.

Meanwhile I've been exchanging wires with Friede about whether I'd have a book ready for this fall. First I thought I could and then I saw plainly that I couldn't, which perhaps was a disappointment to him. But a book a year wouldn't leave a person any time to try experiments. Mine haven't amounted to much yet.

Since there'll be no book this fall, it's possible they'll not be in such a hurry for the pamphlet. I don't know.

Friede also talks about a limited edition of "Tamar," copies autographed and with illustrations. 15\frac{00}{}$! Boo! He says he has two or three artists making sketches but is not satisfied. Could I suggest someone? I can't of course. Can you? "Black and white, or possibly wash in the manner of Wallace Smith's work—the Aubrey Beardsley's unreality.

I have to answer: two long letters from Friede, two and a book from Ben De Casseres, a letter from Rorty, a book from Witter Bynner, some ten letters from other people, all done up in a nice rubber band. Una does them in a package and puts them where I'm likely to see them. One of my eyes is mildly inflamed from splashing dirt into it when I was planting trees yesterday, and that's helpful. I've solemnly promised by telegraph to have a book ready for publishing next spring. (Hope it will be good enough for dedication to you.) I've planted 20 eucalyptus and 112 tamarack pines the past three days, and have still some seventy cypresses to plant.

You'll be coming down soon, George, I hope. Bring your recipe for having time to do things!

Your tree is growing faster than anything on the place—has shot up a foot and a half since you planted it. It will be ready for the little bronze inscription.   Yours always, Robin

I'm eager to see the poem with the naughty ladies in it, the one you promised to bring. —And to hear of Lilith's appearance. —Una told you Albert Bender was here the other day—he's been good enough to send us "Words for the Chisel." —Rorty writes that Macmillan will publish his poems.

67: TO DONALD FRIEDE

April 30, 1926

Dear Mr. Friede: I owe you an explanation and two letters. I was in a fine state of mind about having to send you that second wire; but when I gave a whole morning to reading the manuscript considerately it became dreadfully clear that it would not do. Better for me to discover this than you, or the public at large. Every story that ever occurred to me had got wound up into this one poem, and it was too long, too complicated, and, from the attempt at compression, neither clear nor true. I should have discovered this a year ago, but was still hoping that the end would justify the earlier part. One has to try experiments, even costly ones.[41]

Now I must pick this thing to pieces; and I promise a book for spring publication, if you want it then, that will make up for all this nuisance. Meanwhile forgive me for disappointing you. I'd have done worse if I'd encouraged you to announce this experiment.

The copy of your letter to Sterling came yesterday. I think he'll like the

[41] *Melba Bennett describes the scraps that remain of "Point Alma Venus" as suggestive of the later "Give Your Heart to the Hawks." See her* Stone Mason, *pp. 115–16.*

suggestion. It's extraordinarily good of you to take so much trouble.
You may possibly want to postpone the pamphlet a few months,—since
there won't be a new book till spring—I shan't be unhappy. Sterling
was coming for a few days' visit last week, and telephoned that he couldn't.
His voice had a queer note in it. "Why, George, are you sick?"—"No,
I'm lit." True poet and true San Franciscan.

The Stallion die that you said you were sending has not arrived, and I'm
rather anxious for fear it's lost. We'd value it highly. Lost or not,
thank you much for having thought of sending it.

Your idea of the little illustrated edition of "Tamar" is most interesting.
Could you really sell copies at that George-Moorish price? My wife has
a feeling against drawings in the Wallace Smith manner—I mean for this
occasion—and has promised to write out her reasons to enclose with
this. But I'm not able to suggest any artist.

The check for royalties has not come yet. There's no hurry of course; I
mention it only for fear of its having got lost in the mail.

The lists of books came and we're very grateful indeed for your offer.
The one this family most wanted—George Moore's latest—was ordered a
month ago. So of the rich list I'll mention only two: —Sven Hedin's Life
as an Explorer, and Travels of Marco Polo—but pray don't send both
or either except as it's convenient for you. Then may I ask you to have sent
me, *not* as a gift, ten copies of Roan Stallion? A man asked me to order
and autograph five for him, and five others I'll need to give away in course
of time. And will you have these charged against my account, or
enclose a bill, whichever is simpler.

Seems to me I've spoken of everything—except to congratulate you on
the pleasantest cure for influenza, and to add my very
warm regards.   Yours, Robinson Jeffers

[*Enclosure in Una's hand*]

I hate making suggestions—they know so much better how to make a
beautiful book and one that collectors will desire—but the name Wallace
Smith frightened me. I know two books illustrated by him Ben Hecht's
"Fantazius Mallare" and De Casseres' "Shadow Eater." I have the
strongest feeling against that type of drawing for Tamar. There is about
those drawings a perverse sensuality— and a profound disillusionment
infinitely removed from the robust simplicity of Tamar's family!

Black and white would be splendid—I wonder if woodcuts could be
managed—only they mustn't be *quaint*. In any case we must plead with the
artist to keep in mind that if these Tamar people are queer—its a *rural*
queerness. They are twisted by a natural train of events arising from
passionate people in conflict in a remote and lonely situation—there mustn't
be a hint of [*perversion?*].

68: TO WITTER BYNNER

May 6, 1926

Dear Witter Bynner: I should have thanked you some days ago for the book and the inscription; I was a little in hope of hearing from you from Santa Fe, whence you were going to say what I might send you in return.
Of course there is nothing of particular interest to send except the recent Liveright book—which is quite long, at least.

"Caravan" I've read with pleasure and admiration; you gathered beauty from distant places and near ones and made it all your own in the utterance. Behind occasional flicks of the Faun's ear, it is the large humanity—humaneness—of your nature that impresses me most; unless perhaps the sensitiveness to beauty, no matter where perceived. I'm very grateful.

Your friend Albert Bender was here briefly ten days ago or so. Another friend of yours, George Sterling, just left us after a sudden four-day visit that suspended this letter in the middle of the second paragraph. An active presence—one doesn't write letters with George in the house—insisting, rather, on one's company and of it.

You'll be here, I hope, some time this summer.   Sincerely yours,
Robinson Jeffers

69: TO DONALD FRIEDE

May 8, 1926

Dear Mr. Friede: Sterling has been here four days, and just left for the city. Soon after receiving your letter he wrote to me that he'd be glad to undertake the job, but I was surprised to learn when he arrived here that he hadn't written to you. He thought I would do it. I said I couldn't discuss terms for him. He was vague at first, when I pressed him for something definite he said he thought $150.00 would be proper.

When he arrived here he was still a bit weak and distraught from two or three days of merriment and a consequent week in bed, but he soon recovered in this spartan household. Your letter arrived while he was still in bed, I dare say he didn't feel up to correspondence just then.

> *"Lucky perhaps that we didn't meet in 1911, I*
> *remember humbly a rather queer young person called by*
> *my name then."*

(Letter 61)

I think I've come to terms with my book at last, discovering a form that is quite new, so far as I know, and the only one possible for the subject. It ought to do pretty well now.   Cordially yours, Robinson Jeffers

70: TO ALBERT BENDER

May 11, 1926

Dear Mr. Bender: You are so generous that I should hardly know how to begin saying thank you if Una had not written you a note a day or two ago. George Sterling says that he calls you "Prince Albert," it seems very natural and proper.

I had read the poem in "Caravan" called "Anne," I thought of Anne Bremer[42] at first reading, and when George was here lately I opened the volume you sent to ask him whether it was she. Yourself answered me, you had written in the name. —Thank you also for "Words for the Chisel"—I've not had time yet to read the long first poem but I saw amazingly fine things among the shorter ones. I had a note from Miss Taggard lately; it will be delightful to write to her about them.

Una has spoken of the magnificent etching, and of the portrait of Shelley; we're very grateful for them. The beautiful violinist's face reminds me a little of Hedwiga Reicher's, who was here a year or two ago, you probably know her.[43]

I wrote for some "Roan Stallions," which should arrive in a few days. We've been several times to see [photographer Johan] Hagemeyer, and he was always either away from home or occupied with a subject; we'll see him very soon however.   Yours most cordially, Robinson Jeffers

71: TO ALBERT BENDER

May 18, 1926

Dear Mr. Bender: The five copies of "Roan Stallion" have come, but when I was about to write my name and yours in them it occurred to me to ask whether that's what you wish, and whether you'd like me to copy into them a line or two of verse besides.

I'm not used to this sort of thing yet. And then about the photograph, if you still want it, —your name on that, and a couple of lines of verse

[42] *Bender's cousin and protégée.*
[43] *Type for* Clytemnestra *and* Cassandra *in* The Tower Beyond Tragedy; *see Letter 160.*

over mine? Month, year and place? —I thought only yesterday that we have
a copy of the photograph you wanted, and I could send you this and give
Una the new one Hagemeyer finishes. He seemed—a few days ago—
a little vague as to how soon it could be done. Temperament—

It was ever so kind of you to quote Genevieve Taggard's letter to me. Her
book is splendid—charm and power, and the extraordinary lift upward
toward the close particularly impressed me—it's been a great pleasure
to write to her about it.

Thank you for sending the Argonaut review, which as you say might have
been better; but it was comprehensive at least. The writer, perhaps a
little distrusting himself, took pains not to appear uncritical.

I'd a considerable letter (hand-written!) the other day from Harriet
Monroe, who had a pleasant and successful tour, on the whole, and
enclosed the proof of her review of "Roan Stallion" for the June Poetry. She
doesn't like the title poem but is otherwise very kind.

The twins thank you eagerly for the lovely cards you sent them—so do
we—they are most charming pictures, and almost as many as your other
benefactions.

Did I tell you that James Rorty wrote that Macmillan are going to publish
his poems? Probably you know it already.   Cordially yours,
Robinson Jeffers

72: TO HARRIET MONROE

June 2, 1926

Dear Miss Monroe: You have been very kind and I should like to have
answered more promptly; I work indoors in the morning and lay stones and
plant trees in the afternoon, expecting always to write letters at night;
comes night and one of my little trees could write a more intelligent
letter. I'm sorry.

The review is very friendly and thank you for it.[44] But "purple pride"?
Nothing so picturesque—something might be said for gray arrogance
perhaps! but I don't think so.

The "Marriage with Space" has a great theme elaborately worked out
and I wish I could think something about it to tell you; but I can't. It
seems to me an attempt to paint all in white on a white ground; but the stars
are children of night, the spirit is a spark fed by the flesh and nothing
without it. This isn't criticism, it's only personal; I have a blind
spot for most of Blake too.

[44] *"Power and Pomp,"* Poetry, *XXVIII (June, 1926), 160–64.*

H. L. Davis's work I admire greatly, and thank you much for sending me the poems. He is a great person, his rhythms, his vision, his manner, like no one else's. The people moving like wistful ghosts, with such vivid gestures, through so intensely real a countryside: it gives one the oddest feeling of the grass being permanent and humanity only a poignant episode:[45] perception the more startling for being implicit and not expressed. It's hard reading, rather; I haven't yet been able to decide whether that comes from a haughty or an evasive reticence; or whether there is something just a little out of focus, in this subjective and individual experience, that might be clarified. But it is splendid.

And thank you for sending the page from his letter; keen virile intelligence, and a mind enviable for its dash and decision. —There is my point perhaps: if more of that cavalry-captain decisiveness were in the poetry, where it rather belongs, one wouldn't wonder whether haughtiness or evasion blurs the composition a little. Not the details: nothing could be more vivid.

We've read with keen interest the story of your lecturing journey, told so vividly. Incredible vitality you must have to endure it—even, as appears, —enjoy it. We enjoyed your visit here, at least, very much; and you, looking back on journeys like this one, must appreciate the extraordinary range and power of your influence on people.

I haven't spoken fittingly of the poems you sent, I have no critical mind at all. We're grateful, though; and it has been a pleasure to write to you.   Sincerely yours, Robinson Jeffers

Carmel audiences are most often bad ones. I'm sorry; but we're not part of the village; even legally outside it. Mrs. Jeffers sends cordiallest greetings with mine.   R. J.

73: TO BENJAMIN DE CASSERES

June 4, 1926

Dear Ben: You know perfectly how delighted we were with that review in the Times,[46] and thank you for sending it. Such a hectic life in such a quiet place has kept me from writing four or five days ago, as I should have done. But indeed we weren't surprised; and though delighted because the Times has so much influence, favorable as the review was I thought there were many more fine things might have been said truly.

[45] J treats this theme in such poems as "What Are Cities For?" "Bixby's Landing," and Part VII of "The Broken Balance."
[46] Anonymous review of de Casseres' Forty Immortals, "Benjamin de Casseres as a Press Agent for Parnassus," New York Times, May 23, 1926, Sec. 3, p. 12.

This is the worst pen there is—or else the worst ink.

Our friend of the Bohemian Club [*Sterling*] says that he too has just written a review of you, which no doubt he'll send. He's due here to-morrow evening for another little visit, and probably we're going over night forty or fifty miles down the coast, which gets more and more wild southward. Don't you wish you were coming along? Great redwood-covered mountains down there, dropping two or three thousand feet straight to the ocean. I wish you were.

Well I'll reserve my curses until I see the article in print. The writer of it is a great person; the victim will try to be submissive.[47] Good luck, with best wishes from us all to you and Bio: and again exultant congratulations on the new book.   Yours, Robin

74: TO ALBERT BENDER

June 6, 1926

Dear Mr. Bender: Your kind letter makes me even sorrier than I was not to have written you sooner, and said thank you for many things. Do you know, I haven't even had time yet to read "For Eager Lovers"? I looked into it enough to know that it is very beautiful poetry, and to think that it is not quite so fine as the later book—we've had enjoyment from it, but neither Una nor I have read it yet.

Your generosity already sent us a copy of Markham's lovely little book; but I think we know somebody here who'd be very pleased to have this second copy with the inscription; if he seems anxious for it we'll pass it on, may we? as from you.

I'm very proud of your kindness to the poems, and of Professor Lehman's[48] opinion, and we'd be happy to see him whenever he comes to Carmel. Two or three months ago a blonde girl—freshman from the University knocked at this door and said she'd come to see me on account of something Professor Lehman had said.

George Sterling is coming here for another little visit, arriving this evening; we shall probably go [*for*] a long drive down the coast with him, to the end of the coast-road. And a man here began yesterday to paint

---

[47] *This may be another reference to Harriet Monroe's "Power and Pomp"; see Letter 72.*
[48] *Benjamin H. Lehman, professor of English at the University of California at Berkeley, was an early sponsor of J's work in college classrooms. It was he who introduced Judith Anderson, then his wife, to J, and who, with her, encouraged J to allow his work to be staged. J's correspondence with Dr. Lehman in this collection begins with Letter 109.*

a full-length life-size portrait of me![49] So the coming week promises to be occupied as usual. In between I do some stone work and water several hundred lately planted pines and cypresses. "Even in a palace life may be led well," Marcus Aurelius said—even in Carmel you can be busy!

The letter breaks off here, lacking close and signature. Appended, however, is a note by Una, explaining, "Robin was interrupted here // I think you'd be amused to spend a week end here with us (with bread and milk and apple sauce for supper!) Think it over when you want a quiet moment in the bosom of a simple blissful household."

75: TO DONALD FRIEDE

June 13, 1926

Dear Mr. Friede: Sterling has just left, after a week's visit taking notes for the pamphlet you spoke to him about. At the same time I've been letting a man paint a picture of me on an eight-foot canvas! so it's been an excessive sort of week. The painting seems fairly good, perhaps I'll send you a photograph of it next letter.

Enclosed are four short poems ["*Soliloquy*," "*Ocean*," "*Love-Children*," *and ?*] I promised to send you when there were any, but probably you'll agree with me that none of them is fitted for magazine publication. Except the one called LOVE-CHILDREN they are more in the nature of notes for the long poem to come. I have copies.

Probably the long poem will be called "ANTICHRIST"—if you think that's a good name for a book. [*This has been crossed out, with "Name won't do; I'll find a better one" written after it.*] I've just finished a story called "THE CHOICE," about the length of "ROAN STALLION," same meter and similar manner, the subject of course quite different. You could have it any time, but probably you'll not want it until "ANTICHRIST" is finished. [*This has been changed to "the book is finished."*]

I'm sorry—only for my friend Jim Rorty's sake—to see that the New Masses has sailed into bad weather already.   Cordially yours,
Robinson Jeffers

I'm happy that Dreiser thought well of "Tamar." George Sterling is a friend of his, you probably know, and perhaps have seen the preface that he wrote for Sterling's "Lilith," lately published by Macmillan.

---

[49] *Rem Remsen's portrait now hangs in the Occidental College Library.*

76: TO GEORGE STERLING

July 16, [*1926*]

Dear George: We were sorry when your little letter came saying you
weren't well—paying for being sociable—the convalescence is the sorrowful
part and I hope it's happily complete by this time. They are beautiful poems
you sent, I return them gratefully since you ask me to.

"After Sunset" I think is one of the most beautiful short poems you've
ever written—and those are daring words—but consider the second line, and
the third and fourth of the third stanza—loveliness isn't often so true also.

Don't wear yourself out over the play production. No matter what revision
you agree to, the printed copy will stand, and that's the important one.
Good luck.   Yours always, Robin

77: TO DONALD FRIEDE

July 21, 1926

Dear Friede: It gives me a shock to see the date on your yet unanswered
letter. Sterling descended on us over the fourth with Edgar Lee Masters and
another man, they stayed three days, and your letter arrived, and people
have been coming and going in droves ever since, for no reason except
that it's summer in Carmel. Even an International News-Reel person,
and I've really never had time to write except I was too tired.
But Masters was very amusing and agreeable.

The pictures you sent are exceedingly good—and yet—don't you think
"Tamar" is better off without them? I can't judge. The six or eight people
I've shown them to have been fervid in disapproval. One man, whose
judgment I respect, said that those who thought well of "Tamar" had been
able to silence the others; who, if these pictures were associated with it,
could answer "See! It *is* the sort of thing we thought, after all." He
suggested for a de luxe edition, if that was wanted, some very beautiful
font of type, beautiful spacing, splendid paper, but no illustrations. Said there
are a restraint and austerity in the poem that ought to be emphasized—*I*
don't know where, but that's what he said. He is an art-critic, his wife is an
artist; and she said the pictures are very good indeed but they would be
very bad with Tamar. That is my feeling too. But what do *I* know about it?

Sterling is so involved in having a dramatic poem of his produced at the
annual Bohemian Club festival, I fear his manuscript won't make
much progress this month.

The photograph of a portrait my wife addressed to you—the painter wants suppressed because he thinks he can have a better photograph taken when he takes the picture to San Francisco next week. However, if you've had it reproduced already, his wishes don't matter. He wants to be called Rem Remsen—he's a son of Ira Remsen, Johns Hopkins President-emeritus, who wrote the chemistry text-book.

It's a great pity, the stallion die never arrived here.

I hope you have a delightful time this summer. I should, if people wouldn't come to see me. But I hope *you*'ll come sometime or other, that would make amends for many other people's visits.   Yours, Robinson Jeffers

A marginal note from Una explains, "Remsen is not forbidding the use of the picture—he merely hopes later to get a better photograph of the painting."

78: TO GELBER, LILIENTHAL, INC. (Lantern Press)

July 26, 1926

Gentlemen: I must thank you very cordially for the kindness of Mr. Lilienthal's letter as well as for "The Modern Writer," a book you have good reason to be proud of. James Rorty told me that it was in prospect when he was here two years ago, and spoke highly of you and of Grabhorn at the same time. And of course I have seen and heard praise of your volumes elsewhere.

I should be much pleased to have you publish something of mine. Unfortunately Boni and Liveright have an option on my "two next books." If I were more productive it wouldn't matter, but they wanted a book for publication this fall and I have had to put them off till spring. Probably there's material on hand for a small volume such as you have in mind, but I couldn't submit it without Liveright's approval.[50] I'm writing them about this to-night, but I'm afraid it's hardly likely that they'll consent. If they should, I'll let you know at once. In any case, thank you for the offer, and for the book.   Sincerely yours, Robinson Jeffers

[50] *Leon Gelber and Theodore Lilienthal finally persuaded J to give them a prose piece, since they could not obtain permission to print a collection of his poems. See Letters 81 and 85.*

79: TO DONALD FRIEDE

July 31, 1926

Dear Friede—   Thank you for letting me know that Mencken will take the poem. It's rather astonishing—that one in particular I didn't think could be sold to anybody.[51]

A letter yesterday from Lilienthal (Lantern Press), whose letter I sent you the other day, says that he is a friend of Horace Liveright, and is writing him for permission to publish the little book. I have really no preference, only hoping that you'll publish the one promised for next spring, so you'll do whatever is best for yourselves.

And so you'll do about the Tamar pictures. No doubt it's biological law that neither the author nor his friends ever quite approve of the illustrator.   Yours, Robinson Jeffers

80: TO GEORGE STERLING

August 10, [1926]

Dear George: Thanks ever so much for the brick, which is thrilling to have, and will find a conspicuous place somewhere. [Ira] Remsen brought it several days ago, when we asked whether he's had measles he dropped it and fled, only saying that it was from you, so that we didn't know more until your letter came. We're delighted to hear that Truth was so successfully produced; one wouldn't need to worry if all depended on the author. Miss Welch and Miss Crillow were here and we had a pleasant talk. A Mrs. [Victor David] Brenner, you're perhaps acquainted with or know of (widow of the man that made the Lincoln penny) was here some weeks ago, and when we talked about you she said she'd commissioned her secretary to send her reviews of "Lilith" and she had a whole pamphlet full of splended ones. I'm not surprised at that, but at her interest; she didn't seem extremely acquainted with your work. The Saturday Review article was reprinted in the [Carmel] Cymbal. Una met a man from L.A. to-day who had been at your Grove play [Truth], he had the book with him and every time he could get anyone to listen he read them passages; had been doing so ever since. Una saw Bert Heron's Hamlet and wants to say that it was astonishingly good. It must have been; she doesn't like to see Shakespeare staged, and was glad she went. Heron amazed every body;

[51] "Preface," an early version of part of the Prelude to The Women at Point Sur, appeared in the American Mercury, IX (December, 1926), 434.

David O'Neil was a noble king; program enclosed. Garth has finished his
measles and developed a tonsilitis to keep him company; I expect he'll
be all right in a couple of days and then perhaps Donnan will oblige. Poor
little boys haven't said so, but no doubt they'd rather have these things
when school's keeping. At least they learned to swim this year before
the measles came. Last year they could paddle a few strokes, now
they're quite sure of themselves.

A boy from Kansas came up the hill the other day to ask a question about
Tamar or something, he said he hadn't read Sterling's book about me
yet. I said Sterling hasn't written one yet. "Oh," he said, "it's advertised on
the Roan Stallion jackets." First I'd heard of it. Aren't they enterprising
people!   Yours always, Robin

81: TO THEODORE LILIENTHAL

August 19, 1926

Dear Mr. Lilienthal: It's a pity, but it wouldn't be possible for me to
produce anything in prose during the next half year at least; so there's no
help, I'm afraid, in Donald Friede's suggestions. It's kind of you to
consider it, and I'm sorry that nothing apparently can be arranged at present.

Perhaps sometime in the future we could overcome these difficulties.
Meanwhile I'd be very glad to receive a visit from you if you're ever in the
neighborhood.   Sincerely yours, Robinson Jeffers

82: TO DONALD FRIEDE

August 21, 1926

Dear Friede: Since you're so kind as to offer me choice among the fall
books, may we have Doughty's *Arabia Deserta* when the latest edition is
ready? My wife is a persevering woman and has read it through, (a
borrowed copy), but it's a book one would love to have; perhaps I also shall
read it through before the winter passes. You're very generous. Obviously
there are other fascinating works in the list, but we'll go to the
libraries for them. Not that we never buy!

Gelber and Lilienthal were quite taken with your suggestion that I write
prose for them, but I've had to beg off; I haven't anything to write
prose *about*, and too busy making verses and planting trees.

Sterling writes that he is making progress with *his* prose. I don't
envy him the job.

Thank you for the interesting clipping. I have one from Chicago that makes a curious contrast with it—Harriet Monroe's article—shocked at Roan Stallion but doesn't mind Tamar—morality is a very personal affair.
Yours, Robinson Jeffers

Letter just received from Sterling says that he's finished his manuscript, but I'm not to see it.

83: TO GEORGE STERLING

August 30, 1926

Dear George: I was hoping till the last tide that it would be possible to go after mussels, but it can't be done for a few days yet. Garth isn't allowed to get out of bed until to-morrow, and then only for a half hour or so at a time; probably you don't realize how this complicates a household. The past six days I've been at work again in the mornings, and tried to water the little trees enough to keep them alive—outside of that, not a minute.

That was a nice review Una sent you to-day—"best poetic drama written in America and one of the best in English"—is pretty good for the old N.Y. Times.[52] My own enthusiasm, or Dreiser's, couldn't do *much* better than that.

I haven't yet read "Truth" enough to speak of it with any understanding— only I've seen the terrible significance and the fierce wistful beauty.
Thank you, George.   Yours, Robin

84: TO GEORGE STERLING

Monday night
[*September 13, 1926*]

Dear George: I wrote you half a page last night but it was too late to finish and I threw it in the fire. I suspect it contained imbecilities (bred by sleepiness) about Catullus and Rolfe Humphries. The latter's letter was very

[52] *Percy A. Hutchinson's "Poetic Drama Did not Die with Stephen Phillips . . . ," New York Times, August 22, 1926, Sec. 3, p. 9.*

OVERLEAF:

"It is right to speak in superlatives when one is young; it means there will still be fire in the engine later."

(Letter 243)

worth reading, so was his article. (You remember sending me the Voices it was in.) But I liked the article for the Roman's sake, not the other's. There is no comparison between the people, and I think not in any literary sense between the ages. But it's splendid to have Catullus talked about. Do you remember his Atthis? I don't except that the young Asian castrates himself in the enthusiasm of his worship—I suppose of the Great Mother—and then the pronoun changes; he isn't called "it" as we might say, but "she."

It's all very splendid, choriambics ($\underline{\hphantom{x}}\cup\cup\underline{\hphantom{x}}$). Tennyson imitated the meter in his "Boadicea," and that has a grand long bounding line, but nobody can read it with any resemblance to classical meter since Tennyson died. A fine thunder of its own, though; do look it up if you haven't lately; or else, God help me, I'll read it to you when you visit us next. Those are sweet verses of Tennyson's about Catullus's little home-peninsula in Lake Garda.

And again this afternoon I had wretched luck. We were all from home, the first time I've been away in two weeks, and we returned and there was my chisel on the step. I'm sorry that you bothered about it, but thank you too, but very sorry that none of us was here to be especially nice to your messenger. I wish she might call again sometime, and let me apologize for the horrid burden—though it was neatly done in paper, with your name on it.

The other letters too were most interesting to read, and thank you for sending them. How in the world do you manage so much correspondence? And talking about this person here to so many people—I know your kindness, and am grateful.

I think it was rather impudent of me to ask whether you had considered a certain paragraph in that poem of yours, in prose, for the [San Francisco] Review. No doubt you had considered. You are so royally generous that I don't know how to say thank you, with silence? With disclaimers? With an impudent suggestion?

To-night there are fellows in a car on the little point across the road from us, smugglers no doubt, have been signalling all evening northwestward, switching their headlights off and on, at intervals, in a sort of Morse code. The children, before they went to bed, wanted to help with our flashlight, but I thought we'd better maintain neutrality. When will you come to visit this exciting place again?   Yours always, Robin

85: TO THEODORE LILIENTHAL

September 16, 1926

Dear Mr. Lilienthal: I dislike writing prose, but it would be quite impossible
to refuse two hundred words since you're kind enough to give me the
space. So within a month I'll send you something. It seems an absurdly
long time, but I'm quite occupied, and haven't the least idea
what to write about.[53]
   Thank you for the very interesting Broadside.   Sincerely yours,
Robinson Jeffers

86: TO LOUIS UNTERMEYER

September 17, 1926

Dear Untermeyer: Certainly I'll be happy to have anything of mine that
you please included in the next edition of Modern American Poetry.
   And it is kind of you to ask me to join the next American Miscellany. Yes,
I'll send you twenty pages or slightly less, care of Harcourt, Brace, by
January; and value the privilege the more for that you speak of Aiken,
Fletcher, and Sara Teasdale, as well as yourself, wanting me to. I feel
a sort of personal acquaintance with you through our friend George Sterling,
and am happy to hope it may become closer some day.   Cordially
yours, Robinson Jeffers

87: TO DONALD FRIEDE

September 17, 1926

Dear Friede: Thank you very much for Arabia Deserta, which came sooner
than I expected. It is a beautiful piece of book-making. Thank you also
for "Sweepings," a most powerful story, great I think in its reverberant
tragic irony, and in mass and essential simplicity.
   I have a letter from Untermeyer asking leave to include some things from
Roan Stallion and Tamar in the next edition of his Modern American
Poetry. He also asks me to take part in the next American Miscellany—
biennial to be published middle of next year, manuscript by January.
(No editor: twenty pages at disposal of each contributor.) I've agreed to do

[53] *Gelber, Lilienthal printed "All the Corn in One Barn" in* Lights and Shadows from
the Lantern, I *(November, 1926); reprinted in* Alberts, A Bibliography, *pp. 133–35.*

so, but with some misgiving, as it will subtract something from the book promised you for next spring. The book will be long enough even so; but let me know if you object.

Also at your leisure will you tell me what month this winter you want the manuscript of the book—February, or later or earlier? Or if you think advisable to postpone it to fall I'd be just as well pleased; the choice is yours.

Thank you for writing to Jolas;[54] some people were here the other day who know him and think highly of him. An Alsatian; which accounts for his writing German as well as French.

Thank you too for the statement of royalties, which reached me a couple of days ago.

I'm sorry Carmel gets farther and farther from you. I wish it did from me, but instead it encroaches more and more. There's nothing of particular value here but the coast scenery and that is getting all littered up with people. However, we're too heavy to move, we shall always be here. But I must build a wall around the place. A friend gave us the other day an authentic bit of stone from the wall of China, it's a good beginning. Cordially yours, Robinson Jeffers

88: TO BENJAMIN DE CASSERES

October [5], 1926

Dear Ben: That's a thrilling story of yours about Carmel,[55] Thank you for sending it. I don't know whether to thank you for writing it, it will probably bring the world here, and "the world is too much with us" already. For the talk about me I'm very grateful and overcome with embar[r]assment; you've given me everything, even conversation, which is more than nature did.

A couple of days after your article, came a shout of joy about it from Youngstown [Johnstown] Pa.! from a young man who'd sent me several months ago a review he'd written for his father's paper there, and was very happy to quote you in agreement with him.[56]

Stupidly I hadn't noticed that the article on Coleridge in the N.Y. Times was by you, so hadn't read it.[57] But it was still in the house, on the shelf

[54] *Eugène Jolas, editor of* Transition *and translator of "Roan Stallion" into French; see also Letter 327.*
[55] *"Carmel, the Secret Garden of the Gods,"* New York Herald Tribune Books, *September 19, 1926.*
[56] *Enclosed is a letter from Warren Worth Bailey, Jr., reporter for the* Johnstown Democrat.
[57] *De Casseres reviewed H. I. Fausset's* Samuel Taylor Coleridge, *New York* Times, *September 5, 1926, Sec. 3, p. 8.*

that the waste papers go to, and shan't return there. You have a power all your own, and if I'd read three words I'd have known you, without the name at the top.

Then from Los Angeles came your tremendous manuscript on me, which will not lack publication in course of time, if its subject gets to be a little better known. Meanwhile it's a grand poem, and I'm all the more grateful for it. How beautifully you have done it; I wish I were worthy of such music.[58]

I've just read an article against me by Floyd Dell, in the Modern Quarterly.[59] He's really quite kind, for an enemy, and writes a good article.

I've been trying to persuade Boni and Liveright to wait till next fall for my next book, but they hold me to my promise—publication in April— I'll have to work.

We've had the first rain of the winter, a lovely two-day one, and I've been able to stop watering trees long enough to lay a few more stones. Not on the tower, on the dining-room that's building between house and garage. The more it rains, the more we'll have a dining-room.

Here's the young man's shout of joy about your Carmel article. Don't send it back, I just stopped in the middle of this page and answered it. Yours always—and thank you, Robin

What a magnificent talent you have for titles—"The Elect and the Damned"—a new book of yours is the best news that can be.

89: TO W. ORTON TEWSON

J's answer to the question "Do you care what the Critics say about you?"
a symposium appearing in the "Literary Review" of the New York
Evening Post, *1926.*

October 7, 1926

Dear Mr. Tewson: Certainly I care what the critics say about me. Not enough to arise and sell all and follow them; but a book presumes readers, gentle ones if possible, and as Shelley's friend the Brown Demon said in her poem—

"All, all are men, women and all."

Kind of you to ask.   Sincerely yours, Robinson Jeffers

---

[58] *Begun when Liveright proposed its publicity pamphlet, "Robinson Jeffers, Tragic Terror" was published as an article in* Bookman, LXIX (*November, 1927*), 262–66, *was privately printed as a monograph in 1928, and was finally collected (1936) in the series of essays* The Elect and the Damned, *mentioned below. See also Letters 127 and 128.*
[59] *"Shell-Shock and the Poetry of Robinson Jeffers,"* Modern Quarterly, III (*September–December, 1926*), 268–73.

90: TO GEORGE STERLING

[October 9, 1926]

Dear George: Rorty isn't perfectly kind, but he pays splendid tribute to Lilith, both form and content; and his irritation against Strange Waters, though it blinded him to some beautiful poetry, is quite justifiable if he thought that you were taking a lead from me. Of course you oughtn't, and of course you weren't. To come under Bierce's influence would be natural, and in the days before you were thirty, but I don't believe that even he changed or made your manner to any extent, even though you said he did. I thought your long ago manner remembered Tennyson just a little—perhaps it was only the verse-form of the Testimony of the Suns. —Your later is of course nobody's but Sterling's.

It's pleasing to learn that Rorty isn't editor of the Masses any more, I like and admire him, besides owing him a lot, and I don't want to contribute to any magazine. Also I think that ostentatiously proletarian atmosphere is too slip-shod to be good for any body, at least in this country. Not that it could change him; but I don't think he could change it.

Yesterday we took our Garth to the dentist and had seven baby teeth drawn, the new ones were coming in beside them, three popped out rather easily, four needed novocaine and regular extraction. They were all in condition to last a life-time. But he didn't mind, there are lots more where those came from. Coming home we stopped at the P. O. and found your box of sweets. Garth was as willing as anyone, and the boys thank you much; so do we; they're sharing it. Thank you also for the packages of Nations and Saturday Reviews.

No, I didn't see the reference in Poetry.

The blessed rain gave me three afternoons for doing stone-work, but now I'm watering trees again with the same dogged continuance.

Did we tell you, Col. Wood, Sara Bard Field, her daughter and her daughter's fiancé, were in Carmel awhile ago. We saw them one afternoon and part of another; they are beautiful people.

I must ask Una whether there's any thing else you'd be interested to hear.

She says she'll write her own gossip and not give it to me. —She had a long letter from Masters the other day; she says if Mencken is at all so nice as Masters you must be sure to bring him here if possible.

Weren't you pleased to see Frank Devendorf, philanthropist, in the new Who's Who?   Yours always, Robin

will return R[orty]'s letter and review in Una's big envelope.

91: TO GEORGE STERLING

November 4, [1926]

Dear George: I'm just incapable of reading a review all the way through; the second reading it begins to dawn on me that Rorty's is worse than I thought. Over the proof my mind was focussed on his scolding you for not thinking enough of yourself. There I agree with him. Browning's "eagle and wren" ["A Light Woman"] is funny; but you mustn't invert it, as in that sonnet I never showed anyone and never will. —But Rorty missed all the beauty. Except for his poems and some reviews, what a slop-can this Masses is.

Here's a copy of verses for Overland,[60] the only thing I could find, and I doubt your wanting it. Don't dare let them use it for a frontis-piece, especially with more fitting ones of your own tucked away somewhere toward the back. And don't ask for any more, please, I'm going to do my firmest to keep out of magazines. It isn't good for me. It's good for you but it isn't for me; you can get along in company.

The boys' birthday present is a drive to-morrow to San Antonio Mission ruins, beyond Jolon. I'll mail this on the way. Start 6 AM, 180 miles round trip.   Yours always, Robin

Did you read that Brett Page escaped and hanged himself?

92: TO LOUIS UNTERMEYER

November 10, 1926

Dear Untermeyer: It was pleasant to hear from you returned to these shores, even though the warning wasn't needed. I have it committed to memory that my fifteen or twenty pages must be mailed you not later than Christmas. I'd send them earlier, only there's always the hope that something may yet occur to me. Since you speak of the poem that appeared, rather to its own astonishment, in the Masses[61] —I'll include that, unless there is better.

It's very good of you to speak of looking forward to 'em.   Sincerely yours, Robinson Jeffers

[60] "Post Mortem" appeared in the December issue, which Sterling probably had assembled before his suicide.
[61] The May, 1926, issue of New Masses gave "Apology for Bad Dreams" its first publication.

93: TO BENJAMIN DE CASSERES

Dear Ben: The book of your brother's poems[62] was delayed in the mail—
returned for postage—and has been here only a couple of days, while
I've been thinking what to write to you. I can't believe that comment of mine
could be of importance one way or the other. My literary judgments are
narrow, perhaps, and never enthusiastic; I wish they were, in this
case. I'd give a lot to be able to say something splendid.

But in the first place, I can't go along with your brilliantly written
preface. Suicide is often justifiable, very rarely admirable. As a rejection of
life it is only justifiable; you can't praise a man for going to bed early.

And there was much to praise in your brother. There was talent that
might have developed transcendently; it is simply impossible to foretell a
boy's manhood. If Chatterton had lived he might have been the greatest
English poet; he might have gone silent like Rimbaud; he might have
dwindled into mediocrity.

Walter de Casseres had splendid possibilities; he refused life, as he had
a right to do, and all that you have is a shining memory, and these brief
sweet-blooded poems to share with us. They are musical, clear and
sweet; often they rise to a faint impersonal ecstasy as in the haunting line
"A shadow worshipped and a shadow worshipper"; once at least, in
"The Suicide," to a bare bitter earnestness that captures beauty because it
does not want beauty.

Thank you for having the book sent to me. Indeed I wish I could speak
more fluently about it.

November 17

I wrote this last night and kept it over the day wondering how it could
be bettered. To-day came the tragic news of George's death. I haven't
the heart to rewrite to-night, and I mustn't delay this answer longer.
It appears from the paper that a bottle of poison was found uncorked in
George's room; ironical that I should have been writing that cold paragraph
about suicide last night. You and I have lost a great friend, there was
none more generous or more constant. It seems incredible that we'll have
neither letter nor visit from him.   Yours, Robin Jeffers

---

[62] *Walter de Casseres,* The Sublime Boy *(New York, 1926). Walter de Casseres
died in 1900.*

94: TO ALBERT BENDER

November 19, 1926

Dear Albert Bender: We are very grateful to you for the beautiful letter
and the clippings. It seems incredible even now that he is gone, the
face and voice and personality so vivid in our minds, and to be always, I
am sure, so intimately present in our thoughts of this place and of this
coast. Una and I were looking at some Kodak pictures this evening,
of George and me, and the children.

It seems to me that what happened, however much it may have been
planned for some indefinite future, was purely accidental at this time, as
much as being run over in the street. I mean that I don't think he felt himself
on the wane, nor had any unusual reason for unhappiness nor feeling
of frustration. We hadn't seen him since Masters was here, but there were
several letters from him. He had hoped to bring Mencken to Carmel for
a day or two; if that had been impossible I think he would have
come by himself a few days later.

He was a great man, and generous beyond belief, a master of beautiful
words and thoughts. Perhaps his great misfortune lay in being one of
the foremost and most sensitive minds of a time when romanticism
overlapped materialism—the needs of a spiritual period were still felt and
nothing to satisfy them. But I don't know. The essential is that we love
him, and are sorry, and you and I are very proud to have been his friends.
Yours, and thank you, Robinson Jeffers

95: TO HARRIET MONROE

November 27, 1926

My dear Miss Monroe: George Sterling's death was a grievous shock to us,
and utterly unexpected at the time. I believe he had often anticipated
such an end as desirable, though I don't remember his ever saying so to me.
He had known several cases of suicide and liked to think of them; it was
perhaps a pleasure to feel that he had the key within reach, wasn't
locked in. He assured us for instance that his friend Jack London had died
intentionally, of an over dose of morphine, and not, as reported,
by process of nature.

I don't believe George had suffered any unusual cause for depression
lately. He hadn't been here for several months, but wrote us now and then.
He expected to bring Mencken here or to Monterey for a day or two, but

Mencken was delayed in Los Angeles, and when he reached San Francisco, a few days later than expected, George had fallen into one of those brief illnesses—eclipses—that he dreaded but could not wholly avoid, though they were becoming very rare. He wasn't able to meet Mencken, nor to talk coherently when Mencken saw him in his room. He had looked forward eagerly to the visit, and I imagine that he woke in the night to disappointment and the nervous agony that racked him, of late years, after these seizures; and felt that the time had come for what he had long meditated.

It leaves us sad, but it's no worse death than most others. George disliked the prospect of old age as much as I should hate to miss it. My wife mailed you our village paper a few days ago, with a hastily written but sincere note of mine in it. You won't think that the heading of that poor little article represents my sentiments, nor yet those of the village—"great poet on G. S.!"—only the editor's, who is evidently an enthusiast.[63]

Yes, I was happy to hear from H. L. Davis, and answered, and have received a second letter. I'm the worst correspondent in the world, but this too shall be answered. He reads amazingly; referred to a passage in Dante's Paradiso, I didn't know any body, even the translators, had ever gone so far as that.

Sterling brought Masters here for a couple of days, and we enjoyed his visit. He seemed happy and interested, and in excellent humor. My wife is from a Michigan town, they had a wonderful time talking about places and orchards, and Masters showed her a necklace he'd bought from the desert Indians for his "sweetie"—would she like it? We were interested to read of his marriage: apparently she did.

Thank you for the suggestion that I might contribute to Poetry sometime. I've made myself great promises never more to be printed in any magazine— the reason merely personal of course—publication really distracts and torments me. A book is a necessary evil and you get it finished with, in one lump. However, I sent the Measure something when I was asked, and Palms something when I was asked—nothing to be proud of. It would be stupid not to appear once in Poetry, so I'll try to send something within the next half year, if I may. At present there is really nothing, nothing you'd want.   Sincerely yours, Robinson Jeffers

[63] *J's eulogy for his friend appeared in the* Carmel Cymbal, II *(November 24, 1926), 8. The title was editor W. K. Bassett's; the article is reprinted in* Alberts, A Bibliography, *pp. 135–36.*

December 2, 1926

Dear Bio—   I have so often wished to write you but this summer has been a
busy one—and now the autumn brings its labors too. There are many
people coming to see us and I find it increasingly difficult to do my part—
which is to keep Robin undisturbed. Many people work best I think
when they are stimulated by outside influences and clashing with other minds
but not my husband who gets quite *numb* when he cannot pursue his own
quiet and solitary way. —Then too we had our first serious illness
amongst our young this summer. Garth caught measles which settled in
his tonsils with fever 104+ for several days—afterward it was necessary to
keep him quiet and in bed for a fortnight. We were distracted with
anxiety—. We love them too much for comfort!
    —Now our minds are full of George. He was the dear and special friend
of each of our household. I wonder whether you have correspondents in
San Francisco. At the risk of repeating details you know I will tell you
a little about it all for I know he was fond of you both and would say
he knew of no one who had the lightning-flash of Ben's mind! We had
gotten to know him very well in the last two years. He came down to
see us many times staying from two days to a week and between times
writing often in that big chisselled [*chiseled*] hand of his and sending magazines and clippings—so that he seemed to be with us constantly. —He was
theoretically uncertain whether life was worth the effort but *actually* he
was occupied with a thousand things that interested him tremendously and
I doubt if he ever felt a bored moment. When here with us he was so
eager and buoyant we were always going on little excursions and
pilgrimages—tramping many miles back into the hills and along the coast
and the information he had was extraordinary about the topography,
the geology and the birds and flowers and animals about here. For that reason
our boys found him a fascinating companion. He could describe and
identify tracks and nests—and fish—. One of the visits he paid us
he brought his gun and shot several dozen ground squirrels on our place—
taking keen sportsman joy in stalking them for they got very wary. He
was up early getting abalones off the rocks and mussels and cooking
them for breakfast, chopping wood—making his bed and putting up
lunches for our trips—or scrambling over the rocks looking into the pools—
I am telling you all these things which perhaps were of a side unknown
to you—but his love of talk and discussion of literature and life never
weakened and you know how keen it was! His health was excellent and his
strength and endurance wonderful—*except*—after the drinking bouts—

and they were getting rarer and rarer. He had come to the time when after a few drinks he collapsed to the extent of being taken to the hospital by his friends a nervous wreck—it was a regular routine—then after a few days in the hospital would come the struggle with insomnia which would last for perhaps ten days—then he would be normal again and would then often go for *months* without a drink. His last spell before this was the first part of July. —You see that is over four months. After that he was occupied with his Grove play which was a great success (and George didnt drink at that very wet gathering)—then one thing after another kept him busy until Nov. 14. —He was then expecting Mencken and seemed to be extremely fond of him and looking forward to his visit. He was to stay with George. George expected to bring him down to stay with us for two days. Mencken delayed in Los Angeles to await Hergesheimer and you remember how impatient George was—if it were even a matter of going to the village for a loaf of bread when the time set to go, came, George would prance with impatience if kept waiting. He wrote us that he had saved up seven bottles of prescription sherry during his long dry spell and would devote it to Mencken. —On Sunday— with Mencken due the next day—George went across the bay to call on a friend and he gave George something to drink. —George excited and keyed up and full of plans went back to the [Bohemian] Club—and from then on except for awaking a man in the next room begging for more drink in the night—George kept his room. By Monday morning he was unconscious. *Then* at that moment if his friends had known and got him to the hospital—all would have been well—or at least normal. —On Thursday he must have come to consciousness of his humiliation and in the terrific agony of nerves—took that poison which he had by him, reserved, *as we know* for a time which he thought was still *years distant*. He *talked* of suicide with us—it was pleasant to contemplate for that time when he felt his mind failing or his health precarious—but he was doing some very fine things just now and as for his body—he was instructing us in some intricate gyrations which he considered kept him so fit. One cold day some months ago he made Robin and Hopper both reluctant (and both

"... *you should include in your meditation the grass or weeds in that cemetery, the texture of the stones; and the faces of buildings or mountains, the color of a girl's skin, the colors and shapes and motions of things,—to give the poem body as well as soul.*"

(Letter 243)

wonderful swimmers!) strip and go into the icy water with him beyond Pt. Lobos! He had a great quantity of work planned that we are aware of—He was to do the introduction *con amore* about Bierce for a volume in the Modern Library (I think that is the series). He had bespoken two pages for Jan. Overland for another Bierce article to refute some article in Modern Parade. He had a great deal of verse planned out. He said to us when all the unbound pages of all his books published by Robertson in San Francisco burned a few months ago and we condoled—he said "Dont worry! —I *dont*, I am glad. I have an altogether higher standard for my verse now. I wish to discard a lot—write better—make a new collection." Robertson had all these pages you know and was accustomed to bind up year by year a certain number of copies for sale. Another thing. George had been invited by Gaylord Wilshire to go to England as his guest in the spring. George was fond of that amusing little man—he brought him down here over a week end and felt that it would be very entertaining to meet Wilshire's friend Bernard Shaw! and various other old Fabians—

It is perfectly true George advocated suicide when the proper moment arrived. In a late letter speaking of Brett Page he said "I am thankful that he had the courage to kill himself when he realized his condition. I admire him for it"—

Dear Bio I have gone on and on over pages this rainy morning—We do feel poignantly the loss of this generous and loyal and gentle, eager friend! It has just occurred to me to ask you— do you mind sending this on to Edgar Lee Masters? I meant to write him this morning about George. They were jolly happy companions on their jaunt down here this summer, and I doubt whether he has heard any details of those last days. —It is so difficult to find time for letters with *immediate* tasks pressing on one from all quarters—so if you'll do this friendly and homely favor—send it on to Masters and I will write him a note this morning telling him to look out for it. We have been addressing him at 15 Gramercy Park. It will be forwarded I am sure if his marriage gives him another address.

Perhaps you will think by making this suicide seem *accidental* almost at this time I have taken away its artistic value as a gallant gesture. Perhaps so— but George didnt need to make any gesture to convince his friends of his bravery. And I wont have him played up as desperate and impoverished and senile—he was none of these things and it is not kind to pretend that he was.

One more item about George—even his love affairs were in a pleasant and suitable condition! While he had many gay and young dancing partners—he had had for several years a love—not too violent but charming and pleasant, an Englishwoman, who was devoted to him but not *too* exigent—and always *there*—when he wished! He brought her here twice.

—The San Francisco papers speak of her as a bereaved fiancée. I don't know about that—but I know affairs drifted along contentedly!//

I thought Ben's appreciative article about Robin *splendid*. // Robin was touched by it too but he is shy and uncomfortable when praised, he seems quieter under abuse!

Now goodbye. I have owed you a letter for a long time,—but *when* have you received such a long letter from anyone?   With warm remembrances Una Jeffers//

97: TO ALBERT BENDER

December 8, 1926

Dear Albert Bender: Your article about George seems to me quite the most beautiful, and the most true in essential feeling, of those I have read. I meant to tell you so when I read the manuscript, and again when I read it in print. It is the one that brings him back as one knew him, and as one wishes others to know him. The one by [R. L.] Burgess in the last Overland Magazine is splendid too, but more external than yours, less near its subject. Miss Lee, the Overland editor, writes that she is going to devote her March number to reprinting George's last contributions to the magazine— make it his number. I've promised to send her something for it, probably a poem. The S.F. Review too asked for something about him, and I sent them a sonnet ["*George Sterling*"] the other day, not as good as I wish it were, it couldn't be, but sincere.

Harriet Monroe wrote me a most sympathetic letter of inquiry on first hearing of George's death. Jim Rorty too, a very sad little letter, the first I've had from him in several months.

I'm so overrun with work in-doors and out, besides our servantless bringing up of children, I'm not able to write letters. One or two seem to come every day requiring answer, and I'm desperate to think how many have piled up.

I haven't thanked you yet for "Folkways," which I've read in snatches, and it's fascinating reading; nor for the most beautifully dressed two odes of Keats; nor for Bertrand Russell's little book—I raced through that the other evening. It's very interesting, very true mostly, very English— Anglo-Saxon rather—in its practicality and decency—I mean instinctive healthy morality without speculation or research of novel or individual values. —But I can't talk very good sense without stopping to think! And to talk about "values" sounds like Karl Marx—which Heaven forefend! —Thank you much for the books.

You asked me to inscribe and send you five "Roan Stallions." I've lately received some and will do it to-morrow. I hope anxiously that you haven't been kept waiting too long.

Paul Elder wrote the other day asking me to read or lecture in his gallery—author's afternoon—I answered that it was quite impossible. Now he has written, will I be present while Axtel Clark lectures on me? It is so little to ask that it's hard to refuse, but certainly I wouldn't for a kingdom. That's one of the letters I have to answer!
Yours always, Robin

98: TO MARGARET S. COBB

December 13, 1926

My dear Mrs. Cobb: Thank you much for your letter, and for the poem about our friend's death. It still seems impossible to believe that he has left us. He told me once about your novel, and admired it very sincerely. We too were looking forward to a visit from him.

I should have answered you a week ago, but it seems impossible to find time to write letters. George Sterling was able to get his work done and write letters too; I have often envied him. And felt with admiration the power and generosity of his friendship, toward me and many others. I have never known anyone so instinctively and vitally generous.

He would have loved visiting you on the ranch. I think he was never so happy as out-doors, with wide range, and freedom for that perpetual loving interest of his in every living creature, and from the stars to the stone under the grass. Your poem expresses the eagerness of his attitude toward life and death.   Sincerely yours, Robinson Jeffers

99: TO DONALD FRIEDE

December 16, 1926

Dear Friede: We were quite astonished—not that Mrs. W[——]'s pictures were returned—but that they were returned to this address. She was expected to send them on her own responsibility if she wanted to send them at all, and now it appears not only that she didn't write to you, as she said she would, but that she wrote Mrs. Jeffers' name outside the package! The drawings are on their way to her. I'm sorry that you and we have been bothered with this episode. Mrs. W[——] I think isn't to blame, but the officious friend who began characteristically by signing my wife's name to her own telegram, and who—we've discovered to-day—has been persuading a cousin (I believe) of Horace Liveright to write to him on Mrs. W[——]'s behalf. Her absurdities I hope have now reached an end. —As to the drawings, I haven't seen them; and refused to speak of them the afternoon a few weeks ago when this absurd friend insisted on bringing Mrs. W[——] to see us.

I've been so busy trying to get your book toward completion; I put off from day to day thanking you for the portfolio of Alexander King's drawings, with your very interesting introduction. I'm too rustic to appreciate them properly, but certainly they are powerful and well done. I understand at least your thrill of discovery.

I'm sending to Louis Untermeyer nineteen pages of short poems for his Miscellany of American Poetry. I'm sorry I gave him my promise, for now there are only three short poems left for the "Women at Point Sur" volume, which is to come out before the Miscellany. Perhaps one or two more by February.

Will you do something for me? There was a statement awhile ago of royalties on Roan Stallion—$205.95—due October 31st. No hurry; but as it's past due would you be good enough to remind the proper department?

We're sorry you can't come out here this winter. There's much rain, my trees will grow and the country will be beautiful. —But probably you wouldn't come here for *rain*.   Cordially yours, Robinson Jeffers

100: TO BIO DE CASSERES

December 19, 1926

Dear Bio: We're shamefully late in thanking you and Ben for your very remarkable book "The Boy of Bethlehem." We're up to the eyebrows in all sorts of labor, letters pile up and we can't answer them, late as it is this is the promptest acknowledgment in weeks.

I think there's no doubt that the question of his paternity was a—perhaps *the*—leading factor in the man's life; and you have touched the basic emotional complication of the most influential person since Buddha. (You know of course that Brandes has written a book lately to deny that he was a person at all: I haven't read the book, but I don't think it will prove convincing.) The shock and irony of your conclusion leave one fairly bewildered. How could you forbear working the theme farther, showing the reactions in Jesus' later life—in Mary's, in Pilate's? Perhaps you will

101

some time. Or are you content to indicate, suggest, and leave the noise to tragedians?

Thank you earnestly for the book, and Ben for his introduction. I have another book, not acknowledged yet, with a brief and splendid preface by Ben—that excellent poem of Leverman's, "The Hermaphrodite." To-morrow night if I live I'll write to him.

Una thanks you as I do. —And reminds me to add the best wishes of the season. I was wishing them of course, but had forgotten the season. Cordially yours, Robinson Jeffers

101: TO DONALD FRIEDE

December 29, 1926

Dear Friede: Thank you much for Sterling's little book, which arrived several days ago. He was a noble friend, and I'm grateful to him. To you and your associates I have the satisfaction of expressing my thanks, realizing what trouble you're taking to make a reputation for one who would go about it very left-handedly, if at all, on his own account. I can only impute it to generosity; books of verse are not so likely to sell widely that I could think any thing else.

And thank you for offering to send more copies of the book. My wife ordered a few a couple of months ago, I believe, and no doubt they'll arrive soon.

The manuscript is progressing excellently and will be finished by February, and Mrs. Jeffers joins me in wishing you the best of luck for the year that's coming.   Cordially yours, Robinson Jeffers

102: TO JAMES D. PHELAN

December 29, 1926

My dear Mr. Phelan: Thank you most cordially for the copies of "A Day in the Hills."[64] It is a beautiful little book, and I am very glad to have the poems, the pictures of our dear Sterling, the delightful atmosphere of this day—a Florentine one.   Sincerely yours, Robinson Jeffers

---

[64] *J's "Woodrow Wilson" was anthologized in this privately printed volume, edited by Henry M. Bland.*

*The following questionnaire entitled "Are Artists People?" was published
in* New Masses, II *(January, 1927), 5–9. Albert's* A Bibliography *reprints the
questionnaire, J's answers, and the accompanying note on industrial
Marxism, pp. 138–39. See also Lawrence Clark Powell,* Robinson Jeffers,
the Man and His Work *(Pasadena, 1940), pp. 184–85. The ellipses here
are* New Masses'.

[*December, 1926*]

1. Why do you write, draw or paint?
   That is a subject for analytical autobiography you haven't space. . . .

2. Do you produce for yourself or for an audience? What audience?
   For both. An indeterminate audience. One hopes for intelligence.

3. How would you define literary or artistic prostitution?
   Dishonesty for hire.

4. Do you regard our contemporary American culture as decadent? If so,
   what do you think will succeed it?
   Not yet. What will follow? Centuries of increasing decadence.

5. Does the advent of the machine mean the death of art and culture, or
   does it mean the birth of a new culture?
   "The advent of the machine" changes art and culture, but less than
   people imagine, and will neither kill nor initiate.

6. How should the artist adapt himself to the machine age?
   The machine age is only a partial change; the artist should adapt
   himself to it without ignorance but without excitement. It provides at
   the most, some shift of scenery for the old actors.

7. Can artists unite with each other to secure economic or artistic
   advancement? If not, what group alliance may they seek?
   Artists may find advantages in uniting with each other; it will be
   rather economic than artistic.

8. May society properly demand of the artist, not merely good craftsmanship
   and good reporting, but the "transvaluation of values"—the creation of
   new social values?
   Society may properly wish for it, but it would be fatuous to demand
   what there is only the most exceptional chance of getting.

9. What attitude should the artist take to the revolutionary labor
   movement? Is there any hope of a new world culture through the rise
   of the workers to power? If so, what will that culture be like?

"The rise of the workers to power," if it should reach secure establishment, would produce a quietist, archaizing, lyrical, extremely formal sort of culture. During the time of the struggle and disappointment, any revolutionary labor movement will react on creative work, as a source of power, and a source of disturbance; will break moulds, intensify and pervert ideas, force discoveries. But a really new culture could arise only beyond the Lethe of a new dark ages.[65]

104: TO ALBERT BENDER

January 6, 1927

Dear Albert Bender: The children expect me to read to them every evening for an hour or so—I've been reading your gift, the Microbe-hunters, and they are more deeply interested, I give you my word, than in anything since Treasure Island, two years ago. Meanwhile Una has enjoyed Galsworthy's Caravan, every story I think except half of one that I read aloud to her. So we both, or rather all four, thank you heartily.

I am in a horrid pressure of work just now, having promised to finish a long story in verse by February, and it will be wonderful if I can keep the promise but I'm trying to. I should have written days ago to thank you, and to join Una in appreciation of the very beautiful cards from Yeats's Ireland. —Eight unanswered letters are here before me.

Beautiful days the boys are having now—not going to school because one of them [*Garth's name is inserted above the line*] is to have his tonsils out this month—drawing, reading, their pets (3 bantams, one parrokeet [*parrakeet*] one broken-winged hawk) in the mornings, their Christmas bicycles in the afternoons, your book in the evenings.
Yours always, Robin Jeffers

[65] *Alberts notes, in addition, the following from a letter to Rorty in April, 1932 (see also Bennett,* Stone Mason, *pp. 149–50): "I don't think industrial civilization is worth the distortion of human nature and the meanness and the loss of contact with the earth, that it entails. I think your Marxist industrialized communism—if it were ever brought into existence—would be a further step in a bad direction. It would entail less meanness but equal distortion and would rot people with more complete security. What I think on the subject is only academic, of course. Civilization will have to go on building up for centuries yet, and its collapse will be gradual and tragic and sordid, and I have no remedy to propose, except for the individual to keep himself out of it as much as he can conveniently, as you are doing, and as I am doing, and to exercise his instincts and self-restraints and powers as completely as possible in spite of it."*

105: TO DONALD FRIEDE

January 25, 1927

Dear Friede: This thing that I am working on grows in spite of me, and to omit anything to bring it to a quick conclusion would quite spoil it. So I must just go on thirty lines a day to the end. This is to warn you that the manuscript will be two or three weeks late in spite of my best intentions. Sometime next month it will be finished, I hope early in the month, and nobody will be so pleased as I when that day arrives. It goes on seven days to the week, and I'd like to be at something else.

I'm awfully sorry to be the fortnight late, but if Tamar was any good I think this will be better and perhaps you'll find it worth waiting for. I'll never promise anything again until it's finished.

52 lines this morning (26th).   Sincerely yours, Robinson Jeffers

Does the enclosed need immediate attention? It came a couple of days ago. "Preface"—not under that name—will be a part of a poem in the new book.[66]   R. J.

106: TO DONALD FRIEDE

February 11, 1927

Dear Friede: The thing was finished three or four days ago; I am typing it (nobody else could) and shall send it on in a week or less. Thanks for your benevolent patience. I understood the importance of doing it as well as possible, especially since the theme and dimensions make it—for a poem of this century—rather like a dinosaur in a deer-park. —I think it will do.

Your work on behalf of Antheil is interesting to hear of. Men of various capacity—like you and Ezra Pound—fascinate me all the more because music, art, mathematics, are perfectly opaque to me. Probably music and art and mathematics are none the worse for it.   Yours, Robinson Jeffers

I see (through the bore of copying) that "The Women at Point Sur" is a bit longer than "Tamar." But don't let that alarm you; if it's as long as a novel it's as interesting as a good novel, besides being—I dare say— the Faust of this generation.   R. J.

---

[66] See Letter 79 and note.

105

107: TO DONALD FRIEDE

February 22, 1927

Dear Friede: I finished the manuscript to-day, and shall post it addressed to you—to-morrow, the office being closed to-day. The copying took longer than expected, on account of pauses for revision and efforts to make it shorter; but after all, the changes were of no importance, almost every line that I cancelled had to go in again.

I shall have one or two short poems to add to the four included in the manuscript; I'll send them (or it) in a week or so.

"The Women at Point Sur" seems to me quite a considerable affair—of course it had *better* be, to dare be so long. Now I have cleaned my table of four years' drift of papers, and shall try to do something as different as possible.

We have nothing here but rain and little earthquakes; the rain makes my trees grow, and the quakes do no harm, but there was a gale of wind the other night that broke other people's trees. And thunderstorms— all the weathers that are pleasant to write about.   Yours always, Robinson Jeffers

108: TO ALBERT BENDER

March 1, 1927

Dear Albert Bender: Your kindness is evidently inexhaustible, and I am a poor creature not to have thanked you more promptly. I was in the agony of finishing, then revising and typing, the long manuscript that I promised for the first of February. It is called "The Women at Point Sur" and is so monstrously long that I shouldn't think they'd print it, but probably they will.

We'd read enthusiastic talk about Keyserling's volume,[67] but it is much more interesting than I imagined, especially (but I've only read by fragments yet) Jung's and Adler's articles, and the aristocrat's—von Than's, I don't remember the full name. And it is all quite sane and noble.

Your gift "The Microbe-hunter's" has had an active life too. I read it

[67] *Graf Hermann Alexander von Keyserling,* Book of Marriage; A New Interpretation by Twenty-Four Leaders of Contemporary Thought *(New York, 1926). Jung's article is titled "Marriage as a Psychological Relationship"; Adler's "Marriage as a Task"; the third article J mentions seems to be Paul Thun-Hohenstein's "The Marriage of Convention in Europe."*

whole to the boys and their interest never flagged; and since then
several of Una's friends here have come one by one and asked to borrow it.

We hope you'll stop in to see us some day soon and remain a little longer
than usual.   Yours always, Robin Jeffers

109: TO BENJAMIN H. LEHMAN

March 2, 1927

Dear Mr. Lehman: I was happy to hear from you again, though your
invitation—in spite of the honor—is not one to wake enthusiasm. I mistrust
my own judgment too much. But my wife's critical ability is better than
mine, she has promised to help me, and I'll be glad to do my best. Let me
thank the [Senate] Committee [for the Emily Chamberlain Cook Prize]
sincerely for asking me to serve.

I take for granted that the work can be done by mail, it won't be necessary
for me to leave this place; you don't mention such a possibility. My
favorite quotation, from the forgotten author T. Carlyle: "Any the smallest
alteration of my silent daily habits produces an anarchy to me which you
could not believe unless you saw it!"

But you are of more resolute nature, I'm still hoping that you'll walk in
on us some day.   Sincerely yours, Robinson Jeffers

110: TO DONALD FRIEDE

March 3, 1927

Dear Friede: Here is one more page for the monster; I promise not to send
any more. The title belongs in contents between "The Hurt Hawk" and
"Soliloquy"; the page between 142 and 143.

Did I wish you and Antheil the best of luck? I do, of course.

I shot the hawk two days ago, and buried him in the courtyard.
Yours, Robinson Jeffers

111: TO DONALD FRIEDE

March 12, 1927

Dear Friede: "The Alpine Christ" was useless and absurd, written just ten
years ago.[68] It had some passages of poetry that I can easily understand
may have caught your eye when you saw only fragments, but it was

---

[68] *Una J helps Alberts to date this 1918; see* A Bibliography, *pp. 229–30. See also
Frederic I. Carpenter,* Robinson Jeffers *(New York, 1962), p. 36, and the note to Letter 58.*

vitiated with essential absurdities—exaggerated importance attached to the war that was contemporary then—naïf use of Christian mythology—general childishness. Great men have done their work before they were thirty, but I wasn't born yet. I have no copy of that foolishness, but may sometime use a little of the best of it from memory. —In fact am planning to, in what is being started now.

Your suggestion about an opera libretto was so shocking that it has delayed an answer to your letter. I'm willing enough, if it could be done by mail. My ignorance of music is possibly no great drawback. But I fear that neither composer nor producer could get along with any poem that I'm likely to write.[69]

For instance, I've just drawn up a sort of scenario of what I'm planning to write now. It is to be more or less in dramatic form: but as opera! See enclosure [*a five-paragraph description of* The Song of Triumph; *main characters Attis and Marah*].

This is the only time I've ever drawn up a plan of work before. It will probably put a curse on the work; but at least I keep no copy except in memory.

I have no objection to trying a libretto. But the composer wouldn't like it; and it wouldn't be a King's Henchman.   Yours, Robinson Jeffers

112: TO ALBERT BENDER

March 13, 1927

Dear Albert Bender: I am deeply touched and grateful for the two volumes that preserve so beautifully a little part of your friend's [*Anne Bremer?*] beauty and its impression on other minds. They will be counted among our treasures. Her poems are like crystals full of soft color, through which the courageously and serenely collected spirit reflects its deliverance. It is the rare quality of a few poems to express not only their thought and feeling but something beyond these, that cannot be said in any other words than the poem's, something more even than the writer consciously thought: there are such in this little book—for example the six lines called "Compensation"—and they are rare in the world. Thank you more than sincerely.   Yours, Robinson Jeffers

[69] *See also J's reply to Walter G. Tolleson's proposal to make an opera of* Thurso's Landing, *Letter 364.*

> *"George disliked the prospect of old age as much as I should hate to miss it."*
>
> (Letter 95)

113: TO DONALD FRIEDE

March 27, 1927

Dear Friede: I'm sorry, I can't go east now, in spite of your generous invitation. Reasons: 1. People will like me the better if they don't meet me; I have nothing to say to anyone and don't really like to listen, and can't bear to answer questions. 2. I haven't owned a hat since 1918, nor worn one since 1912. 3. I've begun another book, one I've been impatiently looking forward to, and this is the time for it, while there are still a couple of months of wet weather ahead. Who writes so slowly can't begin too soon. 4. I hate Pullmans more than I can tell you. 5. Here's a quotation from a forgotten author—T. Carlyle: "Any the smallest alteration of my silent daily habits produces an anarchy to me which you could not believe unless you saw it!"

However, I'm sincerely grateful to you for asking me. No doubt I'll see you within a year or two, for we still meditate a journey to Europe, and that can include two stops in New York.

If you want the pencil manuscript sufficiently, I'll send it as soon as we get a proof; keeping it here till then to guard against the loss of the other. I'd hate to have to write the thing from memory.

Thank you for sending me the catalogue. The title is misprinted; it should read The Women *at* Point Sur. No matter, of course, at present. Your list is very interesting.

Enclosed is the page that I spoke of in a former letter, to be added to the book. (Any other short thing that gets written may as well be saved for future occasions.) "Birth-dues" should go in the contents between "Soliloquy" and "Day after To-morrow"; and in the text, as indicated, between pages 143 and 144.   Yours, Robinson Jeffers

114: TO ALBERT BENDER

March 31, 1927

Dear Albert Bender: Your gift of Masefield's letter is indeed treasured, for my admiration of his poems and still more because it was written for George. The letter that came with it from you will be kept with it, a beautiful letter though so hastily written. I should have acknowledged it much sooner. I finished a book last month (as well as I could) and have been hanging in the air on the verge of something new, not getting a line written that was worth keeping, but unable to detach my mind from the thoughts that wanted to be made into a plan but are not formed enough yet. Insistent as the phone calls that you say interrupted your letter— though it doesn't show it.

I wish you could have seen Una's delight when your pictures of Yeats' place arrived. She was expecting a lot, but they are beyond her expectation. They hang over her desk; she has been studying them—with a magnifying glass even—and is very happy. I too love to think of his living there, or at least being able to; Dublin wouldn't see me again if I were he. The portrait with his signature is beautiful to have also; and the letter. How kind you are to us both.   Yours always, Robin

115: TO ALBERT BENDER

April 21, 1927

Dear Albert: It was delightful to see you the other evening, though you and your friends stayed really a very short while, for people who had come that day from Yosemite! I wish that Una and I could go up to the Book Club lecture; there is no more admirable figure in American literature to-day than Edwin Markham, no one I'd rather meet or hear speaking; and yet we cannot go. I haven't been in San Francisco since 1918, when the U.S. called me up for an aviator's examination; and even then I had no hat, except an old wreck from the bottom of a trunk, that I carried in my hand.

In other words, I'm set here like a stone in cement. There are many reasons, but I suppose they come down in the end to preserving our serenity and getting my work done, if possible. A natural lover of mankind, like Markham, or yourself, can meet many people and enjoy it; but for me to see more than two or three in an evening would mean a month's quarrel with the whole race. A giant like Markham can travel about and get his work done too, but I have to stay at home. He is a great man, and I wish you would offer him my admiration and most cordial good wishes, and say that I wish I could see him. If we should go to Europe in a year or two, maybe he will let me visit him in New York, since I was unable to in California. Yours, Robinson Jeffers

116: TO DR. JOHN W. NEVIUS

May 15, 1927

Dear Nevius: I was very glad to hear from you, even though it has taken me all this while to say so on paper. But it's true; and I'll be even better pleased if you can stop in and see us this summer.

I also have had "a devil of a time" once or twice trying to explain about "Roan Stallion," but I do so badly that people have quit asking.

Did you make a nice speech at the class reunion?[70] (The curse that prevents me from writing letters—how many days since I began this?) Remember me please to Bardell and the others whenever you see them; even if the drink was quite legal, it was very kind of you.

Writing verses is all very pleasant; as perhaps being famous is—after you're safely dead—I am neither the one nor the other yet, and I am quite sure that a little notoriety in one's lifetime is very inconvenient. People send me books that I don't acknowledge and manuscripts that I don't like, letters that I don't answer; soon everybody will hate me, except you and my wife and my two sons.   Yours, Robinson Jeffers

117: TO MARK VAN DOREN

May 23, 1927

Dear Mr. Van Doren: Colonel Wood and Sara Bard Field were here a week ago, with gifts of wine and a book—your "7 P.M." She said "if you shouldn't like it you needn't write to him of course, for he doesn't know that I am bringing it to you." I should be sufficiently stupid not to like it! So let me thank you as I do her for these secret and beautiful things presented with a quietness that is sometimes terrible and always admirable. I don't know of any more perfect attunement between the eager soul and the essential moods of landscape; and think of you as the only American who loves his country—articulately at least. With this, and the incisive calm acceptances of your psychology, it is no surprise to find you understanding Emerson from within, and beyond the barrier.   Sincerely yours, Robinson Jeffers

118: TO ALBERT BENDER

June, 1927

Dear Albert: Didn't you receive my letter of very sincere regret about not being able to go up to Edwin Markham's lecture? There's nobody I'd rather meet; but life is only an inch long; and a journey like that would destroy three days of it; and if we should go to San Francisco we'd have to meet other people and they would destroy other days. It is true without exaggeration that I wouldn't drive over to Monterey to meet William

[70] Dr. Nevius and the friend, Bardell, mentioned below, had been J's fellow students in medical school.

Shakespeare; this doesn't imply lack of admiration, or anything more foolish than contentment at home.

Of course I'd be glad to write something more about George for your issue of the Overland. There has been so much said that it will be difficult for one like me, who loved him but knew him only his last two years, and then only at long intervals of meeting, to say much about him that could interest people. He was so sociable and active, and I so much the reverse, that our friendship, though deep and cordial, lacked all the incidents and conversation that make a story. But I'll be glad to do two or three pages. If you have a particular subject to suggest for me, let me know; if not, I will just speak of him as I knew him. I think you said this issue of the Overland was to be in the fall: so if I send you my pages within a month it will be time enough.

Thank you very much for "Revolt in the Desert" and for "Tristram." I haven't read the former yet because I intend to share it with Garth and Donnan, to whom I read an hour or two every evening, and we are in the midst of a library book that has to be finished and returned, while "Revolt" will stay here. From extracts that I've seen I know it is a great story, and will interest them and me too. "Tristram" I haven't read through yet, but have looked into it, and Una especially was wanting to see it, and your gift came as if in answer. One expects a great deal of the poem that undertakes to tell over again that epic love-story. It was a surprising thing for Robinson to attempt, and I'm afraid not a very wise thing, but many think otherwise.

My unwisdom—"The Women at Point Sur"—has the advantage of not being published yet; but I returned the proofs three or four weeks ago, and probably Boni and Liveright will have it out this month. They seem not to be in a hurry—but neither am I. Una has heard that it is to be out the fifteenth.

I have at last persuaded myself to dive into a trunk and find two or three bits of manuscript for you. If you want a few more you may have them. I'd be glad to have you keep the draft of the poem about George for yourself,—whatever you may do with the others. I burned up the Tamar manuscripts when the book was published.   Yours always, Robinson Jeffers

119: TO DONALD FRIEDE

July 1, 1927

Dear Friede: It was delightful to hear from you again, and to hear that you may possibly come to California this summer. As usual, I wasn't able to think of any fitting thing to write in your book, but scribbled your name and mine and some ineptitude, and have mailed it back to you. The volume seems very beautifully made, and I must thank you and the firm most cordially.

Aren't you going to send me any copies to give to friends—the customary half dozen? I'm told that one of the shops in this village has a copy in the window, so the book must be out already, but yours is the only one I've seen.//

I'm keen to hear about your experiences in Boston, and wish you the best of luck of course, whenever it comes to trial.[71] They let themselves in for an incredible absurdity in trying to suppress the American Tragedy there; but the world is full of fools. No doubt I'll see reports of your affair in the N.Y. Times—perhaps in the San Francisco paper. Good luck, and glad you're back in this country.   Yours, Robinson Jeffers

120: TO BENJAMIN DE CASSERES

July 1, 1927

Dear Ben: I am one of those fishlike objects that can't write a letter—you know it already—I postponed letters while I was finishing the new book (of which I'll send you a copy as soon as I can get one) and since the book was written I have been "so languid and so base," trying to get something new started, I really haven't had energy. The thing is published, apparently, for Donald Friede, just back from Europe, sent me his copy the other day, which he wished I'd please autograph and return; but the wretches haven't sent me any copies for myself. I wrote yesterday to ask why not? As soon as any reach me I'd like to send you and Bio one, though I feel rather queerly toward the thing, a sort of astonished hatred, as if I'd fished for salmon and caught an octopus.

We enjoyed Bio's visit tremendously. She still spoke of leading you back to this coast and village, I hope it will happen sometime. Point Lobos is still the same; and our five acres; but everywhere else is breaking out in a rash of houses.

The quicklime portraits were splendid and rather terrible—what a talent you have—many talents—but they all have a unity.

Una has just received a letter from Bio; but I haven't seen it yet.
Yours, Robinson Jeffers

[71] *In April a policeman on the Boston Vice Squad bought a copy of* An American Tragedy *from Friede in an attempt to test the legality of Boston's earlier banning of it and eleven other novels. Boni and Liveright lost the case, Friede was fined, and the book was ruled immoral.*

121: TO ALBERT BENDER

July, 1927

Dear Albert: Thank you much for the Seneca, which is translated in just the right manner, and a most interesting edition, and the sort of grand copious book, like Montaigne, that leaves me never at a loss. Your check for the books came; you are very generous in that way too. Una is sending you this afternoon the remaining five each of the fifteen each that you asked for.

George West was here a couple of days ago; a little doubtful of the Point Sur poem, which didn't surprise me, but he understands its intention and spoke very kindly. He says Lincoln Steffens is in Carmel and wants to come to see us. Anita Whitney came in the other afternoon, with Anne Martin and Dr. Lang; a delightful visit.

I made beginnings both in prose and verse for your issue of the Overland; but have had bad fortune; but something will be done this month.
Yours, Robin

122: TO MARK VAN DOREN AND JAMES RORTY

Alberts includes the letter addressed to Rorty on pp. 37–39 of his A Bibliography; *Bennett on pp. 118–19 of* Stone Mason; *Adamic on pp. 26–32 of* Robinson Jeffers. *The copy which Alberts used varies in certain minor respects from the copy which follows.*

[*August 5, 1927*]

Dear Mark Van Doren: Self-explanation is an invidious task when there are so many more interesting things to think of, but since I undertook it for Rorty it seemed unreasonable not to send you a copy. You have been too kind to my verses to be left in the dark as to my intentions, whatever you may think of the book in question.

Rorty thinks I ought to make a trip east. I shan't; but if it were all like your New England farm I would gladly.   Cordially yours, Robinson Jeffers

Dear Rorty: You were right evidently about the need of an explanation. I have just read Mark Van Doren's article,[72] and if he, a first-rate critic and poet and a good friend of my work, quite misunderstands the book, it is very likely that no one else will understand it at present.

You remember a couple of letters ago I spoke of the morality—perhaps I said old-fashioned morality—implied in "Point Sur." "Tamar" seemed to my later thought to have a tendency to romanticize unmoral freedom, and

[72] *Review of* The Women at Point Sur, Nation, *CXXV (July 27, 1927), 88.*

it was evident a good many people took it that way. That way lies destruction of course, often for the individual but always for the social organism, and one of the later intentions of this "Point Sur" was to indicate the destruction, and strip everything but its natural ugliness from the unmorality. Barclay incited people to "be your desires . . . flame . . . enter freedom" [*Chapter XX*]. The remnant of his sanity—if that was the image of himself that he met on the hilltop—asks him whether it was for love of mankind that he is "pouring poison into the little vessels?"[73] He is forced to admit that if the motive seems love, the act is an act of hatred.

Another intention, this time a primary one, was to show in action the danger of that "Roan Stallion" idea of "breaking out of humanity," misinterpreted in the mind of a fool or a lunatic. I take the idea to be what you expressed in "the heart is a thing to be broken," carried a little farther perhaps. It is not anti-social, because it has nothing to do with society; but just as Ibsen in the Wild Duck made a warning against his own idea in the hands of a fool, so Point Sur was meant to be a warning; but at the same time a reassertion.

Van Doren's criticism assures me that I was quite successful in this intention and in the one about morality; only I proved my points so perfectly that he thinks—and therefore other intelligent people will think— that they are proved against me and in spite of me. I confess I didn't think of this; I didn't think about myself at all. So I have written in these respects well but not wisely.

For the rest, the book was meant to be

(1) an attempt to uncenter the human mind from itself. There is no health for the individual whose attention is taken up with his own mind and processes; equally there is no health for the society that is always introverted on its own members, as ours becomes more and more, the interest engaged inward in love and hatred, companionship and competition. These are necessary of course, but as they absorb all the interest they become fatal. All past cultures have died of introversion at last, and so will this one, but the individual can be free of the net, in his mind. It is a matter of trans-valuing values, to use the phrase of somebody that local people accuse me quite falsely of deriving from.

I have used incest as a symbol to express these introversions, and used it too often, though it is the most appropriate symbol.

(2) The book was meant to be a tragedy, that is an exhibition of essential elements by the burning away through pain and ruin of inertia and the unessential.

[73] *Chapter XXI; the line reads, " 'To what purpose / Have you been dropping wine and fire in the little vessels?' " Jeffers may remember an earlier version, but he is customarily cavalier in quoting even his own work.*

(3) A valid study in psychology; the study valid, the psychology morbid, sketching the growth of a whole system of emotional delusion from a "private impurity" that was quite hidden from consciousness until insanity brought it to the surface.

(4) Therefore a partial and fragmentary study of the origin of religions; which have been necessary to society in the past, and I think remain necessary whether we like it or not, yet they derive from a "private impurity" of some kind in their originators.

(5) A satire on human self-importance; referring back to (1).

(6) A judgment of the tendencies of our civilization, which has very evidently turned the corner down hill. "Powers increase and power perishes." Our literature, as I said in answer to the New Masses questionnaire, is not especially decadent (because in general it is not especially anything); but our civilization has begun to be.

(Some of you think that you can save society; I think it is impossible, and that you only hasten the process of decadence. Of course as a matter of right and justice I sympathize with radicalism; ["*and as a matter of expedience" follows the semicolon, but is crossed out*] any way I don't oppose it; from an abstract viewpoint there is no reason that I know of for propping and prolonging the period of decadence. Perhaps the more rapid it is, the sooner comes a new start.)

There were more intentions, but these are the chief ones that can readily be said in prose. Too many intentions. I believe they all carry over to an intelligent reader, as results though not as intentions, but no doubt I was asking him to hold too many things in mind at once. I had concentrated my energies for a long while on perceptions and expression, and forgot that the reader could not concentrate so long, nor so intensely, nor from the same detached and inclusive view-point.   Yours, R. J.

123: TO ERNEST HARTSOCK

August, 1927

Dear Mr. Hartsock: I opened your book [Narcissus and Iscariot?] when it came and was troubled by what seemed to me an affectation of sonorous words, and put it aside for a clearer hour that has just come. There is still some rebellion in my mind against the too brilliant and sought-out phrases, sown so liberally that they diffuse rather than concentrate attention; but the range and frequent intensity of thought and emotion more than make amends. You have read Poe and Swinburne, and have not entirely found yourself, but often yourself emerges and then there is real achievement, the other is splendid promise. A complex and important mind takes longer to develop than a mere faculty; you have both, and I have enjoyed the poems and value the inscription, and shall watch your development with interest and expectation, there is no limit apparent.[74]

Thank you much for the book, and thank you for writing the review and sending it to me.   Sincerely yours, Robinson Jeffers

124: TO ALBERT BENDER

August [8], 1927

Dear Albert: Thank you much for your kind and wise letters about the "Point Sur" book. I didn't expect anybody to like it, and the letters and favorable reviews that came in all seem to me to indicate more disinterested wisdom and tolerance than one has a right to count on. The book concludes a train of thought that began with Tamar; it was meant to complete the ideas but also to indicate the dangers and abuses of them, which it does pretty thoroughly. Just as Ibsen wrote the Wild Duck to show how his ideas could be perverted by a fool: I set a lunatic to work with the same object in mind. It puzzles people; but will be understood eventually.

My next book will be chiefly shorter poems, I think. After that perhaps a poem in dramatic form, with thoughts and emotions quite different from the Tower beyond Tragedy series.

There are already a number of short poems finished, but the one I want most to write is something dedicated to George Sterling, something more memorable than the little verses I have written about him as yet. I am afraid it cannot be accomplished in time for your Overland. I've written four pages of prose, called A Few Memories,[75] which I can send you at any time, but I have been delaying it, hoping something better would come. Let me know if it's needed at once; it is typed ready to send, but it might be better to wait three weeks yet.   Yours always, Robinson Jeffers

125: TO ALBERT BENDER

August 24, 1927

Dear Albert: Let me thank the Book Club most cordially, and you as a member of it, for the distinguished honor you have done me in conferring honorary membership. Some day I hope it will be possible for me to be in San Francisco and thank some of my friends in person. For the present the concentration involved in staying at home seems to be necessary for

[74] Hartsock founded and edited the little magazine Bozart.
[75] Overland Monthly, *LXXXV (November, 1927), 329, 351; reprinted in Alberts, A Bibliography, pp. 143–46.*

getting done whatever I have to do, but I value your kindness all the more.

Una and the children were in San Francisco last Saturday; they drove up with a friend in the morning and returned that night. Una called you at your various telephone addresses, only to say "hello," but wasn't able to find you. The boys enjoyed a marvellous day; it was their first sight of San Francisco. They ferried across the bay and back, with their mother, and have been telling me about that and the city ever since.

Yours always, Robinson Jeffers

126: TO EDWIN BJÖRKMAN

August 26, 1927

Dear Mr. Bjorkman: I was very glad to hear from you, and indeed I never felt injured that you never acknowledged the Tamar volume.[76] There are so many little books flying about; some of them have been coming my way the past couple of years, and it's a great burden to give them a look and a letter, though I always intend to, and usually do in course of time.

Hopper's report of your approval was encouraging to me at a time when I was quite unable to find a publisher, and indeed was doubtful whether I had anything worth publishing; though I thought I might have sometime.

So there are no amends needed. Too I owe you cordial thanks for your most generous and thoughtful review. Soon after receiving it I saw an announcement of your new book; I am very glad that you are back in the swing of your work again.

Hopper has been in this village for some months and was in to see us a few days ago, but talks of returning to New York; he has to go and come. It is evidently in the modern destiny; I and my household seem to be the only persons in America, except a few old farmers, who can take root in a place.

Thank you most sincerely for the review, and for your letter.

Sincerely yours, Robinson Jeffers

127: TO DONALD FRIEDE

September, 1927

Dear Friede: No, the manuscript was not sent back to me, I returned it with the proofs and haven't seen it since. I hope that you can find it. The pencil manuscript is still in my hands, since you asked me to save it for you. You may have it if you want.[77]

---

[76] *I mailed Björkman a copy of* Tamar *on May 23, 1924.*
[77] *The manuscript of* The Women at Point Sur *is among those in the Beinecke Library at Yale.*

I'm very sorry indeed that the Roan Stallion special edition volume was stolen.

A dozen or so short poems have accumulated, but I doubt whether any of them would be suitable for magazine publication. They are more or less specialized to my course of thought, and will be all right in a book, but mixed up with other things in a magazine might not have much meaning. However, I'll look them over and see if I can choose two or three perhaps.

You remember there was a shorter narrative poem called "Home," and six little ones, along with the Point Sur manuscript, which were not printed. I think these should be returned to me, so that they may be on hand when I come to plan out another book. Or if some are not wanted for the book, I'd better keep them here.

This summer I've been working at several things, and am now in the middle of one of them, but can't consider publication next spring. By that time I'll have the book done probably, and you and I can see how it turns out before we announce it in the fall list. The story I'm working at now is called "Give Your Heart to the Hawks"—(provisionally)—and will be more human than usual, without mysticism or scandal, though I hope rather interesting. [*The following sentences have been crossed out.*] The story is the Greek story of Phaedra, transferred to this coast. Desire under the Elms was a variant of it; but in mine the young man is inseductible, as in the Greek.

I hear that Genevieve Taggard was all wrought up the other day against the Point Sur book, but I haven't seen her article.[78] Myself, I have a good deal more confidence in the book than when I sent it to you; it has large faults, but it is worth several Tamars. It will be nice if the next one can avoid shocking anybody.

De Casseres, who told me about Miss Taggard's review, says that he has sold to the Bookman the article that he submitted to you about his visit here.

I had a statement of Roan Stallion royalties up to Dec. 31st, 1926 but have received no check, and no further statement for [?] up to June. Isn't it usual to mail the check when it's done? But I suppose most of your authors live in New York, and walk in and ask for it.

I'm sorry we're not to see you this summer. Perhaps next year, if we go

---

[78] "*The Deliberate Annihilation*," New York Herald Tribune Books, *August 28, 1927, p. 3.*

"I was baptized John R., but nobody ever called me John since that moment, perhaps the baptism didn't take."

(Letter 178)

a-travelling. I don't know whether we shall or not, I don't look forward
to it very eagerly. Though I'd be glad to see you—and the British Isles
again—if it weren't for the trouble of getting there.   Yours,
Robinson Jeffers

128: TO BENJAMIN DE CASSERES

September 21, 1927

Dear Ben: Here are the verses about George ["*Winter Sundown*"] that
you asked for. Some day I hope to do better.

We're delighted that your article is to appear in the Bookman. I'd have
written sooner, but have been trying to keep my mind on some work,
and people keep tormenting me by visit and letter—concentration
isn't permitted in this time and country. I don't mean that I'm not glad to
hear from *you*. I am *very* glad; and to write to you.

Wasn't that an amusing review you mentioned in the Herald [*Taggard's*].
I don't subscribe to a clipping agency, but one of them sent it anyhow,
and the lady is delightful. Fair weather and favorable reviews always
depress me, but now I am becoming quite cheerful again.

I think the book is my best so far, though perhaps unfit for human
consumption, but of course it has serious faults. The worst of them is that
people come and ask me what it means. They'd think I was comparing
it with its betters if I should ask them in return what King Lear means: so
all I can do is to look grim and assure them that my hero was
crazy but I am not.   Yours, Robinson Jeffers

Our best to Bio.

129: TO HARRIET MONROE

October, 1927

Dear Miss Monroe: Thank you sincerely for asking me to send you
something for Poetry. Here are three items ["*The Women on Cythaeron*,"
"*The Trumpet I–V*," "*Birth-Dues*"], probably the best I have just now.
The series of five may be broken if you prefer. I'm sending several things
so as to offer you a little choice, but of course you are welcome to
all if you like.

You were very kind, some months ago, sending me the number of Poetry
with Davis's friendly expression in it, and I was ill-mannered not to thank
you sooner. It is so hard for me to write a letter. My faithful Una took my

correspondence in hand for me last week and answered eight in two
hours. That would have taken me four afternoons, and the little trees I've
planted would have died meanwhile for lack of attention. She offered
to write this one to you but I reserved it for my own hand.
The loss is yours, for *her* letters are amusing.

I can tell you something funny though. Yesterday a young man from San
Francisco called here to say that he is a Catholic, and editor of the
archbishop's weekly paper, the Monitor, and wanted to tell me that at least
one Christian approves of my work. He was intelligent as well as kind
beyond my deserts, but what will amuse you is that he has lent the Roan
Stallion volume to the archbishop, who has already read some of it.[79]

Our trees are growing well; our stonework will begin to grow again as
soon as the rains come to free me from watering the trees.   Yours
always, Robinson Jeffers

130: TO DONALD FRIEDE

October 22, 1927

Dear Friede: Possibly you have heard of the Book Club of California, that
prints expensive little volumes occasionally for sale to its own membership.
They made me an honorary member a couple of months ago. Now they
want to have one of the clever San Francisco printers do a little book
with an introduction by Professor Lehman of the Univ. of California. —
(His second novel has lately been published by Harper's I think. I enclose a
note from him—don't return.)—the booklet to include "Night" and one
or two (not more) yet shorter poems from the Roan Stallion volume,
and the "Prelude" from Women at Point Sur, and some short new poem of
mine if I can find one. Edition of 300 copies; no royalty but a few copies.
I told their secretary, Albert Bender, who was here lately, that I was
willing, and thought you would give them permission to reprint.
It wouldn't do us any harm, the edition being little and expensive.

If you have any objection to the proposal, please let me know. Otherwise
there's no need of an answer until they write or wire you (or I do) for
formal permission.

Thank you for sending off the books to England, and for answering my
wife's questions. She answered eight letters for me in a couple of hours

---

[79] *A* Monitor *article, "Pagan Horror from Carmel-by-the-Sea" (January 9, 1926), did
not approve, but took J most seriously; compared to Shelley and Swinburne,
mere dilettantes at paganism, J seemed to the reviewer "intrinsically
terrible." See Alberts,* A Bibliography, *p. 231.*

the other day,—more than I can write in a month. The Steffenses left this morning for New York, to return in six weeks. That also is wonderful— to travel so cheerfully.   Yours, Robinson Jeffers

I'll send the Point Sur pencil manuscript as soon as we can get it wrapped up properly; that is in a day or two. I hope you found the typed one.

131: TO ALBERT BENDER

October 22, 1927

Dear Albert: This is to repeat in writing what I said when you were here: that I should be honored and pleased to let the Book Club issue the little book you spoke of, of some verses of mine and Professor Lehman's introduction.[80]

I've just written to Boni and Liveright—(Donald S. Friede, vice-president, is my correspondent in the firm)—saying that the Book Club would wish to include "Night" and one or two shorter poems from the Roan Stallion volume, "Prelude" from "The Women at Point Sur," and some short new poem of mine, and asking them to let me know at once if they had any objection. They have been asking excessive prices of anthologies for permission to reprint, but I feel sure they will not make any difficulty of that kind for the Book Club. As soon as the poems and number of copies (I told them I believed an edition of 300) are quite definitely decided on, I'll ask them to write formal permission for you.

A kind note reached me from Professor Lehman yesterday. It was a great pleasure to see you here again, and the young poetess, and [photographer] Ansel Adams.   Yours always, Robinson Jeffers

132: TO H. L. DAVIS

November, 1927

Dear Davis: Thank you sincerely for your libel on northwestern literature ["Status Rerum"], which I read with acute amusement and admiration, too, and should have acknowledged sooner. It seemed [a] rather grimly powerful wheel to break butterflies on, perhaps because I've never smelt their droppings, but certainly your swarm served the cause when they provoked that destruction. Here in California the winters are milder and insects

[80] Poems *was privately printed for the Book Club by the Grabhorn Press in 1928.*

more numerous—are you not tempted? It's too bad to be partial—what a necklace of scalps with antennae on them you might gather between Sausalito and Los Angeles.

I had a telegram this summer from some lady in Seattle—"We want you to deliver the opening address" (to whatever the mass-meeting was they held there) "your expenses will be paid. Please wire subject." —Having no knowledge of the lady nor of the convention nor what it was all about, if I were in the habit of making speeches I might perhaps have taken expense-money and got horridly but finally immortalized in your pamphlet. Luckily I can't talk any more than I can write letters.//
Yours, Robinson Jeffers

133: TO BENJAMIN H. LEHMAN

November 10, 1927

Dear Lehman: As I told Albert Bender, nothing could please me more than an introduction by you to the little book that the Book Club considers having printed. You are very kind to be willing to write it. I should have told you so sooner, but Bender told you no doubt, and my mind instantly collapses whenever I invite it to answer a letter.

I'm getting The Lordly Ones [*Lehman's novel*], and look forward eagerly to reading it within the next few days. A visit from you is equally a pleasure to look forward to. Next Monday apparently we're all leaving for Sequoia Park, to be gone four days if the weather is favorable, but the rest of the years I expect to be constantly at home.   Yours always,
Robinson Jeffers

134: TO BENJAMIN DE CASSERES

November 10, 1927

Dear Ben: That is brilliant writing as always, your article in the Bookman, and exceeding friendly criticism. Thank you most sincerely and cordially. We are very glad to have your earlier manuscript of this article in the archives here; yet condensation seems to have cost you little, and me nothing of your generosity. Aren't you ever coming west again? We think— but I can't say yet whether prophetically—of going to Ireland and perhaps Italy next fall, ten or eleven months from now, for a year or so. If we go I'll see you in New York going and coming.

Did you ever hear of the great (and beautiful) Hindu-Buddhist temple of
Angkor that stands in the deep jungle in Cambodia, and no one knows
where the people who built it have gone to, nor where they came from? An
enormous affair of sandstone, and the architecture as if it came from
another planet. Someone has given us a little stone head of a wall-carving
from there, and I cemented it into the tower the other day. Someone else
has given us a stone from the great pyramid, and one from the Chinese wall.
Then there's a cuneiform tablet in the tower from Babylonia, from a
temple of Ishtar. Imagine us gathering old stones in Italy or Ireland.
It should be an amusing pilgrimage. Love from us both to you and Bio.
Yours always, Robinson Jeffers

135: TO HARRIET MONROE

December 4, 1927

Dear Miss Monroe: Here are the proofs you were good enough to send;
your reading left nothing for mine but two commas. "Eat change"—not eat,
and change—but in the sense of accept change. And "However I
suppose" = although I suppose. No mail goes out from here on Sunday, and
if this returns too late, two commas don't matter.

Thank you for your kindness, and for the generous check. I noticed the
perfectly proper stipulation about giving credit to "Poetry" if there
should be occasion to reprint the verses.

I suppose H. L. Davis sent you a copy of "Status Rerum," which seems
to me as powerful a piece of invective as I've ever read. There seems a
cruelty in using such artillery on butterflies; but it's great work.

We've had a little rain, so I can return from watering young trees to
stone-building again. If you visit us again—I hope cordially you may
sometime—you'll find the house hidden on the land side, and the tower
dwarfed, by a flourishing little forest. And doves in the courtyard;
somebody gave the boys a pair of pigeons lately. They have seven bantam
chickens too; a little red rooster trained to stand in Una's lap in the
house and crow for raisins; and they had a broken-winged hawk but in pity
we shot it at last. Some verses about the hawk I gave to Mark Van
Doren for the Nation when he asked me.

The long poem I'm engaged with seems to promise a little more
sweet-reasonableness than usual, at least I hope so.

Una wants to be remembered to you most cordially.   Yours
always, Robinson Jeffers

136: TO DONALD FRIEDE

December 7, 1927

Dear Friede: I wonder if you'd take the trouble for me to remind your treasurer that $497.26, royalties on Roan Stallion and Point Sur, were due me October 31$\underline{st}$, according to your letter? Indeed some of it has been due longer than that.

My long poem is growing slowly, not too long I hope, and promises to reflect more sweetness and light than usual, which would be a good thing. We made a trip to the Sierras last month and saw some tremendous sequoias—mountain redwoods—and snow on the ground, with very blessed deer and fawns skipping about in it. Besides a granite rock three or four thousand feet high, that I brought home only a little clipped around the edges, to put into coast scenery in my story.   Yours, Robinson Jeffers

137: TO ALBERT BENDER

January 16, 1928

Dear Albert: I wrote to Boni and Liveright just after your last visit here, telling them all I could about your proposal for the little Book Club volume, and asking them to let me know at once if they had any objection. I didn't feel that I could ask their permission more definitely until the contents, number of copies in the edition, etc., were decided on, because they have been quite unmerciful in asking payment of anthologists for leave to reprint, and would probably not give free permission unless they knew exactly what was wanted and how few the copies would be.

I wrote to you the same day, expressing my pleasure in the plan, and saying that I had asked them whether they had any objection— surely you received the letter?

As they haven't notified me of any objection we may suppose that they agree in principle at least, and I'll ask formal permission whenever I can tell them what contents, number of copies, and probable price per copy have been decided on. Their option on unpublished work expires after my next book— to be published next fall I suppose—and then I'll be a free agent, except as to poems they own the copyright of.

My memory is that you thought of including "Night" and perhaps another short poem from the Roan Stallion volume, the "Prelude" from the Point Sur volume, and some new poem. Una is sending you a copy of "Poetry" with some verses in it that I let Miss Monroe have in fulfillment of an old promise. I wonder if any of these would be of use to you?

If you prefer what hasn't been published even in a magazine, let me know, and I can send you a few others to choose from.

I wrote to Professor Lehman a good while ago, telling him how much an introduction by him would be appreciated here. Una and I have been reading his recent novel with deep interest.

Una thanked you, I'm sure, for me as well as for herself for the lovely things that came from you at Christmas. You are very kind. The cigarette case is too fine for a stone-mason to use often, but will be grand when we go travelling, this fall or sometime.

The Overlands are a wonderfully inclusive record of our dear George, from points of view as various as the people who loved him. What a labor, though a labor of love, your editorship must have been.[81]
Yours always, Robin

138: TO ALBERT BENDER

February 24, [1928]

Dear Albert: Here are some unpublished verses from which you and Ben Lehman might possibly make a selection. I should have typed them sooner, and perhaps more of them, for you to choose from, but I am as desperately busy as my nature permits, involved in a long poem, and in the bitter midst of planting two hundred trees and trying to build a dining-room.

If you don't like any of these, send them back and I'll submit two or three others; but these are best suited to your purpose I think.

Of course we hope you can come and see us too.   Yours always, R. J.
Permission is given for the Night, Prelude and Wilson poems of course.

139: TO DONALD FRIEDE

March, 1928

Dear Friede: It was a shock to hear that you're no longer with Boni and Liveright, and I'm very sorry indeed. Thank you for having arranged permission for the S.F. Book Club's reprint; and for many other kindnesses. We'll be anxious to hear of your plans for the future whenever they are decided on.

It would be delightful if you could make a visit to the coast a part of them. We are still more or less in the notion of going to Ireland and England for a year next fall, so if you don't come here it is possible we might

[81] *The November and December, 1927, issues of the* Overland Monthly *were "Sterling Numbers."*

see you there, or in New York. But who knows? I think we are the only family in America that hates to leave home—I am as attached to this rock as if I were a feudal serf with an iron collar. My wife will have to do a lot of filing to get it off me, and she is only half-hearted about wanting to go.

But indeed I hope that we'll see you, some near time, and I wish you all good fortune in your new choices. Let us hear from you sometimes, do.   Cordially yours, Robinson Jeffers

140: TO MARK VAN DOREN

May, 1928

Dear Mark Van Doren: Of course I'm pleased that you can use "Night" and "Continent's End" in your anthology, which interests me much, and the description of it as "composed mainly of translated poems" excites my curiosity.

I can't imagine that you credited [S. Bert] Cooksley's report, but thank you for telling me. Of course I said nothing even faintly resembling the absurdity that you say he attributed to me. He was here a couple of hours one day and talked while I listened; the evening of the same day he reported his conversation to me as mine to him, to Lincoln Steffens and his wife, to whom it sounded so strange that they asked me about it. But this time it isn't even his own conversation, simply nobody's. I don't remember that you were mentioned that day, except that he referred to you as a friend in getting entrance here, and persuading me to write my name in his album. What a fellow.

I've promised Liveright a book to be called "Cawdor," for fall publication, but that must be as God wills, the long poem is not finished yet.

My wife has been leasing houses by correspondence in Ireland and Scotland, so it's possible I may have the pleasure of looking for you in New York, this autumn, on the way thither, and yet I can hardly imagine leaving here, even for a short year.   Yours always, Robinson Jeffers

141: TO DONALD FRIEDE

June 9, 1928

Dear Friede: I was delighted to hear from you, but now it is almost spoiled with regret at not having answered sooner. I've been foolish enough to promise another book before it is finished—after swearing not to— but it was so near done that I felt quite safe. Well, it is going pleasantly, and will be ready for fall—but my mind is rather given to it. My wife has just shown me a horrible sight—a pack of unanswered letters as thick as a book—from the forest of which I selected yours. She asks to be remembered to you most kindly.

Your new alliance promises splendidly, and I'll be happy watching its success.[82] We saw a note yesterday about the Villon, with King's pictures, excellent.

I wish indeed I could undertake Greek tragedy—I simply can't at present, having had something in my mind for months that I want to get written as soon as this "Cawdor" is finished. Something not of this coast and not Greek either, but of course I don't know how it will turn out.

We didn't intend going to Ireland until October or November in any case; and whether we'll go or not is still perfectly undecided—my wife wants to be there and here too, and I suspect that I faintly prefer being here. If we do travel through New York, sometime before Christmas, I shall certainly look for you.

Most cordial good wishes to you and the new firm.   Yours always, Robinson Jeffers

142: TO ALBERT BENDER

June 26, 1928

Dear Albert: Here is the manuscript, which I read over last night, making one or two small corrections. Thank you much.

May I include a few of the new poems in it in the book that I've promised Liveright for this fall? It seems to me that the Liveright book can hardly get along without a few of these short poems to help balance the long one. I promise not to take more than five, and this would leave at least eight of the thirteen for the Book Club volume exclusively.

The Liveright book is to be called "Cawdor." I have promised to send in the manuscript by the first of August, and am having a devil of a time bringing the long poem to an end.

I hope you got home without any more punctures. We love your visits. Yours always, Robinson Jeffers

So sorry I couldn't get this mailed yesterday. I don't think any foreword by me could be an advantage.   R. J.

---

[82] *Covici-Friede incorporated as a publishing firm on June 4, 1928.*

143: TO WITTER BYNNER

August, 1928

Dear Witter Bynner: I was grateful for your paragraphs, and didn't answer in proper time because I am almost perfectly incapable of writing a letter, and was postponing all letters until the book I had foolishly promised for fall should be finished. I didn't "feel harshly"; quite the contrary.

The disgust you complained of comes partly from local circumstances; this was a remotish place when we chose it, and now look at it! Partly from more general circumstance. The old balance between the people and the world is broken, temporarily, and I rather resent it. It is hard to keep on sympathizing with the top dog. Of course that is no excuse for petulance, but only a reason. The rest of my apology doesn't belong in a bad letter-writer's letter. No doubt what I make verses for is the hope of getting it said as well as possible in course of time. Meanwhile, we write out of our conflicts and excesses—you as well as I—if they were quite reconciled we could afford to keep still.

I should feel the honor of being a judge with you again, but I think I mustn't. Your superior resilience would throw off the bad poetry and take the good, but the prospect of having to read manuscripts would depress me all winter. Besides, we talk of going to Ireland and elsewhere next spring, for ten or twelve months. I don't care especially; but I think Una wants to go, and the boys might like it.

Thank you much for your comment too. If it is a fault to be gregarious, it is also a fault to be solitary; we just have to live with our natures. We're sorry the Fickes[83] have settled so far off. I hope that you and they may visit here again some time.   Yours always, Robinson Jeffers

144: TO MARK VAN DOREN

September, 1928

Dear Mark Van Doren: Having lived through another touristry summer here we can't persuade ourselves to spare the more blessed winter; so if we go to Ireland it won't be until next spring. I hope your invitation will hold until we reach New York; I look forward to the evening you proposed. There are not "many flowering islands" on the track of that pilgrimage. —Why Ireland? I hardly know: it rains in summer as well as winter, and there are gray stones in the fields.

[83] *J's friendship with the poet Arthur Davison Ficke and his artist-wife Gladys is represented here, beginning with Letter 155.*

Perhaps I was a little harsh toward Bert Cooksley in my former letter. I knew that he had invented a whole eloquent conversation for me by evening of the day he saw me, and I dreaded what it might have grown to in the course of months. His verses are often very good.

This village has been quite stirred up lately by a visit from [*Alfred Richard*] Orage—of London and Fontainebleau—whom I suppose you've heard of. I didn't attend his lectures, but I met him often enough to respect his mind if not his doctrine's [*doctrines*]—which seem to begin solid and end shadowy, or perhaps they are veiled from the profane.

The summer has been beautiful in spite of the tourists, gray and sunless and starless; now the autumn gold and blue have begun.   Yours,
Robinson Jeffers

145: TO BENJAMIN DE CASSERES

September [*12*], 1928

Dear Ben: I want to answer your letter, and now I can't find it, until Una comes home from the village and tells me where it is.

The brick you dropped into the puddle of Pittsburgh has made its splash; I have had letters with clippings enclosed from there; one of the writers, who seems to be a sort of official historian of the city, had never heard of me and was quite astonished and indignant.

Another person who first heard of me from you was here three or four weeks ago—Paul Jordan[-]Smith from Los Angeles. We had a friendly time, talking about you with admiration.

I begin to fear you're never coming west again; I'd like to show you how much my trees have grown—two thousand of them—the house is backed by a young forest now. And I'd like you to plant a tree for us, as George Sterling did, and Edgar Lee Masters, at George's suggestion. The stonework has grown somewhat too, but not so fast. In summer I don't often get time for stonework, now I have the new trees to water; and there seems almost a continual procession of visitors, horribly tiresome ones mostly, but not all can be snubbed. We have gates, and signs hung on them, "Not at home before 4 P.M." The end of last summer I turned them over and painted simply "Not at home." Now people either tumble over the wall or else write in for appointments. This comes of living in a sweet touristy place by the seaside. Fortunately the sun hasn't shone all summer, and neither flies nor tourists like gray skies.

> *"She was in many ways a mediator between me and the world."*

(Letter 377)

132

A week ago I read and returned the proofs of my new book "Cawdor." I
hope you'll like it.

A friend of ours—James Hopper—told me lately that he had been talking
to a doctor in San Francisco, a member of the Bohemian Club and friend
of George Sterling's, who assured him that George did not kill himself but
was poisoned by bad liquor. A half bottle of whiskey was found in his
room and showed on analysis enough "fusel oil" (Hopper said) to kill
twenty men. That the Bohemian Club knew this, but the report of suicide
had spread abroad already, and they thought better not to contradict it.
That George had not burnt any of his papers, but only torn up a few
pages of something—apparently unimportant—that he was writing at the
time. Hopper, I think, believes the story; I, of course, haven't sufficient
reason to believe or disbelieve; and it doesn't matter much.

We talk of going to Ireland next spring for a year; if we do, I'll see you in
New York, going and coming and that would be worth the journey.
Love to Bio, from Una and me.   Yours always, Robinson Jeffers

146: TO ALBERT BENDER

October 17, 1928

Dear Albert: Una wrote to you about the books, but I have been too
exhausted with trying to keep some difficult work going in spite of a vile
little attack of flu, to feel able to express my deep and cordial appreciation of
your kindness and the Book Club's. The volumes are most admirably
designed and wrought, and we're proud of them; I'm writing Grabhorn Press
a note to-day to say so. Your gift of eight is most generous; so is the
check you sent me, which, as Una told you, we're tucking away with our
little collection for the journey to Ireland. Please tell Ansel [Adams]—
what he knows already—that his photograph is much admired.
How cleverly it is bound into the book.

And don't forget to come and see us again soon; we love your visits.
Yours always, Robin

147: TO MARK VAN DOREN

October 17, 1928

Dear Van Doren: Thank you very much for "Now the Sky." Indeed I find
nothing cryptic in its beauty—only in the inscription—my "other
pole"?— Some of the poems in their passionate foreshortening ask the
reader to contribute a little thoughtful imagination of his own, but readers

Tor House, Carmel, California.
October 17, 1928.

Dear Van Doren:

Thank you very much for "Now the Sky". Indeed I find nothing cryptic in its beauty --- only in the inscription — my "other pole"? --- Some of the poems in their passionate fore-shortening ask the reader to contribute a little thoughtful imagination of his own, but readers aren't always lazy enough to refuse that, and if they're slow-witted they are all the better for reading twice.

I have a criticism, and no doubt from me it will surprise you. I think you are too (vulgar word) pessimistic. "End of Singing" and the others in that section. Civilization is bitter to the singer, it is bitter in that essential way to everyone, but I think we can remember that there was a time before it and will be a time after it, and can keep an important part of us timeless enough to be uncivilized. You have that timeless part, but it feels menaced and is sorrowful; as mine was gnashing its teeth in a rage a couple of years ago. But these fancies are recent and unformed and perhaps nonsense.

It would be better for me to say what I'm sure of, that the poems are beautiful, startlingly acute in vision and perception, deeply sensitive to their persons and to all the forms and green shadows of a country. It is a finer book than "7PM", and you know I was happy with that.

"Tiresias" I saw and admired in Poems. I don't know another poem like "Civil War", that fills half a continent with its weirdness. "The Sphinx" I admit is a bit riddling, but it is like a pattern in chiselled metal.

A couple of days ago I mailed you a beautifully printed little vanity of the San Francisco Book Club's. My wife and I imagine that I don't look like the photograph in it: yet for one moment I must have.

Yours,
Robinson Jeffers.

aren't always lazy enough to refuse that, and if they're slow-witted
they are all the better for reading twice.

I have a criticism, and no doubt from me it will surprise you. I think you
are too (vulgar word) pessimistic. "End of Singing" and the others in that
section. Civilization is bitter to the singer, it is bitter in that essential
way to everyone, but I think we can remember that there was a time before
it and will be a time after it, and can keep an important part of us timeless
enough to be uncivilized. You have that timeless part, but it feels
menaced and is sorrowful; as mine was gnashing its teeth in a rage a couple
of years ago. But these fancies are recent and unformed and perhaps
nonsense.

It would be better for me to say what I'm sure of, that the poems are
beautiful, startlingly acute in vision and perception, deeply sensitive to their
persons and to all the forms and green shadows of a country.
It is a finer book than "7 PM," and you know I was happy with that.

"Teiresias" I saw and admired in Palms. I don't know another poem like
"Civil War," that fills half a continent with its weirdness. "The Sphinx"
I admit is a bit riddling, but it is like a pattern in chiselled metal.

A couple of days ago I mailed you a beautifully printed little vanity of the
San Francisco Book Club's. My wife and I imagine that I don't look like the
photograph in it: yet for one moment I must have.   Yours, Robinson Jeffers

148: TO MARK VAN DOREN

December [14], 1928

Dear Van Doren: It was a pleasure to write about "Now the Sky," but it is
awkward too to discuss a man's work when you feel that he could do it
so much more competently himself. Having but a couple of days to think
about it, I simply expanded from memory my letter to you.[84]

I haven't seen your review of "Cawdor" yet (nor any other) but of course
shall soon see it. Thank you much for what you say in your letter. As to
tragedy depending on the maintenance of the illusion of man's importance
—it would take me awhile to decide. —"As flies to men, so we to the
Gods: They kill us for their sport" or something like that. I think the illusion
of man's importance is Christian rather than either Greek or Shakespeare.
Yet of course, the more important the victim, the more imposing the

[84] *Compare Letter 148 with J's review in the* New York Herald Tribune Books,
December 2, 1928, p. 4. The review is reprinted in Alberts, A Bibliography, pp. 147–50.

sorrow-play, and it's a pity that we have neither magniloquent Kings nor crucifiable Gods at our disposal now.

As to your own work seeming "slight in comparison"—I remember that absurdity from your letter, which isn't before me—no doubt you are thinking about pages per poem. Is Wordsworth's Leech-gatherer any slighter than the Excursion?

We had a nice excursion of our own the other day—father, mother and twin sons—but we'd have taken you along—to San Antonio Mission, ninety miles south of here. Ruinous high walled old building, adobe with a facade of the Roman-looking Spanish bricks, perfectly desolate with its graves about it, for Hearst has bought up all the valley that surrounds it. Three century-old olive trees full of ripe fruit, two tamarisks, two pomegranates, a falling brick arcade that was once a cloister, stone vats for wine and oil, two mill-stones for crushing olives half buried in the graveyard, and neither priest nor other human being within the square mile. Two years ago there was a sign on the door, "Please shut the door to keep out the cattle," but now even that was gone. The altar was decorated, for they say mass there two or three times a year—to whom?—and when we went in a gray owl as big as a sheep flew from the rafters above the altar.[85] When we went away I found an Indian stone mortar, weighing about two hundred pounds, tied into one of Mr. Hearst's fences near by, to stretch the wire, I found a stone that would stretch wire just as well, and put the mortar in the car. We always take home a stone.

Yes, the "Tower beyond Tragedy"—romantic title—meant the state of a mystic to whom tragedy was impossible because he had escaped finally from the sense of his own—not importance exactly—separateness. Thank you again for the kind things in your letter.   Sincerely, Robinson Jeffers

149: TO RICHARD BÜHLIG

December, 1928

Dear Buhlig: Thank you much for your letter; it was very kind, and aside from that I was happy to hear from you. It is delightful to have your promise again to return to this waxing village, Una and I look forward to

[85] In Part V of "The Loving Shepherdess" Onorio Vasquez tells Clare Walker, " 'In the ruin of San Antonio church / I saw an owl as big as one of your sheep / Sleeping above the little gilt Virgin above the altar. . . .' "

seeing you. Play for me? If I were deaf as an adder I should feel the honor, but I expect to enjoy it too. Thank you, and good luck in your travels.   Cordially yours, Robinson Jeffers

I have just read your letter again and find it even kinder and more understanding than I remembered. My eyes sometimes dazzle a little at first reading.

1928-30   *J completed* Dear Judas and Other Poems *for its 1929 publication, then sailed for the British Isles. The trip, largely financed by Albert Bender, lasted almost six months. It marks the first significant pause in the fixed routine of J's life and work in Carmel. While he was in Ireland, J wrote the poems later collected in* Descent to the Dead, *and Una began a journal of experiences and observations of England and Scotland, but especially of Ireland, which J eventually edited for publication after her death.*

150: TO ALBERT BENDER

December, 1928

Dear Albert: Your extraordinary kindness has made our decision for us. It's doubtful whether we'd have gone next spring, though we think we have money enough saved up to manage it, but travelling is such a nuisance and this place is so dear to us. Now we shall go without fail, and I expect it's a good thing. We'll have to let the boys finish their school year before we start, so that they can enter high school when we return. Perhaps we can arrange to go toward the end of May. Garth and Donnan of course are eager to go; though, like their parents, they know that they'd be happy too if they stayed here.

When your letter arrived yesterday Una and I admired the etching, and I had returned up-stairs to work when she called me down and showed me the check. We stared at each other and thought we couldn't possibly accept it. You are indeed too generous. Over night we have both thought gratefully that you really wanted us to have it; and it will be used for no other purpose than the Irish journey. How lovely it would be if you could come visit us in Ireland. We expect to rent an old farm cottage for headquarters, and a Ford perhaps to travel about in.

Your present has surprised and pleased us beyond measure, and has made our decision, and we are very thankful for both, the gift and the decision. Yours always, Robin

151: TO ALBERT BENDER

[1928]

Dear Albert: Thank you much for sending Joyce Mayhew's poem. It is a beautiful crowded rapid thing, with astonishingly fine passages and pictures. There is often a blurring where one scene flows into another, and some lack of clear motive:—especially the boy's death seems neither quite natural nor consequent on the feeling of the rest. But who wants faultlessness? And the excellences of the poem are obvious. There is grandeur in the figures of the three sages from the three quarters of the earth; and the figure of the Madonna is brilliantly painted in its stiff draped grace. Please congratulate Miss Mayhew for me. Ought we to send back the manuscript?[1]

[1] In a letter to the editor dated May 31, 1967, Miss Mayhew apologizes for being unable to date her poem but describes it as a "Nativity poem I wrote for a Christmas gift to Mr. Bender. It was a long poem in blank verse—iambic pentameter— and I remember Mr. Bender was much impressed by it. He had me read it aloud to Ruth St. Denis and her husband, but I did not know he had sent it to Mr. Jeffers. . . . I don't remember what title I gave it, and it was never published."

The page from the Argonaut is very amusing. They have been good enough to send it to us for the past year or so. It seems to me one of the best-written publications in the country—I would say in the English language, but that sounds absurd, though it is true.

We enjoyed your visit more than I can tell you, and the young people with you. Una told you of course how proud I am to rival Erskine Wood in the matter of cuff-links! And thanked you for the steamer rugs, and so many generosities.   Yours always, Robinson Jeffers

152: TO HENRY GODDARD LEACH

[*1929*]

Dear Mr. Leach: I wasn't more than twenty minutes from home, and so sorry to have missed you. Do come again, if you are still in this neighborhood. My son says he enjoyed talking with you, and that you are an "honest man" and admired his blind rooster.

I'd be glad to send some verses to The Forum, but just now I haven't anything that's less than twenty pages long.   Sincerely, Robinson Jeffers

153: TO MARY AUSTIN

January 14, 1929

Dear Mary Austin: The book was sent because I (like thousands of others) have long admired your works and your life; and because your presence is still a vivid memory among a few of our first-met friends on this bit of coast. I'm sorry you have no expectation of coming here again. It is true there are too many idle people here, but I begin to think they are everywhere, and even on the Gobi desert one would have to be churlish or be over-run.

You made me very happy with the gift of your book. Yes, it is a poem, a most beautiful one; but also as true as any mind can run in its main theme. And who knows that Jesus was not so secure in enlightenment and constant in nature as you have drawn him? If we doubt it, it is only because the people we have met are not like that. I am impressed especially because I had just finished a sort of passion-play, to be called (I think) "Dear Judas," in which Jesus is perhaps farther than yours from common life, but not in the serene direction. Though I hope some earlier serenity is suggested.

My wife met you once when you were visiting here, but I have never met you. I devotedly hope to, some time.   Sincerely yours, Robinson Jeffers

154: TO JOHN HAY WHITNEY

This inscription on the manuscript of "Cawdor," mailed to Barnet B. Ruder, January 15, 1929, is now in the Beinecke Library at Yale.

January, 1929

The poem "Cawdor" came from more diverse and rememberable sources than others that I have written. The name occurred to me first for use in another narrative, which was planned and discarded; the story derives of course from the tale of Phaedra and Hippolytus; one of the incidents relates itself to a mountain-lion skin we have in the house; another to a broken-winged hawk that I kept and fed. The emotional atmosphere comes more than half, certainly, from the earth full of sea-shells and chips of flint, left by the Indians on this hillock by the sea where we live, and on the coast southward.

The domed Rock in the poem is one that I saw in the Sierras and only imagined in a coast canyon; but there is plenty of naked granite about here, so that it is not out of place. The great redwoods fill every canyon of the coast southward for fifty miles.

The first manuscripts of all my longer poems have been like this one, scribbled continuously in pencil from beginning to end, and practically unchanged in the typewriting or in the proof. One or two I threw into the fire, it never occurred to me that they were worth keeping; but I am delighted that John Hay Whitney is to have this one.   Sincerely, Robinson Jeffers

155: TO ARTHUR DAVISON FICKE

[*January 19, 1929*]

Dear Ficke: I know you don't think me an intolerable ruffian for not answering sooner, but I can't imagine why you don't. I am always being dragged behind some versified narrative or other, many of them still-born of course, and when I'm out-doors I write you letters in my mind while building a wind-break for little trees, but the ink and paper are not there. Then your letter, and the extraordinary generosity of your gift of books, stopped my correspondence like a clock. "I can't write to anybody until I write to him." It quite saved my life; instead of thirty-nine unanswered letters I had only one to think of.

How interesting that you should quote "mine eyes dazzle," for that is exactly what I was whispering to myself about the kindness of your letter, before I met it there, only I was crediting Fletcher instead of Marlowe.

No doubt you're right. At any rate, between thanks for your kindness and doubts whether it hasn't made drunken your critical sense—"mine eyes dazzle. She died young."

The book that I read first when they came was the April Elegy. It is extraordinarily beautiful, strange and actual at once. The two people *live*, besides their charm, and in the girl you have caught accurately the feverish desirous arrested life of so many deracinees. —The lines about a second death in Mr. Faust *are* strangely parallel to my fancy; they are much more dreadful. Then I read through the play, admiring the poetry and the thought, and the excellent simplicity. —I have not read all of the other books— never doubt but I shall before long—but much in each except Spectra, which I am saving to the end as different. Wherever I open there is beauty, distinction, and your individual voice. So now I ask you: what sort of liar is the person who has achieved beauty like this, strong and sustained and glowing, so [?] many years, and has never written a line to be ashamed of, and dares to talk about "envy," even in a parenthesis? Not a "horrible liar" perhaps—only a blarneying kind-hearted one.

Thank you indeed for the books. For the letter. For your talk to the editor of the Forum. (I couldn't send him anything, I almost never have anything to send, but it was kind of you.) For your conversation with Liveright; he wrote me a note about it, I mean, what referred to me. For many other kindnesses, known and perhaps unknown. The wood-cut of you was admirable.

I expect your strictures on various things in Cawdor are quite right. The eagle's death was a reminiscence in my mind of the hawk's death, which I saw—dealt. When I first thought of the story I thought of it with three little towers on it, like this ⟋⟍⟍ —digressions from the story— the old man's death-dream, Hood's death-dream, the eagle's.[2] Why shouldn't

---

[2] I elsewhere constructed a triad of parallel emotions or experiences: (1) He wrote his publishers, "I think of Cawdor as making a third with Tamar and The Women at Point Sur; but as if in Tamar human affairs had been seen looking westward, against the ocean; in Point Sur looking upward, minimized to ridicule against the stars; in Cawdor looking eastward, against the earth, reclaiming a little dignity from that association" (see Alberts, A Bibliography, pp. 50–51; Bennett, Stone Mason, p. 125; and Powell, Robinson Jeffers, p. 46); (2) He explained for Alberts how "The Loving Shepherdess" complements "Dear Judas": ". . . the shepherdess in the one, and Judas and Jesus in the other, each embodying different aspects of love: nearly pure, therefore undefiled but quite inefficient in the first; pitying in the second; possessive in the third" (Alberts, A Bibliography, p. 57; Bennett, Stone Mason, p. 132. This statement was also the substance of the jacket blurb objected to by Van Doren [see Letter 178]); and (3) He intended "Thurso's Landing" to "make a display of human courage, in Thurso to endure pain, in his wife to endure and end it, but most of all in his mother. I thought of his as volitional and rather sterile, Helen's as imaginative, of the old woman's as instinctive" (notes for an April, 1932, letter to James Rorty; see Bennett, Stone Mason, p. 149). See also Powell, Robinson Jeffers, pp. 46–47.

a predatory animal, as simpler and more passionate though less intelligent, have a more successful ghost, if any, than a pithecanthropoid one? The only ghost I have ever personally known of was our white bull-dog's. He died one morning; the little boys were just beginning to talk then; they knew nothing of his death that day, and in the afternoon both of them saw him plainly running beside the car for a mile on the way to Monterey through the woods, and laughed at him and called to him. He had never stayed at home. They saw him so *really:* it gave Una and me a queer feeling: and they were so merry with him, while we were feeling rather sad.

No, don't wrong me. I don't think about women as Cawdor did, nor I don't hate people neither. I don't respect them excessively, but I do respect and admire you—and your neighbor Miss Millay, to whom I am writing to-day—and am yours with thanks and affection,   Robinson Jeffers

156: TO ARTHUR DAVISON FICKE

February, 1929

Dear Ficke: Thank you devotedly for "Mountain against Mountain." It is as splendid as its title, and I congratulate you. "Paris 1917" expresses better than any verse or prose I have seen—admirably—the scattered mechanical energy and perfectly bewildered confidence of our national share in the war. The poem is written from the intelligent brain and the brave eyes rather than from deeper down, but that is the way the war was witnessed, except by those who succumbed to neuroses. It is splendid work, and the beauty of the older civilization coming up like wrecked ships through it.

"The Return of Christ" is beautifully done and expresses with excellent originality exactly what you intended to say. Your attitude and mine are after all not too far apart to be quite identical—except a shift of emphasis. —I wrote a kind of passion-play a few months ago that will be amusing to send you when it is published with other things—this fall I expect—and the joke perhaps will be that you have made your Christ a little supernatural, preaching against religion, and I have made mine rather subhuman, at least all-too-human, founding one.

The lyrics are lovely—very. I think I like best "To a Lady Singing an Old Song"—or "My Minnow and Me."

I am proud of course to have my insufficient little saying on the jacket. Liveright's people played me exactly the same trick on the first "Roan Stallion" jacket, of quoting without authorization some extracts from letters, though I too had warned them against it, so I fancy it is commonly done, and times are changed since the Whitman-Emerson controversy.

I congratulate you most sincerely, and wish you further luck, all there is. Yours, Robinson Jeffers

157: TO DUDLEY NICHOLS

April, 1929

Dear Nichols: Your visit is the only occurrence this twelvemonth that has made much impression on me—I mean from outside the household and its interests—if I haven't written before it is only because I have no talent that way. Thank you for the stone from Achill Head, which we are awfully pleased to have, and it will find its marked place in the wall—you'll come and see it sometime. Thank you for the books. Your O'Neill introduction is as excellently done as it is right in appreciation, and more than that, magnificent in vision. He deserves your appreciation. —And I read the Emperor Jones to my twelve-year-olds, between great beef-steaks of Walter Scott. It made a great impression. —I haven't read them the Goat-Song yet, but I read it myself. It is admirable, yet it seems to me the persons are not powerful enough to carry the symbolism; —like people under a thunder-cloud, but the people don't stand high enough, or the cloud doesn't come low enough, and that there is a lack of unity, and the end appears insufficient after all. It is not a failure by any means—but if it *were* a failure, I think it is better to fail with such a conception than succeed with a common one. Did you ever read Yeats's "Unicorn from the Stars"? There is an interesting similarity with all the difference—of points of departure, and race, and manner, —intention even.

We have booked passage and sent for a passport, and are to sail from Montreal, June 14$\underline{^{th}}$, for Belfast. I'd rather stay home, but the boys at least want to go, and no doubt it is proper to interrupt one's contentment now and then. We'll probably be half a year in Ireland and half a year in England and Scotland. I'm going to take a Pacific pebble along, to drop it at Achill Head and pay your debt. If by any chance you should go abroad this summer, or even next spring, mightn't we meet? But if you wait a year and come to California again, you'll find a returned traveller, building another stone wall, and settled for life.   Yours, Robinson Jeffers

158: TO ARTHUR DAVISON FICKE

[*April, 1929*]

Dear Ficke: I am a worm—I might at least have said thank you, but I wanted to say more than that, and there is never a corner of time until midnight puts on the extinguisher. If anyone was ever bored, which is incredible, let

> "Recreations: Stone-masonry, dog-walking, interven-
> tion in dog-fights, and the art of being a grandfather."

(Letter 377)

him get five acres and grow a wood on them, and produce a stone house and twins and a book of verses. He will have a hundred unanswered letters on his hands, and be a worm like me about the one letter that he wants to write.

(An interval. I don't know how many days have gone by, but it is still April. Somebody has a nice story about passing along the road below here, an evening in 1921 or so. They looked up in the twilight and saw a stump of a tower, and me on top rolling a stone into place. They went to China, returned to America, went to Italy, returned. In 1924 they were here again and looked up from the sea-road in the twilight to the same stump of a tower, hardly any higher, and me on top carefully rolling a stone into place. They thought there was something bewitched about my stones—but that is how it is with me.)

We were most grateful for the pictures, the one of you and Miss Millay and another of A. D. F. solus are thrilling. And I am an enthusiast for the poems. Such rich, various, and always formed and beautiful energy, is astonishing in one book, or in one man's work. "Like dagger-handles from Etruscan tombs"—is the jewelled impression the shorter poems leave with me;—but handles with the blades attached and uncorroded. From those sombre "Moments from the Lost Years" to "Loreine: a horse" and the moon-and-sea-piece "I alone Keep my soul," I run the book over with admiration in memory. Thank you.

I have half promised to have a book ready for publication this fall, and that is no pleasure, but it will be a pleasure to send you a copy.

We had a pretty fiesta here the other day, I'd like you to have seen. Someone gave us eight or ten gallons of rich red wine, the color and smell delightful but the taste not quite. Fair; but we suspected a dirty barrel. So first we poured libations to each of the old rocks on the place, and then the rest through the gargoyles of the tower. It was a great sight, like blood gurgling from the stone snouts, and what a fragrance.

Mal Paso Canyon, where you think one ought to kill his women, has just been subdivided by a development company. The devils. But come back and buy a lot there, and build a stone wall around it.

I've planted three hundred more cypresses since you were here, in the hollow north of us, and raised the dining-room wall a few inches. Perhaps we'll get a roof on that room before the rains begin again.

The ranch at Point Sur, that I took liberties with in last year's book, has lately been bought by some wealthy person who intends to breed polo-ponies there. Indeed most of the ranches about here are being bought by wealthy people for horse-breeding—which is certainly more decent than subdivisions, and perhaps may interest your Gladys, and entice you back here sometime. Una sends friendship to her, and so do I, and to you.   Yours,
Robinson Jeffers

159: TO ERNEST MOLL

May, 1929

Dear Mr. Moll: I come to you as a penitent. My wife usually is good enough to look at and answer if necessary letters that come for me—because I never can get it done. When yours came several months ago she said "They are very good poems," and I said "Then let me answer the letter." But I did not read at that time; the letter was laid aside for me and I never found it again until to-night. I am very sorry.

They are, as she said, very good poems. So good that I was able quite to forget myself in reading, and not even wish that they had a better subject.[3] Thank you sincerely, and let me congratulate you on the power and music of the lines.

Three weeks from now we are going away for a year to Ireland and England—I hardly know why, unless for the children's sake. After that, if you are south sometime, I hope you will come and see me and my stones.   Sincerely yours, Robinson Jeffers

160: TO SIDNEY S. ALBERTS

Alberts facsimiled this letter in his A Bibliography, *p. 26.*

May [13], 1929

Dear Mr. Alberts: My father gave me a good start in Latin and Greek when I was quite young, both at school and at college I took them as they came, and that was never profoundly. I think most of whatever acquaintance I have with the classic spirit came from reading English poetry.

The origin of "Tower beyond Tragedy" was probably in the rich voice and Amazon stature of a German-Jewish actress [*Hedwiga Reicher*] with whom we were casually acquainted a few years ago. She recited one of the more barbaric Scotch ballads magnificently in private, and her voice suggested Clytemnestra and Cassandra to me, all the more because she rather failed in the usual sort of play.

I had no thought of production when I wrote, and for that reason began

---

[3] *The two poems "Poet in Stone" and "Builder of Tor House" have recently been published in the* Robinson Jeffers Newsletter, *No. 17 (April, 1967), pp. 2–3.*

with some lines of narrative, but of course your advanced class is free to give a private performance if they should wish to.[4]

We turn to the classic stories, I suppose, as to Greek sculpture, for a more ideal and also more normal beauty, because the myths of our own race were never developed, and have been alienated from us.   Sincerely yours, Robinson Jeffers

161: TO MARK VAN DOREN

May 14, 1929

Dear Mark Van Doren: Your letter makes me sad, for I should love to visit the Connecticut farm—and see you. So I hope to, when we come back. But on the way out our passage is from Montreal, for the sake of the St. Lawrence River, and the children, and who knows whether not also from a feeling that it is better to work up gradually from Carmel to N.Y., through London? San Francisco almost destroyed me the other day, when we went up—for me the first time since 1918, —for shopping and British visa. I ground my teeth all the following night, my wife says. —We go straight and in haste to Montreal, to let the children finish their school year and yet get away June 14, before the full summer rush.

Our expectation is to live three months or so in the north of Ireland, where most of our ancestors came from, about as long in the west, and awhile in Scotland, and a cottage in Oxfordshire. "Why she went to Ireland, Doris didn't know"—as Hardy says—but I suspect it is rather an act of penance than a pleasure-trip, except for the twelve-year-olds. We are all most or less feverish with typhoid vaccination, to-day, in preparation for the Irish inns.

I am sending Liveright another book before we leave, but for fall publishing, called "The Gentle Shepherdess."

Your review of Cawdor[5] was both kind and acute. Thank you. We shall really, I think, return through New York, in a year.   Yours, Robinson Jeffers

[4] *As early as May 18, 1926, after publication of* Roan Stallion, Tamar and Other Poems, *in which "The Tower Beyond Tragedy" first appeared, J wrote to Friede: "I just received an interesting letter, but haven't had time yet to read all of it, from a young man [Lincoln Kirstein] in Massachusetts who was so interested in the Tower beyond Tragedy—'more than in any book except Moby Dick!'—that he built and colored a scene and moulded two hundred little clay figures to act it for him, with cut hat-pins for spears, and encloses sheaves of water-color sketches and photographs—very clever workmanship—isn't that an odd undertaking? I wish I knew enough about staging things to answer him intelligently. . . . My friend Jim Rorty of the New Masses wanted to stage it too; but he looked for human actors— clay figures are more amenable." See also Bennett,* Stone Mason, *p. 114, and Letters 214, 278, and 283.*
[5] *"Bits of Earth and Water,"* Nation, *CXXVIII (January 9, 1929), 50. "The Gentle Shepherdess" became "The Loving Shepherdess," companion-piece to "Dear Judas."*

162: TO ARTHUR DAVISON FICKE

Canadian Pacific
S.S. Melita
June 21, [*1929*]

Dear Ficke: Did I tell you that we were going to sail from Montreal? Life grew feverish, our last months at Carmel—what with getting the boys through school and a touch of flu, packing up, tying down the place for a year's vacancy, finishing a manuscript, anti-typhoid inoculations, and a hundred other disorders.

We went straight from home to Montreal, in a hurry between the end of the boys' school-term and a summer rise in rates on the ocean. When we return we'll be in New York a day or two and surely I can see you, though I fear not for long, because then we'll be rushing to use a return railroad ticket before the year's end.

We've travelled very comfortably but I shall never travel again, it would be disgusting to die away from home, except in some great cause, and there are no great causes.

We're now two days off Ireland, and the sky is still gray but the fog has lifted for the first time. Two nights we lay hove to among ice-bergs on account of the fog off Newfoundland. The ice-bergs were glorious to see, so has the ocean been, though its face is exactly like our own, iron-gray and hard and delightful. The gulls are different though, smaller, gracefuller, more swallowlike and less imposing.

I wish with all my heart we might have seen you a little, as we went by.
Yours, Robinson Jeffers

163: TO LOUIS UNTERMEYER

Clarendon Hotel
York Street
Belfast
June 29, 1929

Dear Untermeyer: If the farm and the sugar-maples are astonishing to you, this clattering city of Northern Ireland is to me. We go out, the day-after-to-morrow, to keep house a couple of months in a stone cabin about the size of my thumb, at Knocknacarry—near Cushendun—Co. Antrim—Northern Ireland. Later on we'll live a month or two in Sligo or Galway, and have a wilder address yet. But we shall be home in Carmel by this time next year.

I'm well content with your choices from my verses for the revision of "Modern American Poetry." Probably there are a few better poems in the

"Roan Stallion" volume, or in my last year's one—"Cawdor"—but I hesitate to suggest any because—I'm not a good judge—and I don't know what price Liveright would set—if any—in reprintings, I believe he has been exacting something from anthologists.

Since "The Women at Point Sur" my only books are "Poems—by R. J." published by the San Francisco Book Club for its members only—an edition of 350 copies, I think—but many of the poems are reprints—and "Cawdor and other poems," published by Horace Liveright. Both 1928. I expect Liveright will publish this fall "Dear Judas and other poems."

There was an English edition of "Roan Stallion, Tamar, and other poems" issued last autumn (1928) by the Hogarth Press.

I am sorry indeed to have missed a visit from you at Carmel. Sometime, I hope. —As for us, we did not see New York on the way east, but sailed from Montreal, three weeks ago. Your letter reached me yesterday. Cordially yours, Robinson Jeffers

164: TO BENJAMIN H. LEHMAN

Dromore Cottage
Knocknacarry
County Antrim,
Northern Ireland
August 31, 1929

Dear Ben Lehman: We miss very much your occasional visits, but I imagine we'll be home again about Christmastime, or not much later, then I hope they'll begin again. This tiny cottage, where we've lived two months when not on our motoring journeys, is not too far from the sea, under high green trees, between stone- and thorn-hedged pastures. The country people about are all Catholics and primitive and dirty and very kindly. Antrim is the only county in Ulster that wasn't planted with Scotch and English protestants, therefore it is as wild and almost as shiftless as the west. It is full of myth—(I walked this morning to "Ossian's Grave," a cromlach [cromlech] and stone-circle near here); Ossian and Fingal lived on a mountain-top a mile farther; the sons of Usna, with Deirdre, landed ten miles from here on their return from Scotland; the children of Lir became swans in a river twelve miles from here—and of history more sanguinary even than the myths. One of the finest historical pictures is of fierce old Sorley Boy McDonnell raging at Fair Head, a few miles north of here, while Essex's ships—Francis Drake commanding one of them—were massacring the MacDonnell women and children in Rathlin Island, only a mile off shore, spread out like a mat under the 600 foot basalt precipice of Fair Head. One probably can't convey the feeling without describing the place, the solitude of rock and heather and the sheer enormous cliff.

Meanwhile we've been in every county of Ireland except one, and seen innumerable ruins and loughs and round towers, which I can recommend, and hotels, which I can't. The funniest memory we have is of the hill of Tara. "The harp that once—" We found on the tip-top a monstrous made-in-Italy statue of St. Patrick and two old American women on their knees under it, not praying, passionately searching the grass for a shamrock-leaf. The most impressive thing perhaps was Newgrange hill—you remember—one of three enormous artificial hills on the Boyne, nobody knows how many millenniums B.C. they date from, with narrow passages and high chambers inside them, roofed and walled with cyclopean stone, not shaped, but incised with symbolic spirals and lozenges. I imagine these are the only structures in Europe that resemble the Egyptian pyramids. Of course there are other chambered mounds.

The anguish of getting packed up surrounds me, and we're going to Scotland. After Sept. 19 our address will be as droll as the present one— "Kerry Vor Cottage—Britwell Salome—near Watlington—Oxfordshire— England"—but we shall only be there a month, and then I fear a month in London. Travelling is a very little more interesting than I thought it would be, but to stay at home is more interesting.   Yours, Robinson Jeffers

165: TO ALBERT BENDER

Knocknacarry, County Antrim
August 31, 1929

Dear Albert: I have just come back from a walk to the old stones they call "Ossian's Grave"—a most interesting place about 2½ miles from our cottage. I had to go alone because it was raining as usual, but Una and the boys were there with me once before. The place is on the shoulder of a hill, with a few old thorn-trees about, and a most magnificent view. There is a prehistoric circle of big gray standing-stones, and close beside it an oblong of big stones set on edge to enclose a grave—no one knows how old it is, but 800 or a thousand B.C. at the latest, perhaps much older. This part of County Antrim is full of Ossianic and other Gaelic traditions, and of sanguinary history as interesting as the myths. Being the nearest part of Ireland to Scotland the whole tide of Gaelic stories and migrations swept back and forth through here. And of the older peoples—Picts or whatever they were—the valley our cottage is in is full of their monuments and forts and artificial caverns, —so that we can hear them stirring about at night, if the wind is right.

The first of the Jefferses' several trips to Ireland was prompted by Una's enthusiasm for Irish culture.

I should have written to you much earlier; but Una has written; and whenever we were not in the act of travelling I've been making verses as actively as when we're at home, and consequently as unable to write anything else.

We bought a closed rain-proof new-model Ford, and could not have managed without it. Four or five thousand miles we've motored already, and shall take it next month to Scotland and England, and sell it before we go home. We've been in every county in Ireland except one—Wexford— and seen almost everything, I think, thanks to Una's energy, even Blarney Castle and Killarney, —and the Dublin Horse Show—which one would naturally avoid, but my girl is thorough. Perhaps the most beautiful place is Aura mountain, four or five miles from here; and Fair Head the most imposing—the northeastern corner of Ireland—immense stretches of purple heather and rock, ending in a violent basalt precipice, 600 feet high, with Rathlin Island and Scotland and the sea under your feet. One of the loveliest and most affecting is Glendalaugh, not awfully far from Dublin; the most curiously impressive are the three artificial hills on the Boyne, not far from Drogheda, Nowth, Dowth, and Newgrange. There is nothing like them except the Egyptian pyramids. We went into the Newgrange hill; by candle-light through the long low passage roofed and walled with enormous carved stones to the vaulted chamber of huge stones in the midst of the hill. There is no tradition and no conjecture as to how many thousands of years old these hills are, or who built them.

We have visited some twenty-odd round towers—(the boys have kept count)—all over Ireland, and innumerable churches and churchyards—and hotels—five of the latter we could honestly say were quite decent. We were twice at Yeats' Tower, and twice at Moore Hall on Lough Carra, the standing shell of George Moore's old family home, which was burned in the "troubles," a most beautiful place. —Una has given me half a dozen of her Kodak pictures to send you with this.

Garth and Donnan have just received your generous gift, and are happy and grateful, planning what they will do with so much money. They have a delightful time here, having made friends with all the country people and cattle and sheep and ducks and goats and pigs about our cottage. The people are Irish Catholics here—the only part of Ulster that was never planted with Scotch and English protestants—therefore as primitive and kindly and dirty as anywhere in the west.   Yours always, dear Albert, Robinson Jeffers

166: TO MARK VAN DOREN

This is a postcard mailed from John O'Groats Hotel, John O'Groats, Wick; the date is illegible, but contents indicate September, 1929. See Letter 167.

We left Ireland the other day, and I rather regretted it until we came north of Oban, but this north is not a bit like Walter Scott. Waste and gray, big stones and peat-bogs. Prehistoric barrows and pillar-stones make one quite happy.   Yours, Robinson Jeffers

167: TO BENJAMIN DE CASSERES

7 Lansdowne Road,
Holland Park,
London, Wil.
[*October 6, 1929*]

Dear Ben De Casseres: We lived in Ireland nearly three (3) months, and in Scotland three or four weeks, and have been here a fortnight, mostly in London. I don't like cities, and shall be glad to leave here in a couple of days, to live in the country in Oxfordshire for a month. Perhaps after that we'll get a cottage by the sea in Cornwall—I don't know yet whether we'll go home this winter or next spring. We had quite beautiful times in Ireland and Scotland, we got a tiny stone cottage in Antrim, in a rather wild place called Knocknacarry, with a few very primitive kindly peasants for neighbors, with the sea on one side of us and "Ossian's Grave"—a prehistoric stone-circle—on the other. The grandest of scenery all about, lovely purple hills of heather and sea-cliffs of basalt and chalk. The cliff in Fair-Head is black basalt, 600 feet high. This is in the bloody north east corner of Ireland, where the old migrations broke back and forth between Ireland and Scotland, and most of the field-stones mark the graves of warriors, even before the Danes and the English came. Dear old dirty suburban England is rather a comedown after this, though northern Scotland was not. We got a car soon after we landed in Ireland, and drove more than 5000 miles, back and forth and around, in every county but one, but mostly avoiding things that were less than a thousand years old. Then we shipped the car over to Scotland and did likewise. We were up to John O'Groat's, the farthest north of Scotland, where you can almost touch the Orkney Islands, and we took a boat to Iona and Staffa in the Hebrides. I expect we'll go down to Land's End this fall—the farthest southwest. I've written some verses the times we were quiet, but mostly about prehistoric grave-stones.

Love from us to you and Bio.   Yours, Robinson Jeffers

168: TO ARTHUR DAVISON FICKE

7 Lansdowne Road
Holland Park
London, Wil.
October [7], 1929

Dear Ficke: Surely I've written to you since that scribble on the steamer, but I can't remember. Except that you answered rather jeering at me for a Chinese desire to be buried in my own place. You were quite mistaken—it wasn't to be buried, but for the pleasure of dying there. When we made the house we made a very sweet little panelled bed-room-guest-room—on the ground floor, with a little fire-place, and the rocks and sea in the window, and wrote Spenser's verses on a beam over the bed:

"Peace after war, port after stormie seas,
  Ease after toil, death after life, do greatly please."

"As the child grows up its attention must be drawn
from itself to the more important world outside it."

(Letter 169)

156

I announced then that I wanted the luxury of dying in that bed. But of course I'm willing to postpone it awhile.

Dear old dirty suburban England is rather a comedown after Ireland and the north of Scotland. I've decided that I don't like trees, they make the landscape so soft and fluffy. In Ireland (perhaps I told you) we lived in a tiny white-washed stone cottage at a wildish place called Knocknacarry, near the Antrim coast. A few very primitive very kindly Catholic peasants for neighbors. (This coast was never planted with Scotch and English protestants, like the rest of Ulster.) We had the sea and the hills of Scotland on one side and "Ossian's Grave"—a prehistoric stone-circle—on a hill on the other, besides a lot of ash-trees and thorn-trees and three goats, two sheep, three stirks (i.e., steers—gelded calves) and a lot of poultry. I had to walk a hundred yards to the spring for pails of water, and once it didn't rain for nine days the spring nearly died on us. We burned peat of course in the cottage fire-place, and Una cooked chickens and steak in the peat-smoke. It's wild country, great lonely purple hills of heather, and sea-cliffs of chalk and basalt. The cliff at Fair Head is black basalt, six hundred feet high, twice as high as the Shakespeare cliff at Dover. And every field-stone, almost, marks the grave of a warrior, for this Antrim coast comes within thirteen miles of Scotland, with Rathlin Island between, and the bloody tides of migration went back and forth here, even before the Danes and the English appeared. —Oh, well, it was a nice place.

We got a car soon after we landed and drove 5000 miles in Ireland, which is almost all there is, and shipped the car over to Scotland. We drove up to John O'Groat's and I suppose we'll be down to Land's End before winter. The north of Scotland, Sutherland and Caithness, were as beautiful and lonely as the best of Ireland; so was Iona in the Hebrides. Of course all the while I'd just as lief be at home—and here in London a good deal liefer—such an enormous expanse of mediocrities. Here we've been two weeks, to-morrow we go to a little village in Oxfordshire for a month, but while our trunks are there I think we'll drive down to Cornwall or somewhere and look into a more inspired sort of place for the next month. Oxfordshire is fairly pretty, and there's an old pre-Roman road by the house there, along which Boadicea used to ride up to London to sell horses, besides a couple of unexcavated barrows—not that I want to excavate them, but you like to feel that the kernel of mortality is inside—but the earth is so civilized and acquiescent and pitifully smiling in England—I hope better of Cornwall. We had to spend a day and a night crossing the black country—Yorkshire and Derbyshire mines and factories—on the way south; and it was hideous of course but it was the only English landscape that looked real. London doesn't look in the least real, though a little hideous too, but in spite of their depression and poverty it is feverishly building itself bigger in all directions—

new tenements and unending new rows of uniform brick houses. The northern edges of London look just like southern California—bungalows innumerable and golf-clubs and subdivisions and the wide motor-roads and brown fields—they've had a remarkable drought this summer.

Do remember me to Edna Millay. —Una and I send love to you and Gladys.   Yours, Robinson Jeffers

169: TO RUDOLPH GILBERT

Part of this letter was published as the facsimile frontispiece to Gilbert's Shine, Perishing Republic *(Boston, 1936).*

Swan Hotel
Wells, Somerset
November, 1929

Dear Mr. Gilbert: I was most grateful for your letter and the copy of your article. They reached me just as we were leaving Ireland. I ought to have thanked you at once, but did not; then they were packed in a trunk, and I have not written until now, when we are about to leave England for home. We have been much on the move.

You ask what is meant by "breaking out of humanity." But poetry can't be translated into prose without seeming exaggerated and mystical, or else flattened down to mere common sense. Either way gives a false picture. But I may suggest several things that were meant by the one saying.

(1) We have learned within the past century or so that humanity is only a temporary and infinitesimal phenomenon in a large universe. The knowledge involves a readjustment of values that can only be managed by looking at humanity objectively, from the outside.

(2) The phrase refers also to those moments of visionary enlightenment that I should hate to call "cosmic consciousness" because so much foolishness has been written about them under that name.

(3) It seems to me wasteful that almost the whole of human energy is expended inward, on itself, in loving, hating, governing, cajoling, amusing, its own members. It is like a new born babe, conscious almost exclusively of its own processes and where its food comes from. As the child grows up its attention must be drawn from itself to the more important world outside it.

(4) In a civilization like ours, metropolitanism intensified by machinery, human nature (which was developed under very different conditions) becomes an anachronism. We can't turn back the civilization, not at least until it collapses, and our descendents will have to develop a new sort

of nature—will have to "break out of humanity"—or suffer considerably—probably both.

I could specify a good many more ideas involved in the one phrase, but my letter mustn't go on forever. Indeed I am not sure that I've indicated even now the thoughts that were uppermost in my mind when I was writing.

Thank you most sincerely for your letter, and for the article, which was excellently (though fervidly) done, and certainly most sympathetic and intelligent. I hope we may meet sometime.   Sincerely yours, Robinson Jeffers

170: TO DR. LYMAN STOOKEY

Clarendon Hotel
York Street
Belfast
December 8, 1929

Dear Dr. Stookey: We're sailing for home the day after to-morrow, and I'm trying to remember whether I've written to you before. I fear not.

We bought a closed car when we first landed and have had a good time with it, motoring five thousand miles into all the corners of Ireland and five thousand in England and Scotland, from John O'Groat's to Land's End and other directions. We had a white-washed cottage on the Antrim coast for several months, and then an old house in Oxfordshire. Ireland pleased us most and England least, though it was pleasant enough. If I couldn't live on the Pacific coast I think I'd live in northern Ireland—say on Fair Head, the north east corner, where sheep cry sadly in the heather above a six-hundred foot basalt precipice, and Scotland seems almost within arm's reach across the channel.

—I had to stop writing, and to-day [*December 10*] is our sailing-day. The newspapers say that "the greatest storm within living memory" continues unabated—which pleases our sons more than it does their parents. We crossed in it from Scotland a few days ago.

Yesterday we drove back to look at our little old cottage on the Antrim coast, and to see our peasant neighbors there. Then a long pilgrimage along the peat-cart tracks in the heather of those mountains. They were streaked with ice and snow and looked more lovely and desolate than ever. The black-faced sheep were still there, but the shepherds were beginning to gather them to take them down. All wild and beautiful; and the names match the places. The hamlet we lived in was Knocknacarry, the town we drove to over the mountains was Ballycastle, we came back over Aura mountain, with Trostan on our right, and delivered our car in Cushendall to the man who has bought it. So we took the bus back from there to Belfast. Come and see us in Carmel, won't you? and we'll tell you the names of places here until you think it's Irish we're talking.   Affectionately, Robinson Jeffers

171: TO BENJAMIN DE CASSERES

Clarendon Hotel
York Street
Belfast
December 10, 1929

Dear Ben De Casseres: Thank you much for the book [The Superman in America], which I admire tremendously. It has the lyrical quality, the brilliance, and the gargantuan laughter of your best. As soon as I get home I'll inscribe my latest and send you; probably it's published by this time, though I haven't heard a word, and don't care much.

We are sailing to-day for home. Last week we motored up from Oxfordshire into Scotland, loaded the car and ourselves onto a steamer and came back to Ireland, in the height of what the British newspapers call the "greatest storm within living memory." We were all surprised and indignant to find ourselves sea-sick for an hour or two. To-day's paper says that the storm "continues unabated," so I dare say we'll have a rough night. The past three or four days we've been revisiting the most beautiful and desolate places in northern Ireland, the hamlet Knocknacarry where we lived in a little white-washed stone hut, and the Antrim coast, and the heather-mountains along the peat-cart tracks, Aura Mountain and Trostan and Langhareema. The mountains are streaked with ice and snow now, and more beautiful than ever. The black-faced sheep were still there, but the shepherds were gathering them to take them down. Ireland and northern Scotland are the beautiful places, perhaps Cornwall too; England is comparatively pretentious and tiresome, though amusing enough. Yesterday evening we sold our car to a man in Cushendall, and felt as if we had sold our best friend. It has carried us more than ten thousand miles to all the corners of these islands; without the car we could neither have afforded the journeys nor endured them. I'm almost sorry to leave here, but I'll be very glad to get home. Won't you and Bio come west and see us sometime, in the years after next January? We're not stopping in New York.   Yours always, Robinson Jeffers

172: TO MARY AUSTIN

Canadian Pacific
S.S. Duchess of Bedford
December [20], 1929

Dear Mary Austin: Thank you much for your letter; it is mere platitude to
say that I value it greatly. You are right of course about the unessentialness
of sex as a motive in literature, but practically it's a great help to have
violent emotion of some sort, and fear, hunger, and so forth are rather
narrowing, ambition likely to be too technical, —Oh well, we have to use
what we can manage. But I agree with you in sum.

We're coming home a little sooner than we expected, the days were grown
too short and the country too flooded to make our small journeys in the car
and look at new things—old ones rather—prehistoric stones and burial
mounds being our usual interest.//

I don't know that I have any really Irish blood, but Protestant Irish, which
means of course Scotch and English drawn through Ireland, but the north
seemed very homelike, and the Free State rather like a fairyland. I imagine
they have very bad hotels in fairyland. The finest and greatest scenery
we saw anywhere was near where we lived on the Antrim coast, the
tremendous black-basalt precipice of Fair Head, a few sheep crying in the
cloudy heather above, and Rathlin Island in the grey swirls of sea below, the
shore of Scotland just beyond. I should like to return there.

On an utterly lonely hill near our Antrim cottage was a little prehistoric
stone-circle and cromlach [*cromlech*] that the people call Ossian's Grave—he
was north-Irish originally rather than Scottish—the most pathetic and
loveable gray old fanged stones that I ever saw. We shall be home I think by
New Year's. We have had no second-class mail forwarded, but a friend
piles it up in our house for us, and one of the things that I most gratefully
look forward to is the new edition of "The American Rhythm." Thank you
much. I've read the old, of course, and admired it greatly, and in great
part agreed with it.   Sincerely yours, Robinson Jeffers

173: TO ALBERT BENDER
See also Bennett, Stone Mason, *p. 131.*

Canadian Pacific
S.S. Duchess of Bedford
December [20], 1929

Dear Albert: We are on our way home, and shall be there I think by New
Year's. Ireland was best, and it was like coming home to come back to it
before we sailed. Northern Scotland we loved intensely too, and the moors

162

Out of the charm of their first experiences in Ireland came Jeffers' excellent collection Descent to the Dead *and the beginning of Una's vivid journals, finally published as* Visits to Ireland.

and sea-rocks of Cornwall were very fine. We loved our travel, and are most grateful to you for your share in it. The days were becoming too short to see new places, and the weather too bad for wandering in Scotland, or we'd have stayed longer.

We drove up rapidly from Oxfordshire through Shropshire and Wales and Carlisle into Scotland, through Gretna Green and Carlyle's village Ecclefechan, where he was born and sits on the hill in bronze. We took a boat from Stranraer to Ireland during "the greatest storm within living memory"—the papers called it—and may I say that we were all sea-sick for an hour—the passage took three—we crossed before breakfast. We spent four or five delightful days seeing northern Ireland again, and sailed from Belfast for New York. The storm was still going on, or had revived, and our ship made slow progress the first two or three days, but we didn't mind. Its motion is not so excitable as a channel steamer's. There is only a handful of passengers, and most of these were sick at first, so that we have had the big ship to ourselves. It is the one Ramsay McDonald went home on. Night before last the ship unexpectedly stopped for an hour, to steady it while they operated on our poor cabin-steward for sudden appendicitis. We've told no one in New York the name of our steamer, not wishing to be met, and haven't yet made up our mind to call on anyone. We shall only stay a day or so, and then go to visit Una's family in Michigan for a few days, then home by New Orleans and Los Angeles. Then I'll begin building a round tower or something, and in a few days you'll come and see us. Una and the boys send their love to you.   Affectionately, Robin

174: TO MAURICE BROWNE

Canadian Pacific
S.S. Duchess of Bedford
December [20], 1929

Dear Maurice Browne: We drove up to Scotland through Shropshire and Wales, and pitched across the Irish channel in the storm of the year. You must have tasted it too: the papers reported addresses of yours in Belfast while we were there. I kept thinking of the ancient mariner in our rapid journey—"I pass like night from land to land"—but "I have strange powers of speech" belongs to you.

Una and I were perfectly delighted to see you in London—I think we showed it—and this note is rather to acknowledge your letter from the Aquitania, which I treasure but show to none. Such a traveler as you—we shall surely see you in California again, if only for a day, not too far in the future.   Yours, Robinson Jeffers

1930-37   *When he returned from the British Isles, J found his growing reputation more and more insistent in its demands on his willingness to discuss his work and his opinions. A number of university students elected to write theses on J or to consider his work as a part of broader studies. Critics and scholars sincerely interested in representing J with accuracy depended more and more upon statements they could urge from him. Una began to answer increasingly large numbers of his letters, then, in order to free him for writing poetry. Nevertheless, he personally answered a large number of individual queries and became interested in correspondents such as Frederic Ives Carpenter for the sake of their own stimulating ideas. This developing interest in J's work produced S. S. Alberts'* A Bibliography of the Works of Robinson Jeffers *(New York, 1933), Lawrence Clark Powell's* Robinson Jeffers, the Man and His Work *(Los Angeles, 1934; rev. ed., 1940), Melba Berry Bennett's* Robinson Jeffers and the Sea *(San Francisco, 1936), and Rudolph Gilbert's* Shine, Perishing Republic *(Boston, 1936).*   ❧   *More frequent and active participation in the literary and political world was also asked of J. He was elected to the National Institute of Arts and Letters in 1937 and was invited to join other organizations, though he usually declined, as graciously as he could. His recommendations were solicited for contenders for literary awards and fellowships: Harriet Monroe pressed him to assist the committee for a* Poetry *magazine award in 1932, and he was asked to serve on the Phelan Fellowship Awards Jury in 1936. But J was uncomfortable in the role of judge, and his scrupulosity was clearly exasperating to Miss Monroe. He was just as cautious in his political attitudes and steadfastly refused to commit himself to any of the varieties of politico-economic movements then supported by many of his fellow writers.*   ❧   *In 1933, after J's publisher, Horace Liveright, went bankrupt, J accepted the invitation of Random House to join its list. Bennett Cerf obtained the manuscript of* Give Your Heart to the Hawks *from Liveright for 1933 publication. (Liveright had already given permission to Random House to publish* Descent to the Dead *in 1931.) Between 1930 and 1937 J published, as well as these books,* Thurso's Landing and Other Poems *(1932) and* Solstice and Other Poems *(1935), and Random House issued the Modern Library edition of* Roan Stallion, Tamar, and Other Poems *in 1935.*   ❧   *Mabel Dodge Luhan (Lujan) arrived in Carmel in 1930 and began to press the Js to make a trip to her ranch in Taos. Although J was not pleased to interrupt his work routine again so soon after his return from abroad, he consented to the first of several rather taxing visits to Taos in June, 1930.*   ❧   *In spite of all these interruptions, J completed the manuscript for* Such Counsels You Gave to Me *before the family's second journey to Ireland in July, 1937.*

175: TO ALBERT BENDER

January 7, [*1930*]

Dear Albert: We've been very busy for a week, getting things unpacked
and out of storage, and the house and place cleaned up, but now things will be
quite normal in a day or two. We look forward to seeing you—some
day soon you'll drive in, I hope. Meanwhile how kind you've been. The New
Year's cake was almost too beautiful to eat—but too good not to eat—a
sort of interior decoration!—and now the candy is with us. —We had a
prosperous and delightful voyage, and are also very glad to be home again.
We might have stayed longer, but the English countryside was really a
little flat and monotonous after Ireland and Scotland, and the winter days
were becoming too short and muddy for much travelling.// Every day we read
in the newspaper of the floods covering the roads behind us. —You know,
California owes us something for the good rain that's just come to it.
When we first landed in Ireland there was a drought, and soon the rain began;
and England was thirsty and brown as the desert when we arrived, and we
left it flooded; and here again we've brought the rain in our suit-cases.
—You're welcome. And you'll be very welcome here when you come to see
us.   Yours, Robin

176: TO MARK VAN DOREN

January 30, 1930

Dear Mark Van Doren: I wanted to see you when we landed in New York,
but I saw nobody. The ship—Duchess of Bedford—was three days late
from running half speed through storms; we had to visit my wife's people
in Michigan for a couple of days, and we had to get away from there
before the Christmas festivities began. We went out to the Bronx Zoo to keep
our promise to the children—Saturday morning—a bitter wind blew on the
bisons—and started west Saturday afternoon. I'm sorry not to have seen you.

   Ireland and northern Scotland and the Hebrides were even more beautiful
than we hoped. England is beautiful, (the country) but the people so tired
and the earth so tame, except on the remote edges.[1] And wearily fluffy
with trees. There is nothing like travel to narrow the mind.

   We'd have stayed until spring but the days grew too short for motoring
and too wet for walking, we saw we'd have to go into winter quarters,
and thought we might as well go home for that.

[1] *J's comments on England in these letters are reflected in the images of "Subjected
Earth" in* Descent to the Dead.

167

I read your review of "Judas"[2] since we came home and didn't agree with it, but the affection I confess to feeling toward you is not diminished. Your great anthology must be popular in England—we saw it well displayed in so many London book-stalls.   Yours, Robinson Jeffers

177: TO THEODORE LILIENTHAL

February 28, 1930

Dear Mr. Lilienthal: Forgive me for not answering promptly. My correspondence has degenerated until now it is nothing but a chronic disease.

Your request is an honor to me, and I'd love to write the preface—I simply can't. If you could see the hundred letters that are lying here unanswered you'd understand that I must stick to the oath about writing no more prose until my conscience is clear—probably that means forever.

Your idea of a catalogue devoted to first editions of modern poetry is most interesting and unusual.   With best wishes, Cordially yours, Robinson Jeffers

178: TO MARK VAN DOREN

March 14, 1930

Dear Mark: Is that too abbreviated? As for me, I'm familiarly called by the name of a little red-breasted bird, but perhaps Robin won't seem to you any more fitting than Robinson. I hope it will, because there's nothing else to suggest. I was baptized John R., but nobody ever called me John since that moment, perhaps the baptism didn't *take*.[3]

As to the review of my verses—you take my disagreement too much in earnest. I ought rather to have said "thank you." —All I was thinking was that there had been (this time) no intention of expressing my peculiar ideas in the poem—least of all through the Judas's mouth—the thing was only an attempt to use our only demigod as a mask in a tragedy, and you

[2] *See Letter 178.*
[3] *J, however, signed his full name to Letter 1, to his father; to an undated school essay, "A Proposal for the Civilizing of Warfare," in the Occidental College collection; and to his first published volume,* Flagons and Apples.

". . . the iron passion and beauty of your poem hardly allow
praise, . . . it would be too much like patting an eagle."

(Letter 62)

seemed to impute to me more than I meant. —As to "not writing what you set out to write"—who does? I'm sure that I never have. —But it's true that I ought to apologize for my words on the jacket of that book.[4] Liveright always writes to me for a description for his catalogue, just when a book is half finished and least describable, and I never have the faintest idea what to say, and invent something, and do it very badly no doubt. But it was not meant for a sort of preface on the dust-jacket, only for salesman's talk in the fall list. —It would be a great pity if you were in earnest about not reviewing people's verses any more—I hope that was only the expression of passing impatience. It's a thankless job, no doubt, but most jobs are, and nobody does it better, nor, with intelligence, more good-naturedly.

We've settled into our old habits here as if we had never wandered, and have no news. The past two weeks we've been watching Lindburg fly his kite from the hill south of us and hang in the wind like a sparrowhawk over our point. We beggared ourselves the other day to buy a little more land on our north boundary, because it has a natural granite column on it that we call the "altar-stone"—my wife is as mad about rocks as I am, fortunately, or rather I as she.   Yours on approval, Robin Jeffers

179: TO ARTHUR DAVISON FICKE

April 19, [1930]

Dear Arthur Ficke: Forgive me for not writing—I don't know why it is— I can't write letters when I want to—I'm very sorry. The Road to the Mountain is a great and moving poem. You know that I admired greatly the first draft of it, in your "Mountain against Mountain"—and now the longer version, instead of being diluted, seems to me very greatly strengthened and more beautiful. It should make gorgeous pageantry as well as being great poetry. Thank you much for sending it. —Una and I laughed aloud when we first heard of you and Krishna-murti celebrating, but his history and your play make it all clear—and indeed it is quite admirable in him.

Yes, Eugene Boissevain and Edna St. Vincent Millay were here for a day, and it was a very lovely one. I admired her poetry—especially the latest— more than any woman's and most men's, but it never occurred to me that herself would be so delightful, nor that I'd quite fall in love with her husband. They seemed to think our coast and Pt. Lobos quite beautiful. Will you

[4] *In his review of* Dear Judas, *"Judas, Savior of Jesus,"* Nation, *CXXX (January 1, 1930), 20–21, Van Doren objected to J's jacket remarks on the special interpretation of love controlling the themes of both "Dear Judas" and "The Loving Shepherdess." See the note to Letter 155.*

give them Una's love and mine, when you see them next.

Mabel Lujan came here from Taos some weeks ago, for a rest from the altitude, Tony of course with her, and Spud Johnson lately for secretary. She rented a house just across the hollow from us. An interesting woman. I hear of her mostly at second hand, from Una, to whom she seems much attached, but I've enjoyed two or three times hearing Tony thump his drum and sing—I prefer him to other musicians.

We had a decent rain this month and warm spring weather, so that the country is ablaze with flowers and green grass and very fragrant. I wish you were here. —We hope eagerly to see you.

Lewis Browne was here a few afternoons ago, with a Miss Lissner whom he means to marry. Your "marrying rabbi."

Una sends love to Gladys and you, and I to you and Gladys.   Yours always, Robinson Jeffers

180: TO CAMILLE McCOLE

The original of this letter is in the restricted Robinson Jeffers Collection at the University of Alabama. Melba Bennett's version (in her Stone Mason, *p. 151) differs only slightly from this, which was published in Andrew Smithberger and Camille McCole,* On Poetry *(Garden City, 1931), pp. 165–66. Mrs. Bennett collects a number of J's statements distinguishing poetry from prose and otherwise defining poetry and the poetic process, including J's hitherto unpublished Preface to* Tamar. *See* Stone Mason, *pp. 151–53 and 106–8.*

[*May, 1930*]

The word "poetry" is one of those abstract words covering a complex of things—like the word "beauty"—so various for different persons that the only definition I could give would be a bad one out of a dictionary. I suppose the point is to distinguish poetry from unpoetic verse and from poetic prose.

As to the latter, it seems to me that the word "poetry," at least in English, implies some form of verse. Verse (I should say, without looking in the dictionary) is a form of speech characterized by rhythmic recurrences, so that there is a noticeable and fairly regular correspondence of some sort between the lines, or lines and stanzas.

I think the difference between poetry and unpoetic verse lies in the appeal of poetry to the aesthetic emotion. So that one might say that poetry is beautiful verse. But the beauties of verse may be so various (and disputable)—

171

from sublimity of subject to mere virtuosity of expression—that personal taste must in the end do the distinguishing.

I think the quality I most value in poetry is that of imaginative power activated by strong emotion, so that the imagination is not displayed idly for a show, but as if of necessity and in earnest, under emotional compulsion.

As to practical suggestions for a student beginning the study of poetry—of course there are many ways. It seems to me I'd begin with ballads of action—Scott's Border Minstrelsy, if the dialects were not too difficult. Then short lyrics, as of Shelley, Keats, Herrick, Andrew Marvell. For a study of poetic form, I'd direct the student's attention to accentual imitations of classic meters, like Tennyson's and Swinburne's, and to some well-made rendering in modern English of the old versification of Beowulf and Piers Plowman, as well as to the metrical instances of today and last century. And some Old Testament poetry, to face the Hebrew verse like an echo in the mountains.   Sincerely yours, Robinson Jeffers

181: TO BENJAMIN DE CASSERES

May 7, 1930

Dear Ben De Casseres: Forgive me for not writing. I have a very real affection for you, since the time of your little visit here, besides my often expressed admiration for your work, but it seems to be impossible for me ever to write letters. To-day the northwest wind is howling so that I can't plant trees while it lasts—and here is my chance.

I remember that you've asked me two questions. (1) Whether Liveright's office used the quotation from your Bookman article on the jackets of my books of their own accord or at my suggestion?—Of their own accord. I've never suggested the least detail of that nature; the publishing business is a matter that I don't dare even to think of. —But of course I was glad to see it—and thank you. (2) Where Mayfield is?[5] If I'd known I'd have answered at once; but it must be two years since I've heard from him. I guess he was in Texas then, but you've heard since that. I'm very sorry if he's died or got away with any manuscripts of yours.

I hope you are well and well occupied, and I wish I could see you. In England and Ireland I felt as if I had been gathered to my fathers, wandering in the islands of the dead. I loved it. The verses I wrote there are called Descent to the Dead. Since our return I've written a narrative poem called

---

[5] *J. S. Mayfield, printer, author of an appreciative comment on J entitled* The Artist *(Fort Worth, 1928), also printed de Casseres'* Robinson Jeffers *(Austin, 1928).*

Resurrection, which is more exciting but less pleasant. I can't make up my mind whether to publish anything this fall or not.

Una enjoyed a friendly letter from Bio lately. We send kindest greetings to both of you.   —Yours always, in spite of silences!—Robinson Jeffers

182: TO H. ARTHUR KLEIN

This response to Klein's request for comment on a lengthy quote from Bridges on Milton's prosody is included in Klein's thesis, "A Study of the Prosody of Robinson Jeffers," Occidental College, May, 1930. See also Alberts, A Bibliography, pp. 150–51, and Bennett, Stone Mason, p. 150

[May 16, 1930]

Dear Mr. Klein: People talked about my "free verse" and I never protested, but now I am quite touched to hear that someone at last has discovered the metrical intention in it. Thank you.

I never before read the passage that you quote from Robert Bridges, but a short essay on Bridges' poetry by Arthur Symons made me familiar with the sense of it, fifteen or so years ago, and no doubt it worked in my mind. Before that I had read a prefatory note of Coleridge to his *Christabel*, in which the same idea is produced. —I've just looked it out: "Preface to the 1816 edition. —"Metre not properly speaking irregular—new principle: namely, that of counting in each line the accents, not the syllables"— etc. —Of course, the principle was not quite new, since Anglo-Saxon verse built on it—probably primitive Germanic verse in general—I don't know. No doubt you're already familiar with these instances.

It seems to me (as you have remarked) that the counting of stresses is not enough, without some regard to the quantities of the unstressed syllables, to make well-sounding lines. But there I can't propose any rule, it is a matter of ear and rhythmic sense. A line made up of syllables like "many" or "easy" couldn't balance rhythmically with a line made up of syllables like "storm-bent," "oak-trees," though the number of stresses were the same.

Several modern poets, especially in England—Rupert Brooke for one— have caught Coleridge's and Bridges' thought, or found it out for themselves, but it seems to me that there remains "an infinite field of rhythm as yet untouched" or hardly touched. English is a language of very diverse and tolerably stable quantities besides being a strongly accented language, great and new things might be done with it if we had time and ear.

Thank you for your letter. Let us know if there's anything further you'd like to have spoken of.   Sincerely yours, Robinson Jeffers

183: TO H. ARTHUR KLEIN

La Fonda
Santa Fe, New Mexico
The Harvey Company
[June 11, 1930]

Dear Mr. Klein: Your letters have just reached us, in Taos, New Mexico,
and I'm very sorry for the delay in answering.

Our visit here was entirely unexpected; we'll be home before the end of
this month.

I believe this is the 11th; we expect to start homeward the 19th and arrive
about the 25th. Our address here is c/o Mrs. Mabel Luhan, Taos, N.M.

I remember with pleasure Jake Zeitlin's visit in Carmel.[6] You are free of
course to quote my letter in his publication and in the magazine article.
It was written hastily and most likely could be bettered by revision; if you'd
like to return it, or a copy, I'll look at it again.

But as to autographing the copies of the edition—no—I couldn't. It would
give the book the appearance of being a manifesto of my own and be a
little ridiculous, as if I wanted to start a "school" or something.
I'm sorry to refuse.

You have thought more about quantity than I have, and I agree perfectly
with the answers you suggest to your own questions. I suppose that even in
Latin and Greek the longs and shorts were more or less conventionalized
approximations, some longs much longer than others, some shorts
much shorter. It seems to me possible that a technician in English verse might
make elaborate lyrical measures [*The foregoing incomplete sentence has been
crossed out.*] Yes, I think it is all a matter of ear, in practise; and that
the quantity of the stressed syllables counts, of course, as of the
unstressed.

Thank you much for your study. Really I feel as if I ought to be
posthumous first—but that will come in course of time.

Of course you have noticed that (chiefly in my narrative poems) many
lines are of irregular length—"free" no doubt—as are many lines in
Elizabethan dramatic verse—but it seems to me there is a metrical pattern—
if only, at most irregular, as a background from which to measure
departures from the pattern.

—We wish you a most pleasant and profitable year abroad.   Sincerely
yours, Robinson Jeffers

---

[6] *The Los Angeles printer and bookseller whose poem "To Robinson Jeffers"
prompted Letter 240.*

184: TO MARY AUSTIN

La Fonda
Santa Fe, New Mexico
The Harvey Company
[*June 19, 1930*]

Dear Mary Austin: I had read the "American Rhythm" before, and now I
have read it through again, with admiration and pleasure—a great book—
though I confess that your part in it seems to me more important than
the songs you translate, though they are lovely. With the drum and the voice
these Indian songs are powerful—without them they are more like the
aspens we were admiring this afternoon on the mountain, lovely and gracious.
    And thank you for "The Flock." I've looked through it, enough to be
astonished that an author who knows so much about the subject could
so mould it into graceful form, but I've not read it yet, I'm saving it to read
aloud to the boys and Una.
    Thank you much, too, for the Penitente poem; it excited and pleased me.
You make them loveable. And you know them; better, some ways, than
they know themselves; it is you that ought to write the story and finish the
poem. We are so happy to have seen you, and now I'm afraid that we are
going back to California without being able to see you again—at present, I
mean, —for we'll return. We're probably going the northern way, and
must hurry, we've stayed as long as we possibly can away from home. A very
kind telegram reached me from Bynner yesterday, about his house. —And
for your kindness we're very grateful.
    We wish you—all four of us—a most interesting and successful journey
in Mexico. —As for us, our eyes are swimming in our heads with all the
sights and experiences that Mabel and Tony Lujan have been occupying us
with, this past fortnight, around Taos.   Yours, Robinson Jeffers

185: TO WITTER BYNNER

June 30, 1930

Dear Witter Bynner: You were very kind to telegraph the offer of your
house in Santa Fe; we couldn't stop there, but would have liked to if there had
been more time. Our hosts in Taos kept us occupied until the time when
it became quite impossible to stay away from home any longer—our
trees had to be watered or die—the children's bantams had to be reclaimed
from captivity—we had to look at the ocean again. It's a tremendous country
you have there, around Taos and Santa Fe, and I'm very glad to have

seen the northern end of it, and the southern at least in passing through. The Luhans took us to wild and beautiful places, and to villages (including the pueblo) where you feel much farther from the United States than ever we did last year in Ireland.

We were a funny caravan crossing the Mohave and Arizona on our way to Taos—the Luhans ahead in their Chrysler carrying our sons, and Una and I tagging along behind in the rusty 1926 Ford—which did bravely—over what roads! And the return trip—Una driving a great three-fathom-long Cadillac that the Luhans wanted taken to California—with one boy—I in the Ford with another. Imagine us under the red cliffs this side of Gallup. We had a good time.

I've owed you a letter then another. Forgive me. It was not my will that didn't answer—only my in-born imbecility as a correspondent. I was glad to receive word from you. If we should visit New Mexico again—it is just possible—I hope you'll let us see you. —Our love to the Fickes, if you are still near them, and to Edna Millay and Eugene Boissevain. Yours, Robinson Jeffers

186: TO H. ARTHUR KLEIN

[July 27, 1930]

Dear Mr. Klein: I appreciated your letter, and am sorry that I can't answer it just now as fully as it deserves—nor as promptly as I should have done—my mind is reluctant to leave the story that seems to be arranging itself since we got home. For the same reason, and since my first letter seems to suit your purpose tolerably well, I am returning without amendment the copies that you were good enough to send, with renewed permission to quote at pleasure. And you have permission to quote my verses, so far as my consent covers them. Horace Liveright Inc. has the copyright of the Tamar and Roan Stallion volume, and no doubt some claim on the later ones that they have published, I should think they will give you free permission if you have occasion to ask them. My verses in the American Miscellany, etc., are free to you.

Thank you for the further quotation from Bridges, I'll read it again later, with more attention, for of course it interests me.

You are probably right about Rupert Brooke, I spoke only from vague memory, and have just drawn a line through his name and two words on each side of it in the copy of my letter.

I'm so sorry we were away when you were in Carmel watering our plants! Come again. Meanwhile let me again wish you good luck on your travels, and with the language and a half.   Sincerely yours, Robinson Jeffers

187: TO H. L. DAVIS

[November, 1930]

Dear Davis: Forgive me for not answering you when I ought; it seems to be out of my power. I had a letter from [*Henry Allen*] Moe [*Guggenheim Foundation*], dated October 28, and answered as follows:

"Mr. Davis' work was first brought to my attention several years ago. The poems I saw then were in magazines, and impressed me so much that I tore out the pages to keep—a thing I haven't been tempted to since childhood—and have them still. Reading them again I find my admiration justified, and increased. I can think of no poetry that comes more especially and freshly from American soil, and I don't know of any modern poetry through which the actual unarranged country earth appears with such Virgilian sweetness.

On the other hand, these poems are not much concerned with this year's ideas and what is called "the American scene"; perhaps for that reason they are less well known than they deserve to be. For the same reason—and because they follow no school but are wholly original in manner— they do not grow old.

I have never met Mr. Davis; I exchanged some letters with him several years ago, and retain the impression of a vivid personality, promptness and energy, and an intense intellectual interest in Sophocles and the Divine Comedy. I have had favorable news of him from various people, —Carl Sandburg and others.

It seems to me that the subject Mr. Davis proposes to work on is excellently fitted to his genius and experience. There is no one whom I could recommend more sincerely or hopefully as deserving the [*fellowship?*] and likely to use it well."

I was glad to hear from you; surprised to hear from you in the desert. We were in New Mexico for six weeks last May and June, at Taos. It was very interesting but very sunny, and we were lonesome for the ocean. Yours, Robinson Jeffers

188: TO LAWRENCE CLARK POWELL

February, 1931

Dear Mr. Powell: You were very kind to send me your essay about my poetry, and I have acted—(not acted) very ungratefully. There are several reasons (but no excuse) for my negligence. I'm constitutionally unable to write a letter, besides a natural wish not to speak or hear or think about

past work, as it troubles the future. Then, your subtitle alarmed me—
"prophet"—but my chief fault was just postponement.

The article is excellently written, and I think excellently interprets what my verses meant to express. I agree with you in preferring Cawdor to the Shepherdess, I agree in practically all your literary judgments, except my natural reservation of opinion as to the merits of my own work, and in your philosophical judgments.

This was written a week ago and ought to have been sent off then, because there is really no more to say—by a person who can't talk about his own verses—except sincere thanks and appreciation. I kept thinking there was something more. Sometime you'll come back to California, no doubt, and I'll be very glad to see you if you should have time to visit this sea-cliff. Sincerely yours, Robinson Jeffers

—You ask about my next publication—not for awhile yet—next autumn I think. But Random House will be bringing out a little limited edition of some twenty short poems that I wrote in Ireland and England, in the meanwhile—three or four months from now—I just sent them the manuscript, fulfilling a promise made two years ago. —Ought I to return to you the manuscript of your essay?   Sincerely, R. J.

189: TO T. R. SMITH (Horace Liveright, Inc.)

February 11, 1931

Dear Mr. Smith: Thank you much for your kind telegram at New Year's, and for the beautifully done Marco Polo. And forgive me for not speaking sooner. I have been busy and unlucky with my verses, not wanting to take my mind off them for fear they'd flicker out—and they flickered out just the same, several times, but I expect everything will be all right now.

Let me congratulate you and the firm on your spring list of books. It is very fine. I hope the autumn one may announce one of mine.

Horace Liveright hasn't appeared here yet, but we are hoping a visit from him soon.   Sincerely yours, Robinson Jeffers

190: TO BABETTE DEUTSCH

February 11, 1931

Dear Babette Deutsch: "Epistle to Prometheus" arrived several days ago, and I hoped to have written you something about it before this. It seems to me a splendid poem. Within a week or less I'll send you a talk about it, which could appear as a review if you know where to publish it. I know nobody.

—Except that Suzanne La Follette wrote to me lately asking for verses for the New Freeman, or an article about poetry. I can send neither, but have just written that I'll send a nice review of your book if she wants.

Perhaps I've done wrong and you'd rather see to its placing yourself. Or perhaps she doesn't want my review. Meanwhile I'll send it to you as soon as I can.

Please take the trouble to thank your publishers for me, for sending the proofs.   Sincerely, Robinson Jeffers

191: TO BABETTE DEUTSCH

March 4, 1931

Dear Miss Deutsch: Here is the review;[7] I've been keeping it awhile hoping to make it better, but time passes. Suzanne La Follette says she will print it as soon as the book is published, and I am sending her a cleaner copy than this. She asks that your publishers credit the New Freeman if they should use the review—I'll enclose her letter, don't bother to return it.

My wife enjoyed your review of Yeats' [*Una has corrected J's error* " 'The Tower' " *to* " 'The Winding Stair' "] and gives me a picture of it to send you, which she took when we were in Ireland a year and a half ago. The place was as beautiful and lonely as it ought to be. Yeats wasn't there; nobody was, all the shutters up, so we could wander around freely. I'd like to go back there sometime, it was very lovely.   Yours, Robinson Jeffers

192: TO SELDEN RODMAN

June, 1931

Dear Mr. Rodman: It is absurdly impossible for me to get a letter written, and I'm sorry; it is my only reason for not answering you sooner. The same misfortune has prevented me from thanking your friend Dwight Macdonald who sent me copies of the "Miscellany." If you see him, please tell him that I thank him sincerely, and appreciated his articles; they were very well done.[8]

Your poem, "Departure," I have read with much interest, and more than once. It is splendid in the power with which it gathers many impulses and scenes and thoughts into the rush of one stream; and the rhythmic power of

---

[7] *"The Stubborn Savior," New Freeman, III (March 25, 1931), 43; reprinted in Alberts, A Bibliography, pp. 151–53.*
[8] *Dwight Macdonald, "Robinson Jeffers," Miscellany, I (July, September, 1930), 1–10, 1–24.*

your verses supports the lyrical energy. The thoughts are not always clear through the speed of the stream; some of them are perhaps too personal, and some imperfectly realized perhaps; so that the impression of the whole has not the definition that your later work will achieve. In reading I was unlucky enough to think of De la Mare's line—"Is there anybody there, said the traveller." The similarity is probably of accident rather than reminiscence, and matters very little, but is unfortunate in its small degree because the poems are so unlike in nature.

Now I've been as critical as possible, and have only to thank you for sending me the poem. I enjoyed it much; and was interested in some of the other things in the Review.[9]   Sincerely, Robinson Jeffers

193: TO DONALD FRIEDE

August 20, 1931

Dear Donald Friede: I'm sorry not to have answered more promptly. Your proposal rather tempted me, (although there was clearly too much of it) and I took a few days to think it over, and then a few more days because it is almost impossible for me to sit down and answer a letter.

It was kind of you to think of it, but I can see that I haven't any time for translation. And I'm afraid the majority of Greek tragedies would make tiresome reading, some of them must have been dull even to their authors.

I'd like to have seen you when we came home from Ireland, but we weren't in New York long enough to see anybody. I expect it will be two or three years before we go again; maybe you'll be in California sometime? I'd love to take you a drive along our twisty coast-road, as I did Horace Liveright when he visited us a couple of months ago.   Sincerely yours,
Robinson Jeffers

194: LAWRENCE CLARK POWELL TO J

14, rue du Petit Potet
Dijon, (Côte-d'Or) France
11 Juillet 1931

Dear Mr. Jeffers: Thank you for your kind and encouraging letter of February. I am enclosing a note on an aspect of your poetry which seems to me to be important. There are many things in it which are yet to be

[9] The Harkness Hoot, *founded and co-edited by Rodman at Yale.*

". . . I'm set here like a stone in cement."

(Letter 115)

developed, others may be downright false, and others still are puzzling to me. Please accept it as a tentative essay only. I have left *Californians* untreated, because, having been unable to secure a copy, I have had a friend copy the contents from his volume, and as yet I have not received all of the poems.

Although you wrote me that you do not wish to discuss your poetry, I cannot help from asking you a question or two, the answers to which would help considerably in illumining the path of my work.

Am I right in inferring that you have studied Freud and kindred dream investigators, and that their work has a relation to your increasing interest in dreams? And could I say that your use of incest as a symbol is connected with the marked attention to dreams manifested in your poetry since the war?

In Tamar's dream of the procession of races through the Carmel country, and in 'the ancestral forms' that—'since Barclay was gone'—prelude Vasquez' visions, are you referring to racial memories to which the individual, in his dreams, is heir, in the same way that many adult dreams stem from childhood experience?

On page 10 of my paper, am I correct in postulating Vasquez as a symbol? And is it perhaps his 'careful chastity of mind,' his 'I have kept myself virgin for the sake of my visions,' etc., that make him and those whom he may symbolize, impotent in relation to life? Thus he might be the other extreme from Barclay and his flaming disciples and the Dionysos cult in *The Humanist's Tragedy*, etc., who, by their complete abandon bring destruction on themselves and society in general. Therefore the golden mean—the 'nothing in excess' of the Greeks—may be man's only salvation. Along this same line, is one justified in comparing Vasquez with Jesus?

In the enclosed paper I have spoken of a concept of Time which seems to be inherent in your poetry: may I ask you, is there any contradiction between your concept and the Oriental teaching of the static quality of Time which Western science now appears to be endorsing (I refer in particular to *An Experiment with Time* by J. W. Dunne, as well as to Ouspensky and others), which is called in India the Eternal Now, in which past, present and future are One?

The conclusion of Orestes, his 'extraversion'—'I was the darkness outside the stars, I included them, they were a part of me, I was mankind also . . .', and among other instances, the thought of section IV, *Apology for Bad Dreams:* is this not something akin to a part of Buddhistic thought which says, Could we but see it rightly, we are not our *selves,* not living entities around and about which an alien universal life whirls in never-ending phantom-series; *we are that life,* and more than we shall ever come to know whilst we remain immersed in this all-undermining dream of Selfhood? Man should seek to free himself from self-love, self-desire ('self' meaning humanity as well) and to attain to 'the motionless and timeless

center,' an exact description of which is impossible, for, with Orestes—
and in the different phrasing of certain Oriental teachings—'they have
not made words for it.'

Believe me, sir, I am not seeking to fabricate a 'system' out of your poetry,
nor do I wish to gather a list of 'influences.' It is only that there seems to
be a few more or less absolute riddles around which, thinking man ultimately
arrives—the three-fold problem—metaphysical, spiritual and moral—
which Barclay mentions in the first of the poem.

I meant to ask you only about the dreams and Freud; but it seems almost
impossible to separate them from the problems of Time and Being, and
so my letter has assumed rather large proportions.

My work to date has been accepted by the Université of Dijon; in another
year I hope to have the thesis finished. Again, may I thank you for your
letter, and when in California, may I accept your kind invitation to
come and see you?

In conclusion, any help which you may be able to give me on the above
questions will be deeply appreciated. I am   Yours sincerely,
The letter is an unsigned, typed copy.

195: TO LAWRENCE CLARK POWELL

September, 1931
[Postmarked October 6, 1931]

Dear Mr. Powell: I am very sorry not to have answered sooner. Your study
is most interesting and well thought—I could say scholarly too if you
were writing about a dead author's work.

Your questions: Yes, I read—one could hardly say studied—several books
of and about Freud and Jung, and found the first one rather ridiculous,
but changed my mind. That was probably in 1914 or so. I still think that
Freud pioneered a new sort of knowledge, however limited or fanciful its later
developments. The use of incest as a symbol is no doubt connected with
those dream-studies, but I think an earlier reading of Shelley and Byron had
something to do with it. In "Manfred," and "The Cenci" it is only a sin,
but elsewhere in Shelley's poetry it seems to be a more or less conscious
symbol of human love, reckless and comprehensive, (as in "Laon
and Cythna").

About the racial memories in Tamar's dream and Vasquez's visions I know
but little. Images and thoughts come to a writer's mind, and those that
seem not too inappropriate to the story are let into it.

This was begun a good while ago and has been lying around.
I'll try to finish.

I shouldn't like to generalize on the subject of Vasquez's chastity resulting in impotence in relation to life: a good deduction, but not universal. His fear of any thought that might threaten it, would be sterilizing certainly. —The "golden mean" is certainly the best counsel: I shouldn't say "man's only salvation"—there are many salvations—(if any)—as Blake wrote "If the fool would persist in his folly he would become wise."

The idea of Time as another dimension of space is familiar of course to modern mathematics. I read and was much interested in Dunne's "Experiment with Time," but have never found satisfactory verification, in my own experience at least. But it seems most reasonable that the future is there already.

I feel for much in Oriental thought, though I don't enjoy reading any Oriental book except the bible. But the Indian feeling that the world is illusory and the soul—the I—makes it, is very foreign to me. The world seems to me immeasurably more real. Am I wrong in thinking that the Oriental mystic identifies the world with himself, and my "Orestes" identified himself with the world? The former imposes a human mind on an imaginary world—attributes to it his own "love," for instance, or desire of love; the latter let in the inhuman mind of the world (Deus sive natura—Spinoza's phrase) to obliterate his human one.

Looking again at your "Study," it seems to me that my answers, as above, are rather oblique and unsatisfactory. I am always occupied with new work, and my recollections of the thoughts in former poems must be very imperfect, without the expenditure of more attention than I have time for now. *En effet,* I imagine that you know more about them than I do. Certainly I have nothing to take exception to in your "Study"; it is most intelligent, and flatteringly attentive.

Let me wish you good luck, and thank you sincerely for sending me the copy. I'll try to answer more promptly if you write again.   Sincerely yours, Robinson Jeffers

196: TO WITTER BYNNER

October, 1931
[*Postmarked November 2, 1931*]

Dear Witter Bynner: I am very sorry not to have written sooner. It is constitutional.

Thank you very much for sending me "Eden-Tree." I read it with admiration for its continuity, its courage, the pageant of varied scenery and the splendid lines. A fine summing up of experience. "Indian Earth" was a beautiful book too. I appreciated especially the Mexican poems, the ones of Chapala, like Greek epigrams.

Something interrupted me, and now I see this paper has lain so long that it is covered with dust and ashes, so I'll send it off before worse happens to it. Think of me as one of those friendly natural objects like a tree outside the window, that hasn't much means of communication but all it has is well intended.   Sincerely, Robinson Jeffers

197: TO T. R. SMITH

November 18, 1931

Dear Mr. Smith: I am not at all satisfied to wait nearly a year from now before the publication of "Thurso's Landing"; that would be three years between books, for "Descent to the Dead" is not more than a pamphlet in length.

I want "Thurso's Landing" to be published promptly, partly because it seems to me the best thing I have written yet and I don't want it lying around so long; partly because too long a vacation is not good advertising; my income has been cut a little, like other people's, while taxes increase.

So let me suggest you publish "Thurso's Landing" in the spring, without the shorter narrative poems, which might distract attention from it, but with a dozen short poems of a page or so each. "Thurso's Landing" is 127 pages of typewriting, and with the short poems would make a book considerably longer than the "Dear Judas" volume.

In the fall you would be free to publish "Descent to the Dead," with "Resurrection," "Margrave," and a longer narrative poem that I would have ready by that time. This again would make a book longer than the "Dear Judas" volume.

But if you prefer not to undertake a book of mine for next spring, I think you should agree to my putting "Thurso's Landing" at least in other hands. It oughtn't to be held up so long, and I have reason to think I could place it quickly. I'd be sorry, but it seems unfair to delay it excessively.

Please let me hear from you on this subject as soon as you can conveniently.

Thank you very much for "Mourning Becomes Electra." I have of course the greatest admiration for Eugene O'Neill, and shall read eagerly. Sincerely yours, Robinson Jeffers

P. S. I know the market is bad, and probably will be next spring, but you will have a spring list just the same. Best wishes.   R. J.

198: TO T. R. SMITH

December 2, 1931

Dear Mr. Smith: Thank you for your most obliging letter, which came yesterday, and for the check in advance of royalties. The latter was not really needed quite yet, but was kindly thought, and it would seem an affectation to return it.

I will send you the manuscript in a week or less, and hope you'll have good luck with it sometime next spring.

As for the other, (Descent to the Dead) I signed the pages quite a while ago, and surely it will be out before the end of this month, but anyhow soon enough for our use in the fall.

O'Neill's Electra is very fine, his greatest play, and therefore no doubt the greatest of our time. Thank you again for sending it.

My recent letter seems to me to have been a little petulant, in view of your kindness, but I do think it is wiser to publish "Thurso's Landing" in the spring, and shall send it on in a few days.   Sincerely, Robinson Jeffers

199: TO FREDERIC PROKOSCH

December [22], 1931

Dear Mr. Prokosch: Thank you truly for sending me the copy of "A Passenger to Asia." The poems and pictures too have a visionary beauty, and bear witness to real talents. It was kind of you to give me this one copy out of three.   Sincerely, Robinson Jeffers

200: TO FREDERIC IVES CARPENTER

December [22], 1931

Dear Mr. Carpenter: I am a bad letter-writer, and should have thanked you more promptly for sending me your pamphlet on Jonathan Edwards.[10] I read it with much interest, and some profit, learning things that were new to me, and feeling a new sympathy toward your subject. Your references to my verses were both kindly and discerning, but thank you also for the whole essay.   Sincerely, Robinson Jeffers

[10] *"The Radicalism of Jonathan Edwards,"* New England Quarterly, *IV (October, 1931), 629–44.*

201: TO ALBERT BENDER

[*January 8, 1932*]

Dear Albert: //I was delighted that you like the verses in "Descent to the Dead." Every word of them was written in Ireland or England; they were so long in being published because I was saving them to go in a book for Liveright to publish with other poems; but as that book didn't get finished as soon as I expected, and Random House asked again for the little volume I had promised, Una thought these would make a nice little volume for them, so I sent them in finally. When Liveright reprints them I shall add a shortish narrative poem called "Resurrection" that I wrote soon after we got back from abroad.

Meanwhile I sent Liveright two or three weeks ago the manuscript of a long narrative poem called "Thurso's Landing," and some shorter things with it.

Spencer Mackey was here the other day with Hans and Phoebe Barkan. He said he was to have driven you down this way lately, but it hadn't been possible for some reason. We hope it may happen yet, for we liked him much, and would be very glad of a visit from *you*,—but that doesn't need saying.

Guess what Una and I do often, when we have time, and so do the boys. —We get out the diary of our Irish pilgrimage and read it for pleasure. We had such a nice time. No doubt we shall go again, probably two and a half years from now, when the boys graduate from high school. They will still be young enough for a year's vacation between that and college.// With love from us all, and hope to see you sometime soon, Robin

202: UNA J TO LAWRENCE CLARK POWELL
See also Letter 293.

January 27, 1932

Dear Mr. Powell: Writing for Robinson Jeffers who is too busy for letters just at the moment but begins to feel an answer to yours weighing on his conscience. I will reply to your questions. He says in regard to punctuation He places his marks to indicate if possible how the lines should be spoken with regard to rhythm and expression with no conscious thought of grammatical divisions.

He believes the judgment of his publishers should be regarded in the matter of number of volumes printed. He has no idea how many without going into elaborate calculations.

He knew in Los Angeles John Stephen McGroarty (author of the Mission Play used annually in Mission Festivals at San Gabriel chiefly). McGroarty was affiliated with Grafton Co. and that is how "Flagons and Apples" came into their hands.[11]

No reason at all for Macmillan except that he submitted his ms. to them as to a well-know[n] publishing co. and it was accepted. Several years after "Californians" he submitted ms. to some other publishing co (he can't remember which) and it was rejected.[12] When he had finished "Tamar" he did not send it to anyone but decided to get it printed himself as cheaply as could be done decently and happened to notice the advertisement of Peter Boyle in the N. Y. Times. Mr. Boyle took a great interest in this poem and as soon as he had read it wrote with great enthusiasm. After it had been printed and had made a "stir" Boyle brought it to the notice of Boni and Liveright who immediately negotiated for the right to it and to any other material R. J. might have on hand. Peter Boyle wrote also and said if Liveright did not take it he would like to republish it in better form at his own expense that time. —We have never met Mr. Boyle but our relations with him were most pleasant and he gave us in his letters the impression of an "original" and a warm lover of literature. I believe he retired soon after our connection with him and business was to be taken over by his son. I do not know whether he is living.—

[See Una's genealogical chart on the facing page.]

Consult "Descendents of W^m and Eliz. Tuttle who came from old to New England in 1635 and settled in New Haven 1639" by Geo. Fred Tuttle. pub by Tuttle and Co. official State Printers, Rutland, Vermont and "Fragments of Family and Contemporary History" by T. H. R. Pittsburgh, Printed by Bakewell and Marthens 1867 and "Thomas Robinson and his descendents" by Thomas Hastings Robinson Harrisburg Pub. Co. Harrisburg, Pa.

Yale Univ. is built on the old Tuttle Estate.

Philip Robinson (son of Thomas) born about 1698 came to Pennsylvania from the North of Ireland before 1730. His name appears on the first tax list of Hanover Township, Lancaster Co (now Dauphin Co.). His father had first settled near Conewago Creek farther east. A fort "Robinson Fort" on his farm defence against Indians.

Scotch Irish from North of Ireland. Calvinist.

McCords from Skye, Argyleshire, Scotland originally

Jeffers from Co. Monaghan, Ireland. Joseph Jeffers father of Wm Hamilton Jeffers came over. He was married in America. Think he settled first in Ohio.

Rosenberg—a German from the Palatinate who fought in the Revolution.

Robinson Jeffers never considered becoming a minister. The family moved to Pasadena as to a warm climate for his fathers old age. Lived in Highland Park a suburb of Los Angeles while attending Occidental. On Shatto street, L.A. and at Hermosa Beach while attending U.S.C.

[11] *See Letters 2, 4, and 5.*
[12] *See Bennett,* Stone Mason, *p. 103.*

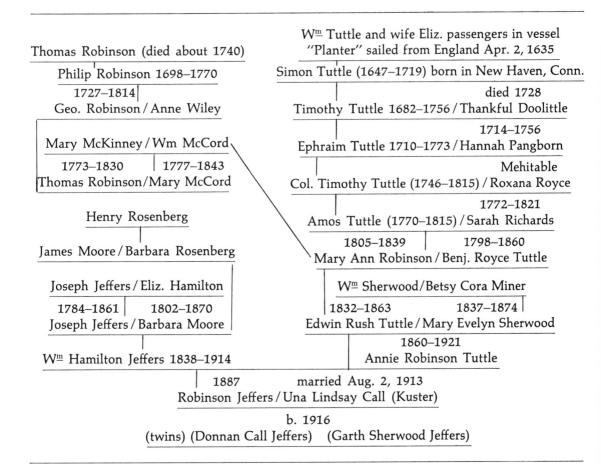

Thomas Robinson (died about 1740)

Philip Robinson 1698–1770

1727–1814
Geo. Robinson / Anne Wiley

Mary McKinney / Wm McCord

1773–1830   1777–1843
Thomas Robinson / Mary McCord

Henry Rosenberg

James Moore / Barbara Rosenberg

Joseph Jeffers / Eliz. Hamilton

1784–1861   1802–1870
Joseph Jeffers / Barbara Moore

Wᵐ Hamilton Jeffers 1838–1914

Wᵐ Tuttle and wife Eliz. passengers in vessel
"Planter" sailed from England Apr. 2, 1635

Simon Tuttle (1647–1719) born in New Haven, Conn.

died 1728
Timothy Tuttle 1682–1756 / Thankful Doolittle

1714–1756
Ephraim Tuttle 1710–1773 / Hannah Pangborn

Mehitable
Col. Timothy Tuttle (1746–1815) / Roxana Royce

1772–1821
Amos Tuttle (1770–1815) / Sarah Richards

1805–1839   1798–1860
Mary Ann Robinson / Benj. Royce Tuttle

Wᵐ Sherwood / Betsy Cora Miner

1832–1863   1837–1874
Edwin Rush Tuttle / Mary Evelyn Sherwood

1860–1921
Annie Robinson Tuttle

1887   married Aug. 2, 1913
Robinson Jeffers / Una Lindsay Call (Kuster)

b. 1916
(twins) (Donnan Call Jeffers)   (Garth Sherwood Jeffers)

The family all were in Seattle, Wash. for a year. Later I was with him there for another nine months.

In Hermosa Beach off and on at intervals from 1905–1912

His brother did preparatory school work in Switzerland and Germany. (Geneva, Lausanne, Zurich, Leipsig)

I took him to Europe the last time—he says thats the only reason. Very sincerely, Una Jeffers

I shall be glad to answer any further questions.

Your friend Harry [*Ward*] Ritchie called ten days ago with interesting talk of people and his work.   U. J.

He has promised Colophon to write a short article on his first book (which he regards as *Tamar*) It will perhaps be in the next number, if I can hold him to it.

203: TO MARY DWYER

March, 1932

My Dear Miss Dwyer: Thank you sincerely for your kind little letter.
—Which of my books best pleases me? None pleases me very much. The
Roan Stallion volume seems the most various, and more distant from
me than later ones. —If I were condemned to read any I should read that
one.   Cordially, Robinson Jeffers

204: TO HARRIET MONROE

March, 1932

Dear Miss Monroe: Thank you much for your letters and suggestions.
I hope to hear from you soon as to whether H. L. Davis may expect the
Guggenheim award this year. If he is to receive it, as you and I hope, might
I trouble you to send me books of Louise Bogan and one or two (or three)
others of the candidates [*for the Sears award*] you have in mind? I am so
seriously ignorant of recent poetry. I'll read and return carefully.
     A friend of ours here speaks of living next door to Louise Bogan a year or
two ago—I think at Groton, N.Y.—and does not believe her to be in need.
But of course many people's circumstances have changed, the past year.
     Mr. [*David*] McCord sent me Margaret McGovern's book, and I do not
altogether agree with your judgment about it, but must hear further
comparisons before forming one of my own.
     Do you know any thing about a woman who writes under the name Clinch
Calkins? I do not, except that a few short poems of hers, seen in the
"Nation" and elsewhere, impressed me enough to make me feel that her name
ought to be mentioned to you and Mr. McCord, on the chance that
either of you knows more about her than I do.
     This letter, and one of similar purport to Mr. McCord, seem to be all I can
contribute to our affair at present. If you'll be kind enough to lend me the
two or three books I spoke of, and will let me know about Davis, and
any further suggestions you may think of, I expect we can come to a decision
very shortly, whether unanimous or not.
     We are very lucky to have your wide acquaintance with recent poetry in
the committee.   Yours, Robinson Jeffers

March 27, 1932

Dear Miss Monroe: Thank you very much for sending me the books. I have
read them all with a good deal of attention, and am returning them with
this. Roy Helton's work, and Maurice Lesemann's earliest poems, seem to
me—(and to Mrs. Jeffers reading independently)—quite the best in the lot. I
cannot get along well with the others: and of Lesemann's I am sorry to
feel that the earliest poems are the best, and the latest the worst in steady
progression. He saw things, at first, rather intensely; now he seems to be
only sitting and thinking, discursively, on a subject of no emotional
importance. We hope he will return to his own again, but meanwhile I don't
think I could vote for him.

And I should sooner vote for Miss McGovern than for Louise Bogan. The
former has had experiences which have moved her and which she tries to
express—often awkwardly—inarticulately—but sometimes she gets it over.
But Miss Bogan seems to me to be just writing poetry, with a good deal of
talent, but without any particular significance.

Roy Helton's work seems to me excellent, and I should be glad to vote for
him, if we had any assurance of his "need"—that is, of his being more in
need than most other people. How could one get that? His notice in "Who's
Who" looks as professionally compe[ti]tive as others.

Fletcher I couldn't vote for, though I know the weight of past opinion is in
his favor. T. S. Eliot seems to me not an American poet, but almost the
only interesting English one,—since Yeats is Irish—and I don't think
the testator, nor most other people, would regard him as American. And I
don't suppose he's—Don't you wish Shelley would knock at the door,
disinherited and starving and recognizably aureoled? [*The interrupting
sentence here has been crossed out.*] particularly in need.

You didn't answer about Clinch Calkins. Perhaps it was not worth while.
My wife says she published a book within the past year or two, but
we haven't seen it.

I haven't heard from Mr. McCord since his first letter. I am sorry not to be
able to say anything definite yet. As far as my enlightenment reaches at
present, I should favor Roy Helton if he were shown to be a special
need.   Sincerely, Robinson Jeffers

OVERLEAF:

"... the only way to become normal again will be to stay at
home as quietly as possible and feel the hills and the sea."

(*Letter 360*)

Juniper Road
Belmont, Massachusetts
January 19, 1932

Dear Mr. Jeffers: —Thank you for your letter about the Jonathan Edwards
article which I sent you. I had not expected one, but now, may I write
to ask concerning your poetry?

—The reason:—There is a book to be called sometime "The American
Idea,"[13] in the back of my mind. The book should attempt an interpretation
of American life and literature in terms of a key idea—namely, *energy*.
—This idea to be differentiated from the European idea of *time*. The problem
is to show how American life and literature have progressively tended to
realize the concept of *energy*—how America has gone one dimension beyond
Europe, so to speak, and worked out the idea of *energy* in all its implications—
physical, mechanical, and human. Your poetry seems to me to represent
the climax of this realization, as expressed in literature.

If all this is false, I'm sorry; but recently re-reading your *Women at Point
Sur* has strengthened my impression. For instance, your Barclay says:
"then I raged against time" (in the past), (but now) ". . . all this energy to
waste? . . . Certainly I shall put out my hands and touch power." —All
the physical imagery in the prologue, too, bears out the idea. The whole poem
seems to me a presentation in artistic symbols of the physical concept of
energy—("the strain, the strain," "stored force," etc.)

—Am I reading something into it not meant to be there? Had you at all
definitely the idea of correlating physical concepts with human actions
in the poem? Again, do you use the word "action" with any implication of its
technical (physical) significance? (as in "God thinks through action.")

Besides all these questions (already too many) there are others of another
sort. Where would you put your poetry in the scheme of American literature,
which I have tentatively projected?—under the heading of "Titanism,"
with Melville, Mark Twain (!) and Henry Adams and E. Hemingway; or
under the heading of "Salvation through Passion" (i. e. suffering) with
Eugene O'Neill, Connelly's "Green Pastures," and (perhaps) E. A. Robinson?
Does your philosophy reject "salvation" (with D. H. Lawrence, for
instance)—and does Barclay speak for it saying "I not his son take him by
violence" ("Titanism"). Or do your characters speak and act only
dramatically, and do you say "Imagined victims *our* salvation."? Is it possible

[13] *See Letters 238, 269, and 312. The theme for this proposed book persists in Carpenter's
evaluation of J's place in American literature in Chapter 5 of his* Robinson Jeffers.

to "fall in love outward" without hating inward first? Do you exaggerate
your emphasis to right the balance, and to force the realization
of the old error?

Or is your whole scheme of tragedies a necessary mold for the expression
of the physical idea of *energy?* —Because hate breeds energy perhaps
more than love, pain more than pleasure. Are all your themes imagined
chiefly to develop "the strain," —to store "the force," with the consequent
violent discharge causing tragedy—the breaking up of the human atom—
the discovery of the ultimate "action" of God? And so, is all this about
"salvation" necessary physical symbolism of your dramatic pieces, and the
conscious explanation of your purpose, as in your "Apology for Bad Dreams."
—Why "apology"? Is this dualism necessary to the American mind—
even yours? Is "law for man" separate from "law for thing" after all?

Please excuse the undue length and frankness of these questions. Your
poetry and your letter induced them. I am trying to gain "energy to
hear effectively," I suppose.   Sincerely, Frederic I. Carpenter

207: TO FREDERIC IVES CARPENTER

March 31, 1932

Dear Mr. Carpenter: Your letter was dated January 19, and you have
probably forgotten writing it. I am sorry not to have answered sooner. The
thesis of the book "at the back of your mind" is most interesting—American
idea *energy*—European, *time*—and looks defensible, though I have not yet
thought about it intelligently enough to speak with much confidence. And per
contra, I think of Arthur Symons writing about Balzac—the "invariable
problem" of his novels—"Man has a given quantity of energy; each man a
different quantity; how will he spend it?" And "Balzac's sentiment of the
supreme value of energy . . ." I had better answer your questions rather than
talk further on a subject that I haven't sufficiently considered.

In "The Women at Pt. Sur" had I "the idea of correlating physical concepts
with human actions?" —Yes. I was thinking of human and non-human as
one substance—or energy!—different (not very different) manifestations of
the same thing. (I am afraid the poem called "Margrave" in my latest
book exaggerates the difference. From that point of view it is just a poem.
I was irritated into extravagance by the excessive value that people seem
to attribute to human consciousness.)

"God thinks through action." Yes, I meant physical action—the lifting of a
hill, and hollowing of sea-beds; the method of "trial and error" in
origin of species, etc.

"Imagined victims our salvation" I think represented two strains of thought—(1) There was a time when human sacrifice was needed to save the people; then a sheep could be substituted, or some kind of Guy Fawkes image. Or an imagined victim in a story, suffering things we all feel liable to but hope to escape. Wasn't this one of the perhaps conscious functions of Greek tragedy? (2) More practically, we endow a person in a story with certain excesses of thought or passion and see what their logic leads to, and are thus perhaps warned ourselves, so he suffers instead of us.

So there might be "salvation through" vicarious "passion."

I shouldn't think of myself among the Titanists. I don't murmur against God, perhaps I do too much against man sometimes.

I think it is quite possible to "fall in love outward" without hating inward. It seems to me the Jesus of the gospels, perhaps, and many mystics have done so. But it is hard if not impossible to make a poem about it; without some hate to balance the love—like painting all in white, with no shadows. As you say, hate perhaps more than love breeds energy; certainly pain more than pleasure makes explosions of energy, though of course it burns it up sooner.

I think one of the most common intentions in tragic stories, from the Oedipus down, is to build up a strain for the sake of the explosion of its release,—like winding up a ballista.

"Apology"—defense—as "Apologia pro vita sua"—not necessarily apologetic.

I shouldn't think of "Law for men" and "law for thing" as separate. Different, as "law for leaf" and "law for stone" are different, but quite the same laws after all. But one is always led into exaggeration, emphasizing a view-point, or for dramatic or poetic purposes.

Your letter interested me much, and I wish my answers were more complete and clear, and had been more prompt.   Sincerely, Robinson Jeffers

208: TO JIM TULLY

April, 1932

Dear Jim Tully: I admire your work and value your opinion. If you paste this scrap into a book, as you threaten, then I'll have a hand in one of your books, which will please me well.

—I hear there's all sorts of symbolism in "Thurso's Landing." —There isn't. The rock and the cable and lime-kilns are twenty-five miles south of here, and I just made up a story about them.[14]   Sincerely, Robinson Jeffers

209: HARRIET MONROE TO J

March 31, 1932

My dear Mr. Jeffers: I confess to depression over your letter . . . . nothing could induce me to base on [*McGovern's book*] any kind of an award.

As for the others mentioned in your letter:

I think Lesemann has size and Miss Bogan depth, and both show impassioned feeling, and achieve beauty to a remarkable degree.

Noctiflora, in Lesemann's latest group, seems to me one of his best and most impassioned poems, and one of the finest poems written by anybody in recent years. And *Sheepherders*, in an earlier group, seems to me amazing in its presentation of great waste spaces and man's loneliness in them. (Also, I know of this poet's "need.")

Of Miss Bogan's very distinguished work, I will merely enclose, with enthusiastic endorsement, my associate's review of her latest book, *Dark Summer.*//

Roy Helton is much older than these, and his work seems to me less interesting than any of the others on my list except perhaps Mr. Corning. Still, he is leagues ahead of Miss McGovern.

Of the "need" of these people, I can speak with complete knowledge only of Mr. Lesemann. Miss Bogan (Mrs. Raymond Holden) is the wife of a small-salaried man; her own income has always been extremely meagre and she is in frail health. Mr. Helton is a 46-year-old-schoolteacher, which doesn't sound affluent. I don't think "need" should mean actual starvation.

You don't mention Kunitz, whom I shd rank after Bogan and Lesemann but ahead of Helton.   Yours sincerely, HM

[14] *This letter accompanied a presentation copy of* Thurso's Landing and Other Poems. *The June 14, 1932, letter to Alberts in his* A Bibliography, *p. 72, describes Bixby's Landing (renamed "Thurso's"): "A promontory of the coast thirty miles south of Monterey is called Bixby's Landing. The cable for carrying lime from the kilns far up the gorge, and a heavy iron skip stuck midway, were still hanging between the headland and the hill when we first saw the place in 1914. Re-visiting it many years later, we found a pair of duck hawks nesting under the headland cliff."*

210: TO HARRIET MONROE

April 11, 1932

Dear Miss Monroe: "Noctiflora" looks better on a second reading, though I cannot feel that it is up to the work set by Lesemann's earliest contributions in Poetry. I have been thinking seriously about our selection, and have talked to a few friends, two of whom suggested Lola Ridge. I'm not an enthusiast for her work, but "Firehead" was much admired, I believe she was ill and poor when it was being written, and no doubt she is still in need. What do you think of her?

The result of all my thought is not very enlightening. I am writing to you and Mr. McCord to say that I should be glad to vote for any one of four that you can agree on: Lola Ridge—Archibald MacLeish—Lesemann—Roy Helton—not named in order of preference. If you can't agree, and the casting-vote is left to me I'll vote for MacLeish, who perhaps has something more like "genius" than anyone else in the list, and is probably in need or he wouldn't be working for "Fortune" magazine.

—That is, I'll choose MacLeish unless further important names or arguments are produced.

I have told Mr. McCord that I couldn't vote for Miss McGovern, though I still like her book. It is true that what it has of originality seems to spring mostly from that one experience.

It will be nice to have this business settled.

Mrs. Jeffers and I admired the dignity and justice of your editorial in the April "Poetry." Thank you for sending it. And thank you again for lending me the books; I hope they have arrived safely.   Cordially, Robinson Jeffers

211: UNA J TO LAWRENCE CLARK POWELL

April 15, 1932

Dear Mr. Powell—   I wish I had time to do a more interesting map but you can get what you want from this perhaps.

"Roan Stallion" was thought of as in Robinson Cañon.

The log cabin of "The Women at Pt. Sur" R. J. moved from the entrance of Palo Colorado to near Pt. Sur. This is a very old two-storied log house very noticeable as a landmark.

"Cawdor" isn't definitely located but thought of as near Little Sur and Mill Creek. Somewhere between.[15]

Woven all through his poems are scattered bits of old legends of the country. I cannot now go into detail because of lack of time, but I will mention a few. "Fawn's Foster-Mother" *true*, told us by an old woman who kept the toll-gate into Del Monte Forest about herself.[16]

In the "Shepherdess"—"he'd ride the furrows at a dead run sowing the grain with both hands"—exactly as we heard of a rancher down there. In "Roan Stallion," California going for the child's toy's [*toys*] and the river rising—that happened to a *native* (Indian-Mexican) girl here who married a Dutchman remittance man—"Love-Children"—one of the group in Untermeyer's "Miscellany of American Poetry 1927" was taken over from an old story here of a couple up near Cachagua—He located the story in his poem below Big Sur.

We were walking up San José Creek one day and came on an abandoned house with some calla lilies growing beside it. It had a desolate tragic look. I found out a man had been killed there years ago by his stallion and the house left empty since—R. J. thus got the *germ* of "Roan St—"

In "Dead Man's Child" the location of Tinajas altas is well known for the deaths which have occurred there—people coming across the desert to this spot for a few drops of water in these stone hollows and finding them as often empty. —The idea of the impregnating dust came from an old legend told in a footnote to Sir Walter Scott's Lady of the Lake. —also the "Loving Shepherdess"—arose from a footnote to Scott's "The Heart of Midlothian"—telling of a girl named Feckless Fannie wandering all over Scotland with her sheep—.

Onorio Vasquez who comes into several of the stories was drawn at the first from a man down the Coast we knew slightly.

In "The Coast Range Christ" O'Farrell the man who dug for the lost silver mine, once worked by the Indians, who hung himself—he was an old inhabitant here. In "Apology for Bad Dreams" the woman who tied up the horse to the tree to lash, with the chain around its tongue—*she* was real and she did just that. (*And* this isnt in the poem we heard later she was killed by one of her horses falling on her as they were crossing a stream. Pinioned her in the water!)

---

[15] *Una's postcard to Powell, dated May 23, 1932, corroborates his hunch that "Cawdor" is set "North of Mill Creek bridge." She also assures him that " 'Manvil's Landing' is Notleys." A letter dated September 13, 1933, informs him further: "Yes, Fraser's Point is Pfeiffer's, reached by going down Sycamore creek, see map." Powell constructed a "Map of the Carmel Coast" from such information; see p. 85 of his* Robinson Jeffers.

[16] *See Letter 14.*

"Continent's End" was published by the "Book Club of San Francisco" a club of wealthy book lovers who issue a few times a year a very *de luxe* edition. They asked Taggard, Sterling and Rorty to edit a book of California poets (or connected somehow with Calif.) Robinson Jeffers contributed a group and one of his poems was chosen for the title of the book.

Yes you may quote from my letters. Kindly edit them if necessary I am always in such a passion of haste.   Very sincerely Una Jeffers

I wish I had time to set down more about the feeling of genius loci in these California poems of R. J. He seems to have drawn it from the very earth and hills of this region and exposed it to our sight.

In the next "Colophon" there is to be a short article by R. J. on his first book.[17] Ward Ritchie is doing the typography.—   U. J.

212: TO FREMONT OLDER

October 26, 1932

Dear Fremont Older: I am very eager for the success of "Barabbas," but I can't write a review. I've written two in my life, the last was four years ago and I swore then never to write another, for the gift of advertisement is not in me.

After seeing "Barabbas" in manuscript I wrote a little statement for the publisher to use. It is on the dust-jacket of the book, and I enclose it here. Perhaps you could print it, with my name, if you think it will do any good, in connection with a review by some more capable person.[18]
Mrs. Jeffers joins me in affectionate regards to you.   Sincerely,
Robinson Jeffers

213: TO JEREMY INGALLS

This letter is included in the Appendix to Miss Ingalls' M. A. thesis, "Metaphysical Aspects of American Poetry," Tufts University, 1933.

November 9, 1932

Dear Miss Ingalls: I am a wretched answerer of letters, but your questions seem few and simple. (1) Poets and poetic forms most satisfying? Shelley, Wordsworth, W. B. Yeats, Milton, Tennyson. Forms—Greek tragedy, Greek lyric. (2) English poetry has more significance for me than American.

[17] *See Letter 58, note 35.*
[18] *Boni's fall book list announced Sara Bard Field's* Barabbas *with J's "statement"; see* Alberts, A Bibliography, *p. 236.*

That is, poetry of the past—certainly not of the present. (3) What poets
in early reading or personal contact most influenced style or philosophy? None
by personal contact. I read and imitated at various times all those named
above, besides Swinburne, Rossetti, and who knows how many others. I am
not qualified to talk about persisting influences on style, indeed I do not
know. "Philosophy" had little to do with any reading of poetry, but came,
such as it is, from life and prose, science and the like. Perhaps a gleam
from Lucretius on one side and Wordsworth on the other. I used to read a
good deal of German and French poetry, having been at school in Europe and
attracted at various stages by Heine, Baudelaire, Hugo, but I think
neither excited nor influenced; nor by Latin either, except the prosody
interested me.

No doubt I should have mentioned Shakespeare and the King James' Bible!
Sincerely, Robinson Jeffers

Poe captured me when I was very young; I had almost forgotten. Emerson
interested me; Whitman never did.

214: TO EDWIN DUERR

*Edwin Duerr, director of Mortar Board Dramatic Group, University of
California at Berkeley, arranged and staged* The Tower Beyond Tragedy
*there on November 8 and 9, 1932. After attending a performance, Una sent
the following verbatim praise from J, which Duerr reported to Walter F.
Higbee on September 30, 1933. See also Letter 160 and its note, and
Letters 278 and 283.*

[*November 10, 1932*]

"My wife says that your production of may [*my*] verses was amazingly
good, and others who saw it tell me the same. But even if it had been
less excellent, I should owe gratitude to you and your players, and some
apology for not having been more attentive about the production. My utter
ignorance of the theatre, and aversion from crowds and responsibility,
were the reason; certainly not distrust of your work. But I don't think my
hands-off attitude was any hindrance to you, but an advantage.

Thank you sincerely. It is astonishing to me that the long verses and
blood-thirsty scenes could be managed so as to satisfy the audience. The
praise that people are kind enough to give belongs to you and your actors—
and to Aeschylus.   Sincerely yours, Robinson Jeffers"

215: UNA J TO PHILIP HORTON

A copy of this letter was also sent to William Gibson.

November 29, 1932

Dear Mr. Horton: My attention has been called to the November issue of
your college magazine. I write to ask you to correct in the next number
an error of fact in your article on Robinson Jeffers.[19] My husband has never
yet read any criticism of his work either in praise or dispraise and does
not care to have me speak of them so I must just digest the bitter with the
sweet by myself. Until this moment I have never commented on any article.
Errors of fact are frequent but unimportant, and as to judgment and taste one
realizes very quickly the personal idiosyncrasy. (I myself have so sharp a
disinclination toward the writings of a certain eminent and contemporary
British man of letters that I cannot discuss them without passionate fury and
abuse!)

Robinson Jeffers has always been extremely interested in the theories of
Freud and Jung, particularly the former but has not been able to concede
any *therepeutical* value to psycho-analysis from cases he has observed. He has
been interested from the standpoint of their broadening the field of
psychological investigation. He has never at any time been psycho-analyzed
by Jung or any one else. He would never have had time or money for such
self-indulgence even if he had needed it! But thats the comical part. Ask
any one who has met him whether or not the first thing one notices about him
is not extra-ordinary serenity and poise of mind and body. —So if you
allow that wrong statement to stand I'm going to have such bundles of letters
to answer—all off on the wrong scent to discover something to explain
his rather turbulent writing. Yes it is violent sometimes, but one cant explain
it so easily by any disharmony in him!

Besides your printed correction I would be interested to hear from you,
your authority for your statement. Very sincerely, Una Jeffers

A dear friend of ours is Dr. Carey de Angulo Baynes who has been with
Jung as patient, pupil and teacher about 8 yrs. and her husband Dr. Baynes
English colleague and translator of Jung.

---

[19] *The November* Nassau Lit *carried two articles, "Robinson Jeffers: Pro" and
"Robinson Jeffers: Con." According to William Gibson, who sent Una the magazine,
"They are the first Jeffers criticisms to appear in a college publication" (draft
of a letter to Una J, November 16, 1932). The correction which Una
requested was made in the next issue of the magazine.*

216: TO T. R. SMITH

January 10, 1933

Dear Mr. Smith: I promised to send you part of my manuscript by January 1, and I am ashamed to have failed. I had a touch of flu about Christmas and couldn't get the copying done. No one but myself can read my pencil manuscript. And "Give your Heart to the Hawks" is taking longer to finish than I expected. The end is in sight, but there are still three or so chapters to do, and if I hurry it I spoil it. I ought never to promise a thing before it is finished.

To-morrow or next day I'll send you the first three chapters of "Give your Heart," and the two poems (about 40 pages) at the end of the book.

I expect "Give your Heart etc." will be finished in February; then I'll send you the rest of it, and the short poems that follow it, and "Descent to the Dead," of which I don't suppose you have a copy for the printer, and I haven't, so I'll have to make a typed one.

I'm very sorry to be so tardy.   Sincerely, Robinson Jeffers

217: TO MARY AUSTIN

March [20], 1933

Dear Mary Austin: Una and I are devotedly grateful to you for "Earth Horizons" with your inscription. We had read it already, of course, with enjoyment and admiration, but it is much to have it from you, and I shall read much of it to our boys this summer, when their high-school work ceases to afflict them. It is a beautiful record of a singularly varied and exciting life.

I am awfully sorry to hear that you have been having difficulty with your health again. I hoped it was stabilized for a long time to come, and still hope it will be. It would be a disappointment to us to find you absent in Mexico, if we should be in New Mexico again this summer, as seems quite likely, but I know that you love the country southward, and have valuable interests there.

I expect I'll have a book out this spring, and shall claim the honor of sending you a copy, but not as a return for yours.   Sincerely yours, Robinson Jeffers

218: UNA J TO THEODORE LILIENTHAL

May 26, 1933

Dear Lilienthal: I am returning your books [*sent to be autographed*], written in, with this. Thanks for passing on to us the Doubleday-Doran letter (that makes the tenth publisher to invite Robin to their lists. Who says poetry isn't appreciated?)[20] When you are writing Mr. Longwell, will you say, please, that R. J. is committed to another publisher—but feels honored that they asked him.   Friendly wishes from both of us to you and Mr. Gelber.   Una Jeffers

219: UNA J TO THEODORE LILIENTHAL

Tuesday, [*1933*]

Dear Lilienthal: We've been busy with house guests from the far north of British Columbia—not a moment to write! They leave tomorrow and we can talk over the poem. Robin says he has in mind only one and that short; but possibly there are others. What is your minimum length— Do you know the Borzoi ones—Siegfried Sassoon's and MacLeish etc—?!

Robin has invariably refused to take part in these little pamphlet things— refused Knopf for that series, because in general he likes his work to appear in larger masses and because he thinks a lot of little items a nuisance to collectors—of whom he fortunately has a number among his readers. However, in these days of depression (financial—nothing else) I mean to try to get him to loosen up on several for two or three of the magazines where requests are neatly docketed here in my desk and have been for a long time! Perhaps one of these will do for your purpose.[21]   Cordially Una Jeffers

To save my time—please hand on my order to your proper department for John Cowper Powys' autobiography just out or just about to be.   U. J.

[20] *Una wrote Albert Bender on August 29, 1933, ". . . eventually thirteen publishers invited Robin to their list. . . . We have gone to Random House who also got Eugene O'Neill,—they took over all Robin's old books and will keep them going, guarantee back royalties, etc. Besides the fine books Random House publishes, they also own Modern Library and I think have wide facilities for selling. I hope we have acted wisely. We thought it all over long and earnestly."*
[21] *Two hundred and fifty copies of* Return, an Unpublished Poem *were printed by Grabhorn for Gelber, Lilienthal in 1934.*

> *"My favorite quotation, from the forgotten author*
> *T. Carlyle: 'Any the smallest alteration of my silent daily*
> *habits produces an anarchy to me which you could not*
> *believe unless you saw it!' "*
>
> *(Letter 109)*

220: TO MELBA BERRY BENNETT

June, 1933

My dear Mrs. Bennett: You must have thought me ungrateful not to answer anything, and I am sorry indeed. Your letter was interesting, and most kind. I failed to answer at once because I was in the cloudy stage of composition when theme after theme presents itself excitingly to be started and abandoned, because the next one seems more attractive. This survival-of-the-fittest kind of contest keeps the mind always preoccupied; whereas after you settle to work you do your little stint and are free for awhile, feeling something done. Yet I should have thanked you sooner. And I am sure you could write very well about my verses, though perhaps too indulgently.[22] I hope this will be forwarded if you should have left Palm Springs by this time. Sincerely, Robinson Jeffers

221: TO C. W. KEPPEL

July 29, 1933

Dear Mr. Keppel: Your interesting letter was forwarded to me in New Mexico, but we have been travelling so constantly since then, to Wyoming and elsewhere, that I could not answer sooner.

The lines you quote were written and printed according to the meter—octameter I suppose—eight feet to the line, that is, eight accented syllables, each with a certain weight of unaccented syllables, or of pause, to make it more or less equal in quantity to its neighbors. All my verses are metrical, or imagine themselves to be, though there is often much departure from pattern in the long poems.

I have no particular objection to your arrangement, but it seems to me that the rhythm is happier in mine; and—since the phrases are formed with regard to the pauses and cadences of the meter—even the meaning appears clearer; but perhaps only to me, because I am used to it.

Whitman of course considered rhythm but not usually meter. Let me congratulate you and your wife on your "lovely evenings" with poetry. It seems to me there is hardly anything more like happiness, except lovely days together with beautiful natural scenery. Sincerely, Robinson Jeffers

[22] Robinson Jeffers and the Sea *was published by* Gelber, Lilienthal *in 1936. See* Melba Bennett's *account of the genesis of her book in her* Stone Mason, *pp. viii–ix.*

222: UNA J TO THEODORE LILIENTHAL

October 14, 1933

Dear Mr. Lilienthal: About my Irish diary. I really *wish* it could be put into permanent form and I think it would be interesting to some people but I simply cannot find time to attend to it just now and this I had to tell an eastern publisher also. The diary is very full and would need to be carefully gone over and condensed and some what rearranged. We sometimes visited some particularly interesting place several times and I would want to group and put the several impressions and observations together. I wrote most of it, but Robin and the boys sometimes wrote in some pages. Of course Robin's pages would be of importance to his public aside from the general interest of the book. I sincerely hope to find time for this before too long a time has elapsed and will remember your request if I do bring it off.[23]

A letter from Random House dated Oct 9 says "Limited edition of 'Hawks' completely sold out with dealers howling for more" and "First Trade Edition of 3000 all gone, second edition on press." That is grand news.

We are much disturbed about Erskines [*C. Erskine Scott Wood's*] illness.
With grand wishes from both of us.   Una Jeffers

I wrote this several days ago but have been busy with Mabel Luhan and Muriel Draper here for a brief visit and forgot to mail.

223: TO LAWRENCE CLARK POWELL

This pencil draft of a Guggenheim recommendation was sent Powell with its appended note.

[1933]

I have known Mr. Powell through correspondence for several years, and was interested in conversing with him during his two or three days' visit here a few months ago.

He seems to me highly intelligent, studious and observant, a very careful and voluminous reader, and capable of independent thought. He is young,

---

[23] *On June 26, 1952, J wrote Lilienthal, "I think I'll edit the diaries, whenever I get time—write an introduction, and reduce the 200,000 words (more or less) to twenty thousand, mostly by leaving out our travels in England and Scotland. Ireland seems enough for once. But I expect the whole thing may be printed in course of time." Una's* Visits to Ireland *was published four years after her death (see Letter 382 and note), but Lilienthal's Quercus Press printed* Two Consolations: with an Excerpt from Una Jeffers' English Journal *in 1940.*

and yet has the advantage of a great deal of various experience and travel. He talks amusingly, writes interestingly and accurately, and with increasing distinction.

I believe there would be a considerable audience for such a work as Powell proposes; and it would be valuable as a book of references. D. H. Lawrence must be recognized as an important figure in any consideration of the English novel.

In spite of the books recently published about Lawrence, and all his own writings, the question of that "message" he felt so burningly impelled to deliver remains quite obscure. If Mr. Powell can solve it I am sure he will solve it interestingly; and—whether the "message" were valuable or not, or merely imaginary—will not lack readers.

Lawrence's early life remains clouded with contradictory stories. But members of his family, and early friends, are still living; Powell is adaptable, persistent, enterprising; I am sure that he can clear up these mysteries also.

Of the witnesses who have written about Lawrence's later life, each has his (or her) own enthusiasm to forward, or defense to make, or enemy to attack. Powell is not personally concerned, and is by nature and education unprejudiced; his account will be clearer and more true.

I think that Mr. Powell is excellently fitted for a work of this nature; and such a work seems to me one of the kinds of enterprise that the Guggenheim scholarships can further most successfully.

This is what I told them, and believe. They asked about your project as well as your ability. Wish you best of luck. —We are having a beautiful rain and wind storm here.   Sincerely, Robinson Jeffers

224: TO FREDERIC IVES CARPENTER

November [18], 1933

Dear Mr. Carpenter: Forgive me for not answering sooner. My less interesting correspondents usually get prompt answers, because my wife writes them; the few that really interest me are left to me to answer, and I do not get it done.

Besides that I dislike talking about my verses, but especially about the meaning of my verses—and I have just been sitting here with an idle pen, wondering why. Partly, perhaps, some relics of false (or even real) modesty; partly because I am a little tired of them after they are written; but it seems to me there is yet a better reason. I think it is the business of a writer of poetry, not to express his own gospel, but to present images, emotions, ideas, and let the reader find his good in them if he can. Not to form a way of thought but perhaps to activate thoughts. So that I feel no impulse to disengage my own meaning—or call it religion—from the web of verses, and even wish not to, in order to keep an innocence of mind on my own account. Not to become too self-conscious about my meanings. There may be symbolism in my verses, but I shouldn't want it to degenerate into allegory.

But your questions deserve answers. When I spoke in my letter to you of Jesus as having "fallen in love outward" I was thinking of "love the Lord thy God with all thy soul"—however it is worded—"and thy neighbor as thyself"—(which might mean *greatly*, or might mean *hardly at all*, the self and the neighbor being recognized as wholly unimportant, and human love swallowed up in divine love).

But when I wrote "Dear Judas" I was thinking of Jesus as a subject for tragedy—the Greeks had many demi-gods; we have only that one—and the subject of tragedy cannot be a perfect person. The perfect man could have no conflict in his mind, and could feel no misfortune; could not even have felt the agony in the garden or the despair on the cross that the evangelists impute to him. However, the two points of view are not contradictory. Mystical vision may be only a momentary experience; one may have it, and then have only a fading remembrance of it, and become a very imperfect person after all. It seems to me that the *having had it* is somewhere indicated in the poem.

I don't remember altogether what Lazarus said in my verses, but it seems to me that he represented only the clear negations and detachment of death, had nothing to do with love.

As to "joy," it has a color, and pain has a color; they are both inherent in life, and seem to me quite exactly balanced. In the complete recognition, such as I imagined for Orestes, might not the two colors cancel or rather fulfil each other, and make a whiteness? There is, of course, the joy of breaking prison; it seems to me rather preliminary than essential, in the recognition we are speaking of.

You ask what I think of Emerson, Thoreau, Melville. I am ashamed to say that I never read anything of Thoreau's; I like to think of his life, though it was rather specialist. Emerson was a youthful enthusiasm, if you like, but not outgrown by any means, only read so thoroughly that I have not returned to him for a long time. Melville: I read Moby Dick aloud to my boys a few years ago and was much impressed. There is greatness in it; there was also much that I resented—the tiresome humor that spoils so much American work—the occasional stilted Shakespeareanisms.

Your essay is very interesting and intelligent, and I think in general very true at least of American literature as a whole. I won't discuss it particularly, wishing, as I said before, to keep my intentions rather instinctive than considered. Thank you sincerely for letting me see it. You did not say that you want it back, but since it is not a carbon copy I return it with this.

I was delighted to hear from you, and shall be if you should write again, and shall try to be decent about answering.   Sincerely, Robinson Jeffers

225: TO (?) PUMPHREY

November, 1933

Dear Mr. Pumphrey: Thank you sincerely for your letter; but I have not time to copy the verses. You lose nothing by that, for my handwriting—you see—is neither beautiful nor easy to read.

And I am sorry not to be able to answer your question. One can say that Mount Everest is higher than Mont Blanc, but there is no way to measure poetry. I cannot even tell whom I prefer to read—sometimes Yeats, sometimes some other.   Sincerely yours, Robinson Jeffers

226: TO E. A. ROBINSON

January 1, 1934

Dear Mr. Robinson: I was sincerely moved by the gift of "Talifer" and the kindness of your letter, and feel ashamed enough of not having thanked you more promptly. It is a moral deformity, that I can never write a letter when I want to. My wife attends to them all, except the very exceptional one that I claim for myself—and then fail to write.

I've read "Talifer" twice through, with enjoyment and admiration. Humor in an atmosphere of cool ironic intelligence is so rare as to be almost unique; and then your characteristic beauty of lines and images, swimming on it like swans on a lake. Thank you very much. My book was sent simply as an oblation that I have long wanted to make; I had no thought of such return for it.

Your letter makes me hope, however faintly, that we may see you here sometime. It would be a great pleasure; and perhaps the coast here might remind you a little of your Tristram's Cornwall. It has been especially lovely the past few days, grand rains and wind, clouds on dark green mountains, our bay white with storm and branded by a long stain from the flooded river.   Sincerely yours, Robinson Jeffers

Tor House, Carmel, California.
January 1, 1934.

Dear Mr. Robinson:

I was sincerely moved by the gift of "Talifer" and the kindness of your letter, and feel ashamed enough of not having thanked you more promptly. It is a moral deformity, that I can never write a letter when I want to. My wife attends to them all, except the very exceptional one that I claim for myself --- and then fail to write.

I've read "Talifer" twice through, with enjoyment and admiration. Humor in an atmosphere of cool ironic intelligence is so rare as to be almost unique; and then your characteristic beauty of lines and images, swimming on it like swans on a lake. Thank you very much. My book was sent simply as an oblation that I have long wanted to make; I had no thought of such return for it.

Your letter makes me hope, however faintly, that we may see you here sometime. It would be a great pleasure; and perhaps the coast here might remind you a little of your Tristram's Cornwall. It has been especially lovely the past few days, great rains and wind, clouds on dark green mountains, our bay white with storm and branded by a long stain from the flooded river.

Sincerely yours,
Robinson Jeffers.

227: TO RUDOLPH GILBERT

March, 1934

Dear Mr. Gilbert: I beg your pardon with sincere regret for having kept your manuscript so long. I always shrink from reading things written about my verses—especially if they are friendly—when the morning's writing is finished I want to forget my verses until the next occasion—and such a not perfectly rational shrinking is just the kind that postpones and postpones. I am very sorry.

My wife answers all my letters but has refused to write about this, saying that it is interesting and very good, and I must read and answer myself. She has been rather constant on the subject lately.

I think you are quite right in feeling that most of what has been written about my verses does not go deeper than the surface; but that is almost invariably the case with contemporary criticism. Only after time and opinion have established a work does it seem worth investigating very deeply. Mine has seemed so to you because you trust your own opinion and are not writing on time. Assuming for the moment that your opinion is justified—·that my poems are worth the trouble you have taken—it seems to me that you have done an extremely good piece of work.

The meanings you find in the poems are not always those that were consciously present to my mind when I was writing—but indeed I am not very conscious of intentions then, of any thing but the immediate story—if there are meanings or symbolisms they are the result of long-previous thought, or unconscious thought. And I do not find any of your interpretations to refuse or deny. No author could ask for a more understanding or more favorable critic than I have in you. And the width of your reading is astonishing—your wealth of quotation and reference from so many diverse authors. The relationships you find for me with other writers would surprise the people who are inclined to blame me for standing so solitary! As to my "philosophy"—Weltanschauung rather—I think you present it very competently. I don't want to think about it too much, for if it were perfectly conscious and a system it would cease to be a source of poetry—which seems to me a better thing than philosophy. [But in saying this I don't mean to suggest an antithesis between *truth* and poetry. They belong together.][24]

I must thank you for your extremely well-done, careful, sympathetic and interesting study of my poems. I am the more remorseful about having kept it so long because you speak of wishing to submit it to a publisher. Of course I should be pleased if it were published—and I don't want to be

---

[24] *The brackets are J's. The manuscript referred to in this letter is "Shine, Perishing Republic," not published until 1936. See Letters 169 and 255.*

discouraging—your work is well worthy of publication and would easily find it, if (or when) its subject becomes better known to more people. In the meantime any publisher may feel that Alberts's "Bibliography" and Powell's "Introduction"[25] are quite all the public wants on this subject at present. However, —the best of luck to you and my sincere thanks.

I was much interested in your quotations from E. Merrill Root and Stephen Spender. They have power and beauty. —I must stop if this is to be mailed to-day.   Sincerely yours, Robinson Jeffers

228: UNA J TO LAWRENCE CLARK POWELL

April 23, 1934

Dear Mr. Powell: Here is the material you asked for. Use as if from a letter: arrange to suit yourself in answer to your questions I Whether R. J. was disillusioned by the war II Ireland but *please* quote exactly if you quote.//

(I About the War.)

It seemed to him that war was unavoidable as the world was (and is) arranged. He thought in 1916 that our entrance into the war on one side or the other was unavoidable. (Is not so sure of that now). He disliked the cant of our neutrality, followed by the cant of our belligerancy [*belligerency*]. My husband felt no conscientious scruples against taking part in the war, but did not enlist in the ranks because we had little money and no immediate expectation of more and our twin boys were infants. After suffering considerable disturbance of mind, he made various unsuccessful applications for training for a commission; he was examined for aviation and rejected for high blood pressure. However he had been provisionally accepted for balloon service and was awaiting instructions when peace was declared.

The conflict of motives on the subject of going to war or not was probably one of several factors that, about this time, made the world and his own mind much more real and intense to him. Another factor was the building of Tor House. As he helped the masons shift and place the wind and wave-worn granite I think he realized some kinship with it and became aware of strengths in himself unknown before. Thus at the age of thirty-one there came to him a kind of awakening such as adolescents and religious converts are said to experience.

(II In Ireland)

//My husband had gone to Ireland for *my* sake; he himself felt very indifferent—but one day after we had walked through the rain some miles

[25] An Introduction to Robinson Jeffers, *the published version of Powell's Dijon Université thesis, 1932.*

213

to "Ossian's Grave," (a dolman and group of standing stones upon a lonely hill) and were coming back along a lane all red with tree-high fuschsias [*fuchsias*] and enchanting with the fragrance of wet briar roses, he confessed he had never been more content, and often now, he who seems so closely knit with this mountainous coast lying all ablaze with sunlight; says longingly, "I wish we could have a little house there too, on the high wild foreland near Bally castle where we could hear the sheep bleating on the hills and watch the rain sweep across that dim heathery moor!"//   [*U. J.*]

229: TO MRS. HUGH BULLOCK (Academy of American Poets)

May 1, 1934

Thank you sincerely for your letter about the proposed Academy of American Poets. The idea seems to me extremely commendable in so far as it aims at enabling good poets to devote themselves to their work without having to seek other sources of income. I am more doubtful of the specially "academy" aspect of the plan. It seems questionable whether the Royal Academy has been really helpful to British painting, or the French Academy to French literature.

I feel honored that you would like to add my name to your list of sponsors, but perhaps it would be better for one who writes poetry not to stand sponsor for a movement that will be seeking funds for the reward and support of poets.   Sincerely yours, Robinson Jeffers

230: TO MRS. HUGH BULLOCK

May 30, 1934

My dear Mrs. Bullock: Forgive me for not answering more promptly. A poet's Academy still sounds to me a little—Druidical—but I can't refuse to sponsor a movement aimed at enabling good poets to attend to their proper business. If you think my name will help you are welcome to it. Sincerely yours, Robinson Jeffers

231: TO GORHAM MUNSON

June 3, 1934

Dear Mr. Munson: Your letter is dated May 13, and I should have answered more promptly. I am sorry.

You ask about "Thurso's Landing." In a previous book (Cawdor, page 144) there is a short piece of verse called "Bixby's Landing," describing the headland of that name, about 25 miles south of here, to which of course I had to give another name when I came to make a story of it.[26] (The canyon was remote and solitary, hung with the old cable of the lime works, when we were first there; now it is spanned by a tremendous rainbow-arched bridge of the new state-highway). —So it appears that the scene impressed me first, and the narrative poem grew out of it. The theme of the narrative is human courage—fortitude, rather—I think (without any assurance) that it was suggested by the powerful and rather cruel depth and concentration of the scene, —perhaps too by the falcons that were nesting there when we first visited it.

Reason for writing the poem? I think the same reason that leads me to call my wife out of doors to look at a sunset. You are excited by something that seems beautiful or significant, —you want to show it to others.

My opinion of "Thurso's Landing"? —I have none, really. It seems neither the best nor the worst of my long poems. Perhaps it is freer than others of my own ideas and "philosophy."

And really I cannot tell how long I was writing it. Six months for a guess; but I cannot remember anything to date the beginning or end.

Thank you sincerely. I shall be glad to have the work that you and Professor W. are writing. I hope this letter does not come too late for your purpose, though it seems to me there is nothing of much importance in it.   Sincerely yours, Robinson Jeffers

232: TO JAMES RORTY

Taos, New Mexico
July 3, 1934

Dear Rorty: My letters to you are forever postponed because of a feeling that I ought to say something reasonable in them, about subjects that interest you and me too, but whenever I feel up to that I begin to think of verses instead. As a matter of fact, you are the only person to whom I can write, except now and then in response to definite questions.

[26] *Compare the excerpt of J's letter of June 14, 1932, to Alberts, quoted in* A Bibliography, *p. 72.*

OVERLEAF:

*"If anyone was ever bored . . . let him get five acres
and grow a wood on them, and produce a stone house
and twins and a book of verses."*

(Letter 158)

215

Thank you very much for sending the book on advertising [Our Master's Voice], and the pamphlet. They have not reached me yet because we are in New Mexico again—guests of Mabel Luhan—and only letters are forwarded, our next neighbor in Carmel is holding all second class material for us. We return within a few days; and though I'd like to see the book at once I don't know how to instruct this neighbor—who is really only an acquaintance—how to choose your book out of the stack.

Before we left home I saw the book (fairly) well reviewed in "Time," with considerable space if not sympathy in the NY Times. That they pay respectful attention to it is something, and there was a faint note of alarm in the Times review that may have pleased you. You have my best wishes, at any rate.

Robert Cantwell (whom you perhaps know) settled in Carmel for a few months stay just before we left; I saw him a couple of times—not much to look at, but intelligent and interesting.

—This has been broken off for days, first by an outbreak in the corrals, here. A big boar broke open the gate of his pen and got among the horses. Our boys heard the noise from a distance; when they reached the place two young mares, one defending her colt, had been horribly torn, and a white gelding (that was altered rather late in life and so has stallion characteristics) was doing battle with the boar, the mares and colts clustered behind him. It was quite bloody and Homeric. The boys and I, and a Mexican gardner, persuaded the boar back to his pen with pitchforks and clubs, (meanwhile Una got our automatic out of the bottom of the trunk and stood by to defend her offspring!) We spent the rest of the day helping an M.D. and a horse doctor sew up horrible wounds in the horses' shoulders and sides, and then had to clean up to go to Frieda Lawrence's ranch for dinner, on a mountainside twenty miles from here—the ranch that Lawrence described in "St. Mawr" and "Death of a Porcupine."

Loud, charming, cordial Frieda lives there with an Italian who loved Lawrence and loves her. She talks continually about Lawrence, and has just written her memoirs of him—"Not I, but the Wind"—the first thousand copies privately printed in Santa Fe and to be published by herself—she hates publishers. $7.50. The books will be ready in a few days, I can't imagine how she hopes to distribute so many. I believe Viking Press will have a trade edition later—The ranch is excessively remote; usually it rains when we go there, and the car travels sidewise or backward or in the ditch of the [slippery?] roads. Frieda and Angelino (the Italian) have built a big log house beside the little one that Lawrence lived in. An Italian flag flies—from the little one—and the paintings of Lawrence's totem, the blazing phoenix, are nailed on several pine-trees. Frieda hopes sometime to bring him home from France and bury him on the mountain above this place. —Angelino is an Italian reserve-officer, a captain of bersaglieri.

*Throughout the 1930's the Jefferses made several
summer trips to Mabel Luhan's ranch in Taos, New Mexico.*

All this sounds fantastic perhaps, but really everything in New Mexico
is more or less fantastic.

Here at Mabel Luhan's strange guests come and go from day to day. We
have been riding ten to twenty miles about every afternoon, we four,
Mabel Luhan, and Myron Brinig who is staying here, sometimes a seventh.
I try to work in the mornings, but probably have accomplished nothing—
too hot, and strange place.

We have been here 3½ weeks, and start home three days from now.

There are lovely thunder-storms, but irrigation water scanty, no snow in
the mountains last winter. The Indians have first right to the water; Mexicans
and others are allowed to fill their ditches "from the hour of pastores"—
does that mean shepherds, the hour of folding flocks?—"on Friday evening
until the morning star rises on Monday." The Indians watch for the
morning star and instantly shut the sluice-gates. I have this from
the village paper.

—Thank you for your review of "Give Your Heart—" It was intelligent,
kindly, and as sympathetic as possible in the circumstances. Una was a
little irritated because you spoke as if I had never known poverty—"economic
struggle"—which she knows too well is quite a commonplace with us. We
get along happily, like a copy-book, by doing everything for ourselves
and not even wishing for luxuries. The only income tax I ever had to pay was
for year before last; at the time I paid it my income was eighty dollars a
month, except royalties, and Liveright, from whom the royalties came, was
bankrupt. We are somewhat better off now but when I was nineteen I

worked in a doctor's office at five dollars a week, and lived on it. However, it is quite true that I have never suffered from poverty. If one of us had been ill, the past two or three years, it might have been a different story.

—It will be a hot drive home. I'll look for your book as soon as we get there.   Best wishes, Robinson Jeffers

233: TO C. W. KEPPEL

July 25, 1934

Dear Mr. Keppel: We have just lately returned from New Mexico, and found your manuscript ["*Souvenirs of Earth*"] and letter delayed here with second class matter. It should have been forwarded; the careless postman judged by the bulk of the package without looking at the stamps, and I am sorry. I like your poem much, and it is astonishing how well your choices cohere—that is what makes it *your* poem. As far as I am concerned, you are free to use the lines that in another context are mine. It is not quite clear from your letter whether my permission would settle the matter with Random House, or whether you were to get mine before they would consider giving theirs. In either case, you have mine.

I like your preface too: it puts the idea in a most interesting and attractive manner; —so do the two little lines of Latin.

I return you the manuscript with this, not at all from lack of interest in it, but because it seems to me you will need a number of copies to show to the various authors whose permissions are to be asked for. I have read it through, and thank you for letting me.   Sincerely, Robinson Jeffers

234: TO FREDERIC PROKOSCH

August 31, 1934

Dear Mr. Prokosch: I was glad to write in your books, and they were mailed back to you the day before yesterday. Thank you for the little poem enclosed with your letter; I liked it much, the lines have a lovely music and strangeness.

My next book will appear next year, no doubt, but I don't know yet what time of the year nor what it will be called. The long poem that is (provisionally) finished is called "Attila's Wife," but I might change the name; and probably the book will take the name of the other long poem, which is not finished, and is not yet named. This one is contemporary; the other begins in Attila's time but seems to have tried to swallow the whole Christian era!   Cordially, Robinson Jeffers

235: TO SISTER MARY JAMES POWER

The mailed copy of this letter is published in Sister Mary James' Poets at Prayer (New York, 1930), pp. 60–61. On the rough draft, which differs little from the final version, in the possession of Mrs. Blanche Matthias, J has written: "Dear Blanche: Of course you can have this first draft if it interests you—scribbled and incomplete—such answers are necessarily incomplete as long as mind goes on experiencing. Affectionately, Robin"

October 1, 1934

Dear Sister Mary James: Your letter should have been answered sooner, but there have been so many visitors and other events the past fortnight.

As to my "religious attitudes"—you know it is a sort of tradition in this country not to talk about religion for fear of offending—I am still a little subject to the tradition, and rather dislike stating my "attitudes" except in the course of a poem. However, they are simple. I believe that the universe is one being, all its parts are different expressions of the same energy, and they are all in communication with each other, influencing each other, therefore parts of one organic whole. (This is physics, I believe, as well as religion.) The parts change and pass, or die, people and races and rocks and stars, none of them seems to me important in itself, but only the whole. This whole is in all its parts so beautiful, and is felt by me to be so intensely in earnest, that I am compelled to love it, and to think of it as divine. It seems to me that this whole alone is worthy of the deeper sort of love; and that here is peace, freedom, I might say a kind of salvation, in turning one's affections outward toward this one God, rather than inward on one's self, or on humanity, or on human imagination and abstractions—the world of spirits.

I think that it is our privilege and felicity to love God for his beauty, without claiming or expecting love from him. We are not important to him, but he to us.

I think that one may contribute (ever so slightly) to the beauty of things by making one's own life and environment beautiful, so far as one's power reaches. This includes moral beauty, one of the qualities of humanity, though it seems not to appear elsewhere in the universe. But I would have each person realize that his contribution is not important, its success not really a matter for exultation nor its failure for mourning; the beauty of things is sufficient without him.

(An office of tragic poetry is to show that there is beauty in pain and failure as much as in success and happiness.)

—There is nothing here that has not been more feelingly expressed in my verses; but I thought that a plain question deserved a plain answer. —Of course you are welcome to photostat this at pleasure.   Sincerely yours, Robinson Jeffers

236: TO BABETTE DEUTSCH

November 7, 1934

Dear Miss Deutsch: I am glad to be one of your references in the application for a Guggenheim fellowship, and wish you good fortune, with that and the poem.

I wonder whether you could lend me a copy of "Honey from the Rocks," so that I can answer a little more intelligently when they write to me? Some of it I remember, of course, but it would be better to see it again, and I am afraid there is no copy in the library here. "Epistle to Prometheus" of course I have. If you can send me a copy of the other I will return it carefully. —At convenience: no doubt it will be some time before the committee writes to me. It is pleasant to hear from you again.   Sincerely, Robinson Jeffers

237: TO GEOFFREY GRIGSON (editor of *New Verse*)

This questionnaire and J's answers were published in New Verse, II *(December, 1934), 18.*

November, 1934

1. Do you intend your poetry to be useful to yourself or to others?
      Both.
2. Do you think there can now be a use for narrative poetry?
      Certainly.
3. Do you wait for a spontaneous impulse before writing a poem; if so, is this impulse verbal or visual?
      Visual, emotional and / or intellectual; not verbal.

4. Have you been influenced by Freud and how do you regard him?
   I think nearly all persons of general intelligence have been influenced by Freud; I regard him as an important (but not epoch-making) discoverer.
5. Do you take your stand with any political or politico-economic party or creed?
   No.
6. As a poet, what distinguishes you, do you think, from an ordinary man?
   Nothing essential; a little specialization.

238: TO FREDERIC IVES CARPENTER

December, 1934

Dear Mr. Carpenter: Thank you for sending me the Contents and last chapter of your "American Idea." I am very much interested; the book is greatly conceived and planned, and the chapter you sent presents a most interesting and attractive view-point, not in the least invalidated by the fact that I don't share it completely.

Of course I agree with you that the European, American and Russian cultures have each its peculiar qualities and values, but I don't think of them as successive but as parts of the same wave, the two latter representing its wash on other shores, which the wave reached later. It seems to be normal for a ripening civilization to pass through the likeness of an increasingly democratic republic, to approximations of socialism combined with dictatorship tending toward empire, —the present phase of the wave—which the more prosperous countries—England, France, America—are able to resist awhile.

But I don't mean to argue, still less to convince you, and am well pleased if verses of mine have helped (as you say) to a mature conception that seems to me original and organic and illuminating. You have certainly not "taken too great liberties" with my images and thought, but quite rightly selected the ones that appealed to you, and it increases my opinion of them.

Congratulations on the book, and on the lucky title too. I hope it will be printed soon, and shall truly be glad if you will send me a copy.[27]
Cordially yours, Robinson Jeffers

[27] *Carpenter did not, after all, publish "The American Idea"; see Letters 206, 269, and 312.*

239: TO ALBERT BENDER

January 31, 1935

Dear Albert: Thank you—and the Book Club—very much for all those copies of the George Sterling folder. It is marvelously done, both typography and the reproduction of the letter—a beautiful thing, that the Book Club must be proud of.[28] Una and I were so much interested in the mining-town series that came out last year.

Una is at present in the Carmel Community Hospital, the eighth day after a little operation, really a minor one, and not dangerous, but she was under the anesthetic for an hour and a half. She is getting along splendidly, and will feel even more energetic than usual when she gets out of bed three or four days from now. She sends you her love; I am writing this by her bedside. She wants to tell you how very much she enjoys the two books you sent, on Irish poetry and Irish place-names. They are both on the little table by her bed.

I have been kept quite busy running back and forth to the hospital, visiting Una and seeing that our boys get their lessons and their meals, besides continuing work on my latest piece of verse, —otherwise I should have answered you more promptly. Our boys are going to Salinas Junior College for their freshman year: they have to get up at 6 AM and drive to Salinas every morning, and I have to see that they do so. They enjoy it, however. Next year they will go up to Berkeley, I think.   Affectionately, Robin

240: TO JAKE ZEITLIN

This letter is facsimiled in Powell's Robinson Jeffers *and privately printed in the brochure announcing Occidental College's "Robinson Jeffers, 1905–1935: An Exhibition Commemorating the Thirtieth Anniversary of His Graduation from Occidental College. . . ."*

March 22, 1935

Dear Jake Zeitlin: Thank you very much for the poem "to R. J." It is beautifully done, and expresses what I suppose is a main tendency in my verses. Sometimes I wish they were not occupied quite so much with it, for though the feeling is true it is less than the whole truth of nature. When I think, I know that pleasure and pain counterbalance each other pretty

[28] *I contributed a laudatory note, "Comment to George Sterling," to the Book Club's special printing in 1935 of a letter from Sterling to Bender, dated November 24, 1914.*

accurately on the average, but when I write verses I am just the opposite apparently of that delightful fellow Ford Madox Ford writes about, who "had tried so hard to be a philosopher, but cheerfulness *would* come creeping in." —However, our ends tend to be rather sad, and we bawl at birth; I suppose my verses are thinking of the ends of life, and with what sort of hard faces to meet them, rather than the way-stations. —At which I wish you and me many pleasant pauses.   Sincerely, Robinson Jeffers

241: TO MRS. HUGH BULLOCK

April 27, 1935

My dear Mrs. Bullock: I hope the enclosed will serve your purpose; it is too long, but there seems to be so much to say. I am delighted to hear that your enterprise is progressing so well. My mind still stammers on the word "academy"—such a supreme-court sound—but I hope the project will redeem the word. It has my best wishes.   Sincerely yours, Robinson Jeffers
[The typed enclosure was solicited for the printed program for the Academy's annual Poetry Ball.]

I'll be glad to say something about the value of poetry, but with the stipulation that any verses myself may have authored are kept out of mind; I do not intend to cry my own wares, now or another time.

Like the other arts, poetry is a source of high and lasting pleasure, but more than most of the others it is capable of affecting life directly; it sharpens the perceptions and emotions, and it can reconcile man to his environment or inspire him to change it. And poetry enriches life, adding overtones of significance and nobility to common things, as for instance wine, honey, horses, gold, bread, are more valuable for the sake of their (even half-forgotten) poetic associations. England is inestimably more beautiful because Chaucer and Shakespeare and Wordsworth wrote; it is almost humorously obvious that Scotland is dearer to her people because Burns made songs.

Poetry stands between prose and music; it is capable of saying things that neither of these can say, and of discovering things that neither can discover. For all the arts—but I think poetry more than others—are instruments of discovery, like a telescope, as well as instruments of expression, like a violin.

And poetry is a test of reality, of emotional and social values, even of conduct. "Is it accepted of song?" But a rather savage test; most of our lives and institutions, as well as our ideals and utopias, ring pretty hollow under it. That is one of the reasons why poetry is sometimes more pleasing to posterity than to its contemporaries.   Robinson Jeffers

242: TO LOUIS ADAMIC

A copy of this letter was sent to Harriet Monroe by Adamic, who noted, "I think this will interest you. . . ." The letter is published in Adamic's My America *(New York, 1938), pp. 474–75.*

May 17, 1935

Dear Adamic: I am ashamed not to have written sooner. I read "Grandsons" soon after it came, with pleasure and deep interest—I that am almost as incapable of reading a novel as of writing a letter. It seems to me an excellent diagnosis of the recent American state of mind. Of course, as you know and say, this restlessness, aimlessness and unrest are present in Europe too. I think they are necessary results of the present stage of civilization—not necessary in any particular person, but in people in general. The individual can conquer them, can make roots and find aims for himself; but I do not think society can, except by letting itself be worked into a quasi-religious intoxication, like Nazism or communism, in which the pleasure of persecution plays a great part, and which I think is worse than that aimless unrest; and they are temporary passages to Caesarism. (It seems to me that Russia has made the passage already.) I like none of these, though I believe we are to taste them if we live long enough.

It seems to me that in a degenerating society the individual has got to isolate himself morally to a certain extent or else degenerate too. He *can* keep his own morals; he cannot save society's, not even though he himself should happen to be Caesar, like Marcus Aurelius (who did all his civic duty and more, but remained isolated in his philosophy, apart from decaying Rome.)[29]

It is no use our turning to the factory-workers, as Tolstoy did to the peasant and Rousseau to the primitive, for what the factory-workers want is exactly what the middle-classes want, and if they got it they would have all the middle-class fatuities; only more so, because they would have less

---

[29] *In 1941 J drafted a response to a question from Herbert Carlin which seems relevant here. See Bennett,* Stone Mason, *pp. 191–92. J comments: "I'm afraid my views have not changed* [since writing 'The Answer' in 1937]. *Certainly the present war and Roosevelt's rhetorical 'four freedoms' do not make them more hopeful. Hitler and Germany can be smashed of course, after years; but I wonder whether anyone realizes what the state of Europe and the world will be by that time? Even if those 'four freedoms' were to be honestly established at a peace conference, nobody but the U.S. could enforce them; and we shall never be Roman nor German enough to police the world for a long time. And if we did— could this be called freedom?*

"One thing seems even more clear than when I wrote the verse:—that it is up to each person 'to keep his own integrity. . . .' It is going to be a very difficult job."

incentive and more security. They might be self-satisfied Peter Gales, instead of searching tormented ones.

Thank you very much for "Grandsons"; it is a fine intelligent illuminating work. What I said above is not criticism, only opinion. And belated congratulations on "Native's Return"—it was splendid.   Sincerely, Robinson Jeffers

243: TO (?) WECHSLER

May 29, 1935

Dear Mr. Wechsler: Thank you for your letter and your expressions about my verses. I can of course neither accept them nor object to them, but only thank you sincerely. It is right to speak in superlatives when one is young; it means there will still be fire in the engine later. But as to "pessimist"; that should mean believing in the worst—that things are as bad as possible. I can imagine them a great deal worse. Things are as they are; and the world is full of wretchedness yet very beautiful. And not all wretched.

I was interested and pleased in reading your sonnets. They are good, and you will do better still. Splendid lines come frequently, and the final line is almost always strong and conclusive. It seems to me that perhaps "Drear as with pain," and "How murmurs deep" are the best, but there are others almost equally good. If I were to suggest anything for your future development, it would be a closer approach to the tangible and visible—that you should include in your meditation the grass or weeds in that cemetery, the texture of the stones; and the faces of buildings or mountains, the color of a girl's skin, the colors and shapes and motions of things,—to give the poem body as well as soul. —But find your way, and don't take advice. Sincerely, Robinson Jeffers

244: TO LOUIS UNTERMEYER

c/o Mabel Luhan
Taos, New Mexico
June 17, 1935

Dear Untermeyer: I am delighted to hear of the new "Modern American Poetry." You are free to use the poems you mention, so far as I am concerned, and I am sure Random House will be easy to deal with. ("Love the Wild Swan" is included in my new book "Solstice," which is being printed for publication this fall.)

As to suggesting two or three more poems—I haven't got my books here, but perhaps can find copies on Mrs. Luhan's shelves this evening—if so, I will suggest two or three titles at the foot of this letter; but I'm not sure that I'm a good chooser. For the same reason I can't speak about the bio-bibliographic note, but I don't remember any error in it, in the copy that you were kind enough to send me a few years ago, which is safe at home. I'll look when we return to Carmel, August first or a few days earlier.

It is delightful to think we may see you in Carmel this December. We'll have the cup of tea for you, or the California equivalent if you prefer. —I'm glad you like the Modern Library "Roan Stallion," etc. —I'll offer something to the Mercury as soon as I have something appropriate—just at present all my verses are gathered into the new book. —This Taos valley is a lovely place: —probably you have been here, or have read Mabel Luhan's "Winter in Taos," which describes it beautifully.   Cordially,
Robinson Jeffers

245: TO ARTHUR DAVISON FICKE

c/o Mabel Luhan
Taos, New Mexico
July 2, 1935

Dear Ficke: I had your card just as we were leaving Carmel, and was so glad to hear from you. There was no time to look for the two letters I have from E. A. Robinson; I feel sure they were preserved but I don't know where they are. At any rate they are only short kindly little notes, and couldn't be important toward his biography.

We have been here three weeks and I have all the while been intending to write to you. We came this time by Yuma and Tombstone and Las Cruces, and shall probably go back through Colorado toward Oregon, perhaps, and south [along] the northern California coast. I expect we'll start home next week. We have the two boys with us, of course, and a school-friend of theirs also—five in the Ford, besides the bull-dog. For the dog I have to take along a bottle of water and keep him wet and evaporating, or he'd die of the heat in the desert stretches. Wet, he gets along very well; though there was one day of our journey here when both he and Una had to wear ice-packs

> "... I wouldn't drive over to Monterey to meet
> William Shakespeare; this doesn't imply lack of
>   admiration, or anything more foolish than contentment
> at home."

(Letter 118)

on their heads. The rest of us don't mind—though the Carmel sea-fog will be pleasant to return to.

Here we have been riding, walking and conversing; camping up in the snow at Blue Lake, swimming a little in the Hot Springs, and the boys playing tennis. Frieda Lawrence was here for lunch to-day, and her daughter Barbara, and the daughter's young Scottish husband. The Indians come and go, quietly, you know how. It is very delightful. One can hardly even pretend to work in this warm golden sunshine—I don't see how Mabel Luhan manages to write so much so well—I suppose in winter; that must be different.

Our boys enter Berkeley this year, as sophomores. It is going to make a change in our lives, their being away from home.

I hope very much that it will be possible for us to see you next summer, if we should go another time to Ireland, as we rather indefinitely expect to. We should probably pass your way early in June. But a year ahead is of course a doubtful quantity, in these rapid times.

Una sends her best to you and Gladys, and so do I.   Yours,
Robinson Jeffers

246: TO H. ARTHUR KLEIN

Klein had offered Dimitrov as a possible character for a poem and had questioned J specifically on MacLeish's statement on metrics, seeing in it much similarity to J's technique as Klein had described it in his thesis for Occidental College.

October 5, 1935

Dear Herbert Klein: Thank you very much for the life of Dimitrov and for the pamphlets. I read with interest and admiration. It still seems to me amazing that he and his friends were acquitted and set free. The Germans, and especially the Nazis, are not usually so sensitive to foreign opinion; and I can't think what other factors in so staged a trial—unless there was really some feeling for justice, and only a few blunderers like Göring were in the plot. I think it was not only Communist morals that upheld Dimitrov—that was a factor, but also Bulgarian toughness, and a power in the man himself.

I'm afraid that the organized hates of the world-war will seem rather trivial compared to what is coming to Europe, possibly even in our time, —there are such wells of accumulated bitterness, and such helpless populations, incapable of self-support if organization breaks down anywhere.

Yes, I read MacLeish's "Panic," and think highly of it, though the end
seemed a little weak and vague. His note on metrics is interesting, but it did
occur to me that it was not particularly novel.

Do come and see us again if you pass this way.   Sincerely,
Robinson Jeffers

247: TO J—— G—— M——

*A copy of this letter was given to Ella Winter; Una mailed another to
Lawrence Clark Powell on November 18, 1935, with some description of the
incident, "since you have been so connected with R. J.'s history. . . ."
J—— G—— M—— sold an article to a small paper in Santa Barbara, presenting a number of claims made by a woman who had heard M—— lecture
on Whitman in Hollywood and who had told him in conversation afterward
that she was J's "first love."*

October 29, 1935

Dear Sir: As my only other letter to you seems to have left some doubt in
your mind, here is a plain statement.

(1) I never at any time contemplated matrimony with your friend L[——] M.

(2) I knew the woman who is now my wife before I met your friend and
we were married as soon as she was free to have me twenty-two years ago.

(3) The verses in *Flagons and Apples* were written mostly for the woman
who is now my wife. A few of them were inspired by other girls; several
of them were of more importance to me than L. M. *Helen* is a name I have
used again and again in my verses with the thought of various woman
real and fictitious in my mind.

(4) The mss. poems you refer to in the possession of your friend were
copies of verses I handed about rather indiscriminately to girls of that period.

(5) I ask you to write no more on this subject.   Sincerely, Robinson
Jeffers

248: UNA J TO SARA BARD FIELD (Mrs. C. Erskine Scott Wood) AND C. ERSKINE SCOTT WOOD

November 13, 1935

Dearest Sara and Erskine: —Erskine's question first of all. I answer equally
happily to *Yew-na* or *Oona*. I came by my name not through my Irish
family who say *Oona* naturally[30] but by way of Spenser's *Una* (Yew-na) in

---

[30] *See the note to Letter 9.*

"Fairie Queene"! I was named after my Father's first wife, a lovely creature who died young. Her name was Una [*Euna*] Lamb. Her father was an old and scholarly doctor [*William George Lamb*]—English—who loved to read Spenser.

That was a beautiful and thoughtful review of Robin's "Solstice" Sara but of course I disagreed in spots![31]

I deny altogether that he is Reactionary, or that he cries "backward" instead of "forward." Where do you find that? I deny that he considers famine noble except in comparison to even more ignoble things (mass life—this horrible entwining of people libidinously listening to *crooners*, etc). He is trying to express his disgust at certain things and says even war is nobler, even famine has more dignity—as one might say even the devil is decent compared to so-and-so. He does not say that war and famine are good or even tolerable. He does think that we perhaps and certainly our descendants are destined to witness a good deal of both and had better view them with a certain amount of historical perspective. We cannot prevent them; the way to postpone them would be to join the League of Nations and make it strong enough to crush nationalism and especially radicalism, which is probably going to cause more turmoil than the others. But he will not advocate that. He likes freedom too well.

He thinks the Russians are naturally a submissive and goodnatured people, but see how much bloodshed and famine and atrocities this revolution cost them! It would cost much more before it could be successful in other countries, and it could not succeed in most of them. He thinks it would only result in empire—what you call fascism—just as the radical movements in Rome and Greece did. And he thinks that Russia itself, as it is at present, is a good example of the same result. It has restored class-distinction and privilege and has less freedom than Germany has, with a few iron-handed strong men at the top, an inevitable result. —In Rome Marius represented the proletariat and became dictator; Sulla represented the upper classes and followed him; Caesar represented the proletariat at first and compromised and took contributions from the wealthy just as Mussolini and Hitler did, and Augustus consolidated the compromise. These dictatorships Russian, Italian, and German and so forth indicate the autumn of an age like yellow leaves on a tree. Dont be misled by words; watch what they do, not what they say, nor what you think, or wish they think and you will see the resemblance between Russia and Germany, Stalin and Hitler. He doesn't like either but they are "on the side of history" as the socialists say.[32]

[31] *Sara Bard Field, "Beauty Dedicated to Reaction," Pacific Weekly, III (November 11, 1935), 226–27.*
[32] *See Letter 257.*

Europe of course cannot properly be compared to Rome, but to Greece in its decline when the proletarian and upper-class tyrannies alternated; because Europe is many states, not one like Rome and must wear itself out with nationalist wars as well as with revolutions—and won't be much of a prize by the time its Caesar comes.

If sometimes you think his verses melancholy "unrelieved pessimism"—remember this is but a faint hint of the historical survey and data which underlies his considered opinion that people dont change much. Get him going on the various Utopias and their outcomes! His desire and inclination for freedom and equality—is as keen as Erskines, but these facts rise up in his mind about the past when he scrutinizes the future. In these paragraphs I have reported to you as accurately as I can shreds of conversation and comments of his while reading of contemporary political and economic movements. You know how he hates to discuss his writing but next time we meet you have some questions ready—not directly intent on his verses—and see what he says. —As for me I cannot tell how cold it leaves me when these crusaders for leisure point with pride to electrical dish-washers and communal nurseries! Not for that would I crusade.

I feel an extreme aversion to the reviewers of today on the left who feel the need of Propaganda in Literature. It makes a temporary pamphlet out of what might be a permanent contribution to Literature. Do you recall the Liberal Leigh Hunt and how he groaned and gnashed his teeth at Wordsworth?—who wasn't devoting his genius as a writer to Causes? —Who cares now in all those marvellous bits of Wordsworth that will live as long as English, —about his omitting the Causes of that hour?[33]

What if Frances Willard or some cultivated W.C.T.U. person of her faith reviewed a book of yours or Erskines and wrote "Alas and alas! such tender hearts and sensitive minds damned beyond hope by their praise of the Vintage!" That's how I feel when I read certain of your passages about Robin! Literature isnt the pleader of a special cause as critic. When alls said and done, though, yours is the lovingest criticism we will ever find in a radical paper. And I love you for being always the sincere and eager advocate you are!//

Fun to discuss all that with you.

And oh *no*—one more thing Robin doesn't "depreciate the intellect"—not

---

[33] *I wrote Elizabeth Bauer in 1938(?), "If I have a 'message' it is expressed perhaps most clearly in the dialogue between Orestes and Electra at the end of 'The Tower Beyond Tragedy' beginning 'Here is the last labor To spend on Humanity . . .' and ending 'No time but spiritual eternity . . .' or in the last line of the last poem in 'Selected Poetry'—the poem called 'Theory of Truth'. . . .*

"But poetry does not necessarily have a 'message' except 'How beautiful things are'—or 'How sad, or terrible'—or even 'How exciting.' These are the only messages that Homer or Shakespeare—for instance—have for us." See also Letter 258.

233

all the time! I suppose you refer to "Return"—Its a temporary need there
to evade thought for the time and let this Being be refreshed and enriched, this
reservoir of Being, refilled by Natural Beauty.   Dearest
love from us both, Una

But your title was a great source of pleasure to Donnan. He said "That's
grand. I'd begun lately to fear father was getting Pinko!"

Another thought: In your letter to me about your review you condemned
the English for exporting rice from India during famine times. What do
you say of the Soviet Russian leaders exporting wheat during famine *there*
and the world led by Nansen trying to collect funds to carry food
into Russia for the starving?

Sara human nature doesn't vary much race by race politics by politics. Its
fine and uplifting to think the mass is noble—it sounds sublime but its
dangerous to act on such a belief too thoroughly.

I shall have lots of second thoughts on the above. —One is I don't mean
of course to divorce Poetry from thought and opinion but I believe it can
reflect contemporary action without *advocating* a line.

Bassett asked if I'd like to write any reply to your article. If you are willing
to send this back to Peter I would let them publish it as a *letter*—and
informal. I haven't time to think it out in better shape and so he is certain not
to see it! —But I am going to ask you—why do almost all Radicals except
Erskine and Sara feel so mean and cross? The very sound of a person
going quietly about his own business and *enjoying* _work_ and not yelling
with anguish because Mr. Rockerfeller has more stuffing in his turkey than
he has turns their blood to gall. Why do they want every poor person to
squirm with envy? I notice that scientists and health crusaders and so on who
are laboring to rectify the mistakes of *Nature* do not have this mean
feeling inside. If they see some one who is not actively fighting a battle against
syphilis and mosquitoes and infantile paralysis, they don't get abusive. If
Robin saw the above he would be very disappointed that I noticed their bile
and now that I have called it to your attention I feel in fact very cheerful
and quit of the unhealthy mess: I put it upon you. Perhaps you
know the answer.//

249: TO CORTLANDT SCHOONOVER

November 18, 1935

Dear Mr. Schoonover: Thank you most cordially for "With Cortes the
Conqueror," and your father for inscribing it. I have already looked through
the text with pleasure, and particularly enjoyed the romantic beauty of

your father's illustrations. Nothing could possibly be too romantic for this most amazing episode of history, and the design and color are delightful.

It was no trouble but a pleasure to inscribe that book of mine for you. Sincerely yours, Robinson Jeffers

250: TO MRS. HUGH BULLOCK

December 16, 1935

My dear Mrs. Bullock: I am sorry, but it seems better to withdraw my name as sponsor for the "Academy of American Poets." I don't mean to ask that it be scratched off letter-heads, etc., only that it be dropped when new ones are printed, and not used in connection with any new enterprise.

I don't ask this in any spirit of criticism, but simply because I live so far from New York that I can't properly undertake responsibility for anything that is done there. For instance, I received a couple of letters about a "Poetry Ball," which the writers seemed not to approve of, and all I could answer was that I had never heard of it, knew nothing about it. I still know nothing about it.

Then again, as was freely admitted in my first letter to you, I don't feel sympathetic toward academies in general. I have nothing whatever against this one, but since I cannot keep au courant of its activities it seems better to withdraw my name—but not in any sense as a protest. Sincerely yours, Robinson Jeffers

251: TO BENJAMIN DE CASSERES

c/o Mabel Dodge Luhan
Taos, New Mexico
[1936]

Dear De Casseres: Thank you very much for the pamphlets and book. I read them all with interest and enjoyment, and wish so much that I could have thanked you sooner. But at home it is practically impossible for me to write a letter, there are so many things to do and experience, and a pleasant hypnotic routine that is perfectly letter-proof.

I like *The Individual against Moloch* best for its thought and substance and *The Muse of Lies* for its poetic value, but all these publications have poetry and truth, beauty and surprise in them. It is fine that you are publishing them at last.

We are visiting here for about a month, as in several previous summers. We ride and watch the thunder-storms and swim in the hot springs; our boys practise their Spanish on the Mexicans and Indians. The country is beautiful and strange, 7000 feet high, going up to 13000, but I would not live permanently except by the ocean.

Congratulations and best wishes on the books you are publishing, full of ideas as the sea is of fish.   Sincerely, Robinson Jeffers

252: TO LOUIS UNTERMEYER

Taos, New Mexico
June, 1936

Dear Louis Untermeyer: I am so sorry not to have written sooner, at least in acknowledgment of your splendid "Modern American Poetry." It is like a narcotic addiction, this inability to write letters. Your anthology is a *noble* work, in scope and variety, in the excellence of its choices and the sanity and good humor of its comment. —Also I owe thanks for your kind and intelligent review of my verses in the Mercury. At least I think it was yours; you said you had written one, so we looked it out.

We were disappointed not to see you last fall, when that wretched accident of the lost manuscripts deferred your journey west. Mayn't we hope that you'll make it yet—this fall perhaps?

We are again visiting in Taos, whence I wrote you last year—beautiful place, though less dear than home. We've been here a month and are en-motoring for home to-morrow morning—two and a half days' journey— and we shall sizzle on the deserts.   Yours cordially, Robinson Jeffers

253: TO MRS. HAAKON CHEVALIER

August, 1936

Dear Miss [*sic*] Chevalier: It is doubly hard to refuse an invitation forwarded by Sara Bard Field, but I cannot serve as sponsor of this Congress of Western Writers. It seems to me quite useless, for writers cannot be organized— except newspaper or film writers—and ought to associate with any or all classes in the community rather than with each other; and if they wish to express opinions they can write them. And I do not think that culture can be maintained or handed down through conventions and committees. I am sorry to write what you must disagree with, but it seems better to speak plainly.   Sincerely, Robinson Jeffers

254: TO OSCAR K. CUSHING AND R. D. McELROY

(James D. Phelan Foundation)

October 13, 1936

Dear Mr. Cushing and Mr. McElroy: Thank you for your letter of
October 6, asking me to serve as a member of the committee of award for the
Phelan Fellowships.[34]

I shall be glad to serve, if the business of the committee is only to read and
judge a number of books or manuscripts, and can be conducted by
correspondence. But if it requires meetings—at least more than one—or to
interview candidates, I must regretfully decline, owing to pressure of
time and circumstances.

I am sorry to make a conditional answer, but really cannot do otherwise.
Yours sincerely, Robinson Jeffers

255: TO RUDOLPH GILBERT

November 29, 1936

Dear Rudolph Gilbert: I am sorry to be late in thanking you for "Shine
Perishing Republic."[35] It is hard for me to persuade myself to read anything
written about my own verses, whether praise or blame or interpretation. I
have almost never read reviews. It is an instinct, and I think a reasonable
instinct, to avoid being influenced in future work by other people's opinions,
and to avoid self-consciousness. But I could not intelligently thank you
for the book without looking through it at least, and it took me some days to
overcome the reluctance.

This evening I have read it rapidly through, and can say that I am sincerely
grateful. I don't know, and don't wish to consider, whether my verses
deserve this studious attention; but I'm glad to believe they have had some
value if they have been an influence in stimulating your mind toward

[34] *I served on the James D. Phelan Fellowship Jury of Award in 1937, 1938, 1939, and
1948. Correspondence acknowledging receipt of manuscripts, agreeing on dates
for jury meetings, etc., was conducted, after this initial acceptance, by Una J.*
[35] *See Letters 169 and 227.*

OVERLEAF:

"Man also is a part of nature, not a miraculous intrusion."

(Letter 307)

the activity and very wide reading that your work evidences. The book is excellently thought and written: let me congratulate you on it. It seems very well manufactured too. There are some errors in the verse-quotations, one or two curious ones, but that is not surprising; I have done much worse now and then with my own proof-sheets.

Your feeling about the meaning or direction of the poems does not always exactly coincide with mine, but it seems to me in almost all cases both intelligent and probable. You do not perfectly comprehend "At the Birth of an Age," and I think no one else does, though the verses are clear enough. All the prevalent religions think of God as blessed, or happy, or at least at peace; even the pantheist mystic finds peace in God; therefore this conception of God as in pain is hardly admitted by the reader's mind. For this reason I built it up through the will-pointing of Prometheus, the self-hanging of Odin in Norse mythology, the personality of Gudrun, and the phantom of Christ, to make it poetically credible. It is a conception that runs through my verses, from "Heautontimorumenos" (the self-tormentor) in "Women at Point Sur" (page 174) down to this latest. If God is ["the universe" is crossed out] all, he must be suffering, since an unreckoned part of the universe is always suffering. But his suffering must be self-inflicted, for he is all; there is no one outside him to inflict it. —I suppose the idea carries psychological as well as cosmic or religious implications. Man as well as God must suffer in order to discover; and it is often voluntary—self-inflicted—suffering.

—I have been too prolix. —Thank you warmly for your book.   Sincerely yours, Robinson Jeffers

256: TO HENRY SEIDEL CANBY (National Institute of Arts and Letters)

January 13, 1937

Dear Mr. Canby: Thank you very much for your letter informing me of my election to the National Institute of Art[s] and Letters. I am sorry that it will not be possible for me to be present at the annual dinner and meeting a week from to-day. May I convey through this letter my thanks to the members of the Institute, and my sense of the honor done me? I am proud to be enrolled in this distinguished fellowship, and with so notable a list of entering members.   Faithfully yours, Robinson Jeffers

257: TO VAN WYCK BROOKS

February, 1937

Dear Mr. Brooks: I would sign this statement[36] if it protested the atrocities committed on both sides, although I feel that these horrors are inevitable in class war, and will come in time to other countries, as they have to Russia and Spain. But I am not willing to go on record in favor of either side. The rebellion, as you know, was not unprovoked; legal democracy was breaking down before it began; in its later development it is a clash of forces which cannot avoid clashing; and whichever side wins, dictatorship will win. Personally I detest dictatorship, right, left, or center; but history favors it, at present and for a time to come. It is impossible for me to sympathize morally with either side.[37]

With best wishes—for I remember the pleasure of meeting you once here— Sincerely, Robinson Jeffers

258: TO MARGERY EVERNDEN

February 3, 1937

Dear Miss Evernden: There are so many kinds of writing—and newspaper writing, fiction, poetry, writing on scientific or economic or political subjects, and a thousand more. Naturally the student should adapt his education to the kind of writing he wants to do. But the writer, perhaps more than other people, ought to know a good deal in a good many directions, so as to have a fairly complete picture of the world. Gaps and blank spaces in the picture are always a nuisance and often worse. —I speak from experience, alas!

Propagandist literature may occasionally be good as literature, but usually it is not. St. Paul was a great propagandist and sometimes a great writer; so is Trotsky; but these are distinguished exceptions. I don't know of any good propagandist poetry. There is good poetry that has streaks of propaganda in it, but the two are not fused; they alternate. There is good poetry that expresses hatred of injustice, love of freedom, and so forth, but it is personal love and hatred, not propagandist.[38]

Now you offer two questions that I can't answer. Whom do I consider the greatest living American poet? I don't consider at all on the subject; it

---

[36] *The text of this protest against the cruelties of the Spanish insurgents and a list of its signers were published in the* New York Times, *March 1, 1937, Sec. 1, p. 7.*
[37] *See Letters 248 and 276.*
[38] *See Letter 248.*

241

sounds too much like statistics. Nor can I guess whether Americans are writing the best poetry of today. I would have to know all foreign literature like a native to answer that one.

Finally, toward which schools do I think American poetry of the future will go? I wish it would avoid schools; that is another word for derivative writing, imitation. I am sure it will soon be avoiding all the schools of the present time. Its future direction cannot be predicted, since it will depend on the genius of writers unknown or unborn yet, and many other incalculable elements.

It has been a pleasure to consider your questions, and even to attempt answers to them.   Sincerely, Robinson Jeffers

259: TO BENJAMIN MILLER

March, 1937

Dear Mr. Miller: I like these poems, but they seem to me a little vague and pale, wistful, rather than vigorous in thought or passionate in feeling. Spender has not the power nor originality of Auden, I think.

The first you mention—"I think continually"—has that characteristic young-England sentimentality which one finds in so many of their novels. —"The Spirit—delight of the blood—demand for love"—all in the same sigh. But there is a fine imaginative lift at the end.

"After they have tired" is interesting, and good poetry, but suffers intellectually from the bright Shelleyan vagueness of its concept of revolution. I think that even poets ought to read the newspapers. And to consider that history—though it rarely repeats the detail—has always repeated the pattern; and Utopia was never included in it. That is what Shelley came at last to recognize, in the final chorus of his Hellas.

—A dissertation on the philosophy of my poetry! Do you remember that seven-times-told story of Ford Madox Ford's, about the man who had tried so hard to be a philosopher, "but cheerfulness *would* come creeping in?" Sincerely yours, Robinson Jeffers

1937-38 *In the summer of 1937, the Js visited unfamiliar parts of Ireland and revisited people and places they remembered with affection. The small collection of correspondence during this period is particularly interesting in its variety and range: here is the longest letter J ever wrote (to his in-laws in Mason, Michigan); here are notes written in third-person response to biographical questions; and here is a letter written to a child in simple courtesy to a parent's request.* ❧ *The Js stopped in Michigan with Una's family, in Taos with Mabel Luhan, and in Palm Springs with Melba Bennett on their way home from Ireland. J had completed* Such Counsels You Gave to Me *before he sailed; he had also begun selecting poems for inclusion in Random House's* The Selected Poetry of Robinson Jeffers, *which was published in 1938.*

260: TO BENJAMIN DE CASSERES

Cunard White Star
"Georgic"
[*July, 1937*]

Dear Ben De Casseres—   We were in New York July 9th, and I telephoned
your address twice, early and late in the afternoon, but neither you nor Bio
answered. So sorry. I hope to see you when we come back, in November
probably. We also tried in vain to reach Edna St. V. Millay and Edgar
Lee Masters. It was horribly hot weather—I hope you were all out of town.

Bennett Cerf, my publisher, lodged and entertained us. He was
extraordinarily kind, and kept our presence a secret from everyone. We
came aboard ship the morning of the tenth, and sailed at noon, and have now
got into lovely gray seas beyond reach of the heat-wave.

Thank you most cordially, Ben, for dedicating "Chiron the Centaur" to me.
It seems to me one of the loveliest of your poems, and I feel the honor.
I read with so much pleasure all your gay wisdom as it is published.

We are going to Ireland and Great Britain again for four or five months—
Una and I and our two sons—we drove across the continent and shipped
the car and are taking it with us. Una has a real need of visiting the British
Isles every eight years or so; and the rest of us are glad to go along.

I hope very much to see you when we return.   Yours, Robinson Jeffers

261: TO FREDERIC IVES CARPENTER

Cunard White Star
"Georgic"
July 14, 1937

Dear Mr. Carpenter: I suppose it must be nearly a year since you sent me
"Puritans Preferred Blondes," and I always meant to thank you for it, and was
sorry to have failed. Here in the long leisures of an Atlantic crossing there
is no excuse for not writing.

Your essay is most interesting, acute and convincing. You speak of the creative impulse failing in Hawthorne and Melville after they turn back toward the ideal of "purity": —the observation sent my thoughts off on a tangent that cannot be developed in a letter, hardly in a book, but I'll try to sketch it, —though probably the thoughts will not be new to you. First it occurred to me that power is with the radicals—the destroyers—in thought and literature, ever since the movement that preceded the French Revolution. The memorable names are mostly the names of men who broke down some set of conventions or "ideals"—Voltaire, Rousseau, Byron— Nietzsche etc.—away down to D. H. Lawrence. Conventions of monarchy, warlike patriotism, Christian dogma, purity, down to reticence even. Many of these radicals were builders of ideals too, or aspired to be; but what they built was temporary and without much influence; what they threw down stays down. Much of their power derives from this catalysis; as an animal's power from breaking down starch and protein. Men like Dante or Thomas Aquinas were more like the plants that preceded the animals and built up the complex molecules that are food for them. (The plants live by power from the sun, the animals by power from the plants.) Perhaps this shift of power, from the builders to the destroyers, is another sign that our culture-age has culminated and turned down again, in a creative sense? —That now its "ideals" and ideas need to be broken up and lie fallow awhile, in preparation for a later age?

Then I thought of—Wordsworth, for instance,—realizing that much of his tendency had been destructive: —he had almost reduced Christianity to nature-worship and pantheism: —so he repented; and lost his creative power and significance, just as you feel that Hawthorne and Melville did when they turned back toward "purity." One could multiply instances, even down to T. S. Eliot, but I'll not go on.

—I haven't answered your letter, only talked thoughts suggested by your pamphlet. I cannot remember what Tamar meant by "We pure have power"— I never thought about it; only it seemed to me that she would say that. —I think you are right in suggesting the ambivalency of the incest symbol.

I think you are wrong in seeing nothing in "At the Birth of an Age" but an old tale of revenge. Revenge was then a moral obligation; the point is that Gudrun's pre-Christian morality broke down; she did *not* take revenge, but was lost between past and future just as the present world is—or your Hawthorne and Melville—but found a vision at the end.

Finally—in spite of this exception!—let me say that you have qualities as a philosophical critic that ought to be very widely recognized, and I think will be.   Sincerely, Robinson Jeffers

I forgot to say that we are en route to Ireland and Great Britain, to return probably in November. No address abroad yet. Letters, if any, will be forwarded from California.

262: UNA J TO FRED B. MILLETT

The following was written on a letter from Professor Millett, dated July 6, 1937, requesting specific information on J's "personal preferences in literature and the other arts; his political sympathies or affiliations, his estimation of American literature in general, or American writers in particular (in contrast, perhaps, to British or Continental literature); and his purposes and methods of writing." In spite of their third-person point of view, the answers are penciled in J's hand.

Dunfarraghty, Co. Donegal
Ireland
July 31, 1937

This letter of yours followed us to Ireland—I asked my husband to make some notes to guide me in my reply. They are so clear I am sending them as he jotted them down. —See over.   Sincerely, Una Jeffers

I (preferences) He has reached the age when he reads mostly for information or amusement. The authors he turns back to (more in thought than in fact)—Homer, Aeschylus, Shakespeare, Milton, Wordsworth, bits of Yeats. In art his taste is averse from "modernism."

II (Politics) Ideally, aristocratic and republican: —freedom for the responsible elements of society, and contentment for the less responsible. This ideal being impractical for the present and the conjecturable future, he is interested in politics but not inclined toward any party, and votes in the sense of a choice of evils.

III He thinks that American and Western European writing *of the present* are products of the same urban culture; there is little fundamental difference between them. American writing is probably more vigorous at present.

IV He is inarticulate about his purposes and methods of writing; has tried intentionally to avoid formulation and preserve a certain degree of unconsciousness on these subjects.

263: TO ISABEL CALL (Una's mother) AND HER DAUGHTERS

Lac-na-Lore House
Ballymore, Donegal, Ireland
August 1, 1937

Dear Mama Call and all at Mason: We have just been swimming, and I came home ahead of the others to write to you. It was lovely clear water, much warmer than our Pacific, and we went in at a gorge in the rocks where the water is about twelve feet deep, so clear and smooth that you can see every shell and bit of seaweed on the white sand at the bottom. Garth swam away out in the bay, and I got dressed as soon as he came back to the rocks.

Life has been very rapid since we landed in Ireland two weeks ago. We arrived without any plan of procedure, and have been darting back and forth in the rain on the little narrow roads, looking at churchyards and mountains and moorlands, visiting round towers and islands, hardly ever stopping two nights in the same place. But now we are settled for three or four weeks. This is a lovely centuries-old farm house, on a hillside with little stone-walled fields of a big woodland and half a mile from the sea. The people are pleasant and intelligent, the food much better than in most hotels. We have breakfast at nine, dinner at half-past one ("half-one," they call it here), "meat-tea" at six, "supper" at ten or so, and shall all be plump and pompous. The name Lac-na-Lore means the "book-stone"—the old name of the place—from a flat rock that lies on the hill above and looks like a huge book.

Near here is the Bloody Foreland, the northwesternmost point of Ireland—drove around there yesterday, a wild rocky solitary place, with some sheep bleating in the sea-wind. Nearer is Horn Head, a still wilder promontory, where we walked and rode a few days ago, above 800-foot precipices, with many sea-birds screaming far down below. The bay we are on is called Sheephaven, and has many long branches and inlets, in which the boys were canoeing day-before-yesterday. They tipped the canoe over in a river and came home streaming wet and got a good scolding from their mother. The canoe belongs to the son of the people here, a boy of nineteen who seems older than our boys, though considerably smaller, and makes a nice companion for them. He has two sisters, a little older than he; their mother is English, from London; the father's family has owned this place for hundreds of years. There are some other guests, six or eight besides ourselves, but more over the weekend. Donnan has been over the guest-book, which dates back for several years, and found no Americans except ourselves; all North-Irish or English, a few from the British colonies.

The other day we went in an eighteen-foot boat to Tory Island, a dozen miles off the coast here, where there is a fishing-village of 200 people or so, very wild and dirty, an ancient round tower, and a lighthouse. The passage was quite smooth on the way out, but two or three people were seasick. We were not. On the way back the waves were against us, they flew over the boat and soaked us to the skin, but nobody was sick. When we were in Galway some days ago we went out to the Aran Islands in a small steamer. That was really a rough passage; the boat nearly stood on her head. All the passengers were sick except ourselves and two American girls. There were a few Aran-islanders on board, and they were sick too. When we landed we got in a jaunting-car and drove six miles at a hard trot over amazing little roads to Dun Aengus, a great prehistoric fortress on a high sea-cliff. Awe-inspiring place, protected on one side by the three-hundred foot cliff, and from the land by three crescents of high thick stone walls, one beyond the other, the inner one about twenty feet high and twenty feet thick, enclosing an acre or two of land. Nobody has any idea who built the place or why. It couldn't stand a siege, for there is no water, and it would take twice as many people as can live on the island now to defend the smallest of the three walls. The islands are all bare and wind-swept, wild rock, hardly any soil. The people make soil by rotting sea-weed, dig a few small potato-patches, and go fishing in their little black canvas skiffs. Some of them can talk English, but never anything but Irish (Gaelic) among themselves. Every where in the Irish Free State we hear Irish spoken, much more than we heard eight years ago. The road signs and signs over shops are in Irish; sometimes with little English translations underneath. All the school-children have to learn Irish, if they don't know it already, and arithmetic, geography, etc. are taught exclusively in Irish. This was almost a dead language twenty years ago, except in the extreme west. The road-signs and shop-signs look very odd, because even the Irish alphabet is different from ours, more like Russian or Greek.

While we were in County Mayo, ten days ago, we climbed up Croaghpatrick—St. Patrick's mountain—one of the highest in Ireland. There is a little locked-up church at the top; St. Patrick is supposed to have prayed and fasted there, and blessed all Ireland from the summit. It was a stiff climb over broken rolling stones, very steep the second half of the way, about 2400 feet high, the summit covered in cloud, but great views of land and water on the way up. Once a year there is a great pilgrimage of Irish Catholics to the summit; it happened just a week ago, three days after we were up there. Una talked to a woman in a shop who said she was going; she would start at four in the morning and hear Mass at the church on top. She had been up seven times, once barefoot. Lots of them go up barefoot, and a few go part of the way on their knees. They all go up fasting, I believe—that is, without breakfast. The woman said, "Oh, I dread it." Una said we were up there the day before, and the woman was very pleased and said, "May it be a benefit to you." Next day we drove by the foot of the mountain and saw thousands of people coming down, thousands of others still going up, like a long trail of ants. The newspapers said that 30,000 people from all over Ireland went up that day. When we were up we picked up several pebbles on the summit to give to our Catholic friends in California.

Just after this we went back to Moore Hall, where Una's literary idol, George Moore the novelist was born. We had been there a few days before, with a letter from his brother Colonel Maurice Moore, and the people there had promised to have a row-boat ready, to take us to the little island in the lake, where George Moore's ashes are buried. It was a weird journey, under the gray clouds on that lonely lake, the stiff reeds hissing and scraping as the boat forced its way through. The caretaker of the place, and one of our boys, rowed the boat. The caretaker is a thoughtful intelligent man with a sense of humor, and Una had a wonderful time gossiping with him about George Moore and his friends. The grave is a hollowed rock on the shore with the ashes in an urn inside it, cemented over, and a great cairn of stones on top. There is also a little stone cross, and a short inscription. We each added a big stone to the cairn and Una and the rest of us thought and talked about George Moore. Then we pushed through the trees and ivy to visit the ruined castle on the island, which is so old that nothing is known about it, except that it was already a ruin more than a thousand years ago. Then we got in the boat and went back through the shallow green water.

To-morrow we are invited for the afternoon and dinner to Glenveagh Castle, which belongs to a friend of our dear friends the Clapps. The people at the house here were quite excited when they heard we were going there, because Glenveagh is the great show-place of this corner of Ireland, and the public used to be allowed to visit it, but not at present.

Una and I are going for a walk now. We all send dearest love to all of you. We'll never forget what a pleasant time you gave us in Mason; and we'll be eager to see you all again.

I've only been able to tell you a few incidents of our first two weeks in Ireland; when we see you again you must make Una read you her diary.   Yours lovingly, Robin

264: TO MARK VAN DOREN

Lac-na-Lore House,
Ballymore (via Lifford)
County Donegal
Irish Free State
August 6, 1937

Dear Mark Van Doren: We have just had a letter from our friend Albert Bender, enclosing your kind little acknowledgment of some verses he sent you. I don't know how he happened to send them, but am glad of the occasion to write to you. At home I can't write letters; here it is a pleasure, on a rainy day like this one.

I think you might love this northwest corner of Ireland; it seems to us the happiest part of the island. The scenery is magnificent, fine mountains and heather and little stone-walled fields, all spun through with lakes and arms of the sea; the people are well-nourished and look you in the eye; there is little history, few antiquities, no industry at all, except weaving in some of the cottages. Thoroughly pastoral place; the name of the bay is Sheephaven, the only meat to be procured is excellent mutton. (With fish for tea, chicken o'Sundays.) There are eight-hundred-foot cliffs at Horn Head, clouded by vast flocks of gulls and sea-parrots, and caverned underneath by the sea. The Bloody Foreland and the beautiful Poisoned Glen are near by, such grand names, with nothing but the faintest little cobweb of legend to explain either of them. And Errigal peak, and Muckish mountain.

Before pitching here for a month we motored intensively for two weeks, avoiding all the places that we visited eight years ago. (Coming third class across the Atlantic—it proved entirely clean and comfortable—we were able to save enough money to bring the car along.) The one great change in Ireland, since we were here before, is the spread of the Irish language. It seems to be really the language of the country now. Amazing, in eight years' time. We have to look for old people now, when we ask directions in the little country lanes, so many of the children cannot speak English at all.

We were out to the Aran Islands off Galway, and Tory Island off the coast here, and [rowed?] out to the little lake island where George Moore's ashes lie under a pagan cairn of stones, opposite the ruins of Moore Hall where he was born. This was specially my wife's pious pilgrimage, but we all—our two boys are with us—added stones to the cairn.

In six weeks or so we shall go over to Scotland. I'd like very much to see you when we return by New York, probably in November.
Sincerely, Robinson Jeffers

265: TO ALBERT BENDER

Melville Hotel,
Londonderry
September 4, 1937

Dear Albert: Please forgive the pencil. Una has the pen and ink, and I am luckier with a pencil anyway.

We left Dublin yesterday morning, spent last night in Belfast, and to-night are stopping here. We don't usually travel such long hops, but yesterday after wandering hither and yon, and then crossing the border into Northern Ireland, we found no tolerable hotels in any of the places we had thought of stopping—or the hotel was full—so we were forced on, finally to Belfast, driving after dark for the first time since we landed in Ireland. To-day we just drove along the coast from Belfast, looking at scenery, and revisiting the cottage and people near Cushendall, where we lived eight years ago. They remembered us and were very friendly. Then we drifted on to Derry, and this evening the boys have gone out to call on some girls here, whom they met in Donegal. To-morrow we shall wander back again through Northern Ireland, stopping in some pleasant place, and in three or four days we expect to go over to Scotland.

We spent several interesting days in Dublin, seeing your friend Kathleen O'Brennan and others, but avoiding parties. We saw your beautiful case of finely printed books in Trinity College Library—not far from the Book of Kells!—and the Augusta Bender room [*named for Bender's mother*] in the National Museum; both were excellently displayed, and we enjoyed them much. Una and Garth visited the gallery of modern art, and saw your contribution of [*John*] O'Shea painting there,—very fine they said.

So now our stay in Ireland is coming to an end; in a week or two we shall be in the Hebrides probably, and then the Orkneys. Una has had a very fruitful time here—you must see her diary when we get home!—and the boys have had a very pleasant time, and I a very lazy one—pleasant too, of course. Especially Donegal was beautiful, with its mountains and seas. Two or three times I thought angrily that it was more beautiful than our own coast mountains, though not so strong, nor so much in earnest. But Fair Head, which we revisited to-day, is the most impressive promontory of them all. It is a pity that no people—not even the Irish!—is equal to its landscape. Except in Homer's Iliad and two or three other poems. With love from all four of us,   Affectionately, Robin

266: TO WILLIAM BERKOWITZ

[*October*], 1937

Dear William Berkowitz: Your father wrote suggesting that you would like to receive a letter from me, and I am delighted to send one. You probably have more amusing things to occupy your time during the long days in bed. One of my sons had to stay in bed for a while after the measles and a

> ". . . I must build a wall around the place. A friend
> gave us the other day an authentic bit of stone from
> the wall of China, it's a good beginning."
>
> (Letter 87)

252

throat infection, and I used to read to him. This was when he was a little boy; he is a big one now, a member of the University of California Wrestling Team.

I am writing from Michigan; we have been travelling in Great Britain and Ireland and we are on our way home to California. Orkney and Shetland, the little islands north of Scotland interested me as much as anything. In the Orkney Islands we sailed through Scapa Flow where the Germans sank the great fleet which they had surrendered to the British at the end of the war. While we were there a German Warship was being brought up from the bottom to be floated south and broken up for scrap iron. In Scotland we saw a man from Iceland, who had sailed from there all alone in a little motor skiff and was going on to Norway. He was a middle-aged man out to see the world a little before he grew too old. They are dark and dangerous seas and he had no charts at all and was navigating with nothing but a compass; had sailed from Iceland before and been beaten back by storms but this time he had gotten through.

It was interesting to see the North Star almost straight overhead as at home in California it is quite low in the sky and as you go North it rises higher. These islands used to belong to Norway and the people are mostly of Norwegian race but they talk English.

I hope this finds you [*better?*]   Sincerely yours, Robinson Jeffers

267: TO HYATT HOWE WAGGONER

November 21, 1937

Dear Mr. Waggoner: I will try to answer the questions in your letter of Nov. 10.

First, as to the importance of science for the artist and for the thinker. It seems to me that for the thinker (in the wider sense of the word) a scientific basis is an essential condition. We cannot take any philosophy seriously if it ignores or garbles the knowledge and view-points that determine the intellectual life of our time. (These data and view-points are not final, of course. A thinker might attack some of them successfully; but he must not be ignorant of them.)

For the contemporary artist science is important but not at all essential. He might have no more modern science than Catullus yet be as great an artist. But his range and significance would be limited accordingly.

Your other questions refer to my own intellectual development. I cannot remember what were the first scientific books that made an impression on me. My father was a clergyman but also intelligent, and he brought me up to timely ideas about origin of species, descent of man, astronomy, geology, etc., so that progress was gradual, none of the view-points of modern science came as a revelation. Studies in university and medical school gave me more room to move in, more points of support, but never, that I remember, any sudden readjustment. —And so with later reading.

In my writing I have tried to avoid the special vocabularies of science (which would seem pedantic or worse) while accepting its influence.

You are welcome to quote anything in this letter, though I fear it is not particularly interesting.   Sincerely yours, Robinson Jeffers

268: UNA J TO CORTLANDT SCHOONOVER

January 11, [*1938*]

Dear Mr. Schoonover: At long last I get to the answering of your letter and discover that while I have the letter in my desk, I have filed away your article and can't get at it tonight without too much trouble. I do not know whether you state definitely which of the small items of Jeffers' you wish to get. —First let me say that we are both of us much opposed to small items. Each one of them has been forced out of us—or come by surprise. (For instance the *Rock and Hawk* was done by Frederick Prokosch before we ever heard of him for his own writing he printed the poem from its first appearance in Scribner's I believe, on his little hand press and sent us all the copies but two I think for a surprise) and so on . . . But we believe that it puts an unfair burden on the average reader and enthusiast to have so many little items to pursue. —If you have no copy of *Stars*, or if you have none of the article on Sterling which was printed with the Sterling *Letter* by San Francisco Book Club, I will give you a copy of each gladly if you let me know. A friend here has a soiled copy of "An Artist" she would part with for $2. —It is the copy used in that special *Carmelite* of circa 1928 [*December 12, 1928*] devoted to R. J. and edited by Ella Winter and Lincoln Steffens—and it got dirty in the press room. —I have a copy of that Carmelite I will give you also if you lack it.

If you name other things you want I may be able to direct you to some of them from time to time.

We arrived home Dec 12, having stopped in Michigan, and two weeks with Mabel Luhan in Taos and again in Palm Springs. —I see that it is a month

tomorrow and it has been a whirlwind of activity only now
subsiding a little.

My husband thanks you for your enthusiastic support.   Sincerely
Una Jeffers

It is possible that within six months a very interesting book will be printed
closely connected with my husband's work. —An eastern friend of yours
now living here has a hobby of photography and is doing marvellous pictures
of landscape. He said lately that so often in the East he is asked "Is that
coast there as Jeffers describes it?"—and his pictures prove that it is!
He asked permission to publish a book of them 40 or 50 and call it "Jeffers
Country." My husband was so enthusiastic when he came to examine
the collection that he agreed to choose captions for the pictures from his own
poems. If this book is published I will let you know.[1]

Thank you for your Christmas greeting!
This coast has never been properly photographed before.

---

[1] *Photographer Horace Lyon describes his uncompleted project, at which he worked from
1936–38, in "Jeffers as a Subject for Horace Lyon's Camera,"* Robinson Jeffers
Newsletter, *No. 18 (June, 1967), pp. 2–5. In 1965 the Sierra Club published* Not Man
Apart, *featuring photographs of the Big Sur coast and lines from J's poems.*

1938-48 *The years 1938–48 were surprisingly productive for J in spite of many interruptions. Never before had he spent so much time away from home and familiar routines: the Js were only just returned from Ireland and their cross-country travel home when Una urged J to accept invitations to the desert as a means to stimulate his exhausted imagination; in 1941 J consented, for financial reasons, to a lecture and poetry reading at the Library of Congress and at several university and college campuses; and in 1947 he reluctantly attended the Broadway opening of* Medea. ❧ *J's poems of the war years demonstrate how gravely World War II distracted him; he served as a volunteer aircraft spotter, while Una did Red Cross work; Garth joined the Marines in 1941; and Donnan left Carmel and settled in Ohio, where he married a Zanesville girl.* ❧ *A new kind of distraction confronted J in the form of several proposals to produce his work dramatically. In 1941 John Gassner adapted* The Tower Beyond Tragedy *as a vehicle for Judith Anderson, who had been interested in the role of Clytemnestra as early as 1937. Gassner's adaptation, starring Dame Judith, was produced by the Del Monte summer stock company in Carmel's Forest Theater. Dame Judith succeeded temporarily in interesting the Theatre Guild in a New York production, but when their interest waned, she and Jed Harris requested that J adapt* Medea *for her. J finished the play in 1945; it opened in New York in October, 1947, a week after Michael Meyerberg's production of* Dear Judas *closed.* ❧ *Random House published* Be Angry at the Sun and Other Poems *in 1941,* Medea *in 1946, and* The Double Axe and Other Poems *in 1948. J had also, during these years, published a considerable amount of prose: his Phi Beta Kappa address, "Thoughts Incidental to a Poem,"* Personalist, *XXI (Summer, 1940), 239–42, excerpted in Bennett's* Stone Mason, *pp. 135–36; "Preface to 'Judas,' "* New York Times, *October 5, 1947, Sec. 2, p. 3; "Poetry, Góngorism, and a Thousand Years,"* New York Times, *January 18, 1948, Sec. 6, pp. 16 and 26; and Forewords to several books.* ❧ *Academic and critical interest continued: J accepted honorary membership in Phi Beta Kappa in 1939, the Helen Levinson Award from* Poetry: A Magazine of Verse *in 1940, and election to the American Academy of Arts and Letters in 1945.* ❧ *Garth, returned from duty in Germany in 1946, bringing with him his bride Charlotte Riederer, and Donnan, married now to Lee Waggener, went home to Tor House and established their families there by 1947.*

269: TO FREDERIC IVES CARPENTER

Dear Carpenter: I am returning the book under separate cover by express.
I read it through with constant interest, and of course reservations of
agreement. My own belief, as you know already, is that the United States
remains culturally a part of Europe, as much as it is (its leadership at least)
racially. You yourself are willing to call your subject the "modern" or
"industrial" idea, instead of "American." "Industrial," I think, indicates the
most recent, and one of the unique, qualities of the culture-age we live
in. Not the beginning of a new age, but one of the qualities of this age.
"Modern" of course means merely recent and contemporary.

I do believe that America may produce a new culture—or new cultures—
but far away in the future. Possibly the obscure seeds are being sown at
present, as the seeds of this age were sown in the time of Augustus and
Tiberius. But meanwhile our culture is Christian (or at least ex-Christian)
and European—more free to develop in some directions, less free in
others—and has the same autumn and winter to endure.

(My disagreement is nothing against your argument: I think that
majority opinion would be on your side.)

The book is uneven, as you know already. Some chapters are excellent—
fine interpretation of Tess of the d'U.s, for instance—others not so good.
"American Idea in Economics" is the least thoughtful of all.

Now—(not for this book especially, but for all books that are general in
scope and suggest social ideals, or ideas of progress)—it seems to me
that some prefatory definition of values would be useful. What does the
author think would be best for men? What is he working toward?

Human happiness? —If a harmless drug were invented, under the influence
of which all people could be intensely and harmoniously happy, only
working enough to provide each other with sustenance and the drug, —would
that be a good goal for men? That would be maximum happiness,
minimum pain.

Goodness? —The modern view—and I think it is yours—makes goodness
a purely human and relative term. Good conduct is the conduct that
conduces to general human happiness. —But then happiness is primary.

Discovery, experience, development of all powers? —But then experience
of sorrow and pain is included. And all hopes of general harmony and
coöperation ought to be cancelled. For man is not only a coöperative animal,
but also a fiercely pugnacious and competitive animal. Unless he annihilates a
whole hemisphere of himself, universal coöperation is not possible. Do we
really want to annihilate half of the powers that have carried us so far?

Would a world of happy saints not be rather ignoble, if it were possible? And would it not lead straight toward degeneration?

—I am not answering these questions,—at present—but I think they are worth considering.

Meanwhile I enjoyed the book very much, and hope you will develop it further and ultimately publish. Perhaps you will finally narrow its scope somewhat. It might be more firmly convincing if you left Russia and India out of the count—they are rather doubtful topics, especially their futures!— and stuck more closely to America, particularly American literature—in which you are strongest.

I was very glad to see you the other day, and hope you'll find a way to return to this coast, and visit here again.   Sincerely, Robinson Jeffers

270: HYATT HOWE WAGGONER TO J

See Letter 271 for an explanation of the marginal numerals.

January 10, 1938

Dear Mr. Jeffers: Questions have arisen since I last wrote you of some importance in shaping my conclusions about the effect of science on your poetry.

(1) Do you agree with Whitehead, Eddington, Jeans, Weyl, et al, in their belief that the "revolution" in physics, which has led to the displacement of the old kinetic-atomic materialism in that science, has important consequences for philosophy? Somewhere in your poetry you say that science has fallen into (2) confusion in its business of understanding the world. Can you see any unity, any general trend, in the tendencies within the many sciences today?

It is my belief that your poetry was in part a source of and is an apt illustration of the doctrines set forth in Mr. Krutch's *The Modern Temper*. (There are, of course, limitations beyond which the comparison may not (3) be pushed; Krutch writes of the impossibility of tragedy now that man has come to see himself as closer to the rat in the psychologist's maze than to the noble creature, first cousin to God, which he once believed himself to be; and yet, many of your poems strike me as being tragic in the very sense which Mr. Krutch says is now impossible.) Such comparison seems to me certainly illuminating, if it is just. Is it? Louis Adamic says in his little book about (4) you that your knowledge of Freud and Jung is second hand. Is that correct?

The question of the meaning and origin of *The Modern Temper* is too vast, involving as it does the whole issue of the decay of Nineteenth Century liberal Christianity, under the impact of science and social disillusion to be treated in the brief study I am now attempting,[1] but I am forced to postulate, without attempting to prove them, four criteria of naturalism. Briefly put, they are: (1) the "debunking" of man; (2) determinism; (3) the idea that man is in an alien universe; (4) the belief that traditional values are illusions. Your poetry seems to me to illustrate all four of these attitudes and beliefs. Such are my conclusions about the effect of science on your philosophy as seen in your poetry. They seem to me to be obvious. I hope they will seem to you fair and accurate.   Sincerely yours, H. H. Waggoner

271: TO HYATT HOWE WAGGONER

February 1, 1938

Dear Mr. Waggoner: To save time and words I have marked the questions in your letter with (1), (2), etc., and return it for reference with my answers— which of course make no claim to authority. I am neither mathematician nor scientist nor philosopher.

(1) Yes, but I do not agree with some of the philosophic corollaries drawn from it. Such, for example, as that famous jump from the *apparently* capricious behavior of electrons to the theological idea of free will.

(2) General advance of factual knowledge, in some cases extraordinarily rapid, but precisely in those cases too scattering as yet to furnish a sound foundation for theory. —When I spoke of "science fallen into confusion" I probably had in mind those essays in cosmic mathematics that burgeoned a few years ago, based on the ideas of curved space, an expanding universe, and so forth. They were so many and contradictory.

(3) I have never read "The Modern Temper." I do not think that tragedy is impossible because man has lost his feeling of importance in the universe. Importance is a relative term; the tragic victim must seem important among other people, but he may be demi-god in Greek tragedy, prince or ex-king in Shakespeare, or only distinguished by personal strength or dignity, or the weight or strangeness of his sufferings. Big-city civilization is certainly hostile to tragedy, but science I think is neutral.

(4) Well . . . I have never been psychoanalyzed, nor performed a psycho-analysis; only read some books.

(5) I cannot pronounce as to naturalism, nor whether my writing belongs in that category.

I certainly do not agree with your third criterion—"alien universe." What

[1] *"Science and the Poetry of Robinson Jeffers,"* American Literature, X (November, 1938), 275–88.

other order of existence could man belong to, or have come from? "Indifferent" might be said, but not "alien."

Nor with the fourth. The belief that traditional values are divinely ordained seems to me an illusion. But to prefer—for instance—courage to cowardice or mercy to cruelty cannot be called an illusion. Traditional values may be thought of as habits or conventions, some useful, others foolish, all subject to change; but not as illusions.

Forgive the typewriter! My sons have taken my good one to college with them.   Sincerely yours, Robinson Jeffers

272: TO BENJAMIN MILLER

February, 1938

Dear Mr. Miller: Thank you for sending the paper:[2] I found it interesting and very well thought and expressed, though the distinction between theism and pantheism—"community of processes which support all of reality"— seems to me unessential.

Now in answer to your questions:—

I did not in my verses intend a distinction between aesthetic experience and what you call sensual mysticism. The intention in poetry is not primarily analytical; in my experience the two feelings were wound together, and so I expressed them. I think there *is* a distinction, and the beauty of things may be felt without any mystical recognition. But in that case it seems to me to be felt incompletely, however keenly. It seems to me that the mystical experience grows out of the aesthetic experience, naturally, almost logically.

I've never attempted a definition of beauty, and the interpretation you quote from Santayana doesn't satisfy me. There is beauty in tragedy, in an ice-berg, a tiger, a disastrous battle-scene,—things into which it is hard to impute any idea of pleasure; —except of course aesthetic pleasure; but that brings us back to where we started from.

When I wrote "beauty is thy human name" I was trying to express the feeling, which still remains with me, that this human and in itself subjective sense of beauty is occasioned by some corresponding quality or temper or arrangement in the object. Why else should a quite neutral thing—a wave of the sea or a hill against the sky—be somehow lovely and loveworthy, and become more so the more it is realized by contemplation? My intelligence

[2] *See Letter 279.*

(such as it is) does not work here; and it is hard to express in prose even my feeling. The feeling of deep earnestness and nobility in natural objects and in the universe: —these are human qualities, not mineral or vegetable, but it seems to me I would not impute them into the objects unless there were something in not-man that corresponds to these qualities in man. This may be called delusion, or it may be called mystical certainty, there is no external proof either way; and it is probably not essential to the religious attitude we are discussing, though with me it is part of it.

   —You call your questions obscure: what of my answers? But I have done as well as I could.   Sincerely yours, Robinson Jeffers

273: TO STUDENTS OF OUR LADY OF THE LAKE COLLEGE, SAN ANTONIO, TEXAS

On January 30, 1938, Sister M. Erasma wrote] asking for an autographed photograph and "a friendly greeting . . ." to the college student body.

February 23, 1938

To the Students of——   It is a pleasure to send you a note of greeting in answer to Sister Erasma's letter. She suggests that I send also "a bit of advice or what you will" but what comes into my mind is a poem by the famous Irish writer, W. B. Yeats. I hope you know his poems; some of them are very fine. This is not one of the best but it is interesting. He tells of visiting a school, I suppose when he was a Senator of the Irish Free State, and he goes about questioning, smiling, approving, but what he is really thinking about is the time when he was young and the woman he loved then and he wonders whether any of the girls here look as she did when she was a little girl. Meanwhile the school-children

> "In a momentary wonder stare upon
> A sixty-year-old smiling public man"

Of course you are not school-children and I am not 60 yet and far from being a public man, but I feel the same amused embarrassment. Perhaps you will let me off [with] a bit of advice and take instead my very best wishes for your present and future happiness.   Sincerely yours, Robinson Jeffers

274: UNA J TO MARGARET PETER ASHELMAN

This letter is facsimiled in Miss Ashelman's M.A. thesis, "The Ethical Fibre of Robinson Jeffers' Poetry," Swarthmore College, 1938.

March 7, 1938

Dear Mr. Peter [*sic*]:   Answering your letter of February 23. Robinson Jeffers father was a Presbyterian clergyman, professor in a theological seminary and for a time the pastor of an important church in Cleveland, Ohio (Euclid Ave Presbyterian church). A man of liberal views which progressively relaxed in creed and dogma. (At the time RJ and I were married—in 1913—his father, then 75 years of age, went each Sunday to a church of different denomination, rotating attendance at about eight churches. He was very scholarly and had travelled widely. He died Dec. 1914.

There were family prayers in RJ's youth, readings from the Bible, and the shorter catechism to learn by heart on Sundays, but all this lapsed and fell into desuetude after some years. RJ is extremely well versed in the Bible. Seldom reads it now, but can quickly locate any reference. His language has been influenced by much Bible reading. His mother was religious and up to her death in 1921 had a great part in church music. She was fond of society and very gay. His father was a recluse. RJ is not conscious of any definite time or any particular feeling of rebellion against religion when he began to feel the unimportance of loving humanity in toto.
Very sincerely, Una Jeffers

275: TO UNA J

J's brother Hamilton's invitation to Death Valley was accepted by Una in an attempt to relieve the inertia J was experiencing; see Bennett, Stone Mason, *pp. 169–70.*

[*Easter, 1938*]

Dear Una—   On account of a dream I had in London—for no one knows what previsions the human mind is capable of—and a 'hunch' I have here, it seems possible that we may crash on the way to Death Valley in spite of Hamilton's flying experience. Therefore this note and the enclosed holograph last will and testament. But a 'hunch' is not an assurance; I wouldn't bet

". . . I suppose my verses are thinking of the ends of life, and with what sort of hard faces to meet them. . . ."

(Letter 240)

money on a 'hunch' and it would be just cowardly to refuse an air-plane ride for one. I say this to avoid misunderstanding because I have no desire to die before writing another poem or two and I should love to know you and the boys for hundreds of years to come, and the beauty of things.

Aside from these considerations I have no prejudice against dying at any time—no desire to but also no shrinking from it so you are not to mourn me if it should happen, but remember that I loved you dearly and wanted you and the boys to be happy—not sorrowful. Remember also that it is vulgar for poor people to spend money on funerals. I wish to be cremated as cheaply, quickly and quietly as possible, no speech nor meeting nor music, no more coffin than may be necessary, no embalming, no flowers. A funeral is only a sanitary measure. Put the ashes a few inches deep in the courtyard near our little daughter's ashes—certainly no gravestone nor tablet.

As to the proposed 'Selected'—in case what I imagine should happen— 'Collected Poems' go ahead with them. I trust your judgment more than I do my own. I will try to get the preface done more or less, and to copy legibly the two or three bits of recent verse that might be added. I really think that the poems are valuable and memorable but how should I know? Don't forget the dedication to U. J. I will copy it out legibly. Finally my dearest love to you and our boys. More than I have ever been able to express.   Robin

276: TO THE LEAGUE OF AMERICAN WRITERS

In May, 1938, Donald Ogden Stewart, President of the League of American Writers, issued a pamphlet titled Writers Take Sides, *which collected letters responding to the League's queries, "Are you for, or are you against Franco and fascism?" and "Are you for, or are you against the legal government and the people of Republican Spain?" Some 400 responses were printed; J's (pp. 73–74) was placed with some uncertainty among those classified as "Neutral." See also Letter 258.*

[*April, 1938*]

You ask what I am for and what against in Spain. I would give my right hand, of course, to prevent the agony; I would not give a flick of my little finger to help either side win.

The legality of the government does not interest me. It did not restrain its supporters from violence and assassination before the insurrection began. It did not represent a majority of the Spanish people, therefore should have moved softly, rather than attempt changes that could only be enforced by violence.

Great changes were overdue in Spain, and the government's supporters
are justified in fighting for them. But Franco's people are justified in fighting
for the older Spain they are more or less loyal to, the religion they believe
in, and the rights they think are theirs, including the rights to life and liberty.
I am not disposed to damn either side for accepting whatever help it can get.

As to the interventionists: I have no tolerance for Italy's intervention and
none for Russia's, which began before Italy's and is less intensive because
Russia is more cautious and farther away.

As to fascism: I would fight it in this country, but if the Italians want
it that is their affair. The same goes for Nazism. The same for communism,
from which the others learned their methods.// Robinson Jeffers

277: TO FREDERICK M. CLAPP

April 24, 1938

Dear Timmie: It is not for lack of appreciation that I am so late in writing
you about "Said Before Sunset." The book delights and holds me as
"New Poems" did. It is more various; I think some of the poems are better
than any in "New Poems." A few are obscure to me (probably just
ignorance), a few seem to me keenly observed but less than poetic, but
perhaps that is my fault—allergy—they are the urban satiric ones, like
"Synchromesh." But "White" is of the same group, and its sudden turn and
irony—"Ah Liberation"—is highly poetic.

If someone asked me what poem in the book most clearly expresses your
special distinction I should probably choose "These Days," not as best
but as most typical; deep, sharp and mature thought in each word, plus
compression, plus the imaginative intensity that forms a picture as if from
inside experiencing it, not from outside observing it. "Shuffling discarded
plans / in the dark chart-room. . . ." It is wonderfully done, and you
are more than ever my favorite author.

I'll name others that have taken my mind. The two on "Mathematics," the
great ending of the first, the image of reality in the second. "The Dead,"
the splendid "Advice to Poets," the truth perhaps more than the fantasy of
"Explosive Mixtures". . . . There are so many others; and those suddenly
terrifying last lines . . . "eyeless sockets have to be met". . . . "The senseless
benedictions that the sea keeps for its dead." It is great work.

And of course the Coast-range Death-dance, which is very beautiful poetry
besides the friendship. "Press their eyes against the windows of men's

minds" is so fine that I wish you had been speaking of Shakespeare.
Yours, Robin

—I don't suppose your publishers would think it worthwhile to quote me
a second time, but if they should wish to I'd be proud to subscribe to
any phrase or fragment of this letter; or to write them another one.[3]
Congratulations and best wishes, Timmie.

278: UNA J TO BENNETT CERF (Random House)

May 29, 1938

Dear Bennett—(or Donald[4]—has Bennett sailed?)   Robin thinks Mr.
Gassner has done excellently well with his arrangement of *The Tower beyond
Tragedy* and hopes that it will be produced as I wired you. I sent back the
play by air-mail yesterday. Also the dramatic production contract by regular
mail. Many people have spoken to us about producing that poem. You
know it *was* produced at the Little Theatre at the University of California
several years ago. Very thrilling—although by amateurs.[5]

Thank you very much for the Freud. Its very well assembled. All the
important things in it—Such interesting reading even though one is familiar
with most of it now.

We expect to start to Taos about June 12 for a month with Mabel. She says
she has many exciting adventures to talk over.   Faithfully, Una

279: TO BENJAMIN MILLER

*The following letter refers first to Miller's thesis, "A Study in Aesthetic
Naturalism . . . ," Pacific School of Religion, 1938, then to Gregory
Vlastos' "Modern Criticisms of the Christian Evangel," Anglican Theological
Review (April, 1938), an assessment of the temptation to the ordinary
middle-class Christian in contemporary society to withdraw from conflict and
seek peace in solitude and romantic "identification with the universe."*

June 10, 1938

Dear Mr. Miller: Thank you for your letter of June third. My son returned
the thesis, and I meant to have written before this; and to congratulate
you on your graduation.

[3] *In promoting Dr. Clapp's* New Poems, *Harper had quoted from J's December 11, 1936,
letter to Eugene F. Saxton, a representative of Harper's: "It is one of the best
books of poetry published in recent years and the most interesting book, whether
prose or verse, that I have seen in a long time."*
[4] *Friede was now with Random House.*
[5] *See Letters 160, 214, and 283.*

I am much interested in your revision of the thesis. It is quite true that religion and ethics are different things, but they are associated almost universally; and religious experience causes some change in the manner of living.

The sentence you quote from Vlastos is typical, as you say. "Middle-class"—because the word is used by his teachers; not because aristocrats—or ditch-diggers either—are immune to "nostalgic solitariness." "Aloof from the struggle"—not because he wants the middle-class to take their own part in it—quite the reverse. And so forth: a typical example of echo-thinking.

We are leaving early to-morrow for a four or five weeks visit with a friend in Taos, New Mexico. I would rather stay here; I think all of us would. But our friend is insistent, and it will be a good change for our boys.   Sincerely, Robinson Jeffers

280: TO UNA J

See also Bennett, Stone Mason, pp. 170–71.

[*1938*]

Una, *I can't write.* I feel completely half-witted (not to diagnose the case) and 'writing'—during the past 30 years—has become one of the conditions of life for me.

You see how morbid!

I believe I'll have a new birth in course of time—not willing yet to grow old at fifty like Wordsworth, and survive myself—something will happen—and *life through this hell come home to me*—something will change, something will happen.

It is a little like my extravagances of 1917 to '19, except that I was uncritical then, and able to keep myself fairly quiet by not writing a lot of foolishness. (Now I know too much.) After that we began to make Tor House—*and that was worth while,*—quite aside from the accidental new birth of my own mind.

Something like that will happen again. You were insensitive in Taos. —You thought too much about yourself, —as I am doing now. Either person of a pair of lovers ought to think of the other—.

(Do you understand? —Our love is something different from the love of people that live in apartments. You might have thought about our own peace here—.)

281: TO HENRY W. WELLS

November 30, 1938

Dear Mr. Wells: "Envy" and the sonnet are beautiful and moving poems;
I admire the sonnet especially; thank you very much for sending them.
And thank you for dedicating "Pursuit of Beauty" to me. Let me wish the
book good fortune, I believe it deserves it.

   Here is the piece of verse you asked for ["*To a Young Artist*"], all copied
out in my cramp handwriting, with best wishes.   Sincerely
yours, Robinson Jeffers

282: TO DOROTHY THOMPSON

*Deeply disillusioned by the disintegration of the contemporary American
democratic and capitalistic society, on October 10, 1938, Dorothy Thompson
wrote a long, troubled letter to J, asking him to organize a poets' movement
and to formulate an inspiring creed through which American civilization
could be renewed, evil could be resisted, and good affirmed. The
following random notes indicate J's struggle to answer her distraught plea, a
struggle which he finally abandoned, according to Melba Bennett, "since
he could offer Miss Thompson no sincere encouragement."*

[*December, 1938*]

   You wrote me nearly two months ago, and I was very much surprised by
your letter, and intended to answer it, but I cannot.

   Several times I have begun to write you the reasons why I cannot; and
they always develop into a volume—which I don't want to inflict on you, even
if we both had time for it.

   In the first place, a poet—if I may be called so—is too untypical an
American to be able to formulate with success or even self-respect—

   Lincoln's words at Gettysburg; and as you say the Ten Commandments
and the Sermon on the Mount—

   Any such movement can only be a rearguard action; or else arrived at some
new culture five centuries ahead.

   You are a highly successful publicist, and I admire you for it; but myself
I cannot think in a crowd, nor for a crowd. You speak of the present
isolation and spiritual despair of the individual; and I must confess that I
value the isolation, and don't feel the despair.

   My own belief is that our civilization has reached its peak and must *necessarily* deteriorate. National conservatism can delay its deterioration; keeping aloof from Europe's dissentions [*dissensions*] can delay its deterioration in America; but I don't expect that we shall be nationally conservative, and I don't expect we shall keep out of Europe.

Germany has poetry on its side—race, blood, soil, the sword, sacrifice, vengeance,—are powerfully moving poetic conceptions (once the civilized insistence is broken down or avoided) even if they are false in fact or vicious in effect.

Whereas democracy, fraternity, equality, civilization, humanitarianism, imagination, conversion, religion—are dangerous things. Christianity did not save the Roman civilization but presided over its destruction.

Justice is a fighting word and so is freedom.

283: UNA J TO BENNETT CERF

January 10, 1939

Dear Bennett—   Robin and I both send you our thanks for the Hollywood Book. Everybody who comes in dashes for it.

Are you a bit relieved when the holidays are over. We've been rushed to death with all kinds of amusing affairs—but Robin does resent too many festivities and each one is a problem for me. Very disappointing that the Guild didnt put on the *Tower*. I hope it will later. . . . Did you meet Judith Anderson? I am eager to hear her report of what actually happened about the Tower.

We've had a very exciting time with high tides and mountainous waves during the past week. The highest except once since we've lived here. Are you coming to California this spring?

You've seemed very far away since you went to Spain. —Have seen Langston Hughes several times lately and heard his talk about Spain.

Well, you won't need our praise of Laura Riding after "Times" proletariat reporter gives her such a puff! and bangs Robin so crossly! The psychology of that reviewer whoever he is and his type is clear. Having for years shown spite toward Robin and any other writer who didnt infuse his work with propaganda—at long last since it is clear to everyone that literature and propaganda dont mix well, the man swings a full arc to the verse most unrelated-to-life, —*actual* life; or to the most *obscure* he can find and sings his paean to that. Riding and Rilke. Rilke is a *poet* I admit that—I've had books both in Eng. and German of his actually in hand every month since June 1934 when a German baron gave me my first ones, but

"Time" reporter gave no indication in his review of any actual knowledge of Rilke's work and chose him for his *obscure* writing. He is very difficult to understand often, and without both translation and German and *copious* notes his "Sonnets to Orpheus" which I am now reading would *never* yield up their meaning.   Love from Una

284: TO JUSTINE LYNN

Miss Lynn, preparing a thesis on J at the University of Kentucky, wrote him on February 6, 1939, asking that he indicate the influence of Freud and Jung on his work and that he respond to an excerpt from Beatrice Hinkle's book The Re-Creating of the Individual (*New York, 1923*).

[*February, 1939*]

Dear Miss Lynn:—   I have read a number of books by Freud and Jung and his disciples but this was mostly twenty years ago and I do not remember the titles of the books, nor which most impressed me.

I have not read Beatrice Hinkle's book, and therefore speak more or less in the dark; but my first reaction to the paragraph you quote "necessity of self-creation"—is to think that man cannot recreate himself, any more than by taking thought he can add a cubit to his stature.

No man can make an invention or a poem by willing it. They come or they do not come. We can only prepare the way a little—sweep out distractions. And I think no man can make himself a new man by willing or desiring it.

As for the present being a critical time for humanity, yes. But no more critical than a dozen former times, most of them prehistoric.
Sincerely, Robinson Jeffers

285: TO WILLIAM K. HUBBELL

*On March 30, 1939, Hubbell, Director of Continuity for the University of Kentucky Radio Studios, preparing a summer series of fifteen-minute broadcasts, asked J some questions on his response to fiction.
See also Bennett,* Stone Mason *pp. 89–90.*

[*March, 1939*]

Dear Mr. Hubbell: I cannot tell you what is my favorite work of fiction, it depends on what I read at the moment. For mere greatness it would probably be the "Karamazov Brothers"—for pleasure and aesthetic enjoyment it would be one of Thomas Hardy's "The Woodlanders" or "Far from the Madding Crowd."

And my favorite chapter of fiction would come from one of these latter books—some description of Gabriel Oak or Giles Winterborne and their activities.   Robinson Jeffers

286: UNA J TO HYATT HOWE WAGGONER

April 27, 1939

Dear Mr. Waggoner: I ought long ago to have thanked you for your interesting article on Robinson Jeffers. He has long made it a rule not to comment on articles on his work, partly because he seldom writes a letter—partly the length of time involved in long discussions. I may say he has what seems to me a curious indifference about *putting over* his own point of view. He says he states things as clearly as he is able in his poetry and has to let it go at that. Your article interested me very much—although I do not agree with some of your opinions. I happen to know for instance that he has never been interested in behaviorism and although he has been tremendously interested in psychoanalysis is very sceptical about the accuracy of diagnosis and almost entirely so about any therapeutic value in it. He does not believe with Mr. Krutch that love has been taken away by scientific analysis—nor does he affirm nihilistic pessimism.—

But I am not going to *attempt* to outline his beliefs. Do come in to see us if you are ever near—and every one does come to California. You can ask him yourself. And in any case look out at some magnificent scenery. Very sincerely, Una Jeffers

287: TO G. WILSON KNIGHT

May 13, 1939

Dear Mr. Knight: It was thoroughly ungrateful of me not to have thanked you for the book and the pamphlet at the proper time. I read them four months ago, with interest and pleasure. I can only plead that it is habitually impossible for me to write a letter. My wife writes them for me, almost always; she leaves to my care only the exceptional or important ones—which consequently never get written, or half a year too late.

To-night I have looked again at "Atlantic Crossing," and again read "Myth and Miracle,"[6] every word. (They have been lying all this while on our

---

[6] Myth and Miracle *(London, 1929) was republished as the first essay in* The Crown of Life; Essays in Interpretation of Shakespeare's Final Plays *(London, 1947).*

273

living-room table, where books come and go like waves of the sea, but these have kept their place, and not neglected.) "Atlantic Crossing" has charm, wide horizons and wisdom, but a little too playful—I should say *smiling*—for my damned serious nature. The Shakespearean essay seems to me to have discovery in it—I mean of Shakespeare's mind and vision—not necessarily of the spiritual world, but perhaps of that too, in a sense. It interests me deeply. Thank you very much, for both books.

Perhaps you will be in California sometime—almost every one seems to arrive here sooner or later. We'd be very happy to see you.

I have this moment found and re-read your letter, and it makes me the more ashamed of not having answered in decent time.

Sincerely yours, Robinson Jeffers

288: TO FREDERIC IVES CARPENTER

June 6, 1939

Dear Carpenter: I read your study attentively and with interest, and of course should be pleased if you decide to print it. It is excellently done, only you are too kind to me, and perhaps evangelize me a little.[7]

Reading "Letters of Lincoln Steffens" yesterday I came on his report of a conversation with me (which I had forgotten, but now remember) concerning an article that a Univ. of Calif. man had written about my verses. —Did I like it?—"Yes." —Didn't I think that he had superimposed some of his own ideas on my poems? —"Yes—but everybody does that." —And I should have added that that is one of the reasons for writing a poem—to give the reader a chance to superimpose his own ideas on it. It seems to me that if it is a good poem—good enough to stand on its own feet—then the author's own understanding of it has no more authority than any other competent person's.

But in general your study does not diverge from my own thought, except sometimes in emphasis and selection. Certainly I find nothing to repudiate; and am well pleased to have been the occasion of such intelligent writing.

—As to my letters, you are welcome to use them as you think best.

Your guess about my ancestry is not so good. My father was a Presbyterian minister, and professor in a theological seminary, but *his* father (Scotch-Irish immigrant of about 130 years ago) was a frontier schoolmaster and farmer in Ohio, and apparently left no records of his ancestry in the old country. (We saw the name Jeffers over a garage in Ireland, near the place of his origin, but did not stop to inquire.) On my father's mother's side

---

[7] "*The Values of Robinson Jeffers,*" American Literature, XI (1940), 353–66.

the line goes back beyond the Revolution; but no clergy. On *my* mother's side the line goes back even farther; and I think they were mostly very religious; but no clergy.

We saw Jim and Kay Caldwell the other evening and they spoke fondly of you. He is very much liked in the English department at U. of C.; she has been lecturing in the Fine Arts building at the S.F. Exposition.

Forgive me for not having told you how much I enjoyed reading your pamphlet on E. A. R.'s Tristram. It is a beautiful poem, and you do it justice. Cordially yours, Robinson Jeffers

289: TO RALPH TYLER FLEWELLING

J received the honorary degree of Doctor of Humane Letters from USC in 1939, the same year he was elected to Phi Beta Kappa. Dr. Flewelling headed the philosophy department there and edited the Personalist, *which published J's Phi Beta Kappa address. See above, p. 258.*

June 16, 1939

Dear Dr. Flewelling: I too was sorry that our conversation was broken off, and I look forward to renewing it at our next meeting.

The note from the secretary of Phi Beta Kappa has not yet reached me, but let me thank you personally for the honor of election; and I shall of course be delighted to accept honorary membership.

As to the poem—God help me! The writing no doubt can be managed, when I learn how many lines would be expected, and what sort of subject; but the reading is a different matter. I have never in my life read my own verses aloud (except to myself alone, composing them)—not even to my wife, but shyly handed her a typescript. Perhaps my spirit and face may toughen, before the time comes.

Thank you very much for sending me the two *Personalists*, with your article and Dr. Wann's.[8] They have just arrived, and I have not yet had a

[8] *Ralph Tyler Flewelling, "Tragic Drama—Modern Style," Personalist, XX (July, 1939), 229–41, and Louis Wann, "Robinson Jeffers—Counterpart of Walt Whitman," Personalist, XIX (July, 1938), 297–308.*

OVERLEAF:

". . . humanity is only a temporary and infinitesimal phenomenon in a large universe."

(Letter 169)

moment to look at either, but shall do so as soon as possible; and certainly shall not expect your conclusions to coincide with mine.

I was much impressed by the mass and pageantry of the commencement exercises, and highly appreciate the honor of the doctorate.

With kindest regards,   Yours sincerely, Robinson Jeffers

290: TO RICHARD J. SCHOECK

July 12, 1939

Dear Mr. Schoeck: Thank you very much for the kindness of your letter, and for "Compensation." It is a lovely poem, and the allusions were immediately clear to me. I am sorry I could not answer more promptly.

As to "solitude"—it is a rather scanty commodity here in the summers, in recent years—but we can make it in our minds, and the cool gray Pacific fog is a great help. I hope you never see more people than just enough, in your beautifully named "Falling Waters" [*Hamburg, New York*].
Sincerely yours, Robinson Jeffers

291: TO LOUIS ADAMIC

This letter is among the Adamic papers at Princeton University, now being catalogued for the University Library by Henry A. Christian. He has published and annotated the letter in the Princeton University Library Chronicle, *XXVIII (Winter, 1967), 90.*

August, 1939

Dear Adamic: Thank you very much for letting me see the manuscript. You have a great subject, and are better fitted to deal with it—by experience, talent, attitude—than anyone I can think of. It will be a valuable book, and may have great influence.

Of course the problem will solve itself eventually in any case, just as it did in Rome, where the "old-stock" Romans became a mixed and unnoticeable minority, while Roman culture, sentiment, prestige and language continued for a long time. Only the Christian ferment made a great change, and that was a contribution of immigrants.

I am sure you will use discretion in discussing the negro and Jewish elements. These are special cases, likely to steal the show unless carefully handled.

278

It might be worth your while to analyze the term "Anglo-Saxon"—
Germanic and Scandinavian + Celtic + the numerous dark-skinned previous
inhabitants, whose language was probably non-Aryan. —Besides all the
mixed bloods of immigration since Roman times.

I remember dimly a satirical poem by Defoe, entitled, I think, "The True-
born Englishman," describing how the sweepings of all Europe combined
to produce him.

—I wish I had more pertinent suggestions for you, but I am too ignorant.
Sincerely yours, Robinson Jeffers

I am keeping your "Plymouth Rock—Ellis Island" to show or give. Good
luck to you.   —R. J.

292: TO JAMES RORTY

October 2, 1939

Dear Rorty: Of course I'll be glad to have you name me as reference [*for a
Guggenheim fellowship*]—and I wish you luck in the new hideout.

We have been [*on*] a wild drive to New Mexico and back. Our boy Garth is
on a vast cattle ranch there (learning ranch management, he hopes)[9] and his
horse charged into a bull, somersaulted over its back, and came down on top
of Garth. Concussion—he was *out* two or three days and pretty fuzzy for
a week—didn't intend to tell us, but a queer misspelled letter from him made
Una think something was wrong. So we drove down there and brought
him home for a week's vacation—through extraordinary floods in the desert,
both coming and going. He's all right now and we have just shipped him
back. He enjoys being a cowboy, but would be safer I think on the Maginot
Line. He hopes to manage a ranch in South America eventually.

Best of luck to you,   Robinson Jeffers

293: UNA J TO JOHN WILSON TOWNSEND

See also Letter 202.

October 12, 1939

Dear Mr. Townsend: Answering your letter of Oct 1. Yes, Robinson Jeffers
had relatives in Kentucky, probably still has distant ones—on his mother's
side the connection came. His great, great, great grandfather George Robinson
(born 1727 died 1814) went from Penn. to Kentucky in 1797 and settled

[9] *After his graduation from U of C in 1938, Garth worked at Bell Ranch from
April, 1939, to July, 1940.*

near Lexington. He was elder in Bethel Pres. Church, Scott Co. was buried there beside the church—his tombstone said "Sacred to the memory of George Robinson who departed this life Mar 6, 1814 in his 87 year.

> "Of softest manners, unaffected mind
> Lover of peace and friend of human kind
> Go! Live, for Heaven's eternal rest is thine.
> Go! And exalt this mortal to divine."

In 1899 his remains were exhumed and buried in Lexington Ky. by his great grandson Thomas H. Robinson (a cousin of Robinson Jeffers' mother). When the above George Robinson moved from Penn. to Ky, eight of his ten grown children settled there also. My husband Robinson Jeffers is descended from his son Thomas who stayed in Northeast, Penn and married Mary McCord.
James F. Robinson a governor of Kentucky was a grandson of Geo. Robinson.
Jonathan Robinson an influential citizen was a son of Geo. R. also. He owned a big farm in Scott Co. (was a capt. in Revolutionary War)
Sarah Robinson a daughter married James Fergus, lawyer and member of Ky. Legislature
Esther Robinson, another daughter married James Logan
Martha   "   "   "   married John Crawford, a judge
John McCracken Robinson son of above Jonathan and Jean Black R. was a U. S. Senator and Judge of U. S. District Court.
He and many others of this family graduated from Transylvania Univ.
His brother James Fisher R. graduated from there—was a Gov. of Ky.
His residence was "Cardome," near Georgetown, Ky.
We are completely out of touch with any relatives in Ky. I daresay there are many descendants of the above mentioned Robinsons in the state. It is nice to register some association with the State of Kentucky. We have never had the pleasure of being there. My husband will be glad to autograph a book for you and try to include a photograph as you desire.   Very sincerely Una Jeffers

294: TO MRS. LYMAN STOOKEY

March 29, 1940

Dear Mrs. Stookey: I was deeply grieved by the news in your letter, but thank you for letting me know. Dr. Stookey was the best friend I ever had, except perhaps Byron; and in all my years in school and college he was the only teacher who ever influenced me or awoke my mind. I remember with joy his lectures and his conversation, and those golden days at your house on the shore. It was long ago, but it does not seem so. These things seem to remain present; and I know that you too have not lost him, though he is gone.

We saw Byron in New York in '37, and Adele was here for a few moments a year or two ago. I hope very much that you will travel this way sometime, and look in here. It is a happy sort of place.

Our twin boys, who were not even dreamed of when I last saw you, are now 23 years old. One of them is with us just now, though leaving soon. He is almost too beautiful to be good, and thinks of becoming an actor. His brother (who graduated in anthropology) is learning ranch-management the hard way, on a huge cattle-ranch in New Mexico. He was a heavy-weight wrestler while at Berkeley; about my height but twice as big and three times as strong; I wish he could have wrestled with Lyman and Byron on the sands at Hermosa.   Affectionately, Jeff

295: TO GRACE BESTHEL

Miss Besthel sent J a questionnaire for her research project on the relationship between imaginary companionship in childhood and creativity in adulthood. J did not check the blanks of the questionnaire, but wrote out his answers as follows. See also Bennett, Stone Mason, *p. 23.*

June 28, 1940

I had little or no companionship with other children and spent much time in day-dreams, but I do not remember imaginary companions (meaning playmates). I was usually alone against the (imaginary) world, astonishing a curious or hostile people by my exploits—a flying man, or an animal companioned man like Kipling's [*Mowgli?*]. This up to 14 years or so, then I found satisfactory companionship of my own age. Occasionally after that when circumstances isolated me again.

At what age began "creative work"? Began to feel poetry strongly and write bad verse at 14.[10]

---

[10] *See Letter 377.*

296: TO GEORGE DILLON (*Poetry: A Magazine of Verse*)

November 26, 1940

Dear George Dillon: Thanks for your friendly letter notifying me of the Helen Levinson Award, and let me express my appreciation, to Poetry and to the donors and judges.

I should have answered instantly, but have been swimming up-stream in a long poem through the wind and fury of Thanksgiving week.
Cordially yours, Robinson Jeffers

297: TO WITTER BYNNER

February 12, 1941

Dear Witter Bynner: Thank you for "Against the Cold," and truly my thanks are not less warm and sincere for being late. I have had a dreadful lot of things to do lately, and—as you know—I am no good at writing letters.

Your poems pleased me so much. "Spring at the Door" is a lovely thing; and "The Sowers," and "Queen Anne's Lace"—but of course I could name dozens. "The Edge" has a fine intensity; and "The Mummies of Guanajuato"—its large dimension and macabre splendor—you could have guessed I would pick that one.

But what I admire especially is the lyric and youthful spirit that never leaves you. You must have a fine "fortitude against the cold" to sustain it in these unpleasant years. I wish it may last forever.   Yours, Robinson Jeffers

298: TO MRS. DAISY BARTLEY

This letter to Una's sister was written on the way home from J's 1941 reading and lecture tour, during which he inaugurated the Library of Congress' Poet's Congress, February 27, and read at several universities. See Una's account to Benjamin Miller, Letter 301, and Bennett, Stone Mason, *pp. 171–87.*

Denver—a nice motor-camp
March 21, 1941

Dear Daisy—and the others at Mason.   Driving in here this evening, Una and I remembered that it was Friday, and Jerry would come home, and you could have a happy time over the week-end. Certainly *we* had a happy time when we were with you—thanks to all of you. It will live long in memory.

I think Una told you what a wild ride we had after leaving you, in the slippery snow and roaring wind, to Fort Wayne and Indianapolis. When we reached the hotel in Indianapolis I had been driving, and consider this!—my hands were so cold that I couldn't roll a cigarette for half an hour! Knowing me as you do—could I say more? Temperature—zero° Fahrenheit.

After my hands unparalyzed, everything was all right. We had a rather nice but fluffy dinner with some young intellectuals, and I said my piece, and we had a nice but fluffy evening at a professor's house, and left in the morning. The next stop was in Kansas City, (Missouri) and we had on the whole a pleasant time. We have some good friends there; and the president of the University, and his wife, with whom we stayed, are charming people, and know how to let guests have free time for themselves. Only I had an hour's signing of books to do, at a "reception" after the "lecture." —In other respects, people were very kind to us.

So we came away yesterday afternoon, and stopped at a place in Kansas, and to-day came on through spring weather but dreary scenery to Denver. We could make Salt Lake City to-morrow if we had to, but shall probably stop somewhere on the way, because our engagement there is for Monday night. I wish it were to-morrow night, and we could go home.

Una is a wonderful companion on our travels, but really she is wasting her time. She ought to be at home writing up her journals of Ireland and Great Britain; you can't imagine how many people every-where—editors, publishers, and so forth—want her to write something for them, based on these journals, and her knowledge of Ireland and its antiquities "and all." But also, people love her and want to talk to her. You Calls are a wonderful family.

And I too feel that I have been wasting my time—pleasantly on the whole— but the visit to Mason, and the dollars earned, make it worth while. Tell Billie to stick to steam-shovels and electric motors—or to being a policeman— very satisfactory occupations. He won't have to inscribe books—and maybe he won't have to make conversation with University professors and their wives.

But the drive across the country would have been amusing—if Kansas weren't so wide and dreary. However—we took turns, driving and sleeping.

Una says it is time to go to bed; and we both send dearest love to you all.   Robin

299: UNA J TO BENNETT CERF AND DONALD FRIEDE

April 4, 1941

Dear Bennett and Dear Donald—   answering both your notes at once. Robin thinks he will be able to get his ms. off to you in ten days. He is up stairs typing at it this moment. He calls it "This Pallid Comet." (I dont know why— haven't read it yet. But thats rather a stunning title. I think)

Robin spent one afternoon at the College of the City of New York making recordings and I with him for help—which he didn't need. I had just now a letter from one of the men in charge, Kimball Flaccus who says ". . . proud of the splendid recordings of your poetry . . . thanks for being so splendidly generous and cooperative in the rather tedious matter of making records. From the standpoint of voice quality and literary interest they are among the finest we possess. —Future generations of students etc."

I hope you had an account of the exhibit at the Library of Congress. Very thrilling. There was some excellent publicity in Washington notably on editorial page of *Wash. Post* of March 3, and article March 1 and in Boston Transcript March 10.

I have no extra copies or I would send you them—He was most warmly received in Harvard. We stayed there some days with Mrs. Kingsley Porter—He gave eight talks altogether

Just saw a cryptic note about *presumed* death of Virginia Woolf suicide.   Una

300: UNA J TO GERALDINE UDELL (*Poetry: A Magazine of Verse*)
April 28, 1941

Dear Miss Udell: Replying to your letter of April 25. Robinson Jeffers agrees to the fairness of limiting the selection to authors of works published during the period of time since Miss Monroe's death. He somewhat favors the selection of a young poet for the award.[11] (In case an older poet were selected, he would vote for Frederick Mortimer Clapp in preference to Cummings.) He is agreeable to Muriel Rukeyser receiving the award, but in case Mr. [*George*] Dillon wishes to recommend some other poet, would be glad to consider another. He thinks regard should be paid to need and special circumstances, other things being equal.   Very sincerely, Una Jeffers

In case he should be asked to consider the work of another young poet, and there is need of haste, perhaps Mr. Dillon would lend him the volume. Sometimes books are not to be had immediately here on the coast.

301: UNA J TO BENJAMIN MILLER

May 1, 1941

Dear Mr. Miller: My husband says he was much interested in reading your review of Amos Wilder's book.[12] I quote him "What you say is true and well put and in regard to my own part in it, I could not want a better defender.

[11] *The Harriet Monroe Poetry Award went to Muriel Rukeyser in 1941.*
[12] Spiritual Aspects of the New Poetry (*New York, 1940*).

You have a very subtle mind but I understand what you mean in your letter by 'mythologically true and not a literal possibility.' Yes, as to Orestes and his complete self-identification with the universe, but in regard to the verses you cite about 'tragic music'; —'to remain part of the music but hear it as the player hears it' seems to me literally possible; —not at all times but certainly at formative moments and as a basis for life. —Thank you for the letter and review."

Our trip was most successful—in fact quite a triumph for Robin. He spoke at U of Pittsburgh (where he did his sophomore year). A lunch for him there and we renewed association with many family connections—*Robinsons*. The Library of Congress hall and the hall connecting with loudspeakers was packed. Harvard and Columbia were equally friendly and enthusiastic. —Also U of Buffalo, Butler at Indianapolis U of Kansas City, U of Utah. Twelve other universities invited him but we could not synchronize dates so quickly. We motored 8063 miles some of it in awful blizzards. We missed engagement at Princeton, bogged down in storm. He made recordings of poetry readings at Harvard and at College of the City of N.Y. Excellent. The Harvard ones are to be sold by Linguaphone Institute Rockefeller Plaza, N.Y.C.

There were thirteen cases of Jeffers exhibit in Lib. of Congress for a month. —Mss., photographs—all kinds of memorabilia. One item was a geneological [*genealogical*] table showing twelve and eleven generations back in America on his mothers side (Robinsons and Tuttles). A distant Tuttle kin of his noticed it and has written to me some very interesting family history. —A bit that may interest you—Jonathan Edwards is a blood kin of my husband. When he heard that he acted as if he'd been given a charming present! This letter is all news about us. You must tell me news of you— and that you and your wife are happy!   Cordially, Una Jeffers

302: UNA J TO FREDERIC IVES CARPENTER

May 2, 1941

Dear Mr. Carpenter: My husband is busily typing his new book (probably to be called "Be Angry at the Sun.") and seems unable to write letters. I have the following statement from him in answer to your question. "As to the hawk-verses, note first—"except the penalties." The penalties did not mean only hanging or imprisonment, but also the inner revulsion, the disgust and emotional discord, which, however, would spring from training, not nature. For people can be trained to kill as easily as they can be trained not to. The average hawk seemed to me (and still seems) a more beautiful and nobler creature than the average man; besides that men swarm by millions and hawks are rare. So if I had stopped to ask myself, 'Is that a true statement?' I should have said 'Yes—*except the penalties.*' There was no misanthropy involved, but only a comparison. And there was no question of inflicting pain, —that would put a different face on the matter, —but only of sudden death. And I think it was a salutary statement, for certainly men overvalue themselves and their lives."

That is practically word for word his answer//   Cordially, Una

303: UNA J TO BLANCHE MATTHIAS

Blanche Matthias offered J a copy of R. W. Short's article "The Tower Beyond Tragedy," Southern Review, VII (Summer, 1941), 132–34, urging him to comment on it. Una returned it with the following note, and J's jottings, along with brief marginalia of her own.

[1941]

Dearest Blanche: I couldn't get Robin to give his serious attention to this article but he did jot down a few thoughts.   Love—U. J.

p. 133—1$\underline{st}$ ¶ [*Short, in explaining J's philosophy, asserts, "He believes that matter, existing in eternity, passes through cyclic changes . . ."* unconcerned with humanity, which is "but an accidental manifestation of this matter"; and he remarks that sentiency, though it distinguishes animate from inanimate, is, in J's view, no special gift.] Matter?—No—energy. Sentiency?—Not exclusive to man and animal, (*and* vegetable)— also attributed to "matter"—e. g. "drawing the *planetary* consciousness up to bright painful points."[13]

134—[*Short refers to J's use of pathetic fallacy in* Solstice *and to his insistence upon presenting 'agonizing' experiences.*] "gas-line dripped stinking blood . . . etc." —Just an ordinary metaphor, same as "car's eyes" for headlights. Metaphor is of the essence of poetry. [As to Madrone's little self-tortures—I was presenting a person who likes to bear and inflict pain. There are such people, and they are interesting.][14]

—Foot of page—[*Short doubts the validity of ll. 57–58, XV, of "Thurso's*

[13] *In 1938 J had noted for Benjamin Miller: "No, I don't feel human consciousness alien to the rest. The animals are aware of external things and inner sensation; no doubt all life is, in some degree; and as life shades down into chemical and physical processes, so it seems to me that consciousness shades down into something not alien to it. This is often indicated in my verses—as in 'consciousness drifting home from the cell to the molecule'—after the young man has died, in 'Margrave' in the Thurso volume. I don't remember the words exactly.   R. J."*
[14] *This set of brackets is J's.*

Landing," since, he says, pain can be of no greater significance than any other human act in J's eyes.] "Shining" is another metaphor. The lines mean "In the presence of these great things the small human being can offer intensity instead of greatness. Pain is probably his most intense experience."

135—last ¶ [*Short complains that J "is unable to construct an artistic substitute for the rejected concept of life after death," allowing "disembodied souls" to wander the earth as Gudrun does in "Come, Little Birds."*] Common ghost-stories and seances, and the Homeric, and in general the primitive view of death—all suggest a shadowy and rather brief survival by some fractional part of consciousness. "Forty years is a long life for a ghost." I don't believe nor disbelieve in this, but use it as mythology. It is certainly more probable than the Christian mythology.

137—[*Short comments on "At the Birth of an Age" that the Young Man's hopes and the Hanged God's negations are simply "two views . . . left, not in tension or conflict, but simply hanging."*] Christ and the Hanged God. The hope that Christ expresses is simply the ethical "Christianity" of our own time, that remains for a while after faith in the supernatural has died. Some of this hope has been justified, though not permanently. It is my Christ's view; not mine.

138— [*Short suspects that J does not understand his own poem "9, 19, 1939."*] Last two lines of Hitler poem were intended humorously, as "quotes" from certain critics. I thought they were rather amusing. [*Short finds it "odd, yet not surprising" that "Tamar" is included in the volume of* Selected Poetry *while "The Women at Point Sur" is omitted.*]Tamar—Point Sur—the reason was simple and I explained it in the foreword. People like the one, disliked the other.

Finally—I don't think I ever referred to my narratives as "tragedies." —The most reckless attribution was—the title that heads this article—"*beyond tragedy.*"

304: TO SELDEN RODMAN

Bakersfield, California[15]
November, 1941

Dear Selden Rodman: Certainly I admired Fleming McLiesh's poem in your anthology; but I know nothing else of his work, and I do not know the man, and cannot appraise him nor speak for him. Also I seem to be committed to another poet for this year's crop of scholarships. But I should be very glad if McLiesh can find some luck when he needs it.

[15] *J was visiting his son Garth, who was working at the time in a gold mine near Bakersfield.*

Your poem about T. E. Lawrence is greatly conceived and admirable; its one misfortune is that it has Lawrence's very articulate and more personal prose to compete with; —and your poem about Flight—excellently wrought and an orbit as wide as a planet's—too spacious perhaps for epic unity. Homer didn't describe the war at Troy, but a short arc of it; and I think as you grow older you will condense your splendid powers and scope. This is not advice but expectation. —The anthology is fine too.

Sometime I hope to send a poem to Common Sense, but at the moment there is nothing finished that has not been published. I'd be very happy if you should appear in Carmel some day, as Samuel Barber did.   Sincerely yours, Robinson Jeffers

305: TO HENRY W. WELLS

December 14, 1941

Dear Mr. Wells: Thank you very much for your letter about my recent verses. I am late in answering, but not from lack of appreciation; only because I am a bad letter-writer. I don't in the mornings and can't in the evenings, and this is the first heavily rainy afternoon this season.

Yes, I read "New Poets from Old" with interest and enjoyment, and mostly agreement, so far as my knowledge reaches. It is a fine subject, and you have the scope to deal with it. The humor also, I liked the passage about a California poet "striding morosely over the hills with a copy of Aeschylus in one hand and a shilling shocker in the other." This is paraphrased from memory, and of course incorrectly, but the picture pleased me. So did the book.

You are quite right about cultivating one's garden. Ours is rocky and sea-salted, but the rock is fairly sane. Someone said the other day, looking

> "—I awoke this morning idealizing Anglo-Saxon
> words . . . admiring the big heavy vowels, like rocks in
> a hissing surf of consonants. . . . It seemed to me
> that people who used such words might spend a whole
> winter rolling in mind one big thought or passion,
> instead of playing with a thousand little ones a day as
> we do now. —One rock versus a thousand pebbles."

(Letter 311)

at these misty promontories and ocean, "Why can't people be like that?" The answer, of course, (which I did not give) is that the earth too has its periods of convulsion; there is an extinct volcano-throat half a mile from here; and people have their periods of repose. Selfishly, one likes these little excitements; it is only if you let your sympathies go—which one ought to do, according to endurance.   Sincerely yours, Robinson Jeffers

306: TO GARTH J

[1941]

Dear Garth—   I was talking to a couple of soldiers who were *bird-watching* with me at Yankee Point the other night, and they said you should by all means play up your typewriting, Spanish, college degree, etc., when you land in the army. Typewriting especially would help make you a non-com sooner, (better pay) and they said definitely that you can always refuse a desk-job, because most of the eligible boys want just that; but typing is useful in the field too. As to cavalry service, they said apply for it and you'll get it, because most people don't want it. You'd probably be sent to Missouri for training; but anyhow it's the army policy to train men a long way from home. (I think too that you might ultimately be sent to places that would interest you more—Latin America, for instance—than infantry or tanks will. As to your College degree and year of ROTC, I should think you might apply for officer's training in six months or so.) Anyhow, take care of yourself and try to get what you want.

Mother and I are really quite troubled about your relations with your draft-board—(which *is* your draft-board, Monterey or Bakersfield?)—for fear of your not getting notice in time, and finally landing in the army under suspicion of irregularity. We don't want you in, of course, but your name must have got lost in some kind of clerical slip-up; or perhaps some notice hasn't reached you. Do be careful. We'd go over to Monterey and inquire, but feel it might be unwise to stir them up without consulting you. —Also— have you heard that men are popped into the army instantly now when their number comes up? Army doctors examine you and you're in. It would be too bad if you couldn't be at home a couple of days first. —Write to us when you can. Come home as soon as you can. And all the love in the world from Mother and me and Winnie [*the Js' English bulldog*].   Father

307: TO JACK WILSON

A senior at Connecticut Teachers College, Wilson wrote J on January 22, 1942, for information to help him prepare a term paper on "The Philosophy of Robinson Jeffers." The following are notes made for a response.

[*February, 1942*]

This is a brief and incomplete abstract of some of the things I have tried to say in my verses:

First: Man also is a part of nature, not a miraculous intrusion. And he is a very small part of a very big universe, that was here before he appeared, and will be here long after he has totally ceased to exist.

Second: Man would be better, more sane and more happy, if he devoted less attention and less passion (love, hate, etc.) to his own species, and more to non-human nature. Extreme introversion in any single person is a kind of insanity; so it is in a race; and race has always and increasingly spent too much thought on itself and too little on the world outside.

Third: It is easy to see that a tree, a rock, a star are beautiful; it is hard to see that people are beautiful unless you consider them as part of the universe—the divine whole. You cannot judge or value any part except in relationship to the whole that it is part of.

308: TO UNA J

Una was visiting Donnan and his first wife in Zanesville, Ohio.

Tuesday, November 24, [*1942*]

Dearest: Your sweet letter from the train came this morning and I let Winnie sniff it before I read it through, but I think the odors of the train confused him, he was bewildered and questioning, though of course excited when I said "Granny." The moonlight and snow must have been beautiful; we have had terrific moonlight here too. I'm glad your air-conditioning worked so well, and that you could be shut away from the mob; and thanks to yesterday's wire I opened the letter with a comforting assurance that all was well. Take care of yourself in that weather.

Winnie and I have lately returned from lunch at the [*Ellis*] Robertses'//

Winnie in the window-sill has just seen a cat walking down the shell path, and is roaring and dancing with rage.

Darling, does the cradle look nice in its new home? —Love to Donnan and Patty—I seem to be sending it to them every day now.//

(A soldier and a woman with light brown hair just knocked at the door. Winnie and I hid in the bed-room—I can't identify them). —Yesterday's letter I told you Noel [*Sullivan*] asked me to dinner Thursday. Later I called him to tell about your telegram, and discovered Thursday was Thanksgiving. Begged off, saying I was already engaged with Ellen [*O'Sullivan*]. (Times don't conflict, but one dinner will be enough.) So he said Friday.

Yesterday I struggled with draft-questionnaire—to-day with application for extra gas to Yankee Point, difficult to fill out in your absence. —To-morrow Ellis's Guggenheim—when revolution comes to this country the important thing will be to burn all the paper—and paper-factories.//

All my love, dearest, Robin

309: TO UNA J

Thanksgiving Day
1942

Dearest, I am beginning to wonder how many more daily letters to send to Zanesville; you know how vague I am about place and dates, —and yours are slightly cloudy. I think to-morrow and Saturday I'll send a couple to Mason [*Michigan*], and hope to have heard more about your plans by Sunday. If letters go wrong you can be sure that my love and Winnie's are still following you like hounds of heaven—or hell—which is which?

This being the last to you in Zanesville, I want to send special love and good wishes to Patty and Donnan, and some *Thanksgiving* that they found each other and are so happy together.

An hour ago Winnie and I came back from Ellen's dinner—very pleasant—Winnie poor boy didn't have any, but lunch beforehand. MacDuffys look very well, especially the statuesque lady. Her mind is almost totally occupied with USO etc. but she is nice. When I left the house, about three, Winnie was sitting at the wheel! First time I know of that he's climbed over from the back seat.

No mail to-day of course. This morning I drove to the Highlands and worked a full half day with Philip MacDougal, felling trees and sawing them—8–noon, and promised for some day next week, in return for more wood. Poor Winnie had to sit in the car, with his jacket on mostly, it was cool. We came home and dressed, and were not late for Ellen's dinner. Did you know it was her birthday too?

This afternoon I went to turn over the signs at the gates—*not* at home— and Jim Greenan called to me from his car below—down for the day with his children—he has developed a *Tin* mine and sends love to you.//

The clock stopped yesterday, though the watches are going, and I think I began this letter later than I believed, because twilight is coming. So I must take this up town and mail it, and see if I can get Winnie a little meat. He lived from a can to-day and last night.   I love you dearest Una, —Robin

310: TO FRANCIS GARDNER CLOUGH

A portion of the first paragraph of this letter is footnoted on p. 60 of Mr. Clough's Sentenced: A Book of Poetry *(New York, 1965).*

February 24, 1943

Dear Mr. Clough: The poems are very good, sincere and moving. Thank you for letting me see them. [*Sonnet*] XLIX is Elizabethan in its cadence and rich simplicity; I comes next in my preference; but I like them all.

As to publication I can't advise you, but I think it would be better to wait a few years, until the war is over or has changed its shape, and people will be able to see it more objectively, and to distinguish more clearly between poetry and exhortation. I know no publishers really except my own, and it is certain that they would not undertake to publish the poems, at least at present.

Good luck to you in any case, and if anything in this note can be of assistance, you are welcome to it.   Sincerely, Robinson Jeffers

311: TO FREDERIC IVES CARPENTER

September [*18*], 1943

Dear Frederic Carpenter: I read your letter and meant to answer, and now I look with horror at the date. Months have gone by like drops of water, and it isn't because I am particularly occupied with anything. Writing verses and usually burning them, and cutting firewood and heaving stones, with

Time and the newspapers for an anesthetic in the evenings. We don't
often see the coast mountains any more, except from the window, on
account of gas-rationing. I might walk to them, and in them, but don't
like to leave my wife and bull-dog alone; and we miss our sons; one of whom
is a military police-sergeant in Hawaii, guarding an internment camp, and
the other is in Ohio, delightfully married, and has lately sired us
a grand-daughter.

Yes, there *is* a little vacuum. One would like to be excited by literature, as
in years long past, or by new landscapes, which are hardly come by at
present, or by something new and large in science. And the continual sense of
planet-wide grief and pain and terror saps one's energies. But spring will
come again. And, to speak literally, a good winter storm here is something
to look forward to. That will come sooner.

—Yes, there are two sides to the medal of civilization, and no doubt I have
made too much of the wrong one. But think how few are the "organizers,
the purposeful and the powerful," as compared to the dough which they
agitate. And the larger the community the fewer they become per million; and
our civilization envisages a worldwide community. So the increasing rifts
and the future breakdown are not altogether unwelcome.

—However, there isn't much to be said for barbarism either! These
different facets turn and return, (though never the same); we can't stay them
nor speed them; and it seems to me that a good life is the affair of private
persons, rather than of society. But also, it requires luck as well as morals.

—Why "The Torchbearer's Race" was omitted from "Selected Poems"—
much had to be omitted. I chose hastily to save myself trouble; I had a
feeling the thing was too long for its weight, and too obvious. Not too
"optimistic" but too young. But just now I looked at it again and rather liked
it—I mean in comparison.

—I awoke this morning idealizing Anglo-Saxon words that I have
practically forgotten—a semester nearly forty years ago—admiring the big
heavy vowels, like rocks in a hissing surf of consonants, thinking how much
our language has lost in gaining its atomic fluidity. It seemed to me that
people who used such words might spend a whole winter rolling in mind one
big thought or passion, instead of playing with a thousand little ones a
day as we do now. —One rock versus a thousand pebbles. —I suppose this
dream represents as well as possible the hardly logical reasons for my
scunner against civilization. —Your thoughts about Man's Coming of Age
interest me very much. I hope you'll make the book.

—My wife sends kind thoughts to you and yours. We both have the
fondest memories of you, in Cambridge and elsewhere.   Sincerely,
Robinson Jeffers

312: TO FREDERIC IVES CARPENTER

[*November, 1943*]

Dear Carpenter: Thank you for letting me read; the ideas are most interesting. Since you ask, I suppose I should choose No. 2 of the philosophies of history. But, like other philosophies, they are mostly a putting of names and analogies on a series of facts. Their significance is in their attitudes toward the future, and even in that regard they are not so widely divergent.

I should not call No. 2 "pessimistic." Civilizations rise and fall, ours has risen and will fall, so will others in the future—is no more pessimistic than to say that men are born and die. —Whereas the conceptions of adolescence and maturity seem to me a little too specialized. I cannot see any more maturity in the mind of the present than in the minds of Athens and Rome at their summits. More knowledge—but that is a different thing. —Also, some kind of culture (fire, flint, language, tradition, probably religion) has been going on for several hundred thousand years; and the centuries you assign to cultural adolescence would seem much too brief for so long a childhood.

About the American frontier, I think its importance has been over-emphasized, as you suggest. Certainly the free land acted as a safety valve, for Europe and ourselves, but this only means it postponed processes that have now come into play again.

December 7, 1943

—What precedes was written I dare not think how long ago, and I am heartily ashamed of having kept your ms. so long. It is partly because I can't concentrate in brief on so big a subject. One may be reckless in verse, but there ought to be some system about history or philosophy, and my thoughts fly away over the hay-stacks.

No doubt from one point of view civilization is a single cumulative process. It tends to grow richer and bigger—because some knowledge is inherited across the gaps—but not therefore better—nor worse. Greek civilization was poorer and smaller than Egypt's before and Rome's after, but certainly not worse than either. Ours is immensely richer and bigger; but not better. All I can conclude is that "Each for its quality / Is drawn out of this gulf."

As to a stable world-civilization in the future—I don't believe in it—any more than in a world-state. People do not unite effectively except against enemies. They may live together in a heap, amorphous and passive, as **China** used to do; but if there is the energy to organize there is the energy to divide.

But indeed I don't *want* to believe in it. The small social groups—the few thousand of a Greek city or Israelite tribe, the few hundred thousand that made a nation when Europe was young—have produced the best part of our literature, art, religion, basic science. The big agglomerations are sterile by comparison—though big armies, big architecture, big engineering no doubt have their uses.

But there is that famous law of diminishing returns, and it seems to me that a few years from now, when Anglo-America and Russia will stand looking at each other, we shall have become about as "global" as Providence will permit. The images will split and fall apart, the kaleidoscope will turn and make new patterns.

Forgive this damned prophetic kind of writing. It is a bad return for yours. —Good luck with the book. If you have written any more chapters I should be very glad to see them. I hope we'll meet again when the wars are over—and may it be soon.   Yours, Robinson Jeffers

313: TO OSCAR WILLIAMS

November 9, 1944

Dear Oscar Williams: Sorry not to have answered you sooner. Here is the authorization. If I can think of any comment about poetry and the war I'll send it to you shortly; but that is doubtful, and it wouldn't in any case be more than a paragraph.

There hasn't been any photo for a long time.

I haven't seen New Poems 1944. If a copy was sent me it must have got lost in the mail.

The War Poets is a most interesting project—I wish you all good luck with it.   Sincerely, Robinson Jeffers

At the bottom of the page, a note, probably by Williams, indicates that no comment on poetry and the war was sent.

314: UNA J TO BENNETT CERF

In spite of the disappointing response of the Theatre Guild to Judith
Anderson's promotion of a 1937 stage version of The Tower Beyond Tragedy
and in spite of a disappointing audience response to Charles O'Neal's 1941
Del Monte summer theater production with Dame Judith starring, she
and Jed Harris were able to interest J in adapting Euripides' Medea *as a*
vehicle for Dame Judith in 1945.

April 23, 1945

Dear Bennett: We are tremendously interested in the "Medea," too. Its
going to be fine reading whether it makes a great stage success or not. I hope
it will go over—and Jed Harris feels it will. We found him a very stimulating
companion. Perhaps he told you he and Judith Anderson were in Carmel
a couple of days with much discussion—

We will let you have the ms. when completed—it will be several weeks
yet. What is the usual procedure for this kind of affair—to print the play as
soon as its ready or to wait for publication until the production is
announced or under way?

We go on all right. Garth is at the front in Germany and never out of our
thoughts. I hope you and your[s] continue happy.   Love from us both Una

Jed brought with him five stage sets—tentative sketches—by Bobby Jones
who is deep in this too!

315: TO (?) HALTER

May 29, 1945

Dear Mr. Halter—   The book that I enjoyed writing, and am most tolerant
of, is a series of short poems called "Descent to the Dead," written in Ireland
and Great Britain in 1929. It was published by Random House in a limited
edition, and then in the volume called "Give your Heart to the Hawks."
I like it because it is cool and quiet as the North Irish hills were at that time.

Of course I have no idea which is the best of my books. The worst are the
first and second.   Sincerely yours, Robinson Jeffers

August 14, 1945

Dear Garth—   There have been a few false armistice alarms here, none of
which moved us, though the Monterey fishing-fleet lost a night's work to
celebrate. Now the real news has come, and I have just put up the flag on the
tower. Mother has been at Fort Ord R[ed] C[ross] duty, and I am waiting
for her to phone me from the village when she returns. —She has just
called. She was crying. —Monterey whistles are making a great noise, and
a few Carmel car-horns. I was filling the pool—*your* pool under the trees—
now stocked with mosquito-fish—when I heard the first car-horns, and
came in and turned on the radio, then put up the flag and began
to write to you.

August 15—Mother came home at this point yesterday. Said it was quite
exciting at Fort Ord; was especially interested in the German PW's
reactions—neither glad nor sorry, but extremely alert and attentive, watching
everyone's face to see how Americans acted in victory. She was also
interested—for your sake—in the truck-loads of MPs being rushed all over
the place to keep the boys in order. —After talking to her I went down to the
shore and got a big stone to commemmorate [*commemorate*] the day—nice flat
surface to carve a date on. We were asked to the Fishes' for dinner, moderate
whiskies before and after. Also asked to Marie Short's, and stopped there
for a moment at midnight; many people were drunk but we were not—and
so to bed. We hope you had as pleasant a day—and now I am very
hopeful that you'll be home within a few months—we have enjoyed
tremendously the letters and pictures you have sent. You seem to be in fine
shape, and look a little younger than when you went away, in spite of
hard work and action. I don't know exactly why we feel so proud of you, but
we do. —Yes, Mother expected you to come home with some particularly
outrageous dialect of German; but I predict two dialects, and excellent
Hochdeutsch besides. I have always heard that the best German is in Hanover,
perhaps you will meet some displaced girl from there. —I hope you are
taking good care of yourself. One of Mother's staff assistants very kindly told
her that she knew a young man who was engaged in the same kind of
work as yours in Germany, and he was killed by a sniper the other day. —Old
Mr. Schoeninger reports that Joe is teaching economics somewhere in
England! Do you suppose he's on the faculty at Shrivenham? If so you didn't
lose much when you didn't get there—or, if you do, don't take economics.
Dick Tevis is supposed to be teaching something somewhere in Belgium.
—Our neighbor Ben Stillwell, the general's youngest son, has a Cooper's
hawk and a duckhawk (peregrine falcon to you) and he is trying to teach them

falconry. It is quite thrilling to see them flying around our woods and tower, uttering wild cries, and each jingling a bell on her leg. The pigeons used to be terrified, and the herons would fly up with angry shouts, but the poor hawks were discouraged or something, nothing ever happens, and now the pigeons just sit and look at them. The peregrine struck one of our herons once, but seemed to get the worst of it. B[——] C. is here, came to call day before yesterday, and I think we'll take her a ride down the coast tomorrow. Very sweet and intelligent girl; but we don't commit you to anything—nor tell her about your Freundinnen.   Dearest love from Mother and Father

317: TO GARTH J

October 3, 1945

Dear Garth—   We are very happy to get your notification about being home by New Year's or sooner—I hope it is sooner—though I'm sure that many a blue eye in Bavaria will weep at your departure.

One of your recent letters about the Bayrische Sprache—is that spelled right?—told about their saying "nimmer" for "never." (That is perfectly good German, of course, though not so usual as nie or niemals.) Curiously, the morning your letter came, I woke up remembering my father, when we were going to Europe about fifty years ago, asking one of the sailors in midAtlantic how deep the water was, and the man answering, "Da Kommt man nimmer zum Grunde." Perhaps he was from Munich.

This morning when we looked out the window there were two big pheasants in the front yard, and I remembered your passion for pheasants a good many years ago. We are almost overrun with quail this year—hundreds—crowding the pigeons out of their own courtyard. And the rock is full of pelicans and the trees of herons.

There have been a lot of fires in Monterey County the past few days—one in Garapatas—a big one at Fort Ord—the air is full of smoke and the sunsets scarlet. It has been fairly hot weather, but the good old sea-damp seems to be coming in again now.

Your dragon-tree in the hollow is making another flower—so is the one

OVERLEAF:

"It seems to me that in a degenerating society the individual has got to isolate himself morally to a certain extent or else degenerate too."

(Letter 242)

by the pool—but the century-cactus there has never flowered yet. I filled up the pool today. It is full of tadpoles and little frogs, and some kind of fresh water shellfish—how did that get there?—besides the mosquito-fish.

I am sorry to see that your General is being replaced, —and I believe you are to blame for it—because one of the things the papers here say is that you MPs call yourselves Patton's Gestapo—and the Germans believe you! You'd better come home before you get to be an SS trooper.//
—Love, Father

318: TO FREDERICK M. CLAPP

Mrs. Hugh Bullock had enlisted Dr. Clapp's aid in urging J to accept the office of Chancellor in the Academy of American Poets, which she sponsored.

December 5, 1945

Dear Timmie: Yes, I will accept the charge, though the office of "chancellor" seems a little heavy to bear. Your approval of the business means very much to me, and certainly Mrs. Bullock's devotion and energy are splendid. Also I like the list of names, MacLeish, Max Eastman and so forth, —it shouldn't be hard to come to an understanding with such men.

Personally, I think $5000 a year is a little extra, even for this inflation. I hope the fortunate poets will not form expensive habits.

We are so happy to hear from you—always. Won't there be another book of poems soon? I've told you before what I think of your work. I enjoy your poems more than any others of this time, particularly for clear sharpness of imagery, and for ascetic intelligence.

Love to you and Maud, from Una and me. Garth has just arrived in California, and we are going to S.F. to fetch him home,—to-morrow probably. Isn't that delightful?   Yours, Robin

I used a bad pen and it sticks in the paper—therefore this crabbedness.

319: TO MARY GLEASON (American Academy of Arts and Letters)

Following his November, 1945, election to the American Academy of Arts and Letters, J was asked for information for a publicity release. See also Letter 320.

December 7, 1945

My dear Miss Gleason: Thanks for your note of November 24, asking about my present and prospective occupations.

Recently I have been making a free adaptation of the MEDEA of Euripides, which the Theatre Guild plans to produce this winter, with Judith Anderson taking the title role. My publishers—Random House—expect to bring it out as a book about the same time.

Meanwhile I have been writing a narrative poem called "Rene Gore," and many shorter pieces, which together will make a book to be published in due time,—probably next fall. I hope to add something to the book before that.

There is nothing else to record. No doubt you have Who's Who, etc., for past history. I have stayed strictly at home since 1941, and published only a few occasional pieces. Probably in 1947, when the congestion clears, we shall make another visit to Ireland and England.   Sincerely yours, Robinson Jeffers

320: TO VAN WYCK BROOKS (American Academy of Arts and Letters)

December 16, 1945

Dear Van Wyck: In conversation with you I spoke of my gratitude for election to the Academy, and now will you let me repeat the expression to you as Secretary, in the hope that you will convey my thanks to our President, Mr. [*Walter*] Damrosch, and our fellow-members. I look forward to meeting them whenever it becomes possible.

Membership in this distinguished body is an honor that I appreciate highly, and wish to be worthy of it.   Sincerely yours, Robinson Jeffers

321: TO VAN WYCK BROOKS

December 23, 1945

Dear Van Wyck: These are distinguished poems [*Theodore Maynard's*], clear, musical and deeply felt. One is happy to listen to such a voice in the present hubbub of the world. Sincerely, Robinson Jeffers

—I am afraid this dull statement is worthless for any purpose; I have read the book carefully and cannot do better, though I should like to.

It was wise of you not to come here the other day. My cold has been merely uncomfortable, but there is always a chance of contagion. We are going to Bakersfield over Christmas, and I should be rid of it when we return—Thursday or Friday—I hope to see you soon after that.   Yours, R. J.

322: TO VAN WYCK BROOKS

January 22, [1946]

Dear Van Wyck: I am sorry—this was written long ago, but it seems impossible for me to get a note sent off:—

—A poet of originality and power, a writer of distinguished prose, and a persuasive speaker, MacLeish is also notable for public service of various kinds. I am sure that he would be a valuable member of the Academy.

—Is this satisfactory? Please amend it in any way that occurs to you.   Sincerely, Robin Jeffers

323: TO MRS. HUGH BULLOCK

February 4, 1946

My dear Mrs. Bullock: Thank you for your letter of December 11th, which should have been acknowledged long ago, —and I hope you will forgive me, I have a great difficulty in answering letters. But I do want to say that I admire your courage and devotion to the cause of American poetry; and it is an honor to serve on your board of chancellors.[16]   Sincerely yours, Robinson Jeffers

324: UNA J TO JUDITH ANDERSON

March 16, 1946

Dearest Judith: Your letter came today. We were not surprised that the Guild had given up the production as we had heard nothing about rehearsals. What we didn't know was what kind of a struggle you were having with the whole thing. I should think you'd be heartily tired of it with all the pressure of your other work. But I hope you wont get too worn out to care about it! I believe the Guild loses its rights to the play if it is not in production April 20th and in rehearsal by March 23. —So in a few days now their option is over. We have no intention of attempting to do anything about it ourselves—and wouldnt know how if we wanted to. Anything that happens to come up about it we will refer to Morris Agency and they should consult you. A few days ago a letter came from the Salkow Agency (by Sarah Rollitts) asking for a script and saying she had a N.Y. producer and

16 *See Letter 318.*

"prominent star" who were very interested in it. I referred her to the Morris Agency.

We are thrilled just to let our mind dwell on the set up you had planned. Patience, my heart, I believe that some wonderful arrangement will yet be arrived at.

I warned Random House some months ago that the Guild were very dilatory, but they went ahead with the printing of "Medea" anyway. And it will be out very soon now. Robin would have been content to save it to include in his next book. However perhaps the reading of it will create a passable audience in advance.

Love from us both. We appreciate fully all the work you've put into this project.　Devotedly, Una

325: UNA J TO SAXE COMMINS (Random House)

April 2, 1946

Dear Saxe:　The book is beautifully done—I hope you saw the note I wrote Bennett.[17] I wanted him to thank everyone in the office who worked on it. Binding, typography and jacket! Two days ago a sculptor who was here went across the room to pick the book off my desk saying "What a thrilling jacket"—not even knowing it was Robin's book. The title looks so tragic and portentous!—

Don't worry if the *blurb* says the Guild is doing it—someone else will be doing it shortly, as Luther Greene has taken an option on it with Judith in the title role. He has tremendous plans about it—Stravinsky has promised to do the music—I'll tell you more about it soon. But we resolved from the start not to think too much about it. The stage is a torment I am told and Poetry is as much bother as we can deal with.

Will there be more *Selected Poetry* forthcoming soon? Dr. Barkan here today from San Francisco tried three book shops in town in vain—they said they couldn't get more, and our Village Book Store here said the same.

I'll send you news as soon as we hear about *Medea*. Morris Agency telephoned us today about it from Hollywood and were preparing the contract with the same terms as the Guild had.

I wonder whether the Guild were scared by *Antigone* which seems to have been rather messy?　Love from Una

17 *Una had written Bennett Cerf on March 26, 1946, "We are delighted with* Medea. *Everything about it is* right—*even the jacket somehow expresses the book. There is a dark threatening look to the title* Medea *and a suggestion of Greek type—I can't quite define it, and the temple—! I wish you would thank all of your Random House people who worked on it and especially Saxe Commins who writes me grand little notes from time to time."*

326: TO VAN WYCK BROOKS

April 18, 1946

Dear Van Wyck Brooks: I don't remember whether we spoke while you were here of our friend Frederick Mortimer Clapp, but very likely you know him. If so, don't you think he would be a credit to the Institute?

Clapp is director of the Frick Collection (—and so forth—see Who's Who if convenient) but he has produced some books of poems that I admire greatly, besides works of art-criticism. His poems will never be popular, but I think they are fairly unequalled at present for profundity of thought, precision of statement and variety of reference.

He is also the best-educated man I know, and one of the most widely intelligent.

It is late to make a nomination now and find seconders, but if you should be present at the April 26th meeting, perhaps you would be willing to suggest Clapp's name for future nomination.

We miss you here, and we hope you and Eleanor are well. Una joins me in sending love to you both, and wishing you here again. I had a nice note from T. Maynard, who says that he too once inhabited your and our log cabin!   Sincerely, Robinson Jeffers

327: TO JULIEN PHILBERT

August 4, 1946

Dear Mr. Philbert:—   I was happy to hear from you again and certainly it is most interesting to see that your translation of "Thurso's Landing" is to be published this Fall. I look forward to seeing the book.

French was once as familiar to me as English, (a long time ago when at school in Switzerland) and I can still read it well, so I shall be able to appreciate your work—the introduction also.

Do you know that Eugène Jolas (editor of "Transition") made a translation of my "Roan Stallion" which was published with some omissions, in an anthology "de Poésies Américaines" ten or fifteen years ago?[18] There was also a woman (whose name I cannot recall just now) who translated "Cawdor" into French and expected to have it published in Paris, but I believe the war supervened.

You ask about "Medea" which our friend Lawrence Powell told you about. It was written at the request of a New York theatrical producer and is

[18] *See Letter 87.*

simply a very free translation of Euripides. It is to be produced in New York this fall—so they *say*—but one never knows. Meanwhile it has been published as a poem and I am sending you a copy.

And now—forgive me for being slow in responding to your kindness. I have no habit of correspondence and it is all but impossible for me to sit down and write a letter, but I did write to you before. I wonder whether you received my letter in answer to your previous one?   Robinson Jeffers

328: TO MICHAEL MEYERBERG

While production difficulties held up Medea, *finally staged in September, 1947, Meyerberg produced* Dear Judas *in Ogunquit, Maine, in August, after a Catholic boycott had prevented its opening in Boston. Then it opened for a short run at the Mansfield Theatre in New York City. See Bennett, Stone Mason, pp. 196–99, and Letter 402.*

[*October, 1947*]

Dear Mr. Meyerberg: I am deeply sorry not to have seen Dear Judas. We met a number of people who had seen it and one or two who had acted in it, and all accounts agreed that it could not have had a more beautiful nor more imaginative production.

We had no intention of going to N.Y. to see Medea, but the pressure mounted until we were practically compelled to go. The day of our arrival, and the next day, we tried to reach you by telephone, and never were able to make connections, and finally decided that you must be out of town. We were in N.Y. only 3 days and our time was terribly preoccupied. But I wish I had seen you—if only to say that I appreciate all you did for the poem and that your labor was not wasted, even if many were not able to understand it.

This note is only an expression of my thanks and admiration.   Sincerely yours, Robinson Jeffers

1948-50 *A trip to Ireland in 1948 was marred by J's illness and necessary separation from Una. His hospitalization forced her to attend alone the opening of* Medea *in Edinburgh. J was not idle in hospital, however; it was there that he wrote* The Cretan Woman, *in fulfillment of a promise made to Agnes Moorehead.* ❧ *During these years, J was preoccupied with the production problems of* Medea, *both here and abroad, with legal and financial difficulties, with his own serious illness, and with the demands of work on an unsuccessful attempt to adapt Schiller's* Maria Stuart *and on a new adaptation of* The Tower Beyond Tragedy. *It was Una's illness and death, however, which finally absorbed all his thought and energy.*

329: TO FELICIA GEFFEN (American Academy of Arts and Letters)

May 1, 1948

Dear Miss Geffen: We have just returned from a journey into Oregon,[1] and I find here your letter and enclosures about the UNESCO Conference in San Francisco, May 13 to 15. I am grateful to our President, Mr. [*Paul*] Manship, for designating me as representative of the Academy, but it is an honor which I must regretfully decline. We are starting for Ireland early in June, and I have a press of work to finish first, and must stay at home and pick away at it.

I have just written to Mrs. Russell, who is a friend and more-or-less neighbor of ours, expressing my regret that I cannot serve; and I hope you will tell Mr. Manship for me that I am sorry.   Sincerely yours, Robinson Jeffers

330: TO ROBERT WHITEHEAD AND OLIVER REA (producers of *Medea*)

May 12, 1948

Gentlemen: As my wire of May 12th informed you, I am not willing at this time to consent to any actress except Judith Anderson playing in America the title role of my adaptation of Medea. I do not know in fact that such a move is under consideration, but this has been suggested to me; and I object to it because the play was written for Miss Anderson, and without her genius it might not have had any success; and the tour projected for the coming season could hardly do well without her. She is certainly the person whom people want to see in this part. Also she is an old friend of ours, for whom we have great affection, and knowing that she wants to play the part, I must do my utmost to see that she gets it. I earnestly hope that you may be able to work out some agreement with her.

Let me say also that my own relations with you have been altogether satisfactory. I want to thank you again for your consideration and kindness. Sincerely yours, Robinson Jeffers

---

[1] *When Garth J first accepted employment with the U.S. Forest Service, he and Lotte settled in McKenzie Bridge, Oregon.*

331: TO NANCY SAYRE (Mrs. William H. Norton)

*While a sophomore at Denison University, at work in English Honors on
"The Personality and Poetry of Jeffers," Miss Sayre wrote J in 1945 and again
on May 6, 1948, asking for information as to purpose, background, form,
etc. of "Roan Stallion," "Tamar," and* Medea, *especially as* Medea
differed from its original.

[*May 17, 1948*]

Dear Miss Sayre: For origins and ideas of Roan Stallion and Tamar—see
Foreword to *"Selected Poetry of R. J."*

As to "Medea," it was written at Judith Anderson's request. The endeavor
was to present Euripides' tragedy in a form and in poetry that might be
interesting to an intelligent but not learned contemporary audience. There is
much in any Greek play that would seem dull or absurd to anyone but a
classical scholar; I tried to omit all this and to emphasize the
essential values of the play.

I am sorry to have neglected your first letter. It is almost impossible for me
ever to answer one.   Sincerely, Robinson Jeffers

332: TO MARION STROBEL *(Poetry: A Magazine of Verse)*

Ballymore, County Donegal
Ireland
June 25, 1948

Dear Miss Strobel: Your thoughtful letter of March 10th, asking for autobiographical fragments or suchlike, should have been answered, though the
answer had to be negative. Here in this raining climate, away from home
and grandchildren, I have time to say that I am sorry, I have never written
nor preserved anything autobiographical, except the bits of foreword to
my "Selected Poetry" and the Modern Library "Roan Stallion," —which were
written at my publisher's bidding. My wife keeps a journal whenever we
travel; it is interesting, and I hope sometime she will edit and publish it, but
it is about Ireland and Britain and so forth, not me. Ireland is beautiful,
particularly here in the northwest; the mountains and seas through gray rain,
and the abject beauty of the brown bogs, with rock biting up through
them.   Sincerely, Robinson Jeffers

333: TO GARTH AND CHARLOTTE J

Lac-na-Lore
Ballymore, Co. Donegal, Ireland
June 26, 1948

Dear Lotte and Garth— [*Una has added "& Sweetheart Maeve."*]   We have
had sweet letters from you—also from the other household—the farewell
letters to N.Y., which were returned and redirected, reached us this morning.
Thank you, and we hope everything goes as well as ever. This place is
little changed, in spite of new rooms and a little new plumbing—attractive
as ever, and we still have to bathe in a wash-basin, with a pint of cold water.
There is a new dog, but apparently the same three ducks, waddling
indignantly over the rocks in the back yard. The same sheep and cows. Some
new building is going on at Portnablagh, but the country has room for it.
The bay at Dunfanaghy is completely silted up—or else the tide is always out
when we are there—nothing but a great mud-flat. Mother got her No.
Ireland driving-license by mail this morning, so we can move on when the
time comes. We are asked to lunch to-morrow—Sunday—by Henry
McElhenny, the new owner of Glenveagh Castle—and of Dunlewy House
too—but he lives at Glenveagh, when not traveling, or home in Philadelphia.
Errigal and Muckish are as fine as ever, but I don't suppose we'll climb
them this time, without you and Donnan and Bertie! to encourage us. Besides
it rains more or less all the time.

Sunday evening

One of three ducks (vide supra) disappeared in the night, it was supposed
that a fox had come; but later the body was found. He had fallen on his
back, couldn't get up and suffocated, like a sheep. Did you know
that ducks do that?
We went to Glenveagh through storms of wind and rain, got horribly lost
in the bog roads, asking our way of a hundred peasants, and arrived half
an hour late for lunch, but it didn't matter. There was only one other guest—
a young man McElhenny knew in the navy, who was staying there for a
week. Navy, Groton and Harvard are their connection—but also our host
impressed us as a person who would not care for young women. It was a little
like Lord Faringdon's household and friends. McElhenny is rather young,
alert, intelligent and active, as wealthy young men ought to be. The guest (I
never hear names) knew Stuyvie Fish at Harvard, spoke of him with
amusement as an odd character. The castle still looks romantic, the lough
was whipped into tempest by the wind, rain fell heavily when we walked in

the garden. We saw a stag beside the road, 200 yds. from the castle, and his antlers were at least as long as his legs. Also a tame doe in an enclosure. McElhenny is to let us know when he goes over to Dunlewy House, so we can visit there too. And I forgot to say—Donnan will be happy to know that Whitesides the perfect butler is still at Glenveagh. (A woman guest arrived while we were there—white hair, young face, first wife of ex-ambassador Bullitt.)//

It is bitterly cold weather, at least for June, besides continual rain. There are jungles of rhododendron in bloom all about Glenveagh, under the Scotch firs, etc. We have seen rhododendron all over Ireland, really growing wild—unplanted—in the wastes of Connemara, and all in bloom. —McElhenny says there is hardly ever frost at Glenveagh. —There is a grove of Monterey pines, all tipped over by the wind, below Marble Hill House here. You remember the Monterey pines and cypress in the Ards monastery park. —Meals at Lac-na-lore are exactly what they used to be— 9 AM, 1, 6, and 10 PM—all sorts of soda-bread—but sometimes there is a little beef instead of permanent mutton as formerly. We had to get ration-cards at the police-barracks for sugar—nothing else rationed—but I think we may be hungry in Northern Ireland and Britain.//
A few grandmotherly remarks by Una end the letter. It is unsigned.

334: TO UNA J

After he became ill in Kilkenny, J was hospitalized in Dublin; Una went on to Edinburgh for the opening of Medea.

[Dublin]
August 20, [1948]

Dearest love—   Afternoon coffee came in two hours ago and almost broke my heart—as almost everything does to-day. Nobody else has come in, except the Matron and a nurse or two—only for moments. It was fun for them to come in and stay, when you were here. —So I have almost killed another novel, in spite of a solid hour's sleep from 2 to 3. Pringle[2] hasn't been here yet—and there is no reason why he should.

I write this sitting up—very warm—sun has been in this window for an

[2] *A Dublin consultant called by J's Kilkenny physician, Dr. Roche.*

"I planted the trees, under Una's supervision, and have probably some right to quote the herons and squirrels that live in them."

(Letter 355)

hour, and still is. But calm yourself; I am wearing all you expect, shoes, stockings and gown.

Laugh! I have just spent five minutes interrogating the Jew's pen in order to address your envelope. At last I know.

I am now back in bed, because the new nurses are spying on me. One cross-questioned me—was I allowed up?—for how long? Soon the tall white one came, to see if I had fainted. —So I have not dared to be up one minute over my hour—and you see I am taken care of! A "hot jar" [*hot water bottle*] has just come in.

How beautiful and brave you looked this morning, dearest. You always do—but more than ever. I think of you constantly—I worry about you— I adore you.

Please give my deep love to the Whiteheads—and urgent good wishes to them and Gielgud, and the others.[3]

To you, dearest—my everlasting love—and admiration! What a cold word.   —Robin

335: TO UNA J

[*Dublin*]
Saturday, August 21, [*1948*]

Dearest—   I am glad you are not flying from here to-day. The weather is the worst yet seen—a raging southeast wind, shark-color sky, continuous fine rain. My window is shut tight.

Last night Dr. Pringle suddenly came in, brandishing his stethoscope; but he didn't use it, the call was purely social, and his talk entirely about you. This morning Dr. Thompson, mostly to reclaim his surgical needles, etc., but did use his stethoscope and expressed his satisfaction. He expects to be there when they X-ray me next week—fluoroscope too apparently, to observe action. (Feels to me as if this pen were running dry—I must save it to address envelopes.)

It is nearly noon, and I have just turned on the light, the day is so dark, more like a wolf's throat now—than a shark's flank. Is it raining where you are? They say the fine Irish harvests are imperilled. Your sweet little letter from the air-port came early this morning, and I shall dutifully observe all your bidding. I love you, dearest. The morning paper also came. Dr. Thompson says I mayn't have even a bed-bath until Monday, on account

---

[3] *John Gielgud remained in the role of Jason, but Eileen Herlie replaced Judith Anderson in the Edinburgh* Medea.

314

of the weather. The nurses—particularly McCarthy—send their love to you, and want me to say that they feel their responsibility. I repeat—in case yesterday's letter should fail to reach you by any chance—my love to the Whiteheads and ġood wishes to them and Gielgud and the others. I am sure they will do well. You are my dearest love forever.   Robin
    —Next letter goes to Norwich.

336: TO UNA J

[*Dublin*]
Monday—August 23, [*1948*]

Dearest love—   I wrote to [*Garth and Lotte at*] McKenzie Bridge yesterday, and began a letter to [*Donnan and Lee at*] Tor House. Finished this morning and sent them off—had a pleasant interview with Dr. Pringle—then shaved and paced the floor, read a couple of letters, and am back in bed, a little tired. It is one PM, and a great tray of food will come presently! About four PM Mr. Maggi will come—he has not yet brought any mail, only newspapers—he is very kind and quite interesting but sometimes stays a little too long, but leaves when I suggest it. —Dr. Pringle did a bit of knocking and listening, and is perfectly satisfied. We spoke sadly of Dr. Roche, whose baby son, born the 18th, lived only 36 hours. (I had already seen the enclosed queer little notice in the paper.)
    Dinner came in, and with it your wire from Edinburgh. Thank you, dearest; I'm glad the letters got there. Yesterday came a cable from Ellen[4] (including Donnan, Lee, Lindsay) with humorous good wishes to "Medea in kilts." This morning a long letter to me from Daisy, and an apologetic note to you from Miss Mooney—I'll try to answer it—she proposes lunch on Tuesday—to-morrow—letter dated Saturday. —Letters the day after you left, from Garth (I mean Lotte)—Maud Clapp (I haven't opened it)—Aunt Carrie—Ella Winter (I haven't opened it). Lotte was unhappy because Garth has to leave her for two weeks, and Maeve had anti-diphtheria inoculation and some blood taken from the sole of her foot. I don't know what the devil that means. —Letters this morning were from R. Mooney and a long one to me from Daisy, mostly about their week-long vacation trip. And she hopes I can stay a long time in Mason and rest, before going home.
    It was so stormy the day after you left that the Mauritania was held up two days off Cobh harbor, waiting until the tender could come out to her. It

[4] *Ellen O'Sullivan, a Carmel neighbor; the "Bess of Hardwick" of Letter 337 is her sister-in-law, who lived in London, where Una went from Edinburgh.*

is 2:25 and I had better sleep—Maggi will come soon. —Coffee came and waked me; now I am up, and no doubt my friend will be in presently, but I could bear it if he didn't. Sun is roaring in this window, over my back and the table I am writing on; it is suddenly hotter than "tunket." But I can't think of any more news—unless Maggi brings some—if he does I'll write a P.S. —Darling, I love you with all my heart—I hope you see everything in East Anglia!—poor child! Come home soon. —Robin

P.S. —Not Maggi came, but Mrs. Hudson [*Una's landlady in Dublin*]; she stayed only fifteen minutes and spent most of them praising your charm and kindness. And how much she misses you. She brought two letters—a very affectionate but newsless one to me from Violet, and (2) a long and hugely complicated claim for exemption from British income tax—a duplicate of which has been sent to Whitehead—from W. Morris Agency. This has to be signed before a notary. It is not instantly pressing, and can wait until you get back and I get *out*. I will study it some more to make sure, but there seems no doubt it can wait a week—or a month. Whitehead has received a duplicate of it to sign; I expect we'll hear from him presently. W. Morris's lawyer—a new one (Leon Kellman)—seems not perfectly sure that it wouldn't be better if signed in America. However, I shall not be in England. —There was no covering letter to me at all—only a copy of the one to Whitehead.

Oh—and Mrs. Hudson brought a sack of oranges—she said you ordered. Thank you darling (I thanked *her* too.) —Your little blonde zany—Kathleen or Catherine—has suddenly disappeared overnight, on vacation, and appointed Nurse McCarthy to bring me the morning paper. I think this is all—except dearest love to you. Robin

337: TO UNA J

[*Dublin*]
[*August 27, 1948*]

Darling— I hope this will reach you. It will have to be the last—until happy 30th. Yesterday evening Dr. Pringle came in with a lot of machinery, saying he would take a second electro-cardiogram in the morning. (You remember he took one in Aut Even [*Hospital, Kilkenny*].) So I expected him all morning, but nothing has happened. I shaved, expecting interruption at any moment, and then read—Edgar Wallace! (First one I ever.) They write better stories now.

All yesterday and this morning not one drop of rain: do you believe me? To-day no wind either: how the Horse-show rejoices!

Recently I read—discovered!—the worst novel that has ever been written and published. It is called "Souci" and was confectioned in the 1890s by a woman named Mrs. Twells!—perhaps American—but I assure you it is worse than even "The Sorrows of Young Werther," which made Goethe's reputation. Mrs. Twells has been undeservedly forgotten—a Thesis for our friend Levy.[5] —Sorry, here is dinner. —1:45—As dinner went out, your wire came in. So glad to hear from you—and especially *so* happy about your day-long visit (yesterday) with all the Pastons. That must make amends for something. Be sure and remember, so you can write it all. —Do you remember at all where the Pastons stopped when they came up to London?

Love to Bess of Hardwick—I mean of Sullivan.

Now, honey, this seems to be the last one to you abroad—yet how long to the 30th! Take care of yourself my dear love, and as Nurse McCarthy still says every evening—"God bless." (When Doyle bids farewell at 8 AM she always says sleepily, "Good-night.") God bless you dearest love, and good-morning!   —Robin

338: TO FREDERICK M. AND MAUD CLAPP

The Js arrived home from Ireland in September, J not fully recovered; then in January, 1949, Una became ill.

January 30, 1949

Dear Timmie and Maud: Una is much better now, and I believe she can come home from the hospital in a couple of days, but I hope she will be willing to rest and be a convalescent for some time. She was exhausted after New Year's—thence the bad attack of flu—and I think she had been over-tired for years. She has such a sense of responsibility—a beautiful thing in moderation—a beautiful thing always—but exhausting, giving herself to me when I was sick in Ireland, and to grandchildren and all of us here. After the flu she was nearly well, and then this obscure abdominal infection appeared—fever again, bad white-blood cell count, and extreme prostration, continued nausea—no food whatever—. The doctors couldn't

---

[5] *William Turner Levy had written his M.A. thesis, "Notes on the Prophetic Element in the Poetry of Robinson Jeffers," at Columbia University in 1947.*

make a definite diagnosis, feared eventual peritonitis, and didn't dare not operate, and see with their eyes what was the matter. They found the rather small area of infection, connected with bad adhesions from the operation of twenty-three years ago, removed some of the adhesions, and packed the place with sulpha-powder. Afterwards a short intensive course of penicillin and streptomycin. The operation was perhaps unnecessary, except as exploration, but it is comforting to know that every abdominal organ was inspected and is normal, no infection remains, and little by little Una is beginning to eat food and drink water again. Her pierced veins are pretty tired of saline solution with dextrose, and blood-transfusions. Today she was able to get out of bed and walk on the balcony, and make loving signals to her grandchild Lindsay and his golden-haired mother (Lee—Donnan's little wife, who has managed the household most competently in her absence, and will manage it when she comes home, as long as we can keep her more or less in bed.) She has never descended as low as I did when I was ill, to the reading of mystery and detective stories, though she tried to; but she allowed me to read Hardy to her all one day, and Weir of Hermiston the next. The latter—as I remembered it—was the most adult but also in spots the most tiresome of Stevenson's.

Well, we are out of the fog now, and going happily.

I want to thank Maud—perhaps again—for her patience and goodness at the New York air-port, when I was supposed to be sick, and could hardly wait for a chance at the charming bottle of whisky she had in store for us. (But I think Una got the larger half.)

And I was terribly sorry—very sorry—not to see you, Timmie. Una assured me that I was ill, and I believed her—perhaps I was at least convalescent— but that is all over now—for you I hope as for me—and for Una in a few weeks.

When will there be another volume of poems, Timmie? I admire and enjoy yours, as I have told you, more than any other of this time. Once or twice in the later volumes they have been a little dark to me—or too erudite for my ignorance—but I still enjoyed them.

Love to you both, from Una and me.   Robin

[*The following is penciled in the margins in Una's hand.*]

Monday. Darlings, so good to get your wire and letter. I've been pretty miserable, but now recovering. Little strength yet. I came down with the flu Jan. 5 and haven't been dressed since. I cannot remember ever having felt so low. I left great piles of unanswered letters on my desk. I felt very sad about not having thanked Wm Levy for a darling unicorn and 3 dozen snapshots of places connected with us in Ireland and Devon. So Robin wrote him for me and sent a message to you. Will you thank him for his note and say we hope soon to be proper healthy citizens—both!

339: TO THE EDITOR, *CARMEL PINE CONE*

See also Bennett, Stone Mason, *pp. 221–22.*

July 20, 1949

Dear Sir: I believe that the Carmel Sanitary Board is acting illegally: first, in opening bids when blocked by a majority of protest; second, in presenting a new estimate (fifty per cent less) immediately after their first one was rejected.//

As to our own place, it is ridiculous to assess us more than six thousand dollars (according to the new cut-rate estimate) for a facility which we shall never need; while a big new house covering a little lot, which therefore perhaps really needs the service, will pay less than one hundred and fifty dollars—more than forty times less. But we shall not press this absurdity; but consider ourselves fortunate as long as we are not actually compelled to hook up with a system that at present shockingly defiles the river-mouth and may in future pollute the bay.   Sincerely yours, Robinson Jeffers

340: TO WILLIAM TURNER LEVY

November 26, 1949

Dear Levy: I was very much interested—and surprised—by the question of your choice of vocation; but of course I cannot advise, only consider. You have talent undoubtedly to make your way in either career; and you like them both; and it is impossible to tell—for you as well as for me—which one would leave you best satisfied at the end, when retirement age comes. For that depends on the accidents of assignment and promotion, war or peace, just war or unnecessary war—accidents which you cannot command nor foresee.

So it becomes simply a question of liking; and if your liking and ability for either course seem equally balanced, one might as well flip a coin, the decision will be as good as any other.

But there are two or three further points to consider. You liked your life in the army: would you have liked it so well in peace-time, when there is a comparative stagnation of the unselfishness and sense of purpose that you felt? And did you not, even then, think sometimes with longing about the quietness and relative freedom of academic life? "When this is over—when I can go back to my proper business—"? It is notorious of course that farther pastures look greener—and so it may be with you now—from the standpoint of academic life the army looks more exciting and refreshing than perhaps it would if you were in it.

Then—to be merely practical—but a point which you must have considered already: is it not true that men from West Point are a kind of well-knit aristocracy in the army, and the others in some degree outsiders? The old school tie and all that? This might make little difference in wartime, and none in social life, but it might in advancement—the normal progress which you have a right to expect. —I don't know.

So I can't advise;[6] I only know which career *I* should choose. And I want to thank you for innumerable kindnesses to Una and myself. —Most cordial good wishes— Robinson Jeffers
[*Una added the sentences which follow.*]
Dear William: Don't trouble to look for the Prokosch poem "The Lonely Unicorn." A friend sent it to me a few days ago. Yrs U. J.

341: TO DR. HANS AND PHOEBE BARKAN

University [*of California*] Hospital
The Medical Center
San Francisco 22, California
January 19, 1950

Dear Hans and Phoebe: Your children heard from you in Paris yesterday, I think, and perhaps you are in Switzerland already. I hope you have a fortunate time there, tho it cannot be altogether happy.[7] Greet the country for me for my school-days' sake. And my best wishes to your mother though of course she won't remember me.

Una is about as she was when you left—a little weaker I'm afraid. The nausea is gone, but she has no desire to eat, and little ability. At least she can

---

[6] *In July, 1951, J commented on Levy's decision to become an Anglican priest: "I am very much interested in your candidacy for Holy Orders—and congratulate you. It is certainly a well rounded mind and education that can choose freely and equally between religion, literature, and a military career. I am glad to have had some part in your decision—as you say—and hope it was for the best. I expect you will be a book-writing Bishop, ultimately, in the manner of Dean Inge— not a Gloomy Bishop—but I have never thought of him as the Gloomy Dean—it seems to me that he just tells the truth, generally, and time proves it."*
[7] *Dr. Barkan's mother was seriously ill.*

drink water. They give her enough narcotics so that she is not much troubled with pain. But the kidneys are not functioning sufficiently; they spoke of uraemia, but now with medication the function is somewhat restored.
But they have ceased for the time giving testosterone, because it increases retention of salt and water; and the x-ray treatments stopped after the first one, because of her pain and weakness. So—the main trouble is not being treated at all. But I am satisfied that everything possible is being done, I am with her all day, and it seems to be helpful to her; and her three nurses are very good; she is quite charmed by one of them.

Dr. Wolfson told me that his expectation when we brought her here was to operate low on the spine and cut the nerves of pain, which he says can be separated from the others: but the x-ray pictures show other involvements higher up. The only other thing is lobotomy, but he doesn't propose it— nor do I. And I don't think she could survive any operation now. I am afraid that she won't even have the two or three years I hoped for, but of course miracles happen. Meanwhile she doesn't know what is the matter, and wonders through the morphine-fog how she ever "got into this mess," but I think still expects to get well. One of the nurses told me today that it is beautiful to see her smile. She is a rare person, as you know. She loves life far more than I do, but she is also far more courageous. She would take it gallantly if we told her what is wrong, but of course we won't.

Little Phoebe and Jack are awfully good to me—and Wong too;[8] I only see them at dinner for an hour or two, but they are very kind. I am interested in the stamp of the Navy on Jack's face—a look of endurance and daring—I have seen it in many other navy men before. I am sorry to trouble them with my continued presence here, though they don't seem to mind it. The doctors tell me that they expect a turn pretty soon, perhaps they mean downward, but perhaps it will be toward life again. Meanwhile she is not suffering much, and seems glad to have me by the bed.

Look across the lake toward the French Savoye, where I had my first adventure—and the first time I was independent of school and parents. Now I have to learn independence again, but this is Una. She is more important to me than my parents (psychologically) and I admire her more.

Does the Dent du Midi still make such a figure along the lake as it used to do?   Sincerely, Robin
To Mrs. Barkan   I spent my childhood looking at the D. du M. Will you pray for Una?

---

[8] *Phoebe and Jack Gilpin, the Barkans' daughter and her husband (see Letter 344); Wong was the Barkans' cook.*

342: TO DR. HANS AND PHOEBE BARKAN

University [*of California*] Hospital
The Medical Center
San Francisco 22, California
February 1, 1950

Dear Hans and Phoebe: I am still here, and hope I am not too much of a
nuisance to your children. Judith Anderson is beginning to stir uneasily down
at Carpinteria—how soon will I be able to get some work done on her new
play?[9] —and Una wanted me to go home last Sunday, when our children
came up to visit. But Sunday was her worst day since the two or three
days of her arrival, and I couldn't possibly leave. All the time the children
were here, and while our other children called up from Oregon, she was lying
very weak, on a somewhat blood-spotted bed, with a needle in her vein,
getting a three-hour dextrose-saline transfusion. To-day is the best day she
has had in a long time. I pray we'll have no more setbacks. We think
she can go home to the Carmel hospital whenever she is strong enough to
stand the ambulance trip. She doesn't suffer too much pain now, and has gone
as much as thirteen hours between hypodermics. It was weakness and nausea
that frightened me last Sunday. Her veins are worn out with transfusions, and
were very little and hard to tap in the first place.

She is well taken care of, three nurses still, of course, and the various
doctors kind and attentive. Dr. Nafziger (new surgeon) comes in most. When
Una said she could eat a little chicken he gave her a wild duck, but that is
still in the deep-freeze. He has also given her a decanter of very choice
sherry, but I think she prefers her tablespoonful of brandy.

Nothing new in the medical situation. Threatened kidney failure has been
averted. X-rays are omitted again since Sunday, (Una says not that Dr. N.
said it wasn't necessary.)—but will be resumed. We'll have her out of this yet.

We have your letters, from the ship and from Montreux. Thank you very
much. We are glad of the good news about your mother, Hans, and
delighted that you both seem to find the trip tolerably interesting. Even your
children didn't know that you plan to go into Germany as well as Venice.
It was a queer feeling I had, seeing Chillon and the tooth of the South
again, on your card, Phoebe.

Your children are very good to me, and I love them. They are wonderful
people. So is Wong, in a different way! I never tasted such flavors.

Una sends dearest love to you—so do I—and gratitude. Also I am
cheerful—Una is like her old self to-day.   Yours, Robin

[9] *A version of Schiller's* Maria Stuart, *proposed to J by Judith Anderson; he
abandoned work on it after the first act. See above, p. 308.*

343: TO MRS. VIOLET HINKLEY

University [*of California*] Hospital
The Medical Center
San Francisco 22, California
February 2, 1950

Dear Violet—   Una was much touched by your call ten minutes ago, and said that she didn't feel able to answer. This morning she could have, but she gets tired toward the end of the day.

Last Sunday she had a very bad day, which came perhaps from too much Xray treatment—now suspended for a week. Since then she has gotten better. Yesterday was the best day in months, and today almost as good.//

I think we'll get her back to the hospital in Carmel in a week or so, and home perhaps in a week or two more. I hope so. This city hospital is an impressive place, huge and full of activity and misery. At first the doctors and consultants came in troops to Una's room. Not so many now; only two or three come regularly.

They are all good men, very kind and attentive, especially the famous Dr. Nafziger, who is in charge of the case, and Dr. Hopper, the laboratory man, whom we have known since he was a little boy in Carmel.

Dr. Nafziger had us up here with the idea of operating but after studying further Xray pictures he decided not to. He gives Una little presents from time to time—a wild duck to tempt her appetite—but it is still in the deep freeze—a decanter of very choice old sherry—and so forth.

Una has three special nurses so that somebody is in continual attendance, and they are very nice women. The hospital is high on a hill, and Una's window looks out over San Francisco across the woods of Golden Gate park; and the channel and great bridge towers of the Golden Gate—wild mountains beyond—and even the distant ocean. But we'd rather be home.

I spend the days at the hospital, and sleep at the house of our friend Dr. Hans Barkan, 2330 Lyon St. S.F. The Barkans are now in Switzerland, visiting his 95 year old mother, who will not live much longer. Their daughter and son-in-law—delightful young people, live in the house while they are gone; also their Chinese cook, who prepares wonderful dinners.

We've had an awful time, but we'll get Una out of this yet and she'll go home and be happy again.

Love to you and Neil from both of us.   Affectionately, Robin

344: TO JACK AND PHOEBE GILPIN

February 28, 1950

Dear "Little" Phoebe and Jack: Una is ever so much better, and we have to restrain her from limping around the house more than five times a day. She is still weak and a little nervous, and the pain returns mildly— no resemblance to what it used to be—but she is looking better than she has for months or perhaps years.

We had a very good journey—home to Carmel. Una came in an ambulance, you remember, to S.F., and suffered on the way; going home she was quite comfortable sitting in her own car. She stayed in the hospital here for about a week, and since then has been in her own bed—whenever she consents to stay in it. Our daughter Lee is very helpful—daughter in law and [in] affection—she has had a little training as a nurse, though very young still—knows how to give a hypo, and so forth—and the touching thing is that she has acquired a big book on the Theory and Practice of Nursing, and studies it. —And for other things—we are proud and happy about Donnan's choice. Besides the beautiful grandson, whom I love almost as noisily—as he is.

Your letter came this morning, Phoebe, I heard about it, and have just— late at night—had my chance to read it. First I want to congratulate you and Jack most devotedly, and to wish you as cunning an offspring as Lindsay is—what more could I say!—and a nice big place to bring him or her up in.

March 3rd —I began this note as dated at the beginning, but have been prevented from finishing it.

Please forgive me for not writing sooner. You were very good to me,— you two and Hans and Phoebe—I'll not forget it. I hope your parents are still finding Europe passably pleasant, and that we'll see you and them soon. Very best wishes to you.   —Robin

". . . I have no desire to die before writing another poem or two and I should love to know you and the boys for hundreds of years to come. . . ."

(Letter 275)

345: TO MRS. DAISY BARTLEY

August 26 (I think) 1950

Dearest Daisy: Forgive me for not writing. There is so little to tell. Una's condition goes up and down, and remains ultimately on the same level. She suffers a great deal, but mostly from extreme weakness and nausea. The pain is very well controlled by morphine and the male hormone injections. I think she hardly ever suffers much actual pain. To-day she has been asleep almost all day, but completely aware whenever she had occasion to talk to me or to the doctor. Or to our daughter, Lee, who has a little training as a nurse, and gives the injections whenever needed. We are very fortunate to have Lee here. She is a sweet and beautiful girl, (from Michigan) better than Donnan or I deserve, but of course Lindsay deserves the best, and all of us try to make Una as happy as we can. Una has a sweet room, looking down on the ocean and rock-islands covered with birds, gulls, pelicans and cormorants; and the sea-lions passing; and the land-birds, quail and the singing sparrows and linnets, in the bushes under the window. Her favorite books are on the walls or near by, and her friends—all over the country—are continually bringing her new books and flowers, and new kinds of food— only hoping to please her—particularly Noël Sullivan and Esther Fish, who come or call almost daily, and the Clapps and others in N.Y., and the Pinkhams in Los Angeles. There are many more. I am sure that Una feels how important and how much loved she is. But she refuses (usually) to see anyone. I don't wonder. I too would want to be let alone.

Harry Teabolt—among others—called up day before yesterday, saying that you sisters of Una's wanted news. I gave him all that I could, but didn't ask him to visit here. We have no visitors now; a few people lay gifts on the door-step; others use the mail.

Love to you, Daisy, and your household, and the others in Mason. Forgive the blots.   Affectionately, Robin

346: TO DR. HANS BARKAN (telegram)

September 1, 1950
9:05 P. M.

Una died this evening—Please tell our friends in San Francisco—With her love to them and to you and Phoebe—Affectionately—Robin

347: TO MR. HUGH BULLOCK

September, 1950

Dear Mr. Bullock: I appreciate your sympathy and thank you for it. She
and I were very dear to each other.   Sincerely, Robinson Jeffers

348: TO FREDERICK M. AND MAUD CLAPP

October, 1950

Dear Tim and Maud: Thank you for your letter, but I know what you felt,
you didn't need to write. Your letter is more real to me than any other of
the hundreds; it isn't sympathy, though I know you feel that too, but *loss*.
We have lost so much that I don't want to speak of it.

I tell myself cold comfort, that her awareness and beauty are dissolved into
the world, and make it more beautiful. But an old superstition keeps
me praying silently: "Make Una joyful, wherever she is."

She enjoyed her little ride with you in the Jaguar; and she enjoyed her ten
days in England and Scotland, when I was convalescent in the hospital in
Dublin, and she was driven out of her lodging there by the Horse-show. And
visiting the old places in Ireland, and some new ones, was a joy to her.
I think of those recent things; after a while, if I live long enough, I shall think
of her life as a joyous whole.

Since the first of January, this year, I have known that she was fatally ill;
and we managed to conceal it from her. She was still in love with life, and
I thought it better not to let her know. Perhaps I was wrong, but I didn't
know how soon the end would come.   Affectionately, Robin

349: TO JUDITH ANDERSON

October 14, 1950

Dear Judith—   Here is the second act [*of the new arrangement of* The Tower
Beyond Tragedy]. I hope it will do, and that it reaches you safely. This is
the only typescript there is.

I enjoyed our telephone conversation this morning. I love you, Judith, and
naturally I wish you good luck on your travels.   Sincerely, Robin

350: TO MRS. DAISY BARTLEY

October 26, 1950

Dearest Daisy: Enclosed is an old letter that I wrote to you and never mailed.[10] Una asked what I was writing, so I gave it to her, and have just found it in one of her drawers here. I think that she read it through. I don't think she thought she was dying, as I knew she was, and the letter suggests, but I had to give it to her when she suddenly asked for it. She knew she was gravely ill; I don't believe she thought any further than that.

Not recently, but very long ago, Una and I told each other what kind of burial we wanted. No funeral ceremony—cremation—and the ashes to be buried in the courtyard of our house here—only a few inches deep, so that the tree-roots might sooner absorb them. That is what we did with the ashes of our little first-born, Maeve. It is now against the law in California, and most other States//

I remember that my worst worry, when I was near dying a couple of years ago in the Dublin hospital, was that there probably isn't a crematory in Catholic Ireland—the Catholics don't approve of cremation—and what a nuisance it would be for Una to have to transport me to England for cremation. An odd fancy!—but it really was my worst worry.

Our Catholic friend Noël Sullivan had Mass said for Una in the old Mission here, and many of our friends attended it. The music was beautiful—and it satisfied their need for some kind of ceremony. Donnan and I went, and Una's doctor sat beside us.

The mail has just come, with your letter of the 23ᵣᵈ. Thank you, dear. You are very kind to write so often; I wish that I could. We saw California poppies highly valued in many English gardens. Their own beautiful red one was regarded as a weed. —Yes, I am very glad that Donnan and Lee and Lindsay are here. —I certainly don't want to go East. If I am forced to, the only pleasant thing about it will be to see you again.

Love to you, Daisy, and my best greetings to your family and your sisters. What a messy writer I am always!   Robin

---

[10] *Since the enclosure duplicates information about Una's condition, contained in other letters, I have omitted it here.*

1950-56 *J's sense of loss persisted throughout the years following Una's
death. He tried to sustain the regular pattern of life that he had led while she lived:
writing in the mornings, laying stone in the afternoons. A group of poems
in a January, 1951, issue of* Poetry *won him the Eunice Tietjens Memorial Award
that year, and when "Hungerfield" appeared in* Poetry *in May, 1952, he
received the Union League Civic Arts Foundation Award. In 1955* Hungerfield
and Other Poems *won the Borestone Mountain Poetry Award. With his son
Donnan's help, J worked at building an annex to Tor House which was not
completed until 1958.* ❦ *Reluctant as ever to appear in public, J nevertheless
consented to fly to New York for Judith Anderson's opening in* The Tower
Beyond Tragedy *on November 26, 1950. In September, 1951, she took*
Medea *to West Berlin to represent American drama in the Festival of West
Berlin; in October 1955, she took* Medea *on tour in Australia.* ❦ *J's
correspondence-friendship with his German translator, Eva Hesse, began in
May, 1951. Her work on his poems began with a German version of* The Tower
Beyond Tragedy, *which was radio-broadcast by the Bavarian Broadcasting
Company in 1951 and 1952. No new volume of J's poems appeared until*
Hungerfield and Other Poems *in 1954. He wrote the Foreword to Una's travel
journal,* Visits to Ireland, *which he also edited for 1954 publication.*

351: TO LUTHER GREENE

November, 1950

Dear Luther: I have just received your letter from New York. Thank you for it, and thank you for bargaining on my behalf. The cuts in the manuscript will be all right, if Judith approves of them. I am glad that you have such fine people in the show, and of course I know beforehand that Judith's Clytemnestra will be superb. I should like to be there, but my almost total inexperience of the theatre—I should only be useless or in the way. I told Judith that I couldn't afford to go. That was not absolutely true, but near enough. All my earnings, from Medea and various books, were put into accounts that Una initiated in the names of our sons when they were babies—quite right too—// Of course I have a small inheritance and so forth to get along on; but I felt I ought to explain to Judith—through you— why I pleaded poverty so soon after Medea.

I notified the William Morris Agency a few days ago, in answering a note from them, that I probably had a small royalty—1000 dollars had been suggested, but I did not know—to collect from ANTA. I am bound to them as my agents—recommended by Judith, when we began Medea—by a five year contract, which I signed in 1948. Please tell Judith that I love and greatly admire her—but I think she knows it.   Affectionately, Robin

352: TO FREDERICK M. AND MAUD CLAPP

November 13, 1950

Dear Tim and Maud: I haven't any intention of going to N.Y. though it would be a great pleasure to see you two, and Blanche and Russell [Matthias]. Judith Anderson tried to persuade me to go, but I was quite firm on the subject. Of course, if the play should be successful enough to go into commercial production after its four weeks with ANTA, Judith will probably coerce me into going—and in that case Lee and Donnan might come along—but that seems highly doubtful.

I have just written to Robert Breen, executive secretary of ANTA (American National Theatre and Academy), asking him to make 4 tickets available for opening night for you and the Matthiases. I gave him your addresses, and I hope he will act accordingly.

Yesterday Donnan, Lee, Lindsay and I drove up the Valley to the top, Chew's Ridge, about 4,000 feet high. We took lunch along and brought back a lot of those huge coulter-pine pine-cones, besides a few hundred-weight of stones to build with. A very pleasant excursion.

No acting version of "Tower" has been published, and I don't see why any should be; there is very little change, except necessary cancellation of a lot of Cassandra's lament and prophecies. N.Y. Times drama editor asked me to write an article about "Tower," which I did rather unwillingly, and he will print it before the opening.[1]

Please give my love to Blanche and Russell.   Affectionately, Robin

353: TO MELBA BERRY BENNETT

December 30, 1950

Dear Melba: I am deeply sorry that I can't write letters. Hundreds have come, and hardly any of them is even acknowledged. I can't ask Donnan or Lee to do what I am too shiftless to do—though Lee has often offered to. They are sweet children. But Donnan has his job, his writing and his garden; Lee has her baby and the household to take care of.

We'll be delighted to see you when you come here next spring or summer.

I have been more or less stunned since September—very unhappy and useless—but now I must get over it. There have been distractions enough. I had to go to Santa Barbara to see Judith Anderson about the play—I refused to go to New York, but then about a month ago I was compelled to—flew of course—and was there five days. Saw the Clapps and Matthiases and my publisher, after my business was done. Saw the play twice. Judith is of course tremendous, and carried the whole thing on her shoulders. The others were fine actors, but some of them were badly miscast, and it seemed to me that there were other serious errors. So I am glad that they will not re-open immediately, as was planned, after their month with ANTA. (American National Theater and Academy). The talk now is of bringing it to California in the spring.

The reviews were various. Brooks Atkinson, in the N.Y. Times,[2] seemed to say that it was the best thing he had ever seen. His opinion is important, but there were many others who thought otherwise, though all of them praised Judith's extraordinary talent. To me the play seemed less impressive than the production in the Carmel Forest Theater nine years ago. More

[1] New York Times, *November 26, 1950, Sec. II, p. 1.*
[2] New York Times, *November 27, 1950, p. 29.*

Route 1, Box 36, Carmel, California
December 30, 1950.

Dear Melba:

I am deeply sorry that I can't write letters. Hundreds have come, and hardly any of them is even acknowledged. I can't ask Donnan or Lee to do what I am too shiftless to do — though Lee has often offered to. They are sweet children. But Donnan has his job, his writing and his garden; Lee has her baby and the household to take care of.

We'll be delighted to see you when you come here next spring or summer.

I have been more or less stunned since September — very unhappy and useless — but now I must get over it. There have been distractions enough. I had to go to Santa Barbara to see Judith Anderson about the play — I refused to go to New York, but then about a month ago I was compelled to — flew of course — and was there five days. Saw the Clapps and Matthiessen and my publisher, after my business was done. Saw the play twice. Judith is of course tremendous; and carried the whole thing on her shoulders. The others were fine actors, but some of them were badly miscast, and it seemed to me that there were other serious errors. So I am glad that they will not resume immediately, as was planned, after their month with ANTA. (American National Theater and Academy). The talk now is of bringing it to California in the spring.

(over)

The reviews were various. Brooks Atkinson, in the N.Y. Times, seemed to say that it was the best thing he had ever seen. His opinion is important; but there were many others who thought otherwise, though all of them praised Judith's extraordinary talent. To me the play seemed less impressive than the production in the Carmel Forest Theater nine years ago. More polished, of course, but slighter & less interesting. However — I know nothing about the theater.

Never a moment of the day or night that I don't miss Una — Terribly. I try to remember the thought & feeling that made my verses and are habitual to me, and I think that they have sustained me against despair — or rather in despair — and this loss will come into proportion after while. We were married for thirty-seven years, and loved each other longer than that. She was so full of life, and all her ancestors and family lived beyond eighty — I never dreamed she would die before me. But it is true.

Over Christmas, a few days after I returned from New York, we visited Garth and his family, at North Fork, near Yosemite. He is making a career in the U.S. Forest Service. What landscapes — and what driving — mostly on twisted mountain roads at night. We went up to Huntington Lake, so that the babies could put their hands in real snow.

I'll be very happy to see you, Melba, whenever you come here. Please give my good wishes to Frank and Doakie.

Affectionately,
Robin.

polished, of course, but slighter and less interesting. However—I know nothing about the theater.[3]

Never a moment of the day or night that I don't miss Una—terribly. I try to remember the thought and feeling that made my verses and are habitual to me, and I think that they have sustained me against despair—or rather *in* despair—and this loss will come into proportion after while. We were married for thirty-seven years, and loved each other longer than that. She was so full of life, and all her ancestors and family lived beyond eighty—I never dreamed she would die before me. But it is here.

Over Christmas, a few days after I returned from New York, we visited Garth and his family, at North Fork, near Yosemite. He is making a career in the U.S. Forest Service. What landscapes—and what driving—mostly on twisted mountain roads at night. We went up to Huntington Lake, so that the babies could put their hands in real snow.

I'll be very happy to see you, Melba, whenever you come here. Please give my good wishes to Frank and Deedee.   Affectionately, Robin

354: TO MRS. DAISY BARTLEY

January 7, 1951

Dear Daisy: Forgive me for not writing. I just can't write a letter—except on a simple matter of business, and that takes all day. It is ridiculous, and I can't understand it. Una used to attend to most of my letters, but simply because I couldn't. Now all the letters that came during her later illness have been thrown away unanswered. At least two hundred letters of condolence are in a box here, unacknowledged; they come from her friends all over the world. And most of the other letters I have received since her death remain unanswered. They will haunt me until I burn them. Let's change the subject.

I had to fly to N.Y. in December, about the play. I had refused before, but now they said it was necessary. It was not. I was there five needless days, saw the play twice, attended three parties, and flew home. One of the parties

---

[3] *Tor House files contain the following notes for a 1958(?) letter: "I admire the work of Albert Camus and should be glad to do an adaptation of one of his plays. But how could it need adapting? The French and the Anglo-Saxon theaters are not very far apart. And, as for me, I know nothing of the theater. I have seen no more than six or seven plays in my lifetime, and two were in German, one in French, two were my own, and one was Shakespeare's. I like to adapt plays from Greek tragedy, the very few that are interesting enough—but I doubt very much that I could do anything successfully for M. Camus.*
"Please convey to him my most friendly greeting."

was given by our friends the Matthiases at their hotel-apartments. There I saw Noël Sullivan, on his way to Europe for the end of the Roman Holy Year, and to see France and the Mediterranean again, before the Russians take over. With him (but not for Europe) were two pleasant young men and the daughter of India's envoy to the United Nations, Miss ? ? Rau. I believe Miss Rau has written a book lately. She was handsome; and Hindu-color, and beautifully half-Hindu dressed; but six feet tall, and held a glass of whiskey and water in her hand, which is rather unusual for Hindus. One of the young men explained to me that she had lost caste anyhow, by crossing the ocean, so the whiskey didn't matter.

Another, but smaller, party was at Admiral "Bull" Halsey's apartments, to which Judith Anderson took me after I had seen the play. Queer to see him in New York.

The third party was for the cast of the play, at Judith's apartments. They are very nice young people, and excellent actors, but some of them badly miscast.

The play was fairly successful but not good. The direction was bad and the stage-set worse; all that I had thought of as hard had been made soft; and the cutting, for which I had given permission, had cut most of the poetry out of the play. I was amazed that the N.Y. Times—Brooks Atkinson, their most famous critic of drama—said it was one of the best plays he had ever seen. I don't think so. But Judith Anderson, of course, was superb. She had done it magnificently in the Forest Theater here in Carmel, and had always wanted to do it in N.Y.

A few days after I came home we drove to North Fork, California, to visit Garth and his family over Christmas. He is a forester, as of course you know—U.S. Forest Service. He loves his work, especially the out-doors part of it. He has amazing strength and endurance and energy, and loves to spend them in the mountain forest. His only question is whether he ought to go back to college for a year and get a Master's degree in forestry, to insure more rapid promotion. Our Christmas was delightful and a little tiring—long cold drives up to snow-line through magnificent scenery—and rowdy nights when the neighbors came in to play poker. The children— Maeve, Lindsay, Diana—had a wonderful time and wonderful presents, besides the snowy mountains and the white-fir Christmas tree. This was the first time that Lindsay has seen snow—perhaps Maeve and Diana did in Oregon. So we came home. It is a five or six hour drive—250 miles or so— we seem always to do it at night, and in a fog.

New Year's eve we spent quietly at home. We had been invited to parties and refused them. We had a few drinks together and I thought desperately of Una—probably Donnan did too. Her absence—her death—is the worst thing I have ever suffered, or ever shall suffer. I'd better keep still.

What a handsome and talented son you have. Give my regards to him, please. Love to Jerry, and our family in Mason and Lansing—Canada too, when you write. We enjoyed very much that record of the family voices.

January 6 was Una's birthday, as of course you know, and Ellen O'Sullivan, who so deeply loved her, had us with Lindsay for dinner that evening. No one else, of course. Miss O'S. also had a mass said for her that morning, which I attended. Noël had one said for her a few days after her death; and Miss O'Sullivan's servant, Mary McNicholas, had one said for her in Ireland, when she was visiting her old mother there. —Pure superstition, but it shows how they love her.

Affectionately, dearest Daisy,   Yours, Robin

355: TO FREDERICK M. AND MAUD CLAPP

The first of the following letters was mailed with the letter dated August 31; however, it seems less confusing to place it here because of its contents.

January 18, 1951

Dear Tim and Maud: You know that I cannot write letters, and I am sorry. There are more than two hundred here that I should have answered, or at least acknowledged. The letters of sympathy I have piled into a deep box, half of them unopened. I dreamed that I might deal with them in time, but of course I can't. Una was much loved, and they came from everywhere.

I suppose this is a fumbling apology for not having thanked you for your kindness to me in New York, and for not having answered until now— your letter of December 23rd. I do thank you—very much. I hope to write to Blanche and Russell soon—and please thank Mrs. Sweeney for me—who, besides the pleasure of her company, drove me to the air-port. It is wonderful to sit behind a woman driver who never makes a mistake.

As to the play—I saw it twice, and I liked it less and less. It was cut to the bone, most of the poetry cut out—(I had given permission to cut)—but what annoyed me was the miscasting of the actors, and the softness of their stage. Everything that I had thought of as hard had been made soft. And I thought of Cassandra as tall and dark—and some dignity. She was little and blonde and unimportant. I had thought of her as Clytemnestra's equal, when I wrote the poem, but most of her lines had been cut—and of course she could not compete with Judith Anderson.

All the players were good, and Judith was superb. But perhaps for that reason—for lack of balance—the play looked dull to me. If it ever goes on the stage again, I shall try to control it and rearrange it.

August 31

This old letter [*the preceding*] is included, though I never finished nor mailed it—only to show that I did try to write to you. As to the play—I must have been hypnotized by fatigue and theater, or I could hardly have bothered to talk about it.

I had your telegram two or three days ago. It was very sweet to hear from you. Midnight has just passed, and this day is the anniversary of Una's death. Passage of time does not make it more endurable. You were her best friends, besides myself, and your loss is deep. She loved you both, constantly and faithfully. She was very dear to us. I mustn't say more, because the "hysterical passion" that troubles me would look ridiculous in a letter.

There is no news of any importance. My son Donnan and his bright-blonde wife and child live with me here. Donnan is working ten hours a day and interested in his work—Bookkeeping and accounting—amazing what narrow straits the merchants of Carmel manage to survive. Lee, my daughter-in-law, yellow-haired and beautiful, is one of the sweetest girls I have ever known. Their son, Lindsay, with curly blonde hair, is most endearing, and reminds me of what Godwin said about his son-in-law: "Shelley is so beautiful, it is too bad that he is so wicked."

Garth and his family are high in the Sierras, forest-ranging. We visited them this summer—from their porch was the most magnificent panorama of snow-peaks that I ever saw, here or in Switzerland. Lotte (Charlotte) and her babies, Maeve and Diana, are very dear to me. You can see that I am pleased with my sons' choices—and products. Garth is a tremendous fellow, in muscles and mind too, but he was mostly away from home while we were there, chasing runaway pack-mules—and, according to Lotte's letters, has spent most of the later summer in fighting lightning-set forest-fires. When the fire season ends they will come down to see their old place at North Fork, near Yosemite.

So I feel like a stretched Titan, with one foot in the ocean and one in the high mountains. I feel miserable, as a matter of fact, and am writing nonsense to cover it up. Nothing will ever make up for what we have lost. My

> "... I would have each person realize that his
> contribution is not important, its success not really a
> matter for exultation nor its failure for mourning; the
> beauty of things is sufficient without him."

(Letter 235)

business at present is to make verses in the morning, and to add a stone or two to the new house-wall in the afternoon. The tasks that Una would have wanted me to attend to if she were here. But I don't answer letters—which she would have set before me from time to time—and I avoid visitors as much as possible. Lee fends them off for me.

The sea-otters, which were supposed to be extinct south of Alaska—killed off for their valuable fur—are coming back here. There are small herds of them down the coast; and individuals, or pairs, appear often off our own rocks—little playful fellows, less than a quarter the size of sea-lions, that seem to have delight in splashing the water with their webbed hands. Or floating on their backs, munching on abalone, with its shell for dinner-plate held on their bellies. And the night-herons have chosen our woods to nest in—terrific birds, "that brawl on the boughs at dusk, barking like dogs"—if I may quote my own verses. I planted the trees, under Una's supervision, and have probably some right to quote the herons and squirrels that live in them. There is a man who lives on the road behind us—he calls the squirrels every afternoon, with encouraging words and clicking nut-shells, and the swift gray creatures come down and eat out of his hands. Lindsay loves to go out under the trees and fraternize with him and them.

Lindsay expects a brand-new brother or sister next December—I am sure it will be as nice and as wicked as Lindsay, who will be four years old day after tomorrow.

Dear love to both of you. I hope you will return here some-time. You are the visitors (besides Blanche and Russell and one or two others) whom I *don't* want to avoid.   Sincerely,—(I mean with deep affection—)   Robin.

356: TO RADCLIFFE SQUIRES

February 3, 1951

Dear Mr. Squires: Thank you—I'll be glad to see the second volume of your poems, to be published this spring.[4] I confess that I have no remembrance at all of the first one—but you write as if that may not be displeasing to you. Probably I didn't even acknowledge it. Writing letters has always been ridiculously difficult for me; I can't answer a quarter of those that come; but I'll do my best to write an answer about your book.   Sincerely,
Robinson Jeffers

[4] *See Letter 370.*

357: TO MRS. LYMAN STOOKEY

February 14, 1951

Dear Mrs. Stookey—   We received the Wrestlers [*a small sculpting*], and
I am glad to have it, and grateful to you. I can't apologize sufficiently for our
silence, and the trouble it has caused you. Una Jeffers always took care of
my correspondence—it is almost impossible for me to write a letter—but I
should have been more attentive.

Una was very ill when you first wrote to us. She did not know it, but I did,
and could hardly think of anything else. We were in and out of hospitals,
here and in San Francisco. Una died last September first, and it is as if
the world ended then. But it goes on; and we have five grandchildren, so I
suppose we go along with it.

Your gracious hospitality, and our days at Hermosa are a wonderful island
to look back to. Dr. Stookey—Lyman—is the only teacher I ever had who
interested or influenced or excited me. And Byron was my best friend,
except Lyman perhaps.

I have a thick-necked son—in the U.S. Forest Service—who would gladly
have shared our wrestlings and beaten any of us; but I do not include
myself among the wrestlers; it was only flattery, and Lyman's good will.

I must tell you that I have wanted to write to you several times in recent
months, but your address was completely gone. Una had noted it, of course—
or had it in memory—but I could not find any notation. We saw Byron
in New York—twice, I think—I mean two different trips of ours to Ireland
and England. We had dinner with him and saw his family. Once he came
to a literary cock-tail party for my sake, and once he took me to see one of his
operations on the spinal cord. It was beautifully done; but I had a horrible
cold at the moment, and couldn't help myself under the gauze mask—I
didn't enjoy it any more than the victim did.

Please let me know if you ever come near Carmel. I should love to see you
again.   With all good wishes, Robinson Jeffers

358: TO MRS. HUGH BULLOCK

March 3, 1951

Dear Mrs. Bullock: I am grateful to the Academy of American Poets, and to
you, for the beautifully shaped and golden-hued gift which arrived here
day-before-yesterday.[5] The proud inscription troubles me just a little, because

[5] *A plaque commemorating J's five years of service as Chancellor for the Academy;
it was inscribed with his name and the dates of his term.*

341

I have been—not negligent—but deficient—in fulfilling my duties as Chancellor. I am not much acquainted with contemporary poets, and therefore quite sterile in making nominations, whether for the awards or for Chancellorship. Nearly all I can do is to vote on those whom others may nominate, and I am sorry.

Thank you, Mrs. Bullock, for your kind note of sympathy on the subject of my wife's death last September. I answered your husband's note but unhappily not yours. I have not been able to answer more than a few of the hundreds that came. The loss was bitter for me to bear, and will always be.   Sincerely yours, Robinson Jeffers

359: TO THE AMERICAN HUMANIST ASSOCIATION

The following is J's response to a query from the American Humanist Association, which defined several types of humanism, suggested that moderns all tend to think of themselves as humanists of one kind or other, and asked an application of the term to his own philosophy. The response was one of forty published in Warren Allen Smith's article "Authors and Humanism," Humanist, *XI (October, 1951), 193–204. J's reply was placed in Section IV of the article, among the "Ambiguous or Equivocal," pp. 200–1. The reply had no salutation or close.*

March 25, 1951

The word Humanism refers primarily to the Renaissance interest in art and literature rather than in theological doctrine; and personally I am content to leave it there. "Naturalistic Humanism"—in the modern sense—is no doubt a better philosophical attitude than many others; but the emphasis seems wrong; "human naturalism" would seem to me more satisfactory, with but little accent on the "human." Man is a part of nature, but a nearly infinitesimal part; the human race will cease after a while and leave no trace, but the great splendors of nature will go on. Meanwhile most of our time and energy are necessarily spent on human affairs; that can't be prevented, though I think it should be minimized; but for philosophy, which is an endless research of truth, and for contemplation, which can be a sort of worship, I would suggest that the immense beauty of the earth and the outer universe, the divine "nature of things," is a more rewarding object. Certainly it is more ennobling. It is a source of strength; the other of distraction.

360: TO KARL SHAPIRO (*Poetry: A Magazine of Verse*)

April, 1951

Dear Mr. Shapiro—   I am sorry not to be able to accept the invitation to give
a reading for Poetry Magazine in Chicago. It is an honor, and it would be
a pleasure to meet you and other friends of Poetry. And I should be glad to
serve the Magazine, if my presence could be of any value to it.

But my life was badly shaken last year by my dear wife's death—I haven't,
for instance, been able to write a line of verse since then (if it matters!)—
and the only way to become normal again will be to stay at home as quietly as
possible and feel the hills and the sea. —Besides this I am a bad lecturer
and a reluctant one; I tried it ten or eleven years ago, and I don't like the job.

Forgive me for not having written sooner. It was not because I hesitated,
but only because I am drowning in a sea of unanswered letters.
Cordially yours, Robinson Jeffers

361: TO LAWRENCE CLARK POWELL

May 2, 1951

Dear Larry Powell: Thank you very much for the beautifully printed little
book of your lecture to Professor Wortham's class in narrative poetry.[6]
It was a graceful and understanding discussion, and it made my verses sound
interesting—even to *me*—which is unusual, except at the moment of
writing. I have missed that interest now for a good while; I have written
nothing since Una's death, last September first, and very little before that,
during her long illness. She was so vital that I never dreamed she would not
outlive me, and it has been like a state of shock, but very likely I'll pull out of
it after while.

I hope you'll call here if you should come north on vacation this summer;
it would be a pleasure to see you and your wife again.   Sincerely,
Robinson Jeffers

---

[6] *"Robinson Jeffers, a Lecture to Professor James L. Wortham's Class in Narrative Poetry
Given on May 22, 1949," was printed by the Press of Los Angeles City College in 1951.*

362: TO EVA HESSE

May 15, 1951

Dear Miss Hesse: //I give you full permission to adapt "The Tower beyond Tragedy" as a radio-play for the Bavarian Broadcasting Corporation.

I also give you permission to translate it, as a poem, or to adapt it as a play; but before publication as a poem it would be necessary to have permission from my publishers also—Random House, 457 Madison Avenue, New York 22, N.Y.

Judith Anderson produced "The Tower" last December in New York. It was much talked of, but was not successful like "Medea"; it only went on for three weeks. I did the adaptation, but did not like it when I saw it on the stage, and I have no copy of my adaptation.

I am mailing to you (under separate cover) the stage version of "Medea," and give you permission to translate.

As to "The Double Axe"—I gave permission two years ago (more or less) to Mr. Otto Schütte, Haarbachstrasse 21, Wetzlar, and he sent me last February his translation of the first part of the poem. But he says that he has not been able to interest any publisher. My permission to him was not exclusive, and there is no reason why I cannot give permission to you also, and particularly if you have a publisher in mind. I am not familiar enough with German to be able to judge Mr. Schütte's translation. It is literal, and is written not in verse but in prose paragraphs.

I like very much your translations of three short poems, Kassandra, etc. which you sent me in June 1949. It seems to me that you reproduced most excellently both the meaning and the rhythm. I am very sorry to have neglected to answer the letter.

I have a friend here, Mr. Bruno Adriani, who is "echt deutsch" in spite of the Italian name, and he agrees with me about the excellence of these translations. Mr. Adriani was connected with the Ministry of Fine Arts under the Weimar Republic, but lived after that in Switzerland, and now here. He was so much interested in your letters, which I showed him, that he is sending you a photograph of me, taken by his wife, saying that it might be convenient for you to have it in case of publication, or magazine articles, or something of the sort.

With best wishes,   Sincerely, Robinson Jeffers

363: TO JOHN HAY WHITNEY

May 24, 1951

Dear Mr. Whitney: It is kind of you to let me know that you are giving those manuscripts to the Yale University Library.⁷ I'm afraid they are rather

⁷ *The manuscripts are those mentioned in Letters 46 and 58.*

messy palimpsests, but if they are worth preserving I cannot think of any more honorable place for them—though indeed I always liked to think of them as in your possession. It was a little romantic to remember that the money you paid for them encouraged and partially financed us in our first and most enchanted trip to Ireland, in 1929.

It is a pleasure too to remember meeting you in the crowded house at Pebble Beach, I can't remember how many years ago.

You speak of my wife, and I am bitterly sorry to have to tell you that Una Jeffers died, after a rather long illness, the first of September last year. She was so vital, and so loved, that I still can't believe it, except with the surface of my mind. One of my sons, and my bright blonde daughter-in-law and their baby, live with me here. If you ever return to this end of the world we should be very glad to see you.   Sincerely, Robinson Jeffers

364: TO WALTER G. TOLLESON

June 14, 1951

Dear Mr. Tolleson: I am sorry to be so slow in answering—I just can't write letters. The evening at Noel Sullivan's was delightful. I was happy to meet you, and proud of your music. We enjoyed it indeed, although we are not a musical family—so did Mr. Sullivan, and the others who were there.

I shall be glad if you can make an opera out of Thurso's Landing, or any other narrative poem of mine, but I can't promise to collaborate. I know nothing about opera, and very little about the stage; I'd be quite unable to make suggestions—besides that I don't like to give my mind to former verses of mine; it is more interesting to start something new.[8]

But of course I'd be delighted to see you again.

This is written in haste. We are starting to the Sierras to visit my son who is in the U.S. forestry service—and your letter has been on my conscience. I am sorry to say that there are a dozen others of some importance that won't get answered.   Sincerely, Robinson Jeffers

365: TO EVA HESSE

September 5, 1951

Dear Miss Hesse: I give full permission for the radio production of your adaptation of my poem "The Tower Beyond Tragedy" by the Bavarian Broadcasting Corporation.

I have no idea what payment—if any—should be made to me. Therefore I relinquish to you the German radio rights, for this occasion, and if any

[8] See also Letter 111.

payment to me seems appropriate I may trust you to send it on, or to let me know.

Have you heard that my "Medea" is one of the American plays to be produced for the "Festival of West Berlin" this month? It will be in English, however. The superb actress Judith Anderson, who played the title role here, has gone over to do it there.   Sincerely, Robinson Jeffers

366: TO EVA HESSE

November, 1951

Dear Eva Hesse: I should long ago have answered your letter about the broadcasting of "Die Quelle" [*German translation of* The Tower Beyond Tragedy]. My only excuse is that it is practically impossible for me to write or answer any letter. A week or two later, $190.00 was deposited for me in the local bank by the Bavarian Broadcasting Company. It is more than I expected, and I wonder whether you—who did the work—received any proper compensation. If not, I should be glad to send back to you at least $90.00.

The clipping which you enclosed with your letter was nice and amusing. "Der Weise von Mt. Carmel"—sagt man!

Your translations—those that I have seen—are very good indeed, and if any book of mine should be translated into German I should wish you to do it.

With best wishes,   Cordially, Robinson Jeffers

367: TO KARL SHAPIRO

November 7, 1951

Dear Karl Shapiro: Let me thank you most cordially, and the others of the editorial staff, for your award of the Eunice Tietjens Memorial prize to my verses in Poetry last January, and for your kind letter.[9]

On impulse—perhaps because I have to-day finished typing it—it occurs to me to offer for publication in Poetry my narrative poem "Told to a Dead Woman"—the first piece of verse I have written in a year and a half or more. But it is probably too long for your convenience—twenty-five pages of double-spaced typescript—which I guess would be nearly thirty of Poetry. Let me know if you care to see it.   Sincerely yours, Robinson Jeffers

[9] *"Fire," "The Beauty of Things," "Animals," "The World's Wonders," "Time of Disturbance," "The Old Stone-Mason," "To Death,"* Poetry, LXXVII *(January, 1951), 187–96.*

368: TO KARL SHAPIRO

November 17, 1951

Dear Karl Shapiro: Here is the poem: you will notice that I have changed
the title [to "Hungerfield"]. You are kind to wish to see it—and please
remember that it was offered on impulse, and it doesn't matter to me whether
Poetry can use it or not. It is really too long for a magazine, and I shall
have it in my next book—probably next fall, if I should get some more written
to make a book's length.

For that reason it ought to appear in Poetry not later than mid-summer if
at all. If you don't use it, please send it back pretty soon, and I'll reimburse
you by return mail with a lot of three-cent postage stamps.

With best wishes, to you and Mrs. Shapiro, and to the magazine—
Sincerely, Robinson Jeffers

Sunday, November 25—This was held up for some changes, but will no
doubt be mailed to-morrow.   —R. J.

369: TO RAYMOND J. PFLUG

[195?]

Dear Mr. Pflug: I'm sorry to be so slow in answering your letter. Most
letters I can't—couldn't—answer at all, and I hope it may be considered one of
the disabilities of old age. I was more prolific when I wrote those letters
to George Sterling. Oh yes, you may quote from them. I don't remember what
I said, except a vague suspicion of two or three florid paragraphs, but if
I've been foolish I won't try to keep it hidden.

As to what you call my Harvard speech,[10] I never knew nor asked where
it was dug up from. I knew it was not the Library of Congress reading,
because that had some mild suggestions that it would be stupid to let
Franklin Roosevelt trick us into war. And so it was.

Walter Clark's work interests me. I didn't know about his thesis at
Vermont.[11] I met somebody a few days ago who said Clark's latest book was
not good—"He can write stories about animals, not about human beings." I
said, "The Ox-Bow Incident"?   Sincerely, Robinson Jeffers

---

[10] *The Bancroft Library at the University of California catalogs a "typed copy of a
lecture delivered March 3, 1941, at Harvard University."*
[11] *Walter Van Tilburg Clark, "A Study of Robinson Jeffers" (unpublished Master's
thesis, University of Vermont, 1934).*

370: TO RADCLIFFE SQUIRES

May, 1952

Dear Mr. Squires: I enjoyed your book—"Where the Compass Spins"—
and was much interested. But it is practically impossible for me to write
letters. I have resolved, time after time, to write at least the more important
ones—and it always fails. My wife used to answer some of them for me,
and now my daughter-in-law does—a few—but she has a family of her own.

Your doctoral dissertation—as you describe the tension of your thought—
must be very interesting.[12] And perhaps disturbing, as you say. I should
normally like to see it. But what can I do or say about it? —I will make
a great confession: My particular desire has been to be dead—or at least
unconscious—before people begin to talk about my verses. —Not that they
are bad—not that they are good. I have given them to the world, if it
wants them; and perhaps I shall write more in the future; but I wish that this
particular aggregation of cells—myself—were not concerned.   Best wishes,
and sincerely, Robinson Jeffers

371: TO KARL SHAPIRO

May, 1952

Dear Karl Shapiro: Thank you for the two copies of POETRY, which have
just reached me; and for the check, which was—for a magazine of
verse—munificent.

I was quite overwhelmed to find myself alone in the book, as a verse-maker.
I didn't realize that the poem was so long. But the critical articles were
excellent, as mostly they have been, ever since Harriet Monroe's time.

And I was slightly overwhelmed by Selden Rodman's somewhat ruinous
photograph of me. I was feeling like hell the day Rodman and his friend
were here, but I didn't know it was that bad. It doesn't matter, of course. I
remember that "Poetry" asked me to send a photograph, and I found one for
you and forgot to send it.

The eight copies that I asked for have not yet arrived. But most of the
people to whom I intended to give a copy seem to have got one already.

I hope you enjoyed your European visit, besides the duties accomplished.

My best greetings to Mrs. Shapiro—and to you.   Cordially,
Robinson Jeffers

[12] *"Robinson Jeffers and the Doctrine of Inhumanism" (unpublished Ph.D.
dissertation, Harvard University, 1952).*

372: TO EVA HESSE

Dear Eva Hesse: //Several weeks—or perhaps months—ago I sent you
"The Women at Point Sur," my most ambitious and longest poem, and
certainly the least liked—except perhaps "The Double Axe," which naturally
expected to be unpopular when it was published. I should have sent you
"The Women—" when you first asked for it; but it is out of print, and
I thought I had only one copy. Later my daughter-in-law discovered two
others in the house, and sent you one of them. But I don't think it
will be useful to you.

It is interesting that the Bavarian radio wants to use your "Die Quelle"
again. —Another letter I haven't answered; but I hope you have made
arrangements with them. Now Radio Bremen wants to use it, and I will
answer their letter to-day or to-morrow, though German is very difficult for
me; it is more than 45 years since I have used it, except to read.

Mr. Scz—— I can't spell it, but he pronounces it "Chessny"—was here
awhile ago, and later sent me the manuscript of "Die Quelle" from Germany.
I haven't read all of it, but it seemed excellent as translation. If you see
Dr. "Chessny" please thank him for me. I enjoyed seeing him and his friend.[13]

I am sending you (but not air-mail) a copy of my poem "Hungerfield,"
printed in the May issue of the magazine "Poetry." It is the only thing I have
written—and finished—since my wife's death.   —Cordially yours,
Robinson Jeffers

373: TO FREDERICK M. CLAPP

The letter is written on cut half-sheets.

Dear Timmie: Please forgive the paper—it is all I can find at the moment,
and evidently my little grandson, Lindsay, has worked on it. He loves tools in
action. He loves shears.

I am very sorry that Ted Lilienthal bothered you about a foreword to the
poem called "Hungerfield." He spoke of it when he was here, and I meant to
write and warn you, but it is almost impossible for me to get letters
written. It was never worth your trouble. I have said, and I repeat, that I
would rather have written "Said before Sunset" or any other of your later
poems, than any of mine. And I told Ted Lilienthal that I would not let

---

[13] *Dr. Gerhard Szczesny was at that time head of the "Abendstudio" at the
Bavarian Broadcasting Company.*

"Hungerfield" be printed by the Book Club unless Random House (my publisher) consented to it. The thing seems not to be covered by contract, but yesterday I had an apologetic letter from them, saying that they do not consent. So that's off.[14] They want "Hungerfield" for the title-poem of a new volume, whenever I have enough verses to make one. I have not been fruitful recently.

Of course the "Hungerfield" poem is important in my life, because it remembers Una. That is why I sent to you and Maud a copy of the magazine, although someone here told me that you had already seen it. The ten copies I ordered were late in arriving, but I hoped that my poor inscription might make it mean something, though you had seen it already.

My little grand-daughter, for whom I am baby-sitting while her mother is at the dentist's, has exactly Una's great blue eyes. Their intelligence scares me. And her secret smile, as if she were saying "You and I know." But otherwise she is not like Una, she has flame-colored hair and a different skull formation, but a dear baby.

Do you realize that Una and I have now seven grand-children? Two of Donnan's here—this little extraordinary girl and green-eyed Lindsay with his blond curls—and two who live with Donnan's divorced wife in Ohio, very dear children, who write to him from time to time—and Garth's three little daughters. Garth lives up in the Sierras, in the wild-wood, with his Munich-born wife and the sweet children. And two dogs, a pit-bull and a bull-mastiff—both of whom collectively Donnan's English bull-dog wants to kill—but it might be the other way around. We have to keep him imprisoned in the Tower when Garth visits us. His name is Heathcliff and he looks the part, but Lindsay calls him Teethcliff.

I don't know why I can't write with a pen—lack of practice probably. And a desk piled high with abortive manuscripts—in pencil—and unanswered letters. I must really make a clearing and a burning—some day.

A curious thing—my "Tower beyond Tragedy" has been twice performed as a "Hörspiel," translated of course, on the Bavarian radio. And now Bremen wants it. The curious thing is that they pay real money for it— American dollars to me, and the same in German marks to the translator—a very intelligent young woman named Eva Hesse. Who never writes to me if she can avoid it, having learned that she will probably get no answer. She is translating other things of mine—also Walt Whitman and Eliot and Ezra Pound. There was a man to whom also I gave permission to translate, and the poor fellow did a lot of work, but I finally had to tell him that she was better. I probably have an enemy now, in Wetzlar where he lives.

---

[14] *Grabhorn Press did, however, print a limited edition of* Hungerfield, *with a Foreword by Dr. Clapp, in 1952; see Letters 374 and 375.*

I can't imagine why I bore you with all this. My interest is to know about you and Maud—how you are, and whether you will ever come again to this coast. You have many friends and admirers here, of whom I am perhaps the least, but we all wish to see you and Maud again.

(Lindsay cut this paper so crookedly that my pen is bewildered on each new page.)

Why don't you drive your latest Jaguar across the country? It would find a compatriot here: Donnan drives a Morris Minor, and scorns my much-battered old Ford sedan. (The door of the stone garage is narrower than the width of the car, and every time I go in I knock something. Or peel off the strips of chromium.)

My dear and remembering love to Maud, and to you.
Affectionately, Robin

Postscript: —I intend to have Una's travel-diaries printed fairly soon, or at least the Irish part of them. If you are willing to write any foreword I wish it would be for that. I shall probably have to write an introduction, but your preface will be better. I told Lilienthal, when he first came to see me, that I had no interest in letting "Hungerfield" be reprinted; my interest was in the diaries. They bring me to her! and I noticed that both our sons, just after Una's death, spent their time reading them, although they were sufficiently acquainted with the contents.   Sincerely again—Robin

374: TO FREDERICK M. CLAPP

September 5, 1952

Dear Tim: Thank you with all my heart for the "Foreword." It is beautifully done, and all too kind an expression of your constant friendship for Una and me, so that my eyes wept a little as I read it through. It is very good of you to have taken the trouble.

I was happy and surprised to hear your voice and Maud's on the telephone —but also it reminded me that I ought to write a letter from time to time. Letters were always difficult for me, but now—I don't know why—they have become practically impossible; even the merest letters of business. But I might change!

We are going on as usual here. Donnan is working quite hard at his accounting business, and I suppose will become a C.P.A. next year, and go into partnership with one of his present employers. He likes the work, and is extremely good at it. Lindsay is just five years old and will be starting to school in a few days. His little sister, Una Sherwood, has seven months I think, and is the happiest baby I have ever seen. She has at last produced a crop of hair—flame-color—or carrot-color if you like vegetables—and she has Una's great intent blue eyes. One of her particular pleasures is to sit in the courtyard in her baby-carriage and watch the birds.

I wish you and Maud were nearer to us—I wish you could come in and see us sometimes. It has been a pleasant summer, with the right alternations of sun and cloud—i. e. mostly cloud. Last night we had a small thunderstorm and the first rain of autumn, if this is autumn.

Please give my affectionate good wishes to Maud, and greetings from all of us.   Devotedly, Robin

375: TO THEODORE LILIENTHAL

September, 1952

Dear Ted: Tim Clapp sent me a copy of his "Foreword" the other day, as he has to you and Noël [Sullivan]. I think it is beautifully done, and all too kind. It was good of him to take the trouble.

I have just remembered a precaution to be taken with Grabhorn, if he should print the poem. A good many years ago he printed for Random House a book of mine called "Solstice," and did a beautiful job of course, but he cut up my long lines into phrases, making secondary verses, which changed and I think spoiled the rhythm that I intended. I didn't see any proofs until the final ones, and then didn't have the heart to make him do his work over again—for he is an artist—but I wouldn't want it to happen again. The lines have to be broken, of course, because they're too long for a page; but they ought not to be broken to indicate sound or sense, but merely according to space, as in the magazine. (By the way—I was able to get five more copies of the magazine, so I could give you an extra one if you need it.)//

It will be delightful to see you again, and I hope Fran also, when you come down here.   Best wishes, Robin

376: TO KARL SHAPIRO

November 20, 1952

Dear Karl Shapiro: Let me thank you sincerely, and the others of the editorial staff, for the Union League Civic and Arts Foundation award given to my poem "Hungerfield." And through you I should like to thank the donors also. I am sorry to be a little late in acknowledgment: I have been away from home a few days, visiting my son in the Sierras.

"Hungerfield" will be the title-poem of my book to be published in the fall of next year by Random House, and I'll not forget to make acknowledgment to "Poetry" for permission to reprint. I am sorry that I had nothing to contribute to "Poetry's" anniversary number.   With best wishes, Robinson Jeffers

377: TO JEAN ENNIS (Random House)

[*1953*]

Dear Miss Ennis: It is more than a quarter century since I last sent "biographical material" to my publishers, but really there is little to add that could be of interest to a reader. We have made three long visits to Ireland and Great Britain, but no farther, and it is unlikely that I shall travel any more. My wife, Una Jeffers, died three years ago; it was for her pleasure that these pilgrimages were undertaken. She was in many ways a mediator between me and the world.

I was born in Pennsylvania, Jan. 10, 1887. My parents lugged me to Europe several times while I was a child; I was too young to remember much but the seasickness. When I was nine years old my father began to slap Latin into me, literally, with his hands; and when I was eleven he put me in a boarding-school in Switzerland—a new one every year for four years— Vevey, Lausanne, Geneva, Zurich. Then he brought me home and put me in college as a sophomore. I graduated accordingly at eighteen, not that I was intelligent but by sporting my languages and avoiding mathematics. Then, I took postgraduate studies in English and European literatures, even a little forestry, finally three years in medical school—not knowing what else to do; and then drifted into mere drunken idleness. I was married in 1913. In 1914 we came to Carmel, having heard that it was a beautiful place. In 1916 our twin sons were born; in 1919 we built a little stone house here. Further dates, books published, etc. may be found in Who's Who.

I wrote verses ever since I was eight years old, but they were no good. I still try to avoid meeting people, and find it practically impossible to answer letters. I still do stone-work—granite sea-boulders—to enlarge our house; for there are several grandchildren.

I still live in the same place, and open my eyes every morning on the same rocks and ocean, ever new under the restless weather and flighty sea-fowl.

Recreations: Stone-masonry, dog-walking, intervention in dog-fights, and the art of being a grandfather.

As to photographs, any of those you sent me will do, except the one that has its eyes turned up like a dying duck. I am returning them in this package. I enclose with them two others taken by a friend which are better looking

Random House files contain one of the photographs, by Sadie Adriani, which Jeffers recommended to Jean Ennis in Letter 377.

but it doesn't matter. Would you mind returning to me these latter two, if you don't use them? Thanks for the trouble you are taking. (Sadie Adriani, if you give credit for publicity pictures).

Sorry I can't be more interesting. Will this help you?   Sincerely,
Robinson Jeffers

378: TO THEODORE LILIENTHAL

This letter was used as the Preface to the special printing of "De Rerum Virtute" by the Grabhorn Press in 1953.

February 2, 1953

Dear Ted: Your wife telephones and gives me some family gossip: that you will attain the robust age of sixty on February twenty-fifth. From my height of sixty-six I am not impressed. But no doubt it marks an era, and Fran has thought that a poem of mine, printed by Ed Grabhorn, who is probably the best printer in the world, might be a birthday gift from her to you. I am glad to dedicate to you the poem that follows. It has just to-day been finished, and seems to be the best I have written lately. The Latin title is stolen from Lucretius, as you will recognize, but I suppose DE RERUM NATURA has become "public domain" by this time. I will trespass again on "public domain" in wishing you from my heart many happy returns of the day. Sincerely, Robinson Jeffers

379: TO BENJAMIN H. LEHMAN

April 23, 1953

Dear Ben: Forgive me for not answering promptly. I have had a wonderful dose of flu, and am convalescent but still semi-conscious.

I cannot find any letters of George Sterling's here. I believe that Una gave all that we received from him to our friend (though I have only seen her once) Mrs. Wilford Holman, who collects Sterling as well as me. But it is possible that Una retained one or two of them; I never pay attention to such things, and can't find anything among our papers. Melba Bennett, whom you have probably met, expects to be here sometime this spring, and no doubt can answer the question; she has all our mss. etc. sorted and indexed—but it does *me* no good.//

It was pleasant to hear from you, though I am so horribly lame at answering—and I hope to see you again pretty soon.   Yours, Robin

380: TO FRASER DREW

September 1, 1953

Dear Fraser Drew: I am very sorry not to have inscribed your books more promptly. Or at least I should have acknowledged receipt. The package has lain unopened in our living-room, and every day I have thought "To-morrow"—and every five days my son has reminded me of it. I have inscribed so many hundreds of books—it is no task—I can't imagine why I kept postponing. —Perhaps because it was such a neat and well made package—if you had come to the door I'd have done it instantly.

It has just been done, and the books will be mailed at the same time as this note.   Sincerely, Robinson Jeffers

381: TO GENE DE WILD

This explanation of The Cretan Woman *was made for the members of the Pasadena Playhouse; the final version of the letter may have been altered slightly. See Bennett,* Stone Mason, *pp. 228–29.*

[*1954*]

Hippolytus rashly incurred the anger of Aphrodite and was destroyed by her. That is the Greek story, and more interesting I think than to put all the blame on Phaedra. It provides another dimension. As to Artemis, she didn't interest me. She is only a goddess, Aphrodite is a force of nature.

As to my Hippolytus being homosexual—I thought I got a hint of it from Euripides. Anyway, it came to my mind and seemed appropriate. You don't write with conscious reasons but take what comes to mind.

As to Hippolytus' horses running away, scared by a sea-beast, in answer to prayer—it seems a little funny, a sort of superfluous miracle. I don't like miracles, they distract attention from the play. And Theseus, with his record of homicide—it is natural for man to kill his son with a sword, not a prayer.

I quoted the prayer (in reverse sense) in order to say: "Yes, I know, I am changing the story a little. I think this way is more likely!"

382: TO FRASER DREW

September 25, 1954

Dear Fraser Drew: I hope you didn't pay too much for those little books. Certainly one of them is nearly worthless, except maybe as a curiosity, and even its author didn't have the heart to ask people to buy it.

But I'll be glad to inscribe them for you.

"The Cretan Woman" was not performed in Provincetown, but by a group that calls itself "The Provincetown Players." Apparently it is going to try its luck on Broadway now—theatrical producers are brave men.[15]

I am much interested to hear about the courses you are giving in contemporary literature.   Cordially, Robinson Jeffers

383: TO THEODORE LILIENTHAL

January, 1955

Dear Ted: Forgive me—I just can't answer letters. It is a kind of insanity I suppose—they pile up and paralyze me.

The little book is beautiful, and I feel most truly grateful to you and Noël,

---

[15] The Cretan Woman *was privately performed on the Arena Stage in Washington, D.C., in May, opened at the President Theatre in New York City on March 12, then moved to the Provincetown Playhouse in Greenwich Village on July 7 and ran until September 5.*

who managed it, and to Ward Ritchie also.[16] He sent me eight copies and
I haven't yet acknowledged them, nor sent one of them away; except that I
gave one of them to Garth, when he and his family were here over Christmas.
There has always been a horrible gulf between me and the post office,
but it is growing deeper.

I'll sign your book and return it to you just as soon as my beautiful
daughter-in-law can get it wrapped up.

All my best to you and to Fran, and again thank you.   Robin

384: TO ARTHUR G. COONS (President, Occidental College)

*A copy of this letter was mailed to Remsen du Bois Bird with the attached
note: "Dear Remsen: Here is what I wrote to President Coons—since you are
named in it. I hope you can read the scribble—don't bother if you can't—
but thank you very much indeed.   Yours, Robin"*

May 17, 1955

Dear President Coons: I am very grateful to Occidental College, and to you,
and to others concerned, for wishing to celebrate in some manner the
fiftieth anniversary of my graduation from Occidental. It is a generous
thought, and I appreciate it deeply: I am truly sorry to tell you that I don't
expect to be present there. Indeed I have been troubled about it for months,
knowing that I didn't want to take part, even as one of the audience, and
wondering whether in common gratitude I ought to. A few days ago I took my
troubles to Remsen Bird, asking his advice. He was entirely sympathetic;
he knew of course already that I didn't want to go, and he said I hadn't
promised to go, there was no moral duty, and he thought that you
and others would understand.

I really don't like such occasions; I can't feel that they do much good to any
of the participants. But if my wife were living we should probably go down
there, because it would please her, I think. She had more interest in
such matters than it is possible for me to feel, and I remain ever grateful to
Occidental—and to U.S.C. also—for having pleased her by conferring
honorary doctorates on me. But now I am alone, and slightly growing old,
it seems better for me to stay at home and attend to my own business. If you
have any sort of a day reserved for me down there, it will not be Hamlet

---

[16] *Lilienthal and Noël Sullivan financed the private printing of Una's travel diaries,*
Visits to Ireland, *edited and with a Foreword by J, issued by Ward Ritchie's
press in Los Angeles in 1954. See p. 140 and p. 330; see also Letter 222.*

without the Prince, it will only be Hamlet without the ghost. And my absence will spare me the expense of spirit and waste of time—as Shakespeare didn't say.

Forgive me for not answering your letter until now, and believe me that I am most grateful to you, and to the others concerned.   Sincerely yours, Robinson Jeffers

385: TO EVA HESSE

[1955]

Dear Eva Hesse: I am ashamed and sorry that I can't answer letters—not even to thank you for yours—nor to thank you for the Lebkuchen in their handsome container. The little cakes disappeared like magic, mostly down the throats of my grandchildren; the container is still in service, for home bred cookies. I do thank you.

Two questions of yours I should have answered at once: —Could I make "The Cretan Woman" longer, so as to fill up an evening?—No. I don't see how I could. —Has "The Cretan——" been performed before? —Yes, for several months, in a little theater in New York but "off Broadway."[17] It seems to have been quite successful there. It has been done in other places too. I have congratulated myself that neither "Cretan" nor "Medea" has been performed in Carmel or Monterey, though the place is permeated with little theaters. But now, this summer, two different groups of people are putting on the two plays. I don't like it, but I'll have nothing to do with it; everyone here knows that I do not go to the theaters, nor attend lectures, nor readings by visiting poets. This sounds bad-tempered but it is not; it is only self-preservation.
The copy I used ends here, unsigned.

386: TO WITTER BYNNER

January 3, 1956

Dear Witter Bynner: Forgive me—it is just impossible for me to write a letter—even to write "thank you," though I can say it. I do thank you. I have read the Book of Lyrics with pleasure and gratitude. I hope you feel as Horace did:

Quod si me lyricis vatibus inseres
Sublimi feriam sidere capite.

[17] *See Letter 382 and note.*

—If you count me among the lyric poets (beginning with Sappho) I shall strike the stars with my uplifted head. This is one of the few tags of Latin or Greek that stick in my mind—though it has little to do with my own expectations—and I send it to you with thanks and admiration.
Cordially and sincerely, Robinson Jeffers

Why did I translate the couplet? You probably know it as well as I do, and you know that Sappho was in Horace's mind, as first of poets, though not in his verses.   —R. J.

1956-62 *In 1956 J once again sailed for England and Ireland, but he returned home earlier than he had planned when he learned of the City of Carmel's decision to convert part of his property for use as a public park. He averted condemnation by subdividing some of his land and cutting many trees. Though he had in mind another narrative, "Christane," J's worsening health interfered with purposeful work on it. From 1958 on, his strength failed noticeably; after September, 1961, its failure was rapid. J worked at some shorter poems, however, but he could assemble no new book, even with the help of Melba Bennett, who sorted manuscripts and frequently answered letters for him.* ❦ *In 1958 the Academy of American Poets elected J a fellow, and in 1961 the National Poetry Society gave him their Shelley Memorial Award. Two new studies, Radcliffe Squires'* The Loyalties of Robinson Jeffers *and Mercedes Monjian's* Robinson Jeffers, a Study in Inhumanism, *were published in 1956 and 1958 respectively.* ❦ *Popular interest in J's poetry and drama was greater in Europe than in America during these years. Eva Hesse translated his work into German, Kamil Bednář into Czechoslovakian, Mary de Rachewiltz into Italian; and Julien Philbert's French version of* Medea *extended a reputation earlier established by Eugène Jolas in France. An American film version of* The Loving Shepherdess *was unsuccessfully proposed to J in 1957, and though he agreed to a contract for screen rights to* Tamar, *and* Medea *in 1961, neither was filmed. In 1958* The Tower Beyond Tragedy *was broadcast in Vienna on the Voice of America, and* Medea *was performed at the Bad Hersfeld festival.* ❦ *In 1956 the Book Club of California published* Themes in My Poems, *the text of the address J had read on his 1941 lecture tour, and Random House published a limited edition of* The Loving Shepherdess, *illustrated by Jean Kellogg. After J's death on January 20, 1962, selections were made from his last work for* The Beginning and the End, *for 1963 publication. The Vintage paperback* Robinson Jeffers, Selected Poems, *1963, is the most recent collection of J's poems.*

387: TO HUGH BULLOCK (Academy of American Poets)
On board Holland-America ship Dalerdyk
February 20, 1956

Dear Mr. Secretary: Thank you for the enclosed $100.00 check. I am returning it to the Academy because I am simply not competent to earn it. I don't know enough about contemporary poetry and criticism; I can't make nominations, whether for awards or chancellorships, because I don't know the people who should be nominated.

Therefore it has seemed to me for a long time that I ought to offer my resignation as chancellor of the Academy. And now I shall be traveling for a year more or less, with no fixed address beyond "American Express, London," it will be even more impossible for me to perform my duties as chancellor. So, with sincere regret, I do offer my resignation. I don't insist on it, nor set a date, and I hate to cause you the nuisance of another election; I beg to lay the matter into your hands. Will you please show this letter to Mrs. Bullock, to whom I wish to express my regret, and my cordial greeting.   Sincerely yours, Robinson Jeffers

388: TO FRASER DREW

[Dolphin and Anchor Hotel]
[Chichester, Sussex]
June 20, 1956

Dear Fraser Drew: I am very sorry that your letter of February 14 went unanswered until now. We left home about that time, and it got lost in my disorderly luggage, and has only now reappeared. Some times I thought of it sadly and could not find it. Now we are going home, sailing to-day.

We went on a pleasant Dutch cargo-passenger ship through the Canal, got a station-wagon in London, and proceeded to lose ourselves on almost every unlikely road in Gt. Britain and Ireland. Our only stops were for a week in North Devon and a month in the extreme northwest of Donegal. My fellow passengers were one of my sons Donnan and his wife and two children.

I hope to be home in Carmel within a month from now, and then I'll write my name six times—inscribed for Fraser Drew—on a big piece of typewriting paper and send it to you if you still want it. Or in the books if you'd rather. My mail will not be forwarded now, but wait at home for me.

With best wishes and sincere apologies,   Yours, Robinson Jeffers

389: TO DR. HANS AND PHOEBE BARKAN (postcard)

Southampton
June 25, 1956

Dear Hans and Phoebe: We have been scrambling all over Great Britain and Ireland, then lived about a month near the place pictured. In the forest left of the road there are a few Monterey cypresses three or four times as big as any at Pt. Lobos or Cypress Point, where they belong. —We're now going home.   —Affectionately, Robin

390: TO ALLEN GRIFFIN

The letter refers to the Monterey Peninsula Herald's *reprint of Kenneth Rexroth's "Decline of a Poet,"* Saturday Review, XL *(August 10, 1957), 30, a review of Radcliffe Squires'* The Loyalties of Robinson Jeffers *(Ann Arbor, 1956); see also Letter 391.*

[1957]

Dear Allen: Thanks for your letter. The episode had no importance, and I have no reason to blame your editor. He wants to print the news as he did at the end of the war, and apparently he thought that unpleasant attack on me—to compare very small things with great ones—was also news. But I have suffered the same kind of thing more than once before, and remain mosquito-proof.

We have been very much interested in your letters to the Herald from Europe, and thank you for them. They are brave people in West Germany, and recklessly gay people in Austria; I hope to God nothing happens to them.   Sincerely, Robin Jeffers

391: TO RADCLIFFE SQUIRES

[1957]

Dear Mr. Squires: I owe you humble apologies—a number of them. First for that silly article in the Saturday Review.[1] The hatred was directed of course, against me, but you had to be included in it, and I'm sorry.

Second, and maybe worse, I have to confess that I have never to this day

[1] *See Letter 390.*

read your book. You sent it to me, or someone did, but all those faces on the dust-jacket so frightened me that I put it away unread.

That was pure self-indulgence. I always try to avoid reading about myself, but at least I should have acknowledged the gift, and I'm sorry to have failed. Now I've brought the work out again and turned a few pages. It seems to me well written and well thought, and I thank you for it.

As to Rexroth's article: it is not disturbing but merely obvious. It has happened several times before, and they always say the same things. I'd never have read it—I don't read the Saturday Review—except that our local newspaper, the Monterey Peninsula Herald, reprinted it on their editorial page, with a big bad portrait of me. My daughter-in-law read it first, and said, "You have an enemy." I said "Thousands of them." (So many people I have insulted by not answering their letters, and I blame myself for it.) But the Herald's correspondence columns were thick for several days with indignant letters to the editor. Then they reprinted several poems of mine, on their editorial page, and paid me for the use of them. And the editor wrote me a letter of apology. It is all very funny.

The copy I used ends here; Squires cannot locate the letter.

392: TO DAN MAGNAN (William Morris Agency)

July, 1957

Dear Mr. Magnan: Thank you very much for the trouble you have taken with this unfortunate business about the "Shepherdess." I do feel sorry about it—wasting people's time with my indecision. As to Mr. Murphy's legal expenses: —it was precisely the work of his lawyers that made me refuse the contract. They thought up too much and claimed too much, making me sick of the whole business.

But I think the project would have been a failure, and Mr. Murphy is saving money by not going on with it.   Sincerely, Robinson Jeffers

393: TO EVA HESSE

[November 20, 1957]

Dear Miss Hesse: Judith Anderson was here, but she didn't seem able to help us much. She suggested no names to write to. Finally she said she would lend us her note-books, (but not the most private one). They indicated staging, lighting and so forth—I said "Like those acting editions of Samuel French's?" She said "Exactly. The same thing." She is a little humorously jealous: "I hate every woman who plays Medea!" "But *you* can't play it in German," I said. She said "Why not? I could talk English and let the others talk German."

I remember that you wanted one of those Samuel French "Medeas." Were you able to get it? If not, I'll make a search here. I know that I have one copy, and if I can find it I'll send it to you.

I am sending after Xmas most of the other books you speak of. I can't find any copy of "Cawdor"; and the "Dear Judas" volume seems to be the only one I have, so let's say that it is on loan to you for a few years; though other copies are no doubt obtainable.

The books will go by ordinary mail as soon as I can get them wrapped up and posted. Also Radcliffe Squires' "Loyalties"—the only copy I have. I never read it nor thought of it—scared away perhaps by all those [*dissected?*] pictures on the dust-jacket—until your letter spoke of it.

The letter breaks off here. Frau Hesse informs me that the letter, still in its rough-draft form, was mailed to her only after J's death.

394: TO BENNETT CERF

[*1957*]

Dear Bennett: Thank you for your letter, but I have no book in prospect for at least a year or two. It was seven years between books last time, and next time will probably be my last book, so I might as well make it good.

It's surprising to be nearly seventy-two years old all of a sudden; I'm not sure that I like it. But I'll have a book for you.   Cordially, Robinson Jeffers

395: TO THE VIKING PRESS

Part of the first paragraph of this letter was used by Viking as promotional material on the jacket of the book described and on the Mentor paperback cover.

[*1958*]

Gentlemen: Thank you very much for sending me the proof-sheets of Horace Gregory's new book, his translation of Ovid's Metamorphoses. It is the best poetic translation of a long poem that I have ever known; and Ovid, whom I have always avoided, has suddenly become in my mind one of the first-class Roman poets, who can be counted on one hand's fingers.

Gregory's persuasive and enlightening introduction has something to do with this conversion, but the beauty and clarity of the translated poem, and its deft construction, speak for themselves.

Sorry that I have lost your letter and can't remember who signed it; so I am addressing this simply to Viking Press.   Sincerely, Robinson Jeffers

396: TO WALTER DUCLOUX

On February 3, 1958, Walter Ducloux of the USC School of Music wrote referring a request from Radio Vienna through the Voice of America for an interview with J on the occasion of the Vienna broadcast of "Die Quelle" and suggesting that J contribute some statement in German. J wrote out the following answer; see Bennett, Stone Mason, *p. 235.*

[February, 1958]

It is a great honor for a foreigner to have his play produced in Vienna, that famous city with its proud tradition of the theater.

I recognize the honor, and I hope that you will find the play interesting. I wrote it as a poem, having no idea that it could ever be staged.

Let me speak also of my translator, Frau Eva Hesse of München. She has extraordinary ability in both languages, German and English, and I am glad to entrust the play to her. My own acquaintance with the great languages of Europe has sadly deteriorated. It is nearly sixty years since I went to school in Leipzig and Zürich; and around the Lake of Geneva—Vevey, Lausanne, Geneva, and so forth. In those days I knew German and French as well as I did English. But now I can only thank Eva Hesse for translating the poem, and you for listening to it.

Mein Deutsch ist aber viehleicht doch ausreichend, um ihnen—von meinem haus am strand des stillen ozeans—meine besten wünsche und warme grüsse zu senden.

397: TO EVA HESSE

May 1, 1958

Dear Eva Hesse: Thank you very much for your interesting letters (I wish I had the ability and patience to write a letter).

There is little to tell you in return. Two young men, German or Austrian, were here from Los Angeles the other day with a tape-recorder, wanting me to say something à propos of the Vienna production. They said they were employed by "Voice of America." So I muttered something for their machine about the honor it was for a foreigner to have his play produced in Vienna, with its great tradition of the theater; and I added some words about my translator, Frau Eva Hesse of Munich, and her unusual ability in both languages—I was glad to entrust the play to her. The little speech was so muttered and mumbled that it is worth nothing. I said so, and the men said, "You don't know what electronics can do."

Also I had a cordial letter from the Rowohlt Theaterverlag. (Hamburg—Klaus Juncker) naming the cities and dates of the plays, and asking whether I could come to Germany. I shall try very hard to answer the letter, but I don't think I'll go abroad, though I'd love to meet you. With best wishes—Sincerely, Robinson Jeffers

398: TO KLAUS JUNCKER (Rowohlt Theaterverlag, J's theater agency in German-speaking countries)

May 1, 1958

Gentlemen: Thank you most cordially for your kind and informative letter. Frau Eva Hesse had told me about the list of city and state theaters, but it still surprises me; and your description of the theater at Bad Hersfeld, in the wide ruins of the cathedral, is most interesting. It really tempts me to go there, in response to your kind invitation. But I don't like traveling, I traveled too much when I was a child, and I don't enjoy meeting people. At my age a man ought to stay at home and try to finish his work, or else be quiet.

I am very fortunate, as you suggest, in having Eva Hesse as my translator—and you, I may add, as my publishers. I am glad to entrust the plays to her hands and yours. If I should ever go to Germany—which remains possible, of course, though very unlikely—I should look forward to meeting you. Sincerely, and with best wishes, Robinson Jeffers

399: TO KAMIL BEDNÁŘ

June 7, 1958

Dear Mr. Kamil Bednar: I am truly sorry not to have written to you sooner; it is almost impossible for me to write or even dictate letters. Yet I am eager to send you my greeting and good wishes.

Your book, "Mara," arrived here a few days ago, and I wish I could read it. I learned German and French when I was a child at school in Switzerland, and have nearly forgotten them, but Czech was left out of my education.

"Mara" is an attractive little volume, and the illustrations are most interesting.[2] Thank you for sending it—and also for translating the poem.

I value your interest in my work, and am truly grateful for your expressions of friendship. Perhaps I shall see you some day—who knows?—in spite of the present distances between us.

If I can find any interesting photographs of my two sons and their families, or of this house, I will send them to you.

With best wishes,   Sincerely yours, Robinson Jeffers

400: TO OGDEN PLUMB

On July 1, 1958, Ogden Plumb, apparently visiting in Carmel, wrote asking if J knew why the imported eucalyptus seems to thrive on the coast while the Monterey cypress struggles to survive in its native habitat. A new house between J's property and Point Lobos also aroused his curiosity. See also Bennett, Stone Mason, *p. 231.*

[*July, 1958*]

Dear Mr. Plumb: I can't answer letters but I am interested in trees. This Point was bare to the sea-wind when we first came here, and eucalyptus could not have grown up without cypress to shelter it.

Once in northwestern Ireland we were told that the biggest tree in Ireland grew in a monastery garden near by. It was huge, and it was a Monterey cypress. —Also the south of England is full of them, but mostly clipped into hedges.

—That winged roof—Oh dear!   Sincerely—Robinson Jeffers

401: TO EVA HESSE

July 27, 1958

Dear Eva Hesse: I am grateful for your long and very interesting letter dated July 14. You have a brilliant critical intelligence, and I believe what you say about Hilde Krahl as compared to other Medeas. But I shouldn't like Judith Anderson to hear it.

You ask why I haven't written an Oedipus, and the answer is very simple: because nobody asked me to. Judith asked for Medea, and another actress

---

[2] *Bednář's translation of* Mara *was illustrated by Miloslav Troup, published in Praha, 1958.*

whom I chanced to meet wanted a Phaedra, but lost interest before I finished it. Oedipus of course is a more serious undertaking—and I'd rather tell my own stories than adapt another's—even Sophocles'.

The stage at Bad Hersfeld, in the abbey ruins, must have been wonderfully impressive. I hear that you had an hour and a half of rain to endure, and that audience and actors met it bravely. I'd like to have been there.

My bank account has no number that I know of. I am sure that "Robinson Jeffers, Bank of Carmel, Carmel, California" would be sufficient. But I still feel that you ought to have ten percent extra as my agent.

Your President Theodor Heuss was here a few weeks ago, taking a little rest on his tour of the country. (I see that he is Lord Protector—Schirmherr— of the Hersfeld Festspiele.) He stayed at the same hotel where Adenauer stayed some time ago—not the best hotel but the most beautifully placed one, with mountain and ocean and rocky cliff and deep pine-forest all in the windows.

My son and daughter-in-law send you cordial greeting. Did I ever tell you that my other son, Garth, fell in love with a girl in Munich and brought her home after the war? He is a U.S. forester in the great forest regions of Northern California, a great change from the Gemütlichkeiten of Munich, but Lotte seems to like it.

Thank you again. I wonder where in the world you learned such perfect English.

—A Czech translator, Kamil Bednar, has lately published as a book a narrative poem of mine called "Mara." I had nearly forgotten it—I think it is in the book called "Be angry at the Sun." He also published "Hungerfield," in a magazine called "Foreign Literature"—or something like that.

My best wishes to you.   Sincerely, Robinson Jeffers

402: TO EVA HESSE

September 7, 1958

Dear Eva Hesse: I referred to you the writer of the enclosed letter, saying that you are my agent in Germany, as well as translator, and have full authority to act for me. I don't care what answer you give him—but probably you don't care either, and I shouldn't have bothered you with this.

Thank you very much for your always interesting letters. When I wondered where you had found your English it was not because you use it perfectly, but chiefly because I couldn't guess whether it was good American English or good English English. Usually there is a difference, but you have the language pure, so to speak.

The three hundred and eleven dollars, or whatever it was, for radiobroadcast arrived punctually, and I should have acknowledged it sooner, but I still find it very difficult to write a letter. Don't bother with accountants, at least so far as I am concerned. Your reckoning is quite sufficient.

I remember from your last letter that you were going to visit Ezra Pound, whose work you have had in hand for eight years, didn't you tell me? —An extraordinary man, and ridiculously mistreated in this country. However, in the state of opinion at that time, I suppose he was lucky. I wish I liked his work better, but indeed I have read very little of it. What most impresses me is that Yeats of Ireland, who was a first-rate poet and an arrogant man, seems to speak of Ezra Pound as a disciple might of a master. That is really surprising.

You asked me, some time ago, whether my "Dear Judas" was a play or a poem. It was modelled, more or less, on the Japanese Noh play, a play of dreamy ghosts repeating a tragic action of their lives, which Ezra Pound I think introduced to western literature and Yeats used for his own purposes.[3]

As to "Dear Judas"—a brave man from Hollywood tried nobly to present it as a play. He planned to try it out in Boston and bring it to New York. But the mayor and police of Boston prohibited it as blasphemous, so he brought it straight to New York and it starved to death before the week was up.[4]

Best wishes to you.   Sincerely, Robinson Jeffers

403: TO MRS. HUGH BULLOCK

October 11, 1958

Dear Mrs. Bullock: Thank you very much for your letter, and its precursor on the telephone. You are very kind, and it was a pleasure to hear your voice. I must thank also your Chancellors for electing me a Fellow of the Academy of American Poets, and for the substantial award. I note the names of those who nominated me, and shall try to write to them. You have an illustrious board of Chancellors.

Also I should wish to thank the donors of the fund which makes possible

[3] *J described the form of* Dear Judas *to* Alberts *in the 1930 letter already quoted in the note to Letter 155. He explained on the manuscript that he wrote* Dear Judas *"with the thought of presenting the only divine figures still living in the minds of people of our race, as the hero of a tragedy. The Japanese Nō plays, in which the action is performed by ghosts revisiting the scenes of their passions, no doubt influenced my conception." See* Alberts, A Bibliography, *p. 57;* Bennett, Stone Mason, *p. 132; and J's "Preface to 'Judas,'"* New York Times, *October 5, 1947, Sec. 2, p. 3.*
[4] *See Letter 328.*

these Fellowships; and yourself in particular, for your devotion to poetry and your admirable persistence.

I hope the photograph that my daughter-in-law sent you was passable. It is one of many press photographs that have been given us, but perhaps we could have chosen more wisely. I have no vanity.

It would please us greatly if you could come avisiting here, sometime when you are in California. You might enjoy seeing our sea-boulder house above the ocean cliff, built by my own hands and latterly my son's, and the great mountain-coast south of here.   Most sincerely yours, Robinson Jeffers

404: TO JEAN KELLOGG (Mrs. James Dickie)

October 13, 1958

Dear Jean: It is so hard for me to write a letter that I thought nothing less than that could express my gratitude for your gift [*a drypoint etching of a hawk's head*]. Ever since it arrived I have been mentally putting ink to paper but as usual got nothing done. I should have telephoned.

It is a magnificent hawk's head, with all the stoicism and stored-up fury that are in their blood. I am truly grateful to you.

Laidlaw Williams must be a marvelous bird-surgeon as well as observer. I should be helpless in that respect, perhaps mostly from fear of hurting them; I remember how ignominiously I failed, even in trying to wash clotted tar off a gull's wings.

Thank you, Jean, very much; I treasure the picture.   Sincerely, Robin

405: TO DR. HANS BARKAN

December [27], 1958

Dear Hans: It was a great pleasure for us when Phoebe and Button[5] came visiting the other day; we only wished that you had come along with them. Since then a letter from Phoebe says that you have been in hospital for an operation; and I am very sorry to hear it. I don't like hospitals, except the one I knew in Dublin, where the nurses had Catholic Irish charm and the management had Protestant ability.

I think of you so often, Hans. I think of your kindness and Phoebe's when Una was ill; I think of the fun we had in Oxfordshire, when you were in the Watlington hotel with that maniac landlord and his shooting-irons. But

[5] *The Barkans' daughter, elsewhere called "Little Phoebe."*

I am sorry we never traveled with you in Ireland. What an oversight!
I think of us in the prehistoric earth-works atop of the White Horse hill; and
the bottle of sherry you brought, and Una's ecstatic delight in it. I think
you took a picture of that—she grinning, hoisting the bottle.

And I remember the great block of stone called King Alfred's trumpet?—
bugle?—you blew through a hole in the rock and made a clear loud noise, but
I couldn't evoke even a whisper. You musicians!

I wish I knew why I can't write letters. I love my friends, who are very few,
but I can't write to them; much less to the people unknown to me—my
"fans," Una used to call them, that horrid name out of Hollywood—but that
doesn't matter—except that it makes me many enemies—who cares? But
I can't write to you and Phoebe. I can't write to Tim Clapp, Una's best friend
and mine too, though he has sent me four or five letters that urgently
required answering. It is a stupid predicament. Of course Una used to answer
my mail for me, when she thought it necessary. And she wrote such
beautiful letters.

As for me—my right eye was hurt at birth, and progressively dimmed, and
is now stuffed up with a cataract. And the other feels pretty old. But
that's no excuse, there must be other causes.

Best love to you, Hans. And please give my love to Phoebe, and to Button
and her husband, who were so kind to me.   Yours always, Robin

406: TO THE BESSINGER (?) FOUNDATION

*Melba Bennett identifies these notes as made for a recommendation
requested by the Bessinger Foundation for a fellowship for Eric Barker.*

[1959]

His poems please me more than any others that are being written at this
time. They are natural and quiet, very far removed from the exhibitionist
nonsense that afflicts poetry magazines. Barker's verses go straight, and he
has a great theme in the coast-range mountains above Big Sur. He has
unspoiled imagination, and a good feeling for musical verse.[6]

You ask me to give an opinion on Eric Barker and his work. I believe that
he is worthy of any help the Foundation may give him, and will return
good value for it.

I know that he is very faithful to his calling, and has in effect half starved
himself in order to have room and time for his work.

[6] *Compare J's Foreword to Eric Barker's* Directions in the Sun *(New York, 1956).*

407: TO MRS. HUGH BULLOCK

The first entry below is a copy of the mailed letter; the second is from notes in the Tor House files. The notes vary somewhat from the mailed copy, though the first paragraph is substantially the same. Ned O'Gorman's The Night of the Hammer *was the Lamont Poetry Selection for 1958; the* Poetry Pilot *issues from the Academy as a monthly newsletter for which editors are invited to select several poems.*

January [25], 1959

407A:

Dear Mrs. Bullock: I am very much ashamed of myself. It is almost impossible for me to answer letters, but I meant to answer yours; I read it hastily and have completely lost it. Sometimes, when I leave letters lying around in hope to answer them, my beautiful daughter-in-law picks them up and puts them in a safe place and then forgets where. But in this case that is only a mean suspicion.

Then further, I have been ill—nothing-serious—but it took away my last ounce of energy.

Thank you cordially for the citation as fellow of the Academy, and for "The Night of the Hammer," which I don't understand. Please forgive me for my stupid inability to answer letters.   Sincerely, Robinson Jeffers

407B:

The last two paragraphs of the notes for this letter read thus:

I believe you asked me to serve for a season as editor of something for the Poetry Pilot. I agree to do so, if I am capable of it, and if I come to know what the Poetry Pilot is. The name is entirely unfamiliar to me.

If anything else was spoken of, I'll do my best about that also. Please forgive my stupid inability to answer letters.

On March 22, 1959, Donnan J wrote Mrs. Bullock to say that his father had recovered from his illness but was still very weak, and to add, "However, he is disturbed that your request that he be your Poetry Editor for one of this year's issues of Poetry Pilot went unacknowledged. We presume, that by now, you have filled the need for an Editor, however, at some future time, when my father is stronger, he would be happy to be of service to you. . . ."

408: TO MARK VAN DOREN

Only the appended note and signature are in J's hand; the typed letter was prepared by Melba Bennett.

July 20, 1959

Dear Mark Van Doren: Two months have passed since your visit to our coast, and it has been in my mind to write you, but action lags shamefully behind intention, and I am now not certain that this letter will reach you.

When my daughter-in-law told me of your telephone message, we made every effort to reach you, as Lee called numerous hotels without success. I had been receiving no visitors—trying to regain my strength after a prolonged illness—but I would have enjoyed a visit with you.

Rorty, Van Doren, and Deutsch—the three brave souls who wrote the reviews of TAMAR which lifted Jeffers from obscurity!

It is probably too much to expect that you will be returning to California very soon again, but if you should, we shall look forward to a visit from you at Tor House.

Thank you, too, for sending me the Autobiography, which, I suspect, only half tells the story of an active and constructive life!   Sincerely yours, Robinson Jeffers

P.S.—Dear Mark: —A kind and courageous lady has taken over my correspondence (since I am incapable of answering letters) and the letter above was written by her. Perhaps you noticed a manner somewhat different from my own. But what it says is what I want it to say—that I am very sorry to have missed you, and hope for another chance.   Yours, Robin

409: TO JUDITH ANDERSON

Medea, starring Judith Anderson, was televised for WNTA on the Play of the Week series, October 12, 1959. As early as 1955, Jerry Wald had negotiated for screen rights for Roan Stallion *and* Thurso's Landing *for Columbia Pictures, but the movies were never made.*

October [19], 1959

Dear Judith: Deeply I wish you all the best. To-day is Sunday PM California time, and your job must be gloriously fulfilled. I can imagine what bitter hard work it must have been.

For my part, even now, I don't at all know what's going on. Until your

373

letter I had no information from anybody except Wm. Morris Agency, and they knew next to nothing.

Jerry Wall—is that the name?—made two appointments to call on me, and wired that he couldn't keep either. So all the more I continued knowing nothing, not even whether that had to do with this.

Dearest love to you, Judith. Please forgive the pencil: I answer no letters, and have forgotten how to write with a pen.   Yours always, Robin

410: TO MARK VAN DOREN

The following are notes for a letter which was never finally composed and mailed.

410A:

[*November or December, 1959*]

Dear Mark: Thank you for your letter. I remember the Aptos Inn, and a big beautiful magnolia tree that stood in front of it, perhaps is still there. In flowering time I had to climb on the car's roof to pluck a blossom for my wife.

I won't bore you by talking about your son's trouble, except to send our sympathy and good wishes. The thing is a nuisance, not a calamity, but damn publicity anyhow.   Yours,

410B:

This note is only to assure you of my sympathy with you and your son in his trouble. Ninety nine percent of his detractors would have done the same thing—it was forced on him—or maybe a hundred percent, that is why they are so excited. Now he will have to begin his life over again: which is a privilege, if he takes it right, not a martyrdom.

My best wishes to him—and to you, old friend,   Sincerely

411: TO EVA HESSE

In the upper margin J has written, "Please forgive the pencil—I can't find a decent pen."

June 9, 1960

Dear Eva Hesse: Thank you very much for your letter. It was—*truly*—a great pleasure to hear from you again. I wish I could respond in kind, but that is not possible. I am not well, and I hate to confess it, but perhaps we have a little license to be sick after age seventy. The illness has no name and no pain, no particular symptoms, but it has gone on for years and destroys my energies. Probably it is just the common nuisance of old age coming on. I don't mind that, but I don't like to insult my best friends, here and abroad, by not answering their letters.

The book—"Dramen"—arrived here the day before your letter. It is beautifully made, and I am grateful to you and the Rowohlt Verlag, and thank you for the volumes that you are going to send. I shall never find a better translator.

Thank you for the list of royalty receipts; I wish they were enough to repay you for your labor.

I have just received a book of my short poems translated into Czecho-Slovakian. They translated and published a long narrative poem some time ago—and naturally I can't read a word of either book.

With all good wishes to you—   Robinson Jeffers

412: TO KAMIL BEDNÁŘ

This letter is not in J's hand; probably Melba Bennett or Lee J wrote it for him.

August 28, 1960

Dear Mr. Bednář: We were very pleased to receive your translations of my poems, and I wish I were familiar with your language so that I might express an intelligent opinion. But I am aware of the amount of work and time they represent and appreciate this, and the success of your translations in Czechoslovakia.

I wish also to express my good wishes for your marriage, of which Melba Bennett has informed me.

My warm personal regards.   Sincerely yours, Robinson Jeffers

413: TO THE NATIONAL INSTITUTE OF ARTS AND LETTERS

January 19, 1962

Dated the day before J died, the postcard provided by the Institute for its members to indicate their intention to attend the annual "Dinner meeting of the Institute" is checked in the space after "I shall" and is signed legibly, in J's hand, "Robinson Jeffers."

APPENDIX

The following lists only letters, postcards, telegrams, etc., written by J or transcribed from his notes or dictation. When possible, I have indicated that copies of letters are deposited in more than one collection. Some letters have changed hands since I began compiling them. I have first listed my source and then indicated other known locations. The largest collections of Una J's letters are at Occidental and Yale, but others can be found with her husband's letters.

Date	Addressee	Location	Letter Number
1897 August 23	William Hamilton J	Tor House[1]	1
1912 November 5	Una Call Kuster	Tor House	2
1912 November 15	Una Call Kuster (telegram)	Tor House	
1912 November 23	Una Call Kuster	Tor House	
1912 November 24	Una Call Kuster	Tor House	
1912 November 25	Una Call Kuster	Tor House	3
1912 November 26	Una Call Kuster	Tor House	
1912 December 2	Una Call Kuster	Tor House	
1912 December 2	Una Call Kuster	Tor House	
1912 December 2	Una Call Kuster	Tor House	
1912 December 4	Una Call Kuster	Tor House	4
1912 December 5	Una Call Kuster	Tor House	
1912 December 6	Una Call Kuster	Tor House	5
1912 December 8	Una Call Kuster	Tor House	6
1912 December 8	Una Call Kuster	Tor House	
1912 December 9	Una Call Kuster	Tor House	
1912 December 11	Una Call Kuster	Tor House	
1912 December 12	Una Call Kuster	Tor House	
1912 December 13	Una Call Kuster	Tor House	
1912 December 14	Una Call Kuster	Tor House	
1912 December 15	Una Call Kuster	Tor House	7
1912 December 16	Una Call Kuster	Tor House	
1912 December 16	Una Call Kuster	Tor House	8
1912 December 17	Una Call Kuster	Tor House	
1912 December 18	Una Call Kuster	Tor House	
1912 December 18	Una Call Kuster	Tor House	
1912 December 19	Una Call Kuster	Tor House	
1912 December 19	Una Call Kuster	Tor House	
1912 December 21	Una Call Kuster	Tor House	9

[1] Many of the letters from the files at Tor House have been temporarily deposited at Occidental, though not all are presently accessible to scholars.

Date	Addressee	Location	Letter Number
1912 December 21	Una Call Kuster	Tor House	10
1912 December 23	Una Call Kuster	Tor House	
1912 December 24	Una Call Kuster	Tor House	
1912 December 24	Una Call Kuster	Tor House	
1912 December 25	Una Call Kuster	Tor House	
1913 July 16	Una Call Kuster	Tor House	
1913 August 1	Mrs. Melissa Nash	Occidental	11
1915 December 15	Dr. Lyman Stookey	Tor House	12
1917 January 18	Dr. Lyman Stookey	Tor House	13
1917 January 19	State Librarian, Sacramento	Occidental	
1917 March 6	Marguerite Wilkinson	Middlebury College	
1917 June 26	Una J	Tor House	
1917 June 26	Una J	Tor House	
1917 July 31	Ernest G. Bishop	Occidental	14
1918 October 4	Una J (telegram)	Tor House	
[1919 July 14]	Una J	Tor House	
1919 July 16	Una J (postcard)	Tor House	
[1920 August 21]	Dr. Lyman Stookey	Tor House	15
1921 April 7	Una J (postcard)	Tor House	
1924 May 23	Edwin Björkman	U North Carolina	
1924 July 5	George Sterling	UC, Bancroft[2]	
[1924]	George Sterling	Huntington	17
[1924 July 12]	George Sterling	Huntington	
1924 August 10	George Sterling	UC, Bancroft	18
1924 September 21	George Sterling	Huntington	19
1924 September 23	Dr. Lyman Stookey	Tor House	20
1924 November 22	George Sterling	UC, Bancroft	21
1925 January 21	George Sterling	UC, Bancroft	22
1925 February 11	Maurice Browne	U Michigan	23
1925 February 12	George Sterling	UC, Bancroft	24
1925 March 15	Mark Van Doren	Columbia	25
1925 March 18	George Sterling	Huntington	26
1925 March 26	George Sterling	Huntington	27
1925 April 8	George Sterling	UC, Bancroft	28
1925 April 11	Benjamin de Casseres	Brooklyn Pub	29
1925 April 30	Mark Van Doren	Columbia	30
1925 June 5	Benjamin de Casseres	Brooklyn Pub	31
1925 June 15	Benjamin de Casseres	Brooklyn Pub	32
1925 June 17	George Sterling	UC, Bancroft	33
1925 June 17	Babette Deutsch	Deutsch	34

[2] Letters to George Sterling in the Bancroft Library are copied in the Library of Congress and Stanford University Library collections.

Date	Addressee	Location	Letter Number
1925 June 21	Albert Bender	Occidental	35
[1925] June 23	Benjamin de Casseres	Brooklyn Pub	
1925 June 28	Albert Bender	Occidental	36
1925 August 8	Sara Teasdale	Margaret Carpenter	37
[1925] August 8	George Sterling	UC, Bancroft	38
1925 September 4	Benjamin de Casseres	Brooklyn Pub	39
1925 September 25	Albert Bender	Occidental	40
[1925] September 26	Benjamin de Casseres	Brooklyn Pub	41
1925 October 12	Albert Bender	Occidental	
1925 November	Bayard H. Christy	Dan Burne Jones	42
1925 November	Albert Bender	Occidental	43
1925 November 3	George Sterling	UC, Bancroft	44
1925 November 4	Albert Bender	Occidental	
1925 November 12	George Sterling	UC, Bancroft	45
1925 November 25	Donald Friede	Yale, Beinecke	46
1925 December 1	George Sterling	UC, Bancroft	47
1925 December [19]	George Sterling	UC, Bancroft	48
1925 December 21	Albert Bender	Occidental	49
1925 December 31	George Sterling	UC, Bancroft	50
1926	(?) Long	Paul C. Richards	
1926 January 2	Dr. Lyman Stookey	Tor House	51
[1926 January 16]	George Sterling	UC, Bancroft	52
1926 January 22	George West	Isabelle Percy West	53
1926 January 26	George Sterling	Huntington	54
1926 January 28	Donald Friede	U Texas	
1926 February 5	George Sterling	UC, Bancroft	55
1926 February 13	George Sylvester Viereck	UC, Bancroft	56
1926 February 19	Benjamin de Casseres	Brooklyn Pub	57
1926 February 19	Donald Friede	U Texas	58
1926 February 23	Lyman L. Pierce	UC, Bancroft	
1926 March 9	Donald Friede	U Texas	59
[1926 March 14]	George Sterling	Huntington	60
1926 March 15	Witter Bynner	Harvard[3]	61
1926 March 18	Babette Deutsch	Deutsch	62
1926 March 29	Ridgely Torrence	Princeton	63
1926 April 13	George Sterling	UC, Bancroft	64
1926 April 24	Donald Friede	U Texas	65
[1926 April 30]	George Sterling	UC, Bancroft	66
1926 April 30	Donald Friede	U Texas	67
1926 May 6	Witter Bynner	Harvard	68
1926 May 8	Donald Friede	Tor House	69

[3] Bynner also has copies of J's letters to him.

Date	Addressee	Location	Letter Number
1926 May 11	Albert Bender	Occidental	70
1926 May 18	Albert Bender	Occidental	71
1926 May 18	Donald Friede	Tor House; U Alabama	
1926 June 2	Harriet Monroe	U Chicago	72
1926 June 4	Benjamin de Casseres	Brooklyn Pub	73
1926 June 6	Albert Bender	Occidental	74
1926 June 13	Donald Friede	U Texas	75
1926 June 21	Harriet Monroe	U Chicago	
[1926] July 16	George Sterling	Huntington	76
1926 July 21	Donald Friede	U Texas	77
1926 July 26	Gelber, Lilienthal, Inc.	Lilienthal	78
1926 July 26	Donald Friede	U Texas	
1926 July 28	Miss (?) Purnell	U Texas	
1926 July 31	Donald Friede	U Texas	79
[1926] August 10	George Sterling	Huntington	80
1926 August 19	Theodore Lilienthal	Lilienthal	81
1926 August 21	Donald Friede	Lilienthal	82
1926 August 30	George Sterling	Huntington	83
1926 September 2	Donald Friede	U Texas	
[1926 September 13]	George Sterling	Huntington	84
1926 September 16	Theodore Lilienthal	Lilienthal	85
1926 September 17	Louis Untermeyer	Indiana U	86
1926 September 17	Donald Friede	U Texas	87
1926 October [5]	Benjamin de Casseres	Brooklyn Pub	88
1926 October 7	W. Orton Tewson	L Congress	89
1926 October 8	Theodore Lilienthal	Lilienthal	
[1926 October 9]	George Sterling	Huntington	90
[1926] November 4	George Sterling	UC, Bancroft	91
1926 November 10	Louis Untermeyer	Indiana U	92
1926 November 16	Benjamin de Casseres	Brooklyn Pub	93
1926 November 19	Albert Bender	Occidental	94
1926 November 27	Harriet Monroe	U Chicago	95
1926 December 7	James D. Phelan	UC, Bancroft	
1926 December 8	Albert Bender	Occidental	97
1926 December 13	Margaret S. Cobb	Stanford	98
1926 December 16	Donald Friede	U Texas	99
1926 December 19	Bio de Casseres	Brooklyn Pub	100
1926 December 29	Donald Friede	U Texas	101
1926 December 29	James D. Phelan	UC, Bancroft	102
[1926 December]	New Masses	New Masses	103
1927 January 3	Donald Friede	U Texas	
1927 January 6	Albert Bender	Occidental	104
1927 January 7	Donald Friede	U Texas	

Date	Addressee	Location	Letter Number
1927 January 25	Donald Friede	Tor House	105
1927 February 11	Donald Friede	U Texas	106
1927 February 22	Donald Friede	Tor House; U Alabama	107
1927 March 1	Albert Bender	Occidental	108
1927 March 2	Benjamin H. Lehman	UC, Bancroft	109
1927 March 3	Donald Friede	U Texas	110
1927 March 12	Donald Friede	U Texas	111
1927 March 13	Albert Bender	Occidental	112
1927 March 27	Donald Friede	U Texas	113
1927 March 31	Albert Bender	Occidental	114
1927 April 5	Donald Friede	U Texas	
1927 April 14	James D. Phelan (telegram)	UC, Bancroft	
1927 April 21	Albert Bender	Occidental	115
1927 May 11	T. R. Smith	Occidental	
1927 May 15	Dr. John W. Nevius	Occidental	116
1927 May 23	Mark Van Doren	Columbia	117
1927 June	Albert Bender	Occidental	118
1927 July 1	Donald Friede	U Texas	119
1927 July 1	Benjamin de Casseres	Brooklyn Pub	120
1927 July	Albert Bender	Occidental	121
[1927 August 5]	Mark Van Doren and James Rorty	Columbia	122
1927 August	Ernest Hartsock	Emory U	123
1927 August [8]	Albert Bender	Occidental	124
1927 August 24	Albert Bender	Occidental	125
1927 August 26	Edwin Björkman	U North Carolina	126
1927 September	Donald Friede	U Texas	127
1927 September 21	Benjamin de Casseres	Brooklyn Pub	128
1927 October	Harriet Monroe	U Chicago	129
1927 October 22	Donald Friede	U Texas	130
1927 October 22	Albert Bender	Occidental	131
1927 November	H. L. Davis	U Texas	132
1927 November 10	Benjamin H. Lehman	Occidental	133
1927 November 10	Benjamin de Casseres	Brooklyn Pub	134
1927 December 4	Harriet Monroe	U Chicago	135
1927 December 7	Donald Friede	U Texas	136
1928 January 16	Albert Bender	Occidental	137
1928 January 25	Donald Friede	U Texas	
[1928] February 24	Albert Bender	Mills College	138
1928 March	Donald Friede	Tor House; U Alabama	139
1928 May	Mark Van Doren	Columbia	140

Date	Addressee	Location	Letter Number
1928 June 9	Donald Friede	Tor House; U Alabama	141
1928 June 26	Albert Bender	Occidental	142
1928 August	Witter Bynner	Harvard	143
1928 September	Mark Van Doren	Columbia	144
1928 September [12]	Benjamin de Casseres	Brooklyn Pub	145
1928 October 17	Albert Bender	Occidental	146
1928 October 17	Mark Van Doren	Columbia	147
1928 December [14]	Mark Van Doren	Columbia	148
1928 December	Richard Bühlig	Los Angeles Pub	149
1928 December	Albert Bender	Occidental	150
[1928]	Albert Bender	Occidental	
[1928]	Albert Bender	Occidental	151
[1929]	Henry Goddard Leach	U Kansas	152
1929 January 14	Mary Austin	Huntington	153
1929 January	John Hay Whitney (Barnet B. Ruder)	Yale, Beinecke	154
[1929 January 19]	Arthur Davison Ficke	Yale, Beinecke	155
1929 February	Arthur Davison Ficke	Yale, Beinecke	156
1929 April	Dudley Nichols	Yale, Beinecke	157
[1929 April]	Arthur Davison Ficke	Yale, Beinecke	158
1929 May	Ernest Moll	Moll	159
1929 May [13]	Sidney S. Alberts	*A Bibliography of the Works of Robinson Jeffers*, p. 26	160
1929 May 14	Mark Van Doren	Columbia	161
[1929] June 21	Arthur Davison Ficke	Yale, Beinecke	162
1929 June 29	Louis Untermeyer	Indiana U	163
1929 August 30	Harriet Monroe	U Chicago	
1929 August 31	Benjamin H. Lehman	Occidental	164
1929 August 31	Albert Bender	Occidental; Mills College	165
[1929 September]	Mark Van Doren (postcard)	Columbia	166
[1929 October 6]	Benjamin de Casseres	Brooklyn Pub	167
1929 October [7]	Arthur Davison Ficke	Yale, Beinecke	168
1929 November	Rudolph Gilbert	Stanley D. Willis	169
1929 December 8	Dr. Lyman Stookey	Tor House	170
1929 December 10	Benjamin de Casseres	Brooklyn Pub	171
1929 December [20]	Mary Austin	Huntington	172
1929 December [20]	Albert Bender	Occidental	173
1929 December [20]	Maurice Browne	U Michigan	174
1930 January	(?) Griffith	Columbia	

Date	Addressee	Location	Letter Number
[1930] January 7	Albert Bender	Occidental	175
1930 January 30	Mark Van Doren	Columbia	176
1930 February 28	Theodore Lilienthal	Lilienthal	177
1930 March 14	Mark Van Doren	Columbia	178
[1930] April 19	Arthur Davison Ficke	Yale, Beinecke	179
[1930 May]	Camille McCole	*On Poetry*, pp. 165–66; U Alabama	180
1930 May 7	Benjamin de Casseres	Brooklyn Pub	181
[1930 May 16]	H. Arthur Klein	Occidental	182
[1930 June 11]	H. Arthur Klein	Occidental	183
[1930 June 19]	Mary Austin	Huntington	184
1930 June 30	Witter Bynner	Harvard	185
[1930 July 27]	H. Arthur Klein	Occidental	186
[1930 November]	H. L. Davis	U Texas	187
1931 January 6	Harriet Monroe	U Chicago	
1931 February	Lawrence Clark Powell	Occidental	188
1931 February 11	T. R. Smith	U Virginia	189
1931 February 11	Babette Deutsch	Deutsch	190
1931 March 4	Babette Deutsch	Deutsch	191
1931 June	Selden Rodman	Melba Bennett; Rodman	192
1931 August 20	Donald Friede	U Texas	193
1931 September	Lawrence Clark Powell	Occidental	195
1931 October	Witter Bynner	Harvard	196
1931 November 18	T. R. Smith	Frederic Ives Carpenter	197
1931 December 2	T. R. Smith	U Virginia	198
1931 December [22]	Frederic Prokosch	Occidental	199
1931 December [22]	Frederic Ives Carpenter	Carpenter	200
[1932 January 8]	Albert Bender	Occidental	201
1932 February 27	Elmer Adler	U North Carolina	
1932 March	Mary Dwyer	Occidental	203
1932 March	Harriet Monroe	U Chicago	204
[1932] March 16	Harriet Monroe	U Chicago	
1932 March 27	Harriet Monroe	U Chicago	205
1932 March 31	Frederic Ives Carpenter	Carpenter	207
1932 April	Jim Tully	UC Los Angeles	208
1932 April	[Horace Liveright]	*A Bibliography of the Works of Robinson Jeffers*, p. 77	
1932 April 11	Harriet Monroe	U Chicago	210
1932 September 20	Remsen Bird	Occidental	
1932 October 26	Fremont Older	UC, Bancroft	212

Date	Addressee	Location	*Letter Number*
1932 November 9	Mildred D. (Jeremy) Ingalls	Tufts U	213
[1932 November 10]	Edwin Duerr	Stanford	214
1932 November 11	[Horace Liveright]	*A Bibliography of the Works of Robinson Jeffers,* p. 78	
1933 January 10	T. R. Smith	U Virginia	216
1933 March [20]	Mary Austin	Huntington	217
1933 June	Melba Berry Bennett	Bennett	220
1933 June 13	Ridgely Torrence	Princeton	
1933 July 29	C. W. Keppel	Buffalo, Lockwood	221
[1933]	Lawrence Clark Powell	Occidental	223
1933 November [18]	Frederic Ives Carpenter	Carpenter	224
1933 November	(?) Pumphrey	U Virginia	225
1934 January 1	E. A. Robinson	NY Pub	226
1934 March	Rudolph Gilbert	Stanley D. Willis	227
1934 May 1	Mrs. Hugh Bullock	Academy of American Poets	229
1934 May 30	Mrs. Hugh Bullock	Academy of American Poets	230
1934 June 3	Gorham Munson	U Virginia	231
1934 June [20]	Gorham Munson	U Virginia	
1934 July 3	James Rorty	Rorty	232
1934 July 9	Gorham Munson	U Virginia	
1934 July 25	C. W. Keppel	Buffalo, Lockwood	233
1934 August 31	Frederic Prokosch	Occidental	234
1934 October 1	Sr. Mary James Power	Blanche Matthias; *Poets at Prayer,* pp. 60–61	235
1934 November 7	Babette Deutsch	Deutsch	236
1934 November	Geoffrey Grigson	Buffalo, Lockwood; *New Verse*	237
1934 December	Frederic Ives Carpenter	Carpenter	238
1935 January 31	Albert Bender	Occidental	239
1935 March 22	Jake Zeitlin	Occidental[4]	240
1935 April 27	Mrs. Hugh Bullock	Academy of American Poets	241
1935 May 17	Louis Adamic	U Chicago; *My America,* pp. 474–75	
1935 May 29	(?) Wechsler	U Virginia	243

[4] Copies also at U Texas and San Francisco Pub; also published and facsimiled in Powell, *Robinson Jeffers, the Man and His Work* (see p. 168 and the fold-out facing p. 172).

Date	Addressee	Location	Letter Number
1935 June 17	Louis Untermeyer	Indiana U	244
1935 July 2	Arthur Davison Ficke	Yale, Beinecke	245
1935 July 20	Louis Untermeyer	Indiana U	
1935 October 5	H. Arthur Klein	Klein	246
1935 October 28	J—— G—— M—— (unmailed)	Columbia	
1935 October 29	J—— G—— M—— (copy of mailed letter)	Columbia	247
1935 November 18	Cortlandt Schoonover	U Virginia	249
1935 December 16	Mrs. Hugh Bullock	Academy of American Poets	250
[1936]	Albert Bender	Occidental	
[1936]	Benjamin de Casseres	Brooklyn Pub	251
1936 June	Louis Untermeyer	Indiana U	252
1936 August	Mrs. Haakon Chevalier	Occidental	253
1936 October	Benjamin de Casseres	Brooklyn Pub	
1936 October 13	Oscar K. Cushing and R. D. McElroy	James D. Phelan Fellowship	254
1936 November 29	Rudolph Gilbert	Stanley D. Willis	255
1936 December 11	Eugene F. Saxton (Harper & Row)	Clapp	
1937 January	Mrs. Hugh Bullock	Academy of American Poets	
1937 January 11	Elmer Adler	Breaking into Print	
1937 January 13	Henry Seidel Canby	National Institute of Arts and Letters	256
1937 February	Van Wyck Brooks	U Pennsylvania	257
1937 February 3	Margery Evernden	Occidental	258
1937 March	Benjamin Miller	Occidental	259
[1937 July]	Benjamin de Casseres	Brooklyn Pub	260
1937 July 14	Frederic Ives Carpenter	Carpenter	261
1937 August 1	Call family	Tor House	263
1937 August 6	Mark Van Doren	Columbia	264
1937 September 4	Albert Bender	Occidental	265
1937 [October]	William Berkowitz	Tor House	266
1937 November 21	Hyatt Howe Waggoner	Waggoner	267
1938 January [28]	Frederic Ives Carpenter	Carpenter	269
1938 February 1	Hyatt Howe Waggoner	Waggoner	271
1938 February	Benjamin Miller	Occidental	272
1938 February 23	Sr. M. Erasma	Tor House	273
[1938 Easter]	Una J	Tor House	275
[1938 April]	League of American Writers	Writers Take Sides, pp. 73–74	276

Date	Addressee	Location	Letter Number
1938 April 24	Frederick M. Clapp	Clapp	277
1938 June 10	Benjamin Miller	Occidental	279
[1938]	Una J	Tor House	280
1938 November 30	Henry W. Wells	U Texas	281
[1938 December]	Dorothy Thompson	Tor House	282
[1939 February]	Justine Lynn	Tor House	284
[1939 March]	William K. Hubbell	Tor House	285
1939 May 13	G. Wilson Knight	Mrs. Mollie Harris Samuels (Columbia)	287
1939 June 6	Frederic Ives Carpenter	Carpenter	288
1939 June 16	Ralph Tyler Flewelling	U Virginia	289
1939 July 12	Richard J. Schoeck	Schoeck[5]	290
1939 August	Louis Adamic	Henry A. Christian	291
1939 October 2	James Rorty	Rorty	292
1940 March 29	Mrs. Lyman Stookey	Tor House	294
1940 June 28	Grace Besthel	Tor House	295
1940 November 26	George Dillon	U Chicago	296
1941 February 12	Witter Bynner	Harvard	297
1941 March 21	Mrs. Daisy Bartley	Bartley	298
1941 November	Selden Rodman	Melba Bennett; Rodman	304
1941 December 14	Henry W. Wells	Columbia	305
[1941]	Garth J	Tor House	306
[1942 February]	Jack Wilson	Tor House	307
1942 May 10	Antoinette Cornish	Tor House	
1942 November 21	Una J	Tor House	
1942 November 23	Una J	Tor House	
[1942] November 24	Una J	Tor House	308
1942 November 25	Una J	Tor House	
1942 Thanksgiving	Una J	Tor House	309
1943 February 24	Francis Gardner Clough	Clough	310
1943 September [18]	Frederic Ives Carpenter	Carpenter	311
1943 [November]–December 7	Frederic Ives Carpenter	Carpenter	312
1944 November 9	Oscar Williams	Harvard	313
1945 May 29	(?) Halter	U Virginia	315
1945 August 14	Garth J	Tor House	316
1945 October 3	Garth J	Tor House	317
1945 December 5	Frederick M. Clapp	Clapp	318

[5] Now owned by Robert H. Taylor, Princeton U.

Date	Addressee	Location	Letter Number
1945 December 7	Mary Gleason	American Academy of Arts and Letters	319
1945 December 16	Van Wyck Brooks	U Pennsylvania; American Academy of Arts and Letters	320
1945 December 23	Van Wyck Brooks	U Pennslvania	321
[1946] January 22	Van Wyck Brooks	U Pennsylvania	322
1946 February 4	Mrs. Hugh Bullock	Academy of American Poets	323
1946 April 18	Van Wyck Brooks	U Pennsylvania	326
1946 July 21	Merle Armitage	William Targ[6]	
1946 August 4	Julien Philbert	Tor House	327
1947 July 21	George Dillon	U Chicago	
[1947 October]	Michael Meyerberg	Tor House	328
1948 April 20	Bennett Cerf (telegram)	UC, Bancroft	
1948 April 26	Judith Anderson (postcard)	Anderson	
1948 May 1	Felicia Geffen	American Academy of Arts and Letters	329
1948 May 12	Robert Whitehead and Oliver Rea	Anderson	330
[1948 May 17]	Nancy Sayre (Mrs. William H. Norton)	Norton	331
1948 June 1	Dramatists' Guild	Tor House	
1948 June 25	Marion Strobel	U Chicago	332
1948 June 26	Garth and Charlotte J	Bartley	333
[1948] August 20	Una J	Tor House	334
[1948] August 21	Una J	Tor House	335
[1948] August 23	Una J	Tor House	336
[1948] August 25	Una J	Tor House	
[1948 August 27]	Una J	Tor House	337
1949 January 19	William Turner Levy	NY Pub, Berg	
1949 January 30	Frederick M. and Maud Clapp	Clapp	338
1949 July 20	Editor, *Carmel Pine Cone*	Tor House	339
1949 November 26	William Turner Levy	NY Pub, Berg	340
1950 January 19	Dr. Hans and Phoebe Barkan	Barkan	341
1950 January 23	Mrs. Daisy Bartley	Bartley	
1950 January 25	Mrs. Daisy Bartley	Bartley	

[6] A copy of the letter is at Occidental.

Date	Addressee	Location	Letter Number
1950 February 1	Dr. Hans and Phoebe Barkan	Barkan	342
1950 February 2	Mrs. Violet Hinkley	Hinkley	343
1950 February 19	Edgar Johnson	NY Pub, Berg	
1950 February 19	Hugh Bullock	Academy of American Poets	
1950 February 28	Jack and Phoebe Gilpin	Barkan	344
1950 August 26	Mrs. Daisy Bartley	Bartley	345
1950 September 1	Dr. Hans Barkan (telegram)	Barkan	346
1950 September	Mr. Hugh Bullock	Academy of American Poets	347
1950 September 4	Mrs. Daisy Bartley	Bartley	
1950 September 5	Una's sisters	Bartley	
1950 September 29	Karl Shapiro (postcard)	U Chicago	
1950 October	Frederick M. and Maud Clapp	Clapp	348
1950 October 14	Judith Anderson	Anderson	349
1950 October 23	Karl Shapiro	U Chicago	
1950 October 25	Luther Greene	Anderson	
1950 October 26	Mrs. Daisy Bartley	Bartley	350
1950 November	Luther Greene	Anderson	351
1950 November 1	William Turner Levy (postcard)	NY Pub, Berg	
1950 November 13	Frederick M. and Maud Clapp	Clapp	352
1950 December 30	Melba Berry Bennett	Bennett	353
1951	(?)	Waring Jones	
1951 January 7	Mrs. Daisy Bartley	Bartley	354
1951 January 18– August 31	Frederick M. and Maud Clapp	Clapp	355
1951 February 3	Radcliffe Squires	Squires	356
1951 February 14	Mrs. Lyman Stookey	Tor House	357
1951 February 20	Evelyn Shapiro (Poetry)	U Chicago	
1951 March 3	Mrs. Hugh Bullock	Academy of American Poets	358
1951 March 14	Stanley D. Willis	Willis	
1951 March 14	William Turner Levy	NY Pub, Berg	
1951 March 25	American Humanist Association	American Humanist Association	359
1951 April	Karl Shapiro	U Chicago	360
1951 May 2	Lawrence Clark Powell	Occidental	361
1951 May 15	Eva Hesse	Hesse	362

Date	Addressee	Location	Letter Number
1951 May 18	Hugh Bullock	Academy of American Poets	
1951 May 24	John Hay Whitney	Yale, Beinecke	363
1951 June 14	Walter G. Tolleson	Tolleson	364
1951 July	William Turner Levy	NY Pub, Berg	
1951 September 5	Eva Hesse	Hesse	365
1951 November	Eva Hesse	Hesse	366
1951 November 7	Karl Shapiro	U Chicago	367
1951 November 17	Karl Shapiro	U Chicago	368
[195?]	Raymond J. Pflug	Tor House	369
1952 January 9	Hugh Bullock	Academy of American Poets	
1952 March 12	Karl Shapiro	U Chicago	
1952 May	Radcliffe Squires	Squires	370
1952 May	Karl Shapiro	U Chicago	371
1952 June	U of Alabama	U Alabama	
1952 June 3	Eva Hesse	Hesse	372
1952 June 7	Dr. Lawrence K. Smith	U Alabama	
1952 June 26	Frederick M. Clapp	Clapp	373
1952 June 26	Theodore Lilienthal	Lilienthal	
1952 September 5	Frederick M. Clapp	Clapp	374
1952 September	Theodore Lilienthal	Lilienthal	375
1952 November 19	Theodore Lilienthal	Lilienthal	
1952 November 20	Karl Shapiro	U Chicago	376
1952 December 2	Albert Sperisen (Pine Vine Press)	Occidental	
[1953]	Jean Ennis	Tor House	377
1953 February 2	Theodore Lilienthal	Lilienthal	378
1953 February [17]	Albert Sperisen	Occidental	
1953 April 23	Benjamin H. Lehman	UC, Bancroft	379
1953 June 4	Eva Hesse	Hesse	
1953 September 1	Fraser Drew	Drew	380
[1954]	Gene de Wild	Tor House	381
1954 April	Newton Taylor	Tor House	
1954 July 9	Blanche Matthias	Matthias	
1954 September 25	Fraser Drew	Drew	382
1955 January	Theodore Lilienthal	Lilienthal	383
1955 February 7	Reece Halsey	Tor House	
1955 March	Anne Curtis-Brown (Argosy)	Tor House	
[1955 April 14]	Elizabeth J. McCloy	Occidental	
1955 May 17	Arthur G. Coons	Occidental	384
[1955]	Eva Hesse	Tor House	385

Date	Addressee	Location	Letter Number
1956 January 3	Witter Bynner	Harvard	386
1956 February 20	Hugh Bullock	Academy of American Poets	387
1956 June 20	Fraser Drew	Drew	388
1956 June 25	Dr. Hans and Phoebe Barkan (postcard)	Barkan	389
[1957]	Allen Griffin	Tor House	390
[1957]	Radcliffe Squires	Tor House	391
1957 April 24	Eva Hesse	Hesse	
1957 May 22	Eva Hesse	Hesse	
1957 June 5	Eva Hesse	Hesse	
1957 July	Dan Magnan	Tor House	392
1957 November 5	Eva Hesse	Hesse	
[1957 November 20]	Eva Hesse	Hesse	393
1957 December 8	Eva Hesse	Hesse	
[1957]	Bennett Cerf	Tor House	394
[1958]	Viking Press	Tor House	395
[1958 February]	Walter Ducloux	Tor House	396
1958 May 1	Eva Hesse	Hesse	397
1958 May 1	Klaus Juncker	Hesse	398
1958 June 7	Kamil Bednář	Bednář	399
[1958 July]	Ogden Plumb	Tor House	400
1958 July 27	Eva Hesse	Eva Hesse	401
1958 September 7	Eva Hesse	Hesse	402
1958 October 11	Mrs. Hugh Bullock	Academy of American Poets	403
1958 October 13	Jean Kellogg (Mrs. James Dickie)	Dickie	404
1958 December [27]	Dr. Hans Barkan	Barkan	405
[1959]	Bessinger Foundation	Tor House	406
1959 January [25]	Mrs. Hugh Bullock	Academy of American Poets	407
1959 July 20	Mark Van Doren	Columbia	408
1959 October [19]	Judith Anderson	Tor House⁷	
[1959 November or December]	Mark Van Doren (unmailed drafts)	Tor House	410
1960 June 9	Eve Hesse	Hesse	411
1960 August 28	Kamil Bednář	Bednář	412
1961 March 31	Kamil Bednář	Bednář	
1962 January 19	National Institute of Arts and Letters (postcard)	National Institute of Arts and Letters	413

⁷ Now at the Gleason Library, University of San Francisco.

INDEX

Jeffers, Lee Waggener, 258, 261n, 318, 324, 326, 331, 332, 338, 340, 375
Jeffers, Lindsay, 318, 324, 326, 331, 336, 338, 340, 350
Jeffers, Maeve (1914), 4
Jeffers, Maeve (Jeffers' granddaughter), 315, 336, 338
Jeffers, [John] Robinson, 2, 188, 189; on Aeschylus, 10n; on American culture, 259, 270–71; art, taste in, 247; on artist and society, 103; on beauty, 221–22, 262; on behaviorism, 273; on blank verse, 35; on Christian mythology, 108; on civilization, 104, 159–60, 294, 295; on classics, 149–50; on consciousness, 286n; on contemplation, 342; on contemporary American and European writing, 247; on criticism, 212; on decadence, 103; on Elizabethan drama, 62; on energy, 195; on Euripedes, 10, 297, 303; favorite fiction of, 272–73; on freedom, 226n; on Freud, 223; genealogy of, 189, 285; on Greek drama, 10, 130, 180, 196, 200, 262, 310, 335n; on happiness, 259–60; on hexameter, 35; on humanism, 342; on humanity, 159; on incest, 35, 59, 116; on the individual, 226; influences on, 201; on isolation, 270; on Jesus, 101, 142, 145, 209, 287; on joy, 209; letters received: from Frederic I. Carpenter, 194–95, from Harriet Monroe, 197, from Hyatt H. Waggoner, 260–61, from Lawrence C. Powell, 180–83; letters from: 1897, 2–3; 1912–20, 4–23; 1924–28, 26–139; 1929–30, 140–64; 1930–37, 166–242; 1937–38, 244–56; 1938–48, 258–307; 1948–50, 308–28; 1950–56, 330–59; 1956–62, 360–65; literary preferences of, 247; on machine age, 103; on meter, 28, 35, 54, 57n, 86, 173, 174; on modern poetry, 28; on nationalism, 232; on Oedipus, 10n; on opera, 108, 345; on philosophy, 342; on poetry, 16, 28, 57n, 62, 86, 159, 171–72, 173, 174, 200–1, 206, 208–9, 212, 222, 225, 262; on *Prometheus Bound*, 10; on propagandist literature, 233, 241, 271; on psychoanalysis, 273; on radicalism, 117; relatives of, in Kentucky, 279–80; on religion, 221, 240, 265, 269; on rhythm, 28, 57n, 206; on science, 254, 260, 261; on sex, 52, 59, 162; on Shakespeare, 27–28, 201, 225, 233n; social views of, 232–33, 241, 247, 259, 271; on sonnet, 57n; on

Sophocles, 10n; on Spanish Civil War, 241, 266–67; on suicide, 92, 98, 134; on time, 184, 195; on tragedy, 17, 35, 209, 222, 261, 287, 335n; on *vers libre*, 21; on war, 213, 226 and n, 232, 337
Jeffers, Una Lindsay Call (Kuster), 21, 33, 81, 90, 107n, 111, 119, 122–23, 128, 131, 140, 141, 163, 166, 171, 189, 201, 204n, 219, 224, 231, 237, 258, 283, 291, 298, 310; death of, 326; illness of, 317–18, 320–26; letter enclosures by, 71, 78, 80, 318; letters from: to Benjamin Miller, 284–85, to Bennett Cerf, 268, 271–72, 283–84, 297, to Bio de Casseres, 95–99, to Blanche Matthias, 286–87, to C. Erskine Scott Wood, 231–34, to Cortlandt Schoonover, 255–56, to Donald Friede, 283–84, to Fred B. Millet, 247, to Frederic I. Carpenter, 285–86, to Geraldine Udell, 284, to Hyatt H. Waggoner, 273, to John W. Townsend, 279–80, to Judith Anderson, 304–5, to Lawrence C. Powell, 187–89, 198–200, 213–14, to Margaret P. Ashelman, 265, to Philip Horton, 202, to Sara Bard Field, 231–34, to Saxe Commins, 305, to Theodore Lilienthal, 204, 207; letters to, 265–66, 269, 291–92, 292–93, 312–17; postcard to Powell, 199n. See also Kuster, Una Lindsay Call
Jeffers, Una Sherwood, 351
Jeffers, William Hamilton, 188, 189, 265; letter to, 3
"Jeffers as a Subject for Horace Lyon's Camera" (Lyon), 256n
Jesus, Jeffers on, 101, 142, 145, 209, 287
Johnson, Samuel, 13
Johnson, Spud, 171
Jolas, Eugène, 88, 306, 360
Jones, Bobby, 297
Jordan-Smith, Paul, 132
Joy, Jeffers on, 209. See also Happiness
"Julian and Maddalo" (Shelley), 41
Juncker, Klaus, letter to, 366
Jung, Carl Gustav, 106, 183, 202, 260, 272

Keats, John, 13, 99, 172
Kellogg, Mrs. Jean, 360; letter to, 370
Keppel, C. W., letters to, 206, 220
Keyserling, Hermann Alexander von, 46, 106n
King, Alexander, 101
Kirstein, Lincoln, 150n

THE JOHNS HOPKINS PRESS

THE SELECTED LETTERS OF ROBINSON JEFFERS

Designed by Gerard A. Valerio

Composed in Palatino
by Monotype Composition Company, Inc.

Printed offset by Universal Lithographers, Inc.
on 60 lb. Mohawk Ravenna

Bound by Moore and Company
in Holliston Sailcloth and Strathmore Artlaid